PERSPECTIVES ON

SAFE &

SOUND

BANKING

PAST, PRESENT, AND FUTURE

MIT Press Series on the Regulation of Economic Activity

General Editor
Richard Schmalensee, MIT Sloan School of Management

PERSPECTIVES ON

SAFE&

SOUND

BANKING

PAST, PRESENT, AND FUTURE

By
George J. Benston
Robert A. Eisenbeis
Paul M. Horvitz
Edward J. Kane
George G. Kaufman

*A Study Commissioned by the
American Bankers Association*

*Published in cooperation with
The MIT Press
Cambridge, Massachusetts
London, England*

First MIT Press Edition, 1986

This book was printed and bound in the United States of
America.

Library of Congress Cataloging-in-Publication Data
Main entry under title:

Perspectives on safe & sound banking.

(MIT Press series on the regulation of economic
activity; 12)
Includes index.
1. Banks and banking—United States. 2. Bank
failures—United States. 3. Banks and banking—United
States—Government guaranty of deposits. 4. Banks and
banking—United States—State supervision. 5. Risk—
United States. I. Benston, George J. II. Title:
Perspectives on safe and sound banking. III. Series.
HG2481.P47 1986   332.1'0973   85-23882
ISBN 0-262-02246-X

CONTENTS

Foreword

The American banking system has functioned remarkably well over the past fifty years. The federal regulatory framework, largely constructed during the 1930s, contributed to an environment compatible with a growing banking industry and also fostered public confidence in its safety and soundness. In recent years, however, the historically comfortable fit between depository institutions and the regulatory framework has been strained by rapid changes in the financial services industry and by volatile economic conditions. Thrift institutions have had great difficulty in adjusting to these changes, and hundreds of them are insolvent or nearly insolvent. Commercial banks have adapted more successfully to the changing environment, but the rate of bank failures and the growing number of institutions on problem lists have aroused anxiety among regulators, Congress, bankers, and the public.

Concern over these issues led the Government Relations Council of the American Bankers Association to initiate a project to examine the broad subject of the safety and soundness of the financial system. An Oversight Committee was appointed to see the project through to completion. The Committee was composed of sixteen bankers with expertise in law, economics, and corporate management, representing banks ranging in size from $34 million to more than $100 billion in assets.

The Oversight Committee in turn selected five highly respected academic consultants to undertake a comprehensive study of the issues surrounding the safety and soundness of the banking industry and the efficacy of its regulatory system. The consultants divided the work among themselves, each contributing drafts of one or more Chapters. The authors' primary responsibilities were as follows: Chapter 1, George Benston; Chapter 2, George Kaufman; Chapters 3 and 4, Paul Horvitz; Chapter 5, Edward Kane and George Kaufman; Chapter 6, Robert Eisenbeis; Chapter 7, Robert Eisenbeis and Paul

Horvitz; Chapters 8 and 9, Edward Kane; and Chapters 10 and 11, George Benston.

The draft chapters were circulated among and critiqued by the other members of the consultant team. The members of the Oversight Committee also reviewed and commented on the study as it was being drafted. The consultants were free to disagree with the Committee and in fact did so on several issues. Thus the end result represents a synthesis of the views of all five consultants.

We believe that the consultants' study provides a valuable basis for the analysis of the complex issues surrounding the deposit insurance system and the broader question of safety and soundness of the banking industry. We emphasize, however, that the consultants' work presents their views and does not necessarily represent the position of either the Oversight Committee or the American Bankers Association.

Valuable assistance to the work of the Oversight Committee was given by P. Michael Laub, Director of the Economic and Policy Research Division of the American Bankers Association, and Gail C. Bolcar, Economist in that Division.

A. Gilbert Heebner
December 1985

American Bankers Association Oversight Committee

Chairman
A. Gilbert Heebner
Executive Vice President
Economist
CoreStates Financial Corp
Philadelphia, PA

Vice Chairman
John K. Moore
Chairman of the Board
Chief Executive Officer
The Beach Bank of Vero Beach
Vero Beach, FL

Committee Members:

Richard Aspinwall
Vice President
The Chase Manhattan Bank, N.A.
New York, NY

Joe M. Cleaver
Senior Vice President,
   Corporate Planning
Florida National Banks of
   Florida, Inc.
Jacksonville, FL

William G. Colby, Jr.
Corporate Executive Officer
Sovran Bank, N.A.
Richmond, VA

Jack D. Davis
Chairman of the Board
United Bank of Arizona
Tucson, AZ

Russell A. Freeman
Executive Vice President
General Counsel
Security Pacific Corporation
Los Angeles, CA

Thomas F. Huertas
Vice President
Citibank, N.A.
New York, NY

William E. Kelley
President
Bank of New England-Hancock
Quincy, MA

Robert E. Renner
Chairman of the Board
Citizens State Bank
Hartford City, IN

William W. Rodgers
Chairman of the Board
Chief Executive Officer
Security Bank and Trust Co.
Blackwell, OK

Robert A. Rough
President
Chief Executive Officer
The National Bank of Sussex
County
Branchville, NJ

Sung W. Sohn
Senior Vice President
Chief Economist
Norwest Corp., Minneapolis,
N.A.
Minneapolis, MN

Thomas J. Stanton, Jr.
Chairman
First Jersey National Bank
Jersey City, NJ

Thomas W. Synnott, III
Senior Vice President
Chief Economist
United States Trust Company
New York, NY

Ronald R. Tullos, Esq.
President
Chairman of the Board
Chief Executive Officer
National Bank of Arkansas
N. Little Rock, AR

Acknowledgments

A special acknowledgment goes to Edward Furash and William R. Weber, Principals of Furash and Company of Washington, D.C., who provided constant encouragement and support from the beginning through all phases of the project. Bill attended the various meetings, read the papers, and offered valuable input from both a technical and industry prospective. Furash and Company also provided overall administrative support for the study including meeting space, library services through the capable hands of Jan Regan and typing help from Nina Bishop in preparing the final document.

We would also like to extend our thanks to Joseph Foote, whose diligence and professionalism in editing the manuscript have contributed greatly to this work.

Executive Summary

Banking is now, and has always been, a risky business. The key to success both in operating a bank and supervising a banking system is management of risk. Since the end of World War II, risk management has become more difficult, and, because of several factors, the likelihood of failure of individual banks has significantly increased. These factors include: (1) changes in the economic environment, such as higher and more volatile interest rates; (2) changes in technology, resulting in faster and cheaper transfer of funds and information; (3) a movement toward deregulation; and (4) the subsidies for many institutions imbedded in the flat-rate premium structure of the federal deposit insurance system. The latter three factors have been important in allowing risk-prone institutions access to large amounts of funds.

While the present system of deposit insurance protects depositors from losses due to bank failure and contributes to stability of the banking system as a whole, indirectly it promotes an increase in the riskiness of individual banks. Banks have been able to reduce capital ratios, substituting, in effect, deposit insurance for equity as a means to protect depositors. Deposit insurance has lowered funding costs for all banks, but—more importantly—the system of flat-rate deposit insurance premiums has favored those bankers more disposed toward risk-taking. It has allowed them to be more aggressive and, in the process, to shift risk to the insurance funds. For this reason, reform of the deposit insurance system is needed in several key respects if the insurance system is to avoid being sorely tested in the next few years.

The basic concern is not with the increased risk of individual bank failures, or with the greater number of actual failures in recent years, but with the stability of the banking system. The stability of the system is enhanced by federal deposit insurance, which limits the potentially disruptive contagion effect of an individual failure leading to collapse of other banks, and by the operation of the Federal Reserve System as the lender of last resort to the banking system and to individual institutions. Losses to bank stockholders (and uninsured creditors) are both likely and desirable in the future, as more market discipline is introduced. However, as long as the Federal Deposit Insurance Corporation (FDIC) and, more importantly, the Federal Reserve, meet their responsibilities appropriately, there is no danger of a collapse of the banking system.

Bank Runs

This conclusion is based, in part, on a review of the history of bank failures in the United States, including their causes and impacts on the economy. A key consideration is the conditions under which bank runs become contagious runs and cause the failure of sound institutions. It is important to distinguish between a bank failure that wipes out only stockholders and a failure that results in losses to depositors and the deposit insurance system. For example, a bank that is closed by the supervisory authorities when its net worth is approximately zero represents a total loss to its owners, but negligible loss to depositors. The review of U.S. banking history indicates that actual losses to depositors from bank failures have been very small, even in periods in which failures were more common than today.

While preventing bank runs is frequently cited as a major accomplishment of deposit insurance, contagious bank runs do not seem to have been a major source of disruption in U.S. banking history, except during the Great Depression of the 1930s. Most bank runs involve the movement of funds from one bank to another. This creates liquidity problems for the bank subject to the run, but not for the system as a whole—what one bank loses, another gains. Even if the funds withdrawn are used to buy other assets, such as government securities, the outflow of funds is rarely systemic, because the seller of the securities is likely to deposit the proceeds into the banking system. There is a systemic problem only when the run takes the form of a flight to currency that is not redeposited in the banking system. The increase in currency holdings represents a loss of reserves for the banking system, but one that can be replaced by appropriate Federal Reserve actions, such as open market purchases of government securities or making loans to individual banks.

Such a flight to currency has only rarely been a feature of U.S. banking history, even before federal deposit insurance. (There were, however, temporary periods of suspension of conversion of bank notes into specie or of bank deposits into currency.) Since the establishment of the FDIC, there has not been any such flight to currency, nor is there likely to be as long as the public has confidence in the insurance system. Insured depositors have no incentive to participate in runs or to prefer currency to bank deposits.

It is important to recognize the relationship between the liquidity problem caused by runs and the solvency of individual banks. An economically solvent bank (i.e., one whose assets at market value exceed its liabilities) faced with a run can simply sell assets to meet the demand for cash. The danger is that if such sales must be made at "fire sale" prices (rather than at "fair market value"), a solvent institution can become insolvent. It is the responsibility of the Federal reserve (or the insurance agency with emergency lending authority) to prevent this result by being willing to lend without limit other than that of the amount of good collateral. This need not involve any loss to the government nor subsidy to the bank. It is merely a way to bridge the time imperfection of financial markets, whereby some assets cannot necessarily be sold at their fair market value instantaneously.

Role of Government

It is clear from the above analysis that the efficient functioning of the financial system benefits from appropriate governmental intervention. Much of this Report considers the means both of increasing the effectiveness and minimizing the extent of such intervention, and of harnessing market forces and incentives to maintain bank stability. In particular, eliminating restrictions on the activities of financial institutions and on the pricing of financial services helps consumers and promotes efficiency in the economy. If concern about the safety and soundness of the banking system halts the trend toward deregulation, or leads to "reregulation," these very real benefits to the economy would be lost. Moreover, some traditional regulation conflicts with risk-reduction, particularly as it limits the ability of depository institutions to diversify certain risks.

Achieving these objectives for the financial system requires a central bank with clearly understood responsibilities, a system of federal deposit insurance with appropriately priced premiums, and incentives for risk-monitoring and control by creditors and equity investors. While there is a broad list of options for reform of the deposit insurance system, there is no single solution, or "magic bullet," that is adequate to achieve these objectives. Several changes in the present system, all of which appear in the existing literature, are recommended. Some of these reform proposals have been discussed only superficially up to now, and the Report provides a more complete analysis.

The Report considers the feasibility of private deposit insurance as a substitute for a federal system, and concludes that privatization of basic deposit insurance is not an appropriate step (although there may be a role for private alternatives for supplemental coverage). The Report recognizes, however, that there are significant structural flaws in the present deposit insurance system that should be corrected. In particular, the present structure provides incentives to risk-taking in the form of a cross-subsidy from safe, conservative banks to aggressive, risky banks. Under the current system, risk-taking is controlled neither by market forces nor by the explicit deposit insurance premium structure, but by a system of restrictions and supervision (sometimes referred to as "implicit" deposit insurance premiums) that is cumbersome, sometimes ineffective, and sometimes perverse.

The structural weakness of the present deposit insurance system can be seen in the current problems of the Federal Savings and Loan Insurance Corporation (FSLIC). That system is near collapse, and its continued credibility is ever-increasingly based on presumed governmental support for the system. The FDIC is clearly not in the same condition as the FSLIC, but because the structures are similar, and because of the substantial contingent liability posed by mutual savings banks that the FDIC insures, some see the current state of the FSLIC as a portent of what the FDIC might become.

Market Discipline

A principal focus of the Report is on increasing the effectiveness of market discipline as a means of restraining risk-taking in the banking system. The federal deposit insurance system has always had a nominal role for market discipline by keeping insurance coverage at less than 100 percent. Uninsured depositors have suffered losses in some bank failures, but the incidence has been too low and too unpredictable to lead to significant monitoring of bank safety by depositors.

The FDIC has handled most bank failures by arranging mergers—purchase and assumption (P&A) transactions—with healthy banks, and these transactions protect both insured and uninsured liabilities in full. Some large failing banks (e.g., Bank of the Commonwealth, First Pennsylvania, Continental Illinois) have received direct assistance from the FDIC that allowed them to stay in business with all deposits and other liabilities protected. As a result of this policy, depositors—particularly at large banks—have little incentive to monitor bank condition carefully; they may rationally expect that if a problem develops they will be able to withdraw their funds in time, or that they will be protected, even in case of failure.

This FDIC policy has economic advantages—it preserves the going-concern value of failing banks, and it minimizes the risk of runs that might develop if depositors felt that they were truly at risk. But it surrenders the beneficial effect of market discipline and promotes a concentration of deposits in banks deemed "too large to fail" (more accurately, "too large to be liquidated"). To avoid a "flight to size" as a substitute for flight to quality, competitive equity considerations suggest that if depositors in large banks receive 100 percent protection, then depositors in smaller banks should be treated similarly. But this approach would eliminate market discipline and increase the role of government in the financial system. Alternatively, methods should be adopted that impose costs on uninsured creditors and equity holders, and these costs should be imposed equally on banks of all sizes.

Analysis of the effects of bank runs supports the hypothesis that the FDIC may have overemphasized the danger to the banking system from individual bank runs, particularly because fear of runs may be an effective force leading to bank conservatism. Nevertheless, bank runs are disruptive, and a policy of imposing greater losses on depositors may lead to an increased frequency of runs. One approach to this problem would be 100 percent insurance protection for holders of transaction deposits (plus, perhaps, very short-term time deposits), but only limited insurance on longer-dated time deposits. Holders of such deposits could not participate in a run, but could be expected to be a source of market discipline. (Again, the benefits of market discipline could be dissipated if failures were handled in a way that provided protection for all depositors.)

A better alternative is to require banks to issue some amount of subordinated debentures. Investors in such instruments would have an incentive to choose on the basis of bank soundness, imposing a higher interest cost on risky banks. These investors cannot participate in a run if problems develop; and, in case of failure, subordinated debt provides a cushion that protects depositors (and the FDIC) from loss.

Higher levels of equity capital would also serve as such a cushion as well as reducing incentives towards excessive risk-taking. Subordinated debt is a particularly useful form of capital in that its presence gives the authorities time to determine whether a bank is insolvent and when it should be closed. Appropriate action to close failing banks is important because, as net worth becomes negative, owners have strong incentives to take exceptional risks. That is clearly seen in the savings and loan industry today.

Supervisors attempt to monitor bank net worth through reporting requirements and examination. This is least successful, however, when fraud is involved. Fraud and insider abuses continue to be leading causes of bank failure, but also are responsible for the largest losses to uninsured depositors and to the FDIC, once failure has occurred. More examination and supervisory resources should be devoted to detection of fraud than has been the case in the past.

The Need for Information

If market discipline is to work effectively, depositors and investors need good information on the financial condition of the bank. At least for large banks, a great deal of information is available, and there are incentives for bank management to make those disclosures that are useful to investors. In banking, however, as distinct from most other industries, there are restrictions on voluntary disclosure by the firm. Although the case for additional disclosure requirements for large banks is not entirely clear, restrictions on disclosure should be eliminated. Additional disclosure by smaller banks, to bring them up to the practices of the large banks, may be necessary if market discipline is to be effective.

One type of information especially useful to investors and depositors is the market value of assets and liabilities. Publicly held bank holding companies now disclose the market value of securities held. In principle, management decisions should be based on market values rather than on historical cost or book values. The Report considers the concept and feasibility of market-value accounting for banks. While it does not recommend a requirement that accounting statements be prepared on a current-value basis, it does indicate that greater availability of market-value information for more assets and liabilities could be useful to management itself and the insurance agency, as well as to investors.

Risk-Related Premiums

Market discipline can be simulated by a system of deposit insurance premiums based on the riskiness of the bank. The logic and equity of such a system has long been recognized. Proposals for risk-related premiums in the past, however, have always foundered on the difficulty of measuring risk in an accurate and objective manner, and on the political difficulties of imposing what in some ways is a system based on the judgments of insuring authorities. Other considerations have included the distinction between risk of failure and loss to the insurer (which can be minimized by accurate monitoring and timely closing of insolvent institutions), and the fact that fraud—rather than risky assets—has been responsible for the bulk of FDIC losses. Nevertheless, some aspects of bank risk are measurable (interest rate risk, for example), and a system of risk-related premiums need not be actuarially perfect in order to be a useful constraint on risk-taking. At the least, even if risk is hard to measure *ex ante*, an *ex post* settling-up may be useful. If a bank knows that ventures that turn out badly will be subject to an increased insurance assessment after the fact, it will recalculate the potential costs and benefits from undertaking risky investments.

In the absence of market discipline or risk-related premiums, the allowable range of bank activities has been limited. An appropriately designed insurance system could lead to an easing of these restrictions (which may even reduce risk through greater diversification), although it is recognized that not all restrictions on bank activities can be traced to concern with bank safety and soundness. Restrictions on such activities as real estate or insurance brokerage, mutual fund management, and operating travel agencies bear little relationship to risk. Considerations such as fear of concentration of economic power, "fair competition," and objections to "tied sales" have played a large role, even though they have been inconsistently applied to specific issues. All these considerations have been raised in discussions of whether any expansion of bank activities is better confined to separate subsidiaries of bank holding companies or to the bank itself.

If insurance premiums are geared to the risks of the consolidated entity, there is little reason to prefer one type of organizational structure over another. In the transition to such a system, however, diversification should first be confined to financial activities so as to control monitoring costs and not to stretch management capabilities. Even if an optimal system of deposit insurance makes greater use of market discipline or risk-related premiums, there will still remain a role for bank supervision and examination. At a minimum, even with the optimal degree of reporting of financial information, on-site examination will be necessary to verify the accuracy of reports. In addition, fraud detection is better done through on-site inspection.

The Role of Examination

The record of the examination and supervisory function of the state and federal regulatory agencies has displayed weaknesses. Examiners have sometimes been slow to recognize serious problems, and the follow-up supervisory activity has more frequently failed to be timely. Moreover, the supervisory agencies have been exceedingly slow to implement screening devices, such as "early warning systems" and computer-based data collection and monitoring systems, that could lead to a more effective allocation of limited examiner resources. Finally, in view of the key role of fraud in bank failures (and particularly in FDIC losses), it is surprising that the examination function is not more oriented toward detecting fraud.

It has long been commonplace to point to the exceedingly complex structure of bank regulation in the United States as evidence of costly duplication and, potentially more serious, a sign of "competition in laxity" among the supervisory agencies. There is no evidence that competition in laxity has ever existed to the detriment of the public or of the efficient operation of the financial system. While it would be hard to demonstrate that the present system is an optimal one, there are clear benefits from the existence of more than one route to obtaining a bank charter, and perhaps from the existence of more than a single regulatory and insurance-pricing agency. In this regard, the Bush Task Force* recommendations have little merit, and in some ways (particularly in promoting a greater supervisory role for the Federal Reserve) represent a step backward.

Conclusion

The nation's banking system—the heart of the nation's financial system—is experiencing a number of serious problems. These problems are growing in severity, especially in the area of federal liability for accounts in federally insured banks and savings and loan associations. Solutions are available now, but solutions long delayed may prove not to be solutions at all.

The nation can do nothing, of course, but this will not correct the problems outlined in this Report. In the alternative, the nation can realistically face the fact that change is necessary, and take those steps that promise to ensure the safety and soundness of the banking system.

---

*Vice President's Task Group on Regulation of Financial Services, which issued a report, *Blueprint for Reform*, in 1984.

CHAPTER 1

The Risks of Bank Failure

"Risk" is the probability that any event, or set of events, might occur. It usually denotes a negative or undesired event—one that will cause a financial institution (hereafter generally called a bank) to fail rather than to be very successful. The types and sources of these risks are discussed first in this chapter, followed by an assessment of whether the risk of bank failure is greater now than it was previously. The chapter closes with an analysis of the stability of the banking system and the prospects for a financial system collapse.

Concern about large bank runs and other aspects of risks to individual banks and to the banking system are discussed in succeeding chapters. The consequences of the failure of one or more banks on other banks and on the regional and national economies are examined in Chapter 2. The effects of government-provided deposit insurance, treated briefly in this chapter, are analyzed more extensively in Chapter 3. The role of the lender of last resort, which is important for reducing liquidity risk (discussed briefly below), is considered in Chapter 5. The risk associated with expanded bank powers and the organizational form in which these powers are used (i.e., within the bank or in affiliates or subsidiaries) is analyzed in Chapter 6. The very important role of market discipline in reducing and controlling risk to socially acceptable levels is discussed briefly in this chapter, and is developed further in Chapters 7, 8, and 9.

The risks faced by individual banks come from three, not mutually exclusive, sources:

1. Insufficient diversification—the probability that some event, or group of events, will result in losses (reductions in equity capital) that will cause a bank to be insolvent;

2. Insufficient liquidity—the probability that a bank will be unable to meet demands for deposit withdrawals (a bank run) except at a price that results in the bank's insolvency (when the present value of its equity is negative); and

3. Risk-taking propensity—the willingness and ability of bankers to incur risks.

Diversification is important because many risks cannot be predicted; their effect, however, can be mitigated by reducing the impact that possible losses will have on the ability of a bank to continue operations, or by organizing a bank's activities such that losses are likely to be offset by gains. While liquidity is a banking risk that can be affected by bankers' actions, it also is a function of the banking system and has, in the past, affected the stability of the system. Risk-taking propensity (including risking insufficient diversification) must be considered because bankers can choose among alternative assets, liabilities, and activities such that the probability of both favorable and unfavorable outcomes is increased or decreased.

The types of individual bank risks and the prospects for their being mitigated by diversification are delineated and discussed in the next section of this chapter. Because fraud has been the single most important cause of bank failures, both in the past and in the present, it is distinguished from excessive risk-taking. Risks that can be excessive include interest rate risk, securities speculation, foreign exchange risk, risk-taking by affiliates and subsidiaries, credit (default) risk, operations risk, and regulatory risk. Liquidity risk, which is a function of runs on individual banks, is considered in the following section. (Because of its importance, liquidity is considered further in Chapter 2.)

Types of Individual Bank Risk

Fraud Risk

Fraud has always been a major problem for banks because they deal in very large quantities of the most easily fenced of all commodities—money. In the United States over the period 1865-1931, fraud and violations of the law were cited by the Comptroller of the Currency as the cause most responsible for failures of national banks. Frauds also are responsible for the most costly losses to depositors and the insurance agencies; the assets in other failures usually have substantial liquidation value, while frauds usually result in the almost total dissipation of assets. The ratio of the number of citations for fraud to the total number of identified causes of failures ranges from 63 percent over the years 1914-1920 to 18 percent over the decade 1921-1929 (when local economic depression was identified as the principal cause). (Benston, 1973, Table VII). For the period 1934-1958, the Federal Deposit Insurance Corporation (FDIC) reports that for "approximately one-fourth of the banks, defalcation or losses attributable to financial irregularities by officers and employees appear to have been the primary cause of failure." (FDIC, 1958, pp. 28–9). During 1959-1971, fraud and irregularities were responsible for 66 percent of the failures. (Benston, 1973, Table XI). An overlapping study of 67 insured banks that failed between 1960 and 1974 found that 59 (88 percent) were attributable to improper loans, defalcations, embezzlement, and manipulations. (Hill, 1975).

Data from 1982, 1983, and the first quarter of 1984 show that fraud continues to be the principal contributor to bank failures. Peterson and Scott (1985) analyzed and extended information compiled by the U.S. House of Representatives Committee on Government Operations, Subcommittee on Commerce, Consumer and Monetary Affairs. They found that failures could be ascribed principally to three, sometimes overlapping factors: (1) malfeasance, measured by continuing investigations by the Federal Bureau of Investigation (FBI) or Justice Department in response to all allegations of misconduct or by guilty pleas, criminal convictions, or grand jury indictments of bank officers and directors; (2) rapid growth, measured by asset growth in excess of 40 percent over a two-year period prior to failure; and (3) low performance, measured by returns on assets in the bottom quarter of similar-size banks for three consecutive years prior to failure. They report the following number and percentages ascribed to malfeasance and overlapping other factors among the 33 failures in 1982 and 47 failures in 1983 and 1984 first quarter:

	Number			Percentages of total failures		
	1982	1983-84	Total	1982	1983-84	Total
Malfeasance only	15	9	24	45	19	30
and low performance	6	6	12	18	13	15
and rapid growth	5	8	13	15	17	16
and both	1	3	4	3	6	5
Total malfeasance	27	26	53	82	55	66

The number of ways that frauds can be perpetrated is great, but hardly infinite. Indeed, it seems that the same means have been used time and time again. Simple looting of vaults is rare, probably because it is more profitable and less risky to steal in other ways. When banks' liabilities consisted primarily of bank notes, a simple means was printing, distributing, and making very difficult the redemption of notes for which there was insufficient backing. As Sinkey (1979, pp. 3–5) describes, this was the cause of the first U.S. bank failure, in 1809.

Making loans to associates who either take great risks with or just steal the funds is perhaps the most popular means of defrauding banks and the deposit insurance agencies. This method of removing funds from a bank has the benefit of being similar to ordinary banking practice. Consequently, it may be easily undertaken and, when the "loans" fail, the cause may be ascribed to errors of judgment or bad luck, rather than stealing. Perhaps this is why this method has such a long history. Some recent, rather spectacular examples appear to be the failures of the United States National Bank of San Diego, the Penn Square Bank of Oklahoma City, the United American Bank in Knoxville, Empire Savings and Loan of Mesquite, Texas, and possibly Home State Savings Bank in Cincinnati, Ohio. (See Committee on Government Operations, 1984C, for an extensive analysis and examples.)

Purchasing property from confederates at inflated prices is another method that has been used, but with much less frequency. One reason for its lack of popularity is that banks are not permitted to own property except for operating purposes, which limits the amounts that can be stolen. A second reason is the much clearer trail of wrongdoing that is left, particularly as compared with loans. The selling price and parties to the sale of real property usually are legally recorded, which, when combined with comparable appraisals, establishes a record of inflated values.

Excessive Risk-Taking in General

Excessive risk-taking is defined as risks that a bank would not take were it not for the presence of underpriced deposit insurance or uninformed investors whom the banker need not compensate for the possibility of failure. Excessive risk-taking is distinguished from fraud, because it need not be illegal *per se*. Consequently, it is safer (more profitable) than fraud; it is also likely to be a problem that is exacerbated by underpriced deposit insurance.

The total risk of a bank's failing is not a function of the sum of the individual risks, because one risk can offset another. Indeed, the addition of an activity with high potential cash flows will reduce the risk of bank failure if these flows are negatively or even imperfectly correlated with similarly large cash flows from the bank's other operations. This is why interest rate risk (expressed in the form of an unbalanced total portfolio with respect to duration) is particularly dangerous, because there is nothing to offset a negative event. Consequently, those who practice this form of risk often are described as "betting the bank."

Interest Rate Risk

When interest rates change unexpectedly, the present value of fixed coupon assets and liabilities changes as the promised payments are discounted at higher or lower rates. The greater the difference between the durations of assets and liabilities, the greater the effect that a change of interest rates has on a bank's capital. (See Kaufman, 1984). While the risk due to changes in interest rates has always been a possibility, this source of risk was not considered to be serious as long as interest rates were stable. However, interest rate changes experienced since the late 1970s have shown that the effect of interest rate risk can be very great. McCulloch (1981, pp. 237–238) conducted some simulations, using data on interest rate variations from January 1947 to June 1977. He found that a bank with a capital/asset ratio of 7 percent, liabilities repriced continuously at the market, and a portfolio of 1-year bonds would be likely to fail once in 66 years. But, if it had a portfolio of 20-year amortized mortgages, it would be likely to fail once in 8 years. Indeed, this has been the experience of thrift institutions. The relatively high rates of failure that they experienced are attributable primarily to the greater durations of their assets rather than liabilities combined with increases in interest rates. (See Benston, 1985).

Unbalanced portfolios can provide bankers who want to take excess risks with the opportunity. As Kane (1985, Chapter 5) explains, the presence of underpriced deposit insurance has given thrift institutions, in particular, considerable incentives to gamble that interest rates will decrease rather than increase. Many of them lost this gamble during the past five years. Kane (1985, Tables 4–5 and 4–6) estimates that as of December 31, 1983, the aggregate net worth after deducting unrealized losses on mortgages is negative $12.3 billion for mutual savings banks and negative $73.7 billion for savings and loan associations.

Similarly, investing funds that are borrowed short term in long-term bonds is a means of taking interest rate risk. This gamble (together with loan losses) is what caused the effective failure of The First Pennsylvania Bank. In 1979, the year before it failed, the bank's total portfolio is estimated to have had a duration of between 1.3 and 2.5 years, while almost all of its liabilities were of very short duration. When interest rates went up instead of down, the bank's bond portfolio is estimated to have declined in market value by $89 million, which contributed considerably to reducing its equity to below zero, if measured on a market value basis. (Maisel, 1981, pp. 130).[1]

Another example is the sale of a standby commitment to purchase securities at a fixed rate, price, or yield on a future date, at the option of the purchaser of the commitment. The banker who sells the commitment gets a fee, for which the possibility of a large loss is accepted. Alternatively, the banker could buy or sell a foward commitment that is binding on both parties, thereby hoping for a large gain but accepting the possibility of a large loss. Similar risks can be taken with securities that are sold or purchased with agreements (repos and reverse repos) to repurchase or resell at a fixed price when the transaction is unsecured. This occurs when the banker takes notes rather than possession of the securities that were purchased under a resale (repo) contract (as occurred with Home State Bank and others). These transactions have appeal to the risk-seeking banker because they offer the prospects of quick and large gains and do not require much expertise.

Securities Speculation

Equities are usually considered the principal vehicle for securities speculation because their value generally can change much more than that of bonds. However, the recent issuance of very high-risk, high nominal-yield "junk" bonds, often issued by corporations formed to finance takeovers, has given risk-seeking thrift associations a means to indulge their preferences. Although Federal Reserve member banks are forbidden by the Banking Act of 1933 (the Glass-Steagall Act) from investing in corporate securities, they can invest in mortgage and other asset-backed bonds of varying degrees of risk.

Foreign Exchange Risk

Speculative dealing in foreign exchange is another way in which great risk can be taken in the quest for great gain. Options and foward contracts can be used to increase the potential gains and losses considerably. Franklin National Bank of New York provides the most notable U.S. example of such risk-taking. Before its failure in 1974, it was the 20th largest U.S. bank and the largest in U.S. history to have failed. Other factors caused Franklin's problems, but as its financial situation worsened, it engaged in increasingly risky foreign exchange transactions that included hiding the extent of the bank's positions from Comptroller of the Currency examiners. The loss on these transactions amounted to $65 million for the first five months of 1974, the largest loss ever reported to that date by an American bank. (See Spero, 1980, p. 126). Similar speculations were responsible for the failure in 1974 of Bankhaus I.D. Herstatt of Cologne, one of Germany's largest private banks, and for very sizeable losses by other banks.

Risk-Taking by Affiliates, Subsidiaries, and Related Organizations

Banks are said to use affiliated organizations to take excessive risks. In his analysis of the conditions leading to the passage of the Glass-Steagall Act, Peach (1941) suggests that affiliates were used for this purpose in the late 1920s, but he does not cite any evidence. A more current example is the Hamilton National Bank of Chattanooga, which was the third largest failure and the 195th largest U.S. bank when it failed in 1976. The bank invested heavily and disastrously in real estate loans that were booked by a holding company affiliate, Hamilton Mortgage Corporation of Atlanta. The bad loans were shifted ("sold") from the affiliate to the bank. Thus, the separate corporate form of organization did not shield the bank from the losses incurred. However, because the shifting of loans violated regulations, this example might be better classified as fraud. (Sinkey, 1979, pp. 199–205).

The strength of incentives for a banking organization to accept responsibility for related entities is shown by banks' treatment of the real estate investment trusts (REITs) that they organized. Technically, REITs are not bank affiliates, but separate organizations that banks sponsor and often manage. Although it is not clear whether many REITs were engaged in overly risky investments, were poorly managed, or simply experienced bad luck when interest rates unexpectedly increased, they absorbed considerable losses. Many sponsoring banks "bailed out" their affiliates and sponsored enterprises, particularly where these bore the bank's name, rather than suffer a loss of reputation. (See Sinkey, 1979, pp. 237–255). Thus, the shifting of activities to another related organization did not shield the banks from the losses incurred. (The role of holding company affiliates and related organizations is discussed in Chapter 6.)

Credit (Default) Risk

The possibility that borrowers will not repay their loans as promised is a basic risk that bankers take and manage as an integral part of their business. Indeed, assessing and pricing these risks, determining the optimal amount of collateral, writing covenants and other legal agreements that constrain borrowers from unilaterally changing the risks they presented to the banker, establishing and maintaining the documentation that would support legal actions to collect the loans, monitoring loans, and creating an efficiently diversified portfolio of loans are basic activities in which banks should have a comparative advantage. However, some past and recent failures have indicated that bankers occasionally do not exercise the caution for which they are famous (or, from the viewpoint of rejected borrowers, infamous). An important case in point is the failure of the Penn Square Bank, which wrote more than a billion dollars in multimillion-dollar loans based on nothing more than the unfounded belief of the lending officer that the borrowers "were good for it." Even more astounding, perhaps, was the ease with which Penn Square sold enormous amounts of undocumented loans to such banks as Continental Illinois, Northern Trust, Michigan National, Chase Manhattan, and Seafirst. (Singer, 1985).[2]

Guarantees of acceptances and other obligations of customers represent a sale of the banks' credit evaluation expertise and standing. These off-balance sheet items subject banks to the same sort of risk of loss that they incur when loans are booked. Therefore, they should be taken explicitly into account when the riskiness of a bank's portfolio is assessed.

The risk that defaults will result in the failure of a bank is greatest where the bank does not hold a diversified portfolio. Indeed, lending relatively large amounts to a single borrower or industry has been an important cause of bank failures and an early subject of regulations. Many banks in Renaissance Italy and elsewhere failed as a consequence of loans made to princes and kings who refused or were unable to repay their borrowings. The first three failed U.S. national banks had made large loans to a few borrowers who failed. (Sinkey, 1979, p. 9). The Penn Square failure represents nothing new.

Although the banking regulations of most states and the federal agencies limit loans to any one borrower to 15 percent of a bank's capital and surplus, similar limits are not formally imposed on loans to a single industry. Loans to mobile home dealers were responsible for the 1966 failure of the Public Bank of Detroit, one of the largest failures up to that time. More recently, the concentration of the Penn Square Bank and many Texas and Oklahoma banks in oil-related loans was responsible for their failures. Banks in Oregon that were heavily involved in the timber industry and banks in farm states have experienced relatively high rates of failure, apparently because of the very bad economic condition of the industries in which they specialized. (See Bovenzi and Nejezchleb, 1985). A similar situation explains the high rate of failure in the 1920s and early 1930s of banks in the western grain and southeastern and southwestern farm states. (Benston, 1973, Table III).

"Country risk" is another aspect of default risk. It refers to the possibility that loans will not be repaid as promised because economic conditions in a country have deteriorated to the point where the foreign exchange needed to service loans made in foreign currency is unlikely to be available, or because the government will not permit the loans to be repaid and/or will not repay the loans made to it. This risk has become more visible as a consequence of the inability of several less developed countries to repay their debts as scheduled. The interesting questions are whether: (1) the large banks that made these loans correctly assessed the nonrepayment risk and were sufficiently compensated in the earlier years of the loans to offset the later losses (which is to say, the loans were positive present-value investments); (2) the banks correctly assessed the risks and are carrying a diversified portfolio of loans, of which some of the country loans have turned out badly while others (to which attention is not drawn) turned out well; (3) the banks misassessed the risk because the present situation could not reasonably have been forecast, and they had no way to know the extent to which these countries were becoming indebted; (4) the banks failed to analyze the risks because of incompetence or overconfidence; (5) the banks knowingly took risk because they expected or hoped to be bailed out by the government; or (6) the banks took advantage of underpriced FDIC insurance to take excessive risks.

Operations Risk

Operations risk refers to the possibility that a bank will be operated such that its costs exceed its revenues, thereby depleting its equity capital. In an important sense, all of the risks discussed above, including fraud, are operating risks. Fraud or gross mismanagement can occur as a consequence of an inadequate system of internal control, or a system that is ineffectively maintained and monitored. Such appears to have been the situation that resulted in the massive losses taken by Continental Illinois. (See Report of the Special Litigation Committee . . .,1984). Foreign exchange risk also can be incurred inadvertently when traders' activities are poorly monitored. The managers of affiliates and subsidiaries similarly might take risks greater than those the bank's managers would find prudent, or might excessively overexpand their activities. Default and interest rate risks become a serious problem when lending and investments are insufficiently controlled and diversified. Thus, most risks may be considered to be aspects of operations, and the cost of risk can be reduced with operations controls.

Another aspect of operations risk is related to the operation of the payments system, which is an integral part of banking. One risk is fraud by customers, which can take the form of outright stealing of funds, fraudulent loans, or through unreimbursed use of funds by taking advantage of imperfections in float monitoring. The increasing use of computers to process payments has made both methods of fraud more prevalent and costly. Customers (or computer "hackers") attempt to and sometimes succeed in violating electronically a bank's funds-transfer system. Recently, E.F. Hutton admitted to obtaining billions of dollars in interest-free funds by writing checks on uncollected balances, a form of check kiting made possible on a large scale by computers.

Another payments system-related risk is daylight overdrafts. Banks can use hundreds of millions of dollars in funds that are uncollected as long as the cash letters clear by the end of the day. Should a bank fail during the day, the entire system could grind to a halt; individual claims could be very difficult to assess, resulting in great_cost to the banks and their customers. This almost happened when the Bankaus Herstatt of Cologne, Germany, failed.

"Operations risk" additionally refers to the efficiency with which the bank's activities are conducted. The risk is that the costs of an operation might substantially exceed the revenues generated. A bank might not keep up with technological change, and so miss the opportunity to improve its operations and provide services demanded by its present and potential customers. On the other hand, overly ambitious managers might overextend their banks by expanding branch networks and developing and marketing new products. For example, a major cause of Franklin National Bank's problems was its relatively high level of operating expenses. Compared with a sample of the 50 largest U.S. banks, Franklin's net operating income as a percentage of assets in the years before its failure was significantly lower; Franklin's revenues and expenses separately, however, were not significantly different from the control group, except for 1973 (the year before failure), when its expenses were significantly higher. (Sinkey, 1979, Tables 6.9 and 6.10). It should be noted, though, that this type of operations risk rarely is the major cause of a bank's failure. While Franklin spent more than was justified, *ex post*, on opening and staffing branches in New York City and overseas, (see Spero, 1980), its failure was the result of losses from bad lending practices and from later foreign exchange speculation. (See Rose, 1974).

Similarly, even though bad management has been cited as an important cause of bank failures (although far behind fraud), poor earnings are much more likely to be the result of unexpected (or undesired) changes in interest rates and other results of risk-taking behavior. On the other hand, effectively conducted operations are necessary for a bank to maintain and attract equity capital, which is an important factor in reducing the probability and cost of failure. The propensity of bankers to take operations risk is enhanced by different aspects of regulations and deregulation.

Regulatory Risk

Laws and regulations can have a considerable effect on banks' profitability and ability to survive. Laws that constrain banks from diversifying their assets and liabilities efficiently have been (and still are) an important cause of failures. In particular, laws restricting branching were responsible for a large number of the failures of the small unit banks in the 1920s and 1930s. When the largely farming and timbering activities in these banks' market areas collapsed, the banks suffered simultaneous losses of deposits and defaulted loans. Not having funds and gains from other areas to offset their losses, the banks had to close their doors. This situation is being repeated in the 1980s. While unit banks in farm states could have diversified their assets by purchasing non-local assets, they would have had to limit lending to their customers, which would have cost them their comparative advantage from serving local customers. Sales of participations in loans also is a possibility, but it is limited by the cost of evaluating and monitoring loans; these costs are higher for separate banks than for a single bank with branches. Legislation, such as the Community Reinvestment Act of 1977, that requires banks to lend to particular borrowers or in particular geographic areas (or punishes them for not doing so), also may result in inefficiently diversified portfolios. Consequently, a decline in value of the assets of a group of borrowers in whom a bank has a relatively high percentage of its loans can result in losses that exceed the bank's capital.

Legal restrictions on the products that banks can offer, such as Glass-Steagall Act provisions that prohibit banks from offering corporate security transactions and underwriting, similarly limit portfolio diversification. Product-limiting laws may have been particularly important for thrift institutions. Prior to 1981, most thrifts were not permitted to offer most types of consumer and business loans, and were prohibited from offering variable-rate mortgages. They were also subsidized with lower taxes and underpriced deposit insurance for holding long-term mortgages. Their resulting long-duration, unbalanced portfolios made them especially susceptible to the devastating effects of increases in interest rates. Although they presently can offer a wide range of financial services, they find it very difficult to diversify their portfolios in competition with established commercial banks.

Controls on interest rates that banks could offer to depositors have benefited banks in the short run, but have damaged them as depositors and uncontrolled suppliers of financial services found ways to obtain and offer market rates of interest. Banks were forced to compete in inefficient ways, such as overexpanding branches and other non-interest means of attracting deposits. Although brokered deposits have frequently been criticized and often are associated with failures due to overexpansion, they also offer a cost-effective means for banks and thrifts to obtain funds. Indeed, a careful study of brokered deposits by the staff of the House Committee on Government Operations of the period December 31, 1983, through March 31, 1984, found "no evidence that brokered deposits are more likely to be misused or to contribute to institutions' losses than other kinds of rate-sensitive purchased liabilities." (Committee on Government Operations, 1984b, p. 9).

Thrift institutions, particularly mutual savings banks in New York State, were strongly negatively affected by state-imposed usury ceilings on mortgage loans. State and federal laws made investment in mortgages necessary and otherwise desirable, while restricting investments in other types of loans. Hence, many savings banks invested in bonds. Unfortunately, they chose to take interest rate risk by investing in long-term bonds. When interest rates increased, they suffered losses both on their mortgage and bond portfolios, resulting in multiple failures. Until reserve requirements were reduced, Federal Reserve member banks and their customers suffered from required non-interest-bearing reserves that made bank money more expensive for users than alternatives. These and other regulations have made it more difficult for banks to operate efficiently and effectively.[3]

Mismeasurement of bank capital also may be categorized as a regulatory induced risk. Banks can increase their recorded capital by making risky loans with high up-front fees, where most of the fees are recorded as current income and, hence, as an increase to capital. This appears to be what Empire Savings and Loan of Mesquite, Texas, did. Nevertheless, the Federal Home Loan Bank Board apparently could not "see past" the accounting; Chairman Edwin J. Gray testified that:

> While the . . . examination . . . found violations of regulations and practices that were clearly unsafe and unsound, Empire, at least on paper, did not appear to be heading toward insolvency. Instead, its earnings and assets appeared to be growing. (Committee on Government Operations, 1984A, p. 33).

Liquidity Risk—Runs on Individual Banks

The losses any enterprise incurs are borne by those with claims over its assets. Therefore, people with such claims have considerable incentives to liquidate their claims while sufficient assets remain in the enterprise. Although equity holders and creditors with claims that are not due until a specified date have no legal right to insist that the enterprise pay out assets to them, such is not the case for depositors whose claims are payable on demand. If these depositors believe that their bank's assets are worth less than the bank's equity and nondemand liabilities, they also believe that only the earliest depositors who remove their funds will be fully repaid. Hence, they have reason to remove their balances as soon as possible—which is the definition of a bank run. Of course, those depositors who believe that their claims will be fully met by a deposit insurer have no motive to withdraw their funds precipitously.

Liquidity risk refers to the possibility that depositors will withdraw funds from a bank in excess of the bank's ability to obtain those funds except at a considerably higher-than-normal cost. The higher cost could result from higher borrowing costs or the sale of assets at fire sale prices. These higher costs could be sufficient to cause a solvent bank to become insolvent. In this event (if no other action were taken), the regulatory authorities could force the bank to cease operations as an independent enterprise by closing it or by forcing it to merge with another institution. This action usually causes additional costs, to the further detriment of shareholders, bank employees, customers, and the deposit insurance agencies. Hence, liquidity risk is very important. The means of dealing with it, particularly by the insurance agencies and the Federal Reserve as the lender of last resort, are discussed in Chapters 2 and 5.

Liquidity problems do not occur in the ordinary course of events, because a bank can count on a large proportion of withdrawn funds to be replenished from deposits and loan repayments. The balance usually comes from four sources: (1) sales of assets with very low-selling (transactions) costs, such as U.S. treasury bills; (2) sales of packages of standardized loans, such as Federal Housing Administration (FHA) mortgages; (3) sales of certificates of deposits; (4) borrowing of federal funds; and (5) borrowing from correspondent banks. The first and fifth sources generally are continuously utilized, while, for smaller banks in particular, the rest are not. Because the markets for these types of asset sales and borrowings are efficient, the transactions cost of obtaining funds is low and the amount of funds that can be obtained in a short time is great. But the efficiency with which banks can obtain funds by these means is due to the belief by market participants that they are taking almost no risk in buying many assets from banks or in lending to them. The fact of a bank run is evidence that this confidence does not exist for assets other than those with obvious market values.

Consider first the sale of assets as a means of obtaining funds. A bank experiencing a run has no problem in selling assets about which purchasers need no information, such as U.S. Treasury obligations and other traded securities. However, it often must incur considerable costs to be able to sell assets, such as loans, about which a potential buyer has little trustworthy information, particularly if the bank run has occurred because depositors question the value of a bank's loans (perhaps because of an alleged fraud or the failure of a major borrower or borrowers). The bank's only feasible alternative, then, is to sell loans or participations in loans to correspondent banks that know and trust it, or to discount the loans with the lender of last resort—the Federal Reserve. Indeed, this is the function of the lender of last resort—to step in when a bank is solvent but where the transactions costs of selling assets is high because of market distrust.

Borrowings that are not insured by the FDIC or other federal agency are clearly affected by a loss of confidence in a bank's solvency. The bank can offer higher interest rates, but no rate is sufficiently high if the lender is certain that the money will not be returned. Furthermore, because higher-than-ordinary market rates usually indicate higher-than-ordinary risk, the offering of higher rates often is taken as a signal that the bank is in serious financial trouble. Considering the cost of determining the risk, many lenders are likely to choose the alternative of refusing to lend to a bank that offers high rates of interest, thereby forcing the bank to pay even higher rates to those who are willing to take the risk.

Relationships Among Risks and Banks' Means of Dealing With Them

Tradeoffs Among Risks

Many of the risks discussed above are related and can be dealt with together. Fraud usually is reduced to tolerable proportions by internal control systems. Having many different people responsible for disbursing and receiving cash, for approving a loan, and for obligating the bank is the usual procedure. Monitoring of the control system is an important, indeed vital, requirement. Unfortunately, this obvious step was not taken by the management of Continental Illinois, according to the Report of the Special Litigation Committee of the Board of Directors (1984). Although the bank's regulations required multiple signatures for loans and participations of the type made to and with the Penn Square Bank, and reports of loans that were not approved and performing as required, no one who had the power to do something seemed to be monitoring the system or concerned when irregularities were revealed. While this situation could be the result of incompe-tence or malfeasance, it may represent a tradeoff between incurring the cost of monitoring a control system and risking its breakdown. Smaller organizations may trade off the cost of establishing an effective control system for the risk of fraud or error. While such *ex ante* trade-offs may be cost effective, *ex post*, when a fraud has occurred, the tradeoff decision probably will appear to have been either stupid or conspiratorial.

Risk-taking similarly is subject to tradeoffs. Better control and monitoring systems can reduce unauthorized transactions by foreign currency traders and managers of affiliates. Default risk can be reduced in a similar fashion. Interest rate risk can be reduced by expenditures on asset/liability planning models and by hedges with interest rate futures and options. Adjustable-rate (ARM) rather than fixed-rate (FRM) mortgages can be offered. However, this ARM-FRM substitution involves trading interest rate risk for default risk, unless the adjustable-rate mortgages have greater equity cushions as a conse-quence of higher downpayments or shorter maturities (which is unusual). Regulatory risk can be reduced by expenditures on lobbying and planning. Liquidity risk can be mitigated by large holdings of readily marketable securities and established lines of credit. These alternatives, however, increase operations risk because they all are costly. Management's task is to equate the expected marginal avoid-able cost of risks with the marginal cost of reducing risks. In this respect, risk management is no different from other types of manage-ment.

Diversification

Bankers can reduce risk by diversifying their activities and portfolios. Not putting all the eggs in one basket reduces the possibility that all will be lost if the basket is dropped or stolen. Nevertheless, sufficient diversification often is not undertaken, for at least three reasons. First, bankers may not be permitted to diversify. As noted above (see regulation risk), laws restricting branching and products keep banks from diversifying optimally. If these laws were based on mitigating or preventing the imposition of a negative externality, such as the ostensible concern that the removal of constraints on branching would lead to monopolies, the constraint might be justified. However, the antibranching laws are better explained as protecting banks with local monopolies from competition. Another example is enforced or encouraged specialization by depository thrift institutions, which research and experience have shown to be not supported by concerns for externalities (such as socially desirable housing), while making the institutions excessively subject to interest rate risk. (Recent regulatory changes, such as those permitting thrifts wider powers and adjustable-rate mortgages, have reduced their involuntary proneness to that risk.) Laws that penalize banks for not making investments in particular areas, such as the Community Reinvestment Act, also lead to inadequate diversification.

Second, diversification can be costly if the bank must give up the advantages of specialization, including benefits to the bank's customers. For example, it might be beneficial for a bank in a small farming community to hold only, say, 20 percent of its assets in loans to farmers. But such a policy probably would not give the bank the opportunity fully to use its expertise in farm lending. If there were few banks in the area (which is likely), this policy would seriously inconvenience the local farmers, who would have to bear higher transactions costs from dealing with a distant bank. However, the local bank could diversify by selling shares in its loans to others, although it would have to incur the costs of convincing those investors of the value of those loans. Thus, bankers may trade higher net profits for greater risks.

Third, some bankers may not want to diversify because they want to take risks. Deposit insurance that is not priced to reflect risk fully gives holders of the insurance an incentive to take risks. Furthermore, managers of institutions that are insolvent, in the sense that the present going-concern value of their assets is less than the present going-concern value of their liabilities, have incentives to "bet the bank."

Therefore, one cannot simply assume that bankers will tend to make the socially optimal tradeoffs among the costs and benefits of risk incurrence and reduction, as they would in the absence of restrictive regulation and underpriced deposit insurance.

Incentives Towards Risk-Taking by Bankers

Deposit insurance and presently available technology virtually eliminate the incentive for insured depositors to monitor the banks' risk-taking. They also reduce incentives for monitoring by demand depositors and, subsequent to the extension of insurance to all of Continental Illinois's creditors, by all uninsured depositors in the largest banks. As a result, there is an increased incentive for banks to take risks in the hope of profiting thereby.

An Illustration

The incentive towards risk-taking can be illustrated by means of choices among investments with uncertain outcomes. Assume a banker who has neither a preference for nor an aversion toward firm or career risk. In deciding whether to make an investment, the banker first estimates the expected cash flow. These cash flows are then discounted at an interest rate that is the opportunity cost of not making the next best available investment. Because the cash flows are uncertain, a probability calculation must be made to determine the expected amount, as in the following example for two investments, A and B, each of which has two possible outcomes:

$$\text{Net cash flow} * \text{Probability} = \text{Expected amount}$$

Investment A				
net cash flow	100	*	.1	=	10
possibilities	200	*	.9	=	180
expected value					190
Investment B				
net cash flow	−700	*	.1	=	−70
possibilities	300	*	.9	=	270
expected value					200

Investment B has a higher expected value and higher variance of possible outcomes than investment A. Because higher variances increase the risk of outcomes and make incurring the real costs of bankruptcy more likely, the banker might prefer investment A to investment B. If the costs of uncertainty and bankruptcy just equal the difference in expected values, the banker will be indifferent as to the alternatives. However, the banker probably could reduce the variance and eliminate the possibility of a failure-causing loss by diversifying among many loans and/or by making a large number of such loans, so that there would be a high probability that the losses in a time period would be offset by gains. Then investment B would be preferred and would be profitable. Indeed, the ability of bankers to reduce variance by diversifying among large numbers of loans is a key contribution of banking to the economy.

Assume now that these two investments represent all the investment possibilities, the banker borrows some of the funds from depositors, and the depositors perceive the possible outcomes to be as given above. If the depositors are not insured, they will insist on a return on their funds that compensates them for their share of the risk that a bad outcome might occur, because they normally would not share in the good outcome, should it occur. The depositors' concerns could be dealt with by the bank's owners putting in equity sufficient to absorb the possible loss of 700 from investment B, or by the bank offering depositors an interest rate that is contingent on the outcome of the investments. In the absence of such compensating arrangements, the bank would have to forgo use of depositors' funds, or take investment A rather than investment B.

Now introduce full deposit insurance. The depositors need not be compensated for risk, nor would they have much incentive to monitor the risks taken by the bank. The risk and the concern now would be borne by the insurer. Assume, though, that the insurance is not priced to compensate the insurer for risk and that the banker accepts investment B. Should the 300 cash flow occur, the bank will gain that amount (before interest and other expenses, which are the same for both investments). But if the owners' equity investment in the bank (which includes the value of a bank charter, customer goodwill, and other intangibles) is less than 700, say 200, 500 of the cash flow of -700 will be borne by the insurer. Hence, the expected value of investment B is $-200 \times .10 + 300 \times .90 = 250$. This additional amount would make investment B preferable to investment A.

Of course, many (perhaps most) bankers would find it distasteful to take risks that imposed costs on the FDIC, even though the bank was expected to benefit thereby. Such bankers would suffer psychic or moral costs from excessive risk-taking. These costs, in effect, increase the equity that the banker might lose should the unfortunate outome of -700 occur. But assume that the banker faces the alternative of bankruptcy or loss of job should the bank earn only 100 or 200 from investment A, while earnings of 300 from investment B would save the bank and the banker's job. Is it farfetched to conclude that such investments as B would not be taken? Furthermore, might not bankers in such a situation convince themselves and their boards of directors that the possible negative outcome from investment B is *very* unlikely to occur? In addition, the banker has a moral and probably a legal responsibility to take actions that benefit the owners. Refusal to take a risky investment that has a positive present value could be interpreted as an evasion of this responsibility.

The Role of Uninsured Depositors

Uninsured depositors have reason to be concerned about the risks taken by their bank, with several important exceptions. They may believe that the insurance agency will bail them out by having the bank's liabilities assumed by another bank (as was the common practice before the failure of the Penn Square Bank) or by extending deposit insurance to all deposits (as was done for the creditors of Continental Illinois). Or, the uninsured depositors may have loans outstanding that can be offset against their deposits. These depositors can closely monitor the activities of the bank or they can closely monitor rumors about the bank. Rumor-monitoring is likely to be preferred, because, should a run develop, it is best to remove one's funds quickly to the point where the remaining balances are insured or equal to loans one owes to the bank.

But running from a bank is not a costless procedure. Deposits are kept at a particular bank because it offers convenience and services that are more desirable than those offered by other banks. Uninsured depositors, in particular, often are also borrowers. They have invested in longstanding banking arrangements; they know their bankers and their bankers know them. Hence, against the possible losses from a bank failure, depositors weigh the costs of changing banks. In formal terms, a depositor with funds withdrawable on demand will run only if the present value of the expected loss should a bank fail, times the probability that it will fail, is greater than the cost of establishing a new banking arrangement plus the cost of removing the deposit from the bank.

However, uninsured demand depositors usually maintain deposits in several banks. Hence, they can switch fairly large amounts of funds among banks relatively quickly, should they fear that a bank is insolvent and their deposits are at risk. Therefore, unless all depositors believe that their funds are in fact (if not in law) totally insured, bankers have incentives to maintain uninsured depositors' confidence in their bank's solvency.

Holders of uninsured certificates of deposit (CDs) and other time-dated deposits cannot run until the due date of the obligations. Their concerns about the safety of the bank are expressed in the interest rate on the obligations demanded. Consequently, bankers have reason to be concerned about all uninsured depositors' and other creditors' perceptions about the risks taken by their banks, as is discussed further in Chapters 3 and 7.

The Role of the Deposit Insurance Agencies

If nominally uninsured depositors believe that they really are insured or that they will be able to remove their funds before the bank has run out of funds or is closed, the deposit insurers have greater reason to be concerned about risk-taking by bankers. Furthermore, even if most bankers would not chance or misperceive excessively risky investments because of the presence of deposit insurance, a few are likely to be opportunists or outright thieves. Unless the deposit insurance agency is able to monitor their behavior and charge them an insurance premium that compensates the agency for the risk, these bankers are likely not only to take risks, but may even seek them out. The means by which risks can be taken are extremely diverse, so much so that it is difficult to see how the deposit insurer can prohibit all activities that a risk-seeking banker could employ. The means by which the insurance agency have attempted to control excessive risk-taking and the effectiveness of these means are explored in Chapter 10.

Bankers' Attitudes Towards Risk-Taking

It is risky to comment on attitudes, which can be but imperfectly measured, if at all, and which measurements are not clearly related to actual behavior. Nevertheless, it seems likely that bankers' attitudes towards risk-taking also affect the likelihood that banks will fail. A change away from extreme risk aversion appears to have occurred as a result of most bankers' unwillingness or inability to fear or even imagine a time such as the Great Depression of the 1930s.

In addition, people who have not been trained in traditional banking have entered the industry, in part as a result of improvements in technology that have eliminated many barriers to entry. Entry by new suppliers was encouraged and financed by high interest rates, which enhanced the payoffs to developing ways to avoid the regulations that prevented traditional suppliers from serving the public by offering market rates of interest on deposits.

This situation is not reversible, because the available technology makes inexpensive the almost instantaneous transfer of very large sums of money, and that blurs (if not completely eliminates) the lines between regulated and unregulated banking. Thus it is not feasible to reregulate all possible substitutes for traditional banking services, although it might be possible to constrain chartered banks. However, the rescinding of costly regulations reduces the reward for regulation-avoiding innovations. Thus, if regulations on banking are reduced, such innovations are unlikely to pose a problem.

Changes in Risks Since Federal Deposit Insurance Was Established

The opportunities for bankers to take risks have been more than sufficient for some time. While more volatile interest rates and foreign exchange offer considerable possibilities for great gain or loss, traditional banking offers adequate opportunities for risk-taking. Although some important changes have taken place, the key change is the increased incentive toward risk-taking that has resulted from related increases in deposit insurance and decreases in equity capital.

Fraud

It is sometimes alleged that computers have made fraud easier to accomplish and more difficult to discover. Because an undiscovered fraud is by definition unknown, this hypothesis cannot be tested. However, few (among the frauds that have been discovered) are very different from those perpetrated before computers became prevalent. Most occur because of the absence of monitored controls, even though computers make such controls less expensive. But, the control system may not be used (as appears to have been the situation at Continental Illinois). Indeed, incentives to employ the controls effectively appear to have decreased. (Further discussion of this issue appears in Chapter 10.)

Interest Rate Risk

The unexpected increase in interest rates since the late 1970s has increased the cost of interest rate risk considerably for institutions that held assets with longer durations than their liabilities. The increased volatility of interest rates since 1979 also increased the potential for losses and gains. This phenomenon is new, although the potential for interest rate risk existed as long as thrifts were required and encouraged to specialize in long-term mortgages funded by immediately withdrawable savings.

Changes in the laws that permit thrifts to match their durations better by making loans and investments of shorter durations have reduced their potential exposure to interest rate risk. Market developments, such as interest rate futures and options, also offer some opportunity for banks to come close to neutralizing interest rate risk. Deregulation of interest rates also made it possible for depository institutions to reduce interest rate risk by allowing them to float longer-term liabilities.

Securities Speculation

Speculating on unexpected changes in interest rates and securities prices has long been available to bankers who wished to engage in this form of gambling. However, increased variability of interest rates and the availability of futures and options give risk-seeking managers an opportunity to gain or lose great sums of money in a short time. Although such market instruments can reduce risks by giving bankers an opportunity to hedge the risk of unexpected interest rate changes, they also offer the possibility of creating very unbalanced portfolios. Hence, they represent a different quality, if not a different type, of risk.

Foreign Exchange Risk

Foreign exchange holdings were subject to risk prior to 1973, when exchange rates were fixed, because rates changed in occasional large jumps rather than continuously. The adoption of floating exchange rates, however, increased trading and gave risk-seeking bankers the opportunity to gain or lose large sums more often. But foreign exchange is only one of many means of risk-taking. Bankers who want to take risks can make risky loans, build large office buildings that are only partially used for banking purposes, acquire sites for future branches, and speculate in interest rate movements by investing in or selling long-term, fixed-interest obligations. Hence, it cannot be said that the opportunities for risk-taking have increased.

Affiliate Risk

Affiliated organizations that engage in activities in which a bank legally could engage increase risks to the extent that the affiliate's activities are not monitored by the authorities or the banks as they would be were the activities conducted within the bank. Affiliates, though, have given banks the opportunity to do things they otherwise couldn't do directly. As is discussed in Chapter 6, many of these activities have tended to reduce, rather than increase, the risk of failure. But the requirement that the activities be done in separate organizations has increased bank operating and monitoring costs and reduced somewhat the advantages of diversification.

Credit Risk

Credit (default) risks are a function of the state of the economy and of bankers' ability to assess and price risk. There is no reason to believe that bankers have become better or worse predictors of economic conditions, or evaluators and monitors of borrowers. Given a reasonably high level of credit-gaining expertise, bankers generally can reduce risk by increasing diversification, so that unexpectedly large losses are offset by unexpectedly large gains. It is possible, however, that diversification can lead to greater risk if the activities added are subject to considerably greater variance in returns than the activities previously undertaken. The extent to which risk-reducing diversification has taken place is considered in a following subsection.

Operations Risk

Operations risk has both increased and decreased as a consequence of regulation. Deposit interest rate ceilings encouraged banks to offer services in lieu of cash payments as a means to hold and attract deposits. They also encouraged alternative, unregulated suppliers to enter the market. The removal of those ceilings has resulted in some capital losses as banks' investments in non-cash rewards, such as branches, became less valuable. Branching restrictions similarly imposed operations costs on banks. The removal of Regulation Q and regional removal of branching restrictions have served to reduce operations risk, although at the expense of immediate losses as pre-existing branch networks became less valuable.

Diversification

Banks' opportunities to diversify have increased since the 1930s. Less expensive technology has made nationwide and even worldwide banking cost-effective. Most large banks have loan production offices in all major cities. Funds are transferred electronically around the country and the world. To this extent, the antibranching laws are no longer constraining and have been *de facto* repealed.

While country risk has become a recent public concern, there is reason to believe that banks that make loans around the world have reduced risk, *ex ante*, by having more diversified portfolios. Because the United States has done well economically, particularly as compared with most other countries, it may seem that banks that made loans in other parts of the world were not well advised, either by their own analysts or by U.S. government officials. But such a conclusion does not consider the total returns on a portfolio of offshore loans, nor does it consider that, *ex ante*, one cannot predict economic conditions with much assurance. In addition, it is unclear whether loans to American farmers will fare much better than loans to Mexicans. (It was not very long ago that loans to Mexico, Chrysler, and New York City were equated.)

However, diversification could increase risk if the added activities had a greater variance of cash flows than the other activities, and if the cash flows did not offset each other sufficiently. For example, an additional large investment in oil wells might increase the variance of a bank's total cash flow, while a smaller investment could decrease total variance. Loans to developers of large construction projects might increase total cash flows, while direct investments in many real estate housing projects might decrease the variance of cash flows. Nevertheless, although there is no way to determine the effect of diversification on risk without knowing the assets and liabilities held by a bank, it is true that greater diversification results in less risk, all other things being equal.

Incentives Towards Risk-Taking

Incentives for bankers to take greater risks have increased as a consequence of higher levels of deposit insurance and lower amounts of equity capital (which is largely a consequence of underpriced deposit insurance). Both of these situations are the result, primarily, of high nominal interest rates—not of deregulation, as such. Deregulation of interest rates and some banking powers did not occur until after banking failures increased.

The December 1980 increase in deposit insurance from $40,000 to $100,000 per account in each insured institution, plus the existence of low-cost means to transfer and monitor funds, made it possible for depositors to insure large sums of money, thereby eliminating their incentive to monitor banks and increasing the benefits to bankers from taking risks. Previously, the smaller insured amounts and the higher transactions costs made obtaining large amounts of non-local funds relatively expensive. The removal of ceilings on deposits in the early 1980s made bidding for funds from distant borrowers more feasible, particularly for very risky banks. However, interest rates were not restricted previously on $100,000 insured CDs, and, before 1966, the Regulation Q ceilings generally were not binding. Furthermore, banks competed for deposits with implicit payments, such as convenience in the form of branches and 24-hour automatic teller machines (ATMs) and "free" services. Therefore, it is not removal of explicit interest rate ceilings, as such, that is responsible for the present situation.

Equity capital (measured in economic rather than in accounting values) in banks and thrifts decreased as a consequence of two effects of the increase in interest rates in the late 1970s that resulted from increases in the money supply. One was the entrance of unchartered and unregulated suppliers of banking services into the banks' and thrifts' markets. This occurred because Regulation Q interest rate ceilings prevented banks and thrifts from competing efficiently for savers' funds; brokers and others seized the opportunity to offer savers the alternative of higher-yielding money market mutual funds and interest-bearing checking accounts. This competition decreased the intangible (unrecorded) value of bank and thrift charters. Continuing disintermediation forced the deregulation of interest rates in the early 1980s. As a result, the present value of those deposits on which chartered institutions had been paying less than a market rate of interest increased, which decreased their equity capital. The other related event was the substantial decrease in the market value of fixed-interest assets. Thrifts were particularly hard hit, resulting in negative real (though not book) equities for many. The lower equity capital reduced the incentive for bankers to avoid taking risks. Negative capital gives some bankers incentives to seek out risks.

Equity capital as a percentage of total bank deposits also decreased when the Federal Reserve increased the money supply in the late 1970s. Most of this money must be held in banks in the form of demand deposits. Thus the equity/deposits ratio declined, not entirely because of a rundown of bank capital, but because of a Federal Reserve-determined increase in deposits.

Additionally, the unrecorded value of deposit insurance increased as a consequence of the greater volatility of interest rates. Deposit insurance gave bankers who held assets with greater durations than liabilities an option; they would benefit if interest rates decreased unexpectedly, while the deposit insurance agencies stood to lose if rates increased unexpectedly. The greater the volatility of interest rates, the greater the expected value of the gamble.

Because the increased volatility of interest rates and the increase in deposit insurance coverage took place at about the same time as the deregulation of banks' and thrifts' powers to offer financial services, it must be said explicitly that this deregulation is not a cause of increased incentives towards risk-taking. Almost all of the failures that have occurred were the result of traditional frauds, previously permitted activities, and portfolio imbalances. In particular, thrifts have not failed because they were given the power to offer checking accounts or consumer cash loans or to invest directly in real estate and service corporations. (Benston, 1985). An analysis of bank failures in the post-deregulation period shows that very few failures (17 percent at the most) involved sustained low performance with no malfeasance involved. (Peterson and Scott, 1985). The only new product that banks have been permitted to offer—discount brokerage services—has not resulted in solvency-threatening losses. Indeed, there is reason to believe that the additional activities that have been permitted have improved the ability of thrifts and banks to weather adverse economic conditions.

Financial System Instability

A financial system collapse can bring considerable loss of wealth and personal suffering; hence, it is a very serious concern. A banking crisis occurs when banks—not just a few banks, but banks in general—are unable to meet depositors' demands for their funds. A collapse follows if there is a multiple contraction of the money supply. At that point, because prices tend not to be reduced to a level consistent with the lower money supply, markets do not clear and people and other resources are involuntarily unemployed. Furthermore, when contracts (such as loans) are written in fixed-dollar terms, the later reduction in prices and values, together with the loss of income from un- and underemployment, can result in defaults and insolvencies for borrowers and banks and losses to depositors and other creditors.

The Role of the Federal Reserve

Absent the total bankruptcy of a country (perhaps as a consequence of a devastating disaster such as loss of a war) or a hyperinflation that destroys peoples' willingness to use financial instruments, the financial system cannot collapse unless the central bank (the Federal Reserve in the United States) permits the money supply to contract precipitously. Such a contraction cannot happen as long as the Fed is willing (and legally able) to supply base money (reserves and currency) to the financial system in amounts sufficient to offset increases in the public's desire to hold currency and banks' desire to hold additional reserves. The Fed has three means to avert a reduction in the money supply. It can purchase assets (generally U.S. Treasury securities) on the open market by crediting banks' reserve balances at the reserve banks. It can loan reserves to banks through its discount window. Or it can reduce the banks' reserve requirements. Thus the Fed can replace *any* amount of currency that people wish to hold outside of banks, or supply *any* amount of reserves that banks want to hold. While individual banks can fail, the banking system cannot collapse if the central bank does its job.

Depositors' Confidence in Banks

Depositors' loss of confidence in banks or the banking system cannot, by itself, cause a financial crisis. Consider what happens when depositors run from banks. What can they do with the funds?

If depositors withdraw their deposits by transferring the funds to another bank that is considered safe, the receiving bank's reserves increase by the amount that the sending bank's reserves decreased. If the receiving bank fears that it will face greater-than-normal withdrawals, it might want to hold additional reserves. The Fed (which knows daily what each bank's reserve balances are, because they are held at the Federal Reserve banks) can make additional reserves available.

Some depositors might "run to quality" by purchasing such secure investments as U.S. Treasury obligations. But the result would be a redeployment rather than a reduction of bank reserves. For example, consider the purchase of Treasury bills by depositors who are fearful of a general bank collapse. The sellers of the bills now have checks that bear no interest that were received in exchange for interest-bearing obligations. Hence, they will deposit the checks in their banks (particularly if they fear collapse of the purchasers' banks) and the funds will simply be transferred from one bank to another. Because the funds do not leave the banking system, there is no change in the money supply (assuming that the banks keep the same reserve relative to deposits).

The fearful depositors might be concerned about all U.S. banks and deposit their funds in foreign banks. But foreign banks don't hold U.S. currency; they hold the funds in deposits with U.S. banks. Thus the funds are simply redeployed from one U.S. bank to another.

Finally, depositors might want to keep their funds out of all banks—perhaps in a mattress. But few, if any, large depositors could keep their withdrawn funds in currency; the amounts involved are too large for safety, and bills paid in cash leave very poor audit trails. Hence, large depositors have strong incentives to redeposit their funds in some bank. Individuals, though, or perhaps very fearful foreign banks, might hold currency. In this event, the Federal Reserve could offset the reduction in reserves.

The Role of Deposit Insurance

The Fed might still not keep bank reserves from falling, because it is not legally required to do so. However, enactment of federal deposit insurance and subsequent increases to a sufficiently high coverage to eliminate the people's desire to hold currency outside of banks have practically eliminated the possibility of general financial collapse. There now is no reason for depositors with less than $100,000 per account at any one bank to withdraw their funds from federally insured banks. If they did, they would be faced with the prospect of holding cash and risking its theft. Nor is the presence of uninsured or state-insured financial institutions reason to fear a general financial collapse. Thus, when Home State Savings of Cincinnati failed and bankrupted the Ohio Deposit Guarantee Fund, there was only a shifting of deposits to and among federally insured institutions. (Although depositors in Home State could have lost some of their savings, they were bailed out by the Ohio state legislature.)

Uninsured depositors have reason to withdraw their funds from banks that might be or become insolvent. But these depositors have powerful incentives to redeposit these funds in other banks. Thus, a system collapse can occur only if the Federal Reserve acts to reduce bank reserves or if banks or the public choose to hold large amounts of currency or reserves and the Fed refuses to meet these demands.

Lessons From the Past

Because the financial system has collapsed in the past, it should be useful to know why these collapses occured and why they are unlikely to happen again. At times, such collapses have been triggered by the failure of an important financial institution. However, systemic collapse has more often and more seriously been the consequence of governmental actions that reduced or failed to offset reductions in the nation's money supply, resulting in multiple bank failures.

For example, the 1873 failure of Jay Cooke's banking house and the closing of the New York Stock Exchange contributed to the ensuing depression. But the Treasury exacerbated the situation by retiring greenbacks in 1874, which reduced the monetary base, resulting in a multiple contraction of deposits. (Friedman and Schwartz, 1963, p. 54). In 1884, Grant and Ward (President Grant's firm) and the Marine National Bank failed, sparking runs and the consequent failure of numerous brokerage houses and banks. Friedman and Schwartz found that the panic was attributable, as well, "to an outflow of gold resulting from the sale of foreign-owned securities." (p. 100). In any event, as they state: "The panic, while severe . . . was largely confined to New York." (pp. 99–100).

The very serious panic of 1893 saw the suspension in that year of 491 national and state banks. The prior failure (in 1890) of the London banking firm of Baring Brothers, which specialized in financing U.S. enterprises, resulted in a reduction of the monetary base as Baring's European creditors demanded that Americans pay their debts in gold. Fears in 1892 that the federal government would abandon the gold standard caused individuals and banks to hoard gold, which exacerbated the situation. Commercial failures and a sharp decline in stock market prices caused the public to be concerned about the solvency of banks, which led to further hoardings. The combined result was the suspension by 1894 of more than 600 banks and the failure of 13 of every 1,000 businesses. (Friedman and Schwartz, 1963, pp. 104–113).

The Panic of 1907 was "set up" by the prior successful actions of the Secretary of the Treasury to stabilize interest rates, which induced banks to hold lower levels of reserves. To gain the resources to intervene in the money market, the Treasury had subsidized the importation of gold. The Bank of England retaliated in 1906 by raising its discount rate and by asking British banks not to renew American finance bills. The inability in 1907 of the Knickerbocker Trust Company to meet nervous depositors' demands for gold resulted in its suspension (until 1908) and in runs on several other trust companies. (Cleveland and Huertas, 1985, Chapter 3, pp. 27–28).

The Federal Reserve was created in 1913 so that financial panics would not occur ever again. Rather than banks holding their reserves in specie or as balances with other banks, the Federal Reserve would hold member bank reserves and stand ready to lend to banks in distress as lender of last resort. Thus, the Federal Reserve could offset a run to specie or currency and prevent a multiple contraction of the money supply.

Nevertheless, the greatest U.S. financial disaster was the Great Depression of 1930-1933, when a third of the nation's commercial banks failed, a fourth of the people were unemployed for years, and the gross national product declined by a third. Tragically, the Fed did not act to offset the public's withdrawal of funds from the banking system and the banks' increases in voluntarily held reserves (both of which reduced the money multiplier and, hence, the money supply) for several reasons. One was Congress' concern about stock market speculation, which led the Fed to reduce and, by 1930, prohibit borrowing from the Federal Reserve banks by banks that made brokers' loans. The consequence was a reduction in the banking system's reserves. Another was the economic depression, particularly in the farm states, which resulted in the failure of many small, unit banks that were not members of the Federal Reserve, and hence were not eligible to borrow from the Fed. Warburton (1966, p. 320) explains that:

> As bank failures became frequent, the Federal Reserve banks developed an extremely hard-boiled attitude toward member banks which needed to borrow to meet deposit withdrawals. . . . At the same time the Federal Reserve authorities failed to enlarge the assets of Federal Reserve banks through open-market operations in an amount sufficient to maintain member bank reserves.

The Fed was also constrained by (but did not lobby hard to change) a legal requirement of 25 percent gold backing from issuing unlimited amounts of Federal Reserve notes. However, Warburton (1963) points out that, although the Fed expanded bank reserves following the passage of the Glass-Steagall Act (which reduced the gold-backing requirement) in February 1932, this policy soon ceased "and the hard-boiled attitude of the reserve banks toward rediscounting by member banks faced with deposit withdrawals continued." (p. 321). He observes (p. 321):

> When currency withdrawal on a large scale occurred in early 1933, bank reserves were permitted to contract again . . . by 20 per cent. This contraction, together with the failure of the Federal Reserve Board to use its power to suspend reserve requirements in such a situation, was the immediate direct cause of the March, 1933 banking crisis.[4]

Conclusion

As long as the Federal Reserve is willing (and legally able, as it now is) to supply base money (reserves and currency) to the financial system, there is absolutely no reason for a systemwide financial collapse to occur. Even were the public totally to lose confidence in the banking system, or if foreigners should decide to hold massive amounts of U.S. currency (which would be desirable for U.S. taxpayers, because currency bears no interest), the Federal Reserve can—if it wants—offset the reduction in currency and reserves with open market operations, discount window loans, or decreases in required reserves.

Nor would the failure of large numbers of banks as a result of a collapse of asset values result in a collapse of the financial system. Consider, for example, the consequence of a sharp reduction in farm land values and the failure of hundreds of banks that had loans outstanding to farmers. Uninsured depositors would now be owners of farms (or claims over farms) rather than of cash. They would be poorer than they were previously, just as the owners of equity shares would lose wealth should stock market prices fall. But the money supply would not go down and other banks would not fail unless people held more currency, banks held more reserves, and the Federal Reserve did not supply these demands. With deposit insurance in place, such demands for currency and reserves are very unlikely to occur.

Thus, it seems safe to conclude that there is little or no possibility of a general collapse of the financial system, whether from internal or external causes.

Summary and Conclusions

In brief, risks that are or can be taken by individual banks are considerable. The mispricing of deposit insurance, together with greatly improved funds-transfer technology and the increase in insurance coverage to $100,000 per legal account per insured institution, has created incentives for increased risk-taking and resulted in a substantial increase in the likelihood that individual banks will fail. *De jure* deregulation of banking prices and powers plays a subsidiary role in this increase in the risk of failures. The banking system, however, is not in danger of collapse as long as the Federal Reserve does not permit bank reserves to decline precipitously (a situation over which it has almost complete control).

Fraud and malfeasance were and continue to be perhaps the two most important causes of bank failure. Excessive risk-taking also results in bank failures, and there are many ways in which such risks can be taken. Liquidity risk, though, has decreased as a consequence of deposit insurance, which obviates most bank runs. Risks also can be reduced by diversification that results in a decrease in the variance of a bank's net cash flows. Optimal diversification, however, is constrained by laws that limit branching and products. Diversification also may be insufficient because some bankers want (or find it profitable) to take risks, in part because underpriced deposit insurance imparts incentives toward risk-taking.

The incentives for bankers to take risks is importantly and positively affected by underpriced deposit insurance, which also gives banks incentives to hold relatively low amounts of equity capital. However, the analysis does not conclude that bankers generally will seek risks—just that some bankers have incentives to do so, depending on the extent to which they do not bear the costs of risk-taking.

Fraud, securities speculation, foreign exchange risk, affiliate, credit (default), and operations risk have not changed much, although some of the ways in which these risks can be taken have changed. Opportunities for diversification have increased somewhat. Interest rate risk was realized, although it previously was considered only a potential hazard. The most important change is increased incentives towards risk-taking by banks. Two related factors are responsible: less concern and monitoring by depositors as a consequence of higher insurance coverage and lower transactions costs, and lower real (economic) equity capital in banks due to underpricing of deposit insurance. Both factors are attributable largely to inflation and to the increase in nominal interest rates in the late 1970s. Deregulation of interest rates and banking powers is a response to this situation, and is not a cause, as such, of increased risk-taking. However, expansion of the assets and liabilities in which banks can invest and be liable for has increased the ability of risk-preferring bankers to take greater risks. Nevertheless, the entry of unregulated suppliers of financial services, made possible by improved technology and fueled by past regulations that prevented banks from offering the public market rates of return for their funds, has made reregulation for the purpose of constraining risks not feasible.

Changes in the attitudes of bankers towards risk-taking also affect the likelihood that some individual banks (but not the banking system) will fail. In part this change is the result of most bankers' unwillingness or inability to fear or even imagine a time such as the Great Depression of the 1930s. In part it is a result of technology changes that make inexpensive the almost instantaneous transfer of large sums of money, and that blur (if not completely eliminate) the lines between regulated and unregulated banking, making unfeasible the reregulation of banking services (although perhaps not of chartered banks). But the most important danger to the soundness of banks and the effectiveness with which the banking system can serve consumers is mispriced deposit insurance, which gives bankers incentives to take excessive risks.

The stability of the banking system, however, is not in question. The financial system collapses that occurred in the past are very unlikely to be a problem in the future as long as the Federal Reserve is willing to provide sufficient reserves to the banking system to keep the money supply from declining precipitously. Even then, the existence of federal deposit insurance should mitigate such a situation greatly, because people will have little reason to keep funds in the form of currency, with the consequence that the contraction of the money supply would not be exacerbated as it was during the Great Depression. However, the value of deposit insurance for this purpose depends on depositors' beliefs that the insurance agencies' guarantees will be honored.

A remaining concern is the possible effect of the failure of large banks on other large banks when deposits that can be withdrawn on demand are not fully insured. This concern is considered in the following chapter.

[1] The amount in Maisel is given as $89 billion; presumably, "billion" should read "million."

[2] See Chapter 10, sections 4 and 5, for additional material on frauds.

[3] See Benston (1978) for an analysis of why banks were leaving the Federal Reserve System and why most banks (particularly the large, correspondent banks) chose to remain members of the Federal Reserve despite the tax on required reserves.

[4] The following data illustrate the changes that occurred before and during the period:

Year	ˉ Currency to consumer expenditures	Reserve money multiplier*	Total deposits at all commercial banks
1926-1930	4.8%	12.9	$41.2 million
1930	4.8	12.7	41.1
1931	6.3	11.5	36.1
1932	9.3	10.3	30.1
1933	10.2	8.3	26.5

(Cagan, 1965, Tables F-18, and F-8)

*The inverse of the reserve ratio at all commercial banks.

CHAPTER 2

Consequences of Bank Failure

B ank financial difficulties and failures are both affected by and affect economic activity in their communities. With the exception of fraud, bank losses occur primarily from defaults on loans; increases in interest rates that depress the market values of securities, including loans, by more than deposits; and increased competition. In addition, the value of some assets may decline if the bank has to sell them quickly in order to meet a deposit outflow.

Loan losses, in particular, reflect reductions in economic activity in some sector and transmit the financial difficulties of these borrowers to the bank. Such declines in economic activity are independent of bank behavior and must be analyzed separately from any further declines in activity or spillover effects to other financial institutions that are attributable to any resulting bank problems.

This chapter traces the effects of problems in the economy on banks and the effects of problems of banks both on other banks and on the economy, and evaluates the relative probabilities and strengths of each effect. Particular attention is paid to whether and under what conditions instability in individual banks can spread to other banks and to the banking system as a whole, and how such instability can be contained.

Bank Failures: Theoretical Analysis

In economic terms, banks become insolvent when the market (present) value of their net worth (capital) becomes zero. At this point, the present value of a bank's total assets (including loans and investments, off balance sheet and contingent items, fee-based services, franchise value, benefits of any underpricing of federal deposit insurance, and other forms of "goodwill") is equal to the present value of its deposit and nondeposit liabilities other than equity capital. At least economically, the bank no longer belongs to the shareholders, but to its creditors (including depositors and deposit insurance agencies, if any). Any further losses must be charged against debt, which is in violation of the agreement to repay these claims at face value when due.

To protect the creditors not covered by deposit insurance and the insurance agency, so that all share equally in the remaining value of the bank's assets, the bank is generally declared insolvent by the appropriate chartering agency and is either liquidated or its assets are sold to another new or existing institution that also assumes the liabilities. (Under mergers sponsored by the Federal Deposit Insurance Corporation (FDIC), only some assets may be sold, with the FDIC liquidating the poorer assets and paying the assuming bank the difference less any premium offered by the bank.)

When declared insolvent, the bank is considered to have failed, with penalties accruing to shareholders and possibly also managers and/or uninsured depositors and other creditors. In practice, however, economically insolvent banks need not be declared legally insolvent by the responsible chartering agency. For example, the bank can be supported through financial assistance and/or guarantees by a regulatory agency. A bank may be considered to have failed, whether or not it has been declared insolvent, if there is a regulatory-induced cessation in its operations as an independent entity free of direct intervention and oversight by a regulatory agency.

If the bank is declared insolvent at the exact moment that the market value of its net worth touches zero and is either merged or liquidated promptly, direct losses are suffered only by shareholders. However, indirect losses are suffered by bank customers, who must search for and/or adjust to new banking associations, and by bank employees, who may lose their positions or work for a new organization and face possible changes in their rank or seniority status. Perhaps the most severe losses are those experienced by bank loan customers who did not default and who must rebuild a bank relationship often nurtured over many years. If the bank is liquidated rather than merged, reestablishing customer-bank relationships is likely to be somewhat more severe, although in most instances another bank or branch will be located within reasonable geographic distance.

A bank failure, even of a large bank, that is caught promptly so that no losses accrue to depositors is unlikely to have consequences on the local economy much different from that of the failure of any other firm of comparable size and importance in which shareholders suffer losses, employees are laid off, customers are sent scurrying for other suppliers, and creditors are protected. Indeed, some students of banking have argued that an individual bank failure may be less serious than the failure of other kinds of firms, particularly if the bank is declared insolvent early enough to minimize losses to uninsured depositors or if the losses are shifted to government agencies.

Except for some bank loans, bank products and services are at least as homogenous as for most firms, and shifts among providers should cause relatively minimal disruptions. Bank employees perform substantially the same tasks using substantially the same procedures and equipment in all institutions, so that transfers from failed to healthy institutions should be relatively painless. Where bank loans may be personalized, most medium and large bank business customers and many smaller business and household customers maintain multiple bank affiliations, so that if one is ruptured, greater reliance is placed on the others. A recent survey of households showed that only 2 percent of the households used only one financial institution and that 60 percent used three or more. (Bennett, 1984). A survey of small business firms reported that 50 percent used financial services at more than one financial institution. (Whitehead, 1982). Larger firms are even more likely to use multiple banking affiliations. A number of years ago, Paul Horvitz (1965) observed that:

> It is by no means clear that bank failures are necessarily the disaster they are commonly considered to be. The failure of the textile mill in the one-mill New England town is almost certainly a greater community disaster than the failure of the local bank in a one-bank town.

Similarly, Dale Tussing (1967) argued that:

> The ease with which banks . . . can be closed without serious loss is underlined by comparing their assets with those of manufacturing and other non-financial firms. While long-term governments, corporate term loans, mortgage notes, etc. are classed by banks among their more illiquid assets, they are considerably more liquid than the equipment, fixtures, and even most inventory held by other types of businesses. The other financial assets of banks are even more liquid. . . . Even a bank facing sudden and abrupt insolvency . . . faces circumstances . . . less severe than that faced by most businesses in similar straits.

Moreover, whether the failed bank is liquidated or merged, *de facto* and *de jure* deregulation in recent years have both reduced barriers to the entry of new commercial banks and attracted a wide range of additional players, e.g., thrift institutions, investment bankers, Sears, General Motors, etc., onto traditional commercial bank turf, e.g., transactions deposits, business loans, and consumer loans. This has increased further the number of viable alternatives available to customers of failed banks, and should have lessened even more any adverse impact of bank failures on a community.

If the bank is not declared insolvent when the market value of net worth is zero, but only after it has become negative, the consequences are likely to be more severe for the community than if it were declared insolvent sooner. It should be noted, however, that both because changes in net worth are unlikely to be continuous but occur in jumps and because, even with the best in monitoring, it is not always possible to catch a bank just when its net worth reaches zero, regulators frequently will not be aware of a bank's insolvency until some time after it has actually occurred. Moreover, regulators are often under political constraints—self-imposed or otherwise—to delay declaring banks insolvent, particularly the only bank in a community. Bank closings may be viewed as a blot on their record.

If economically insolvent banks are not declared insolvent, losses will accrue to uninsured creditors and/or the insurance agency as well as to shareholders. The timing of the declaration of insolvency affects the identities of the parties, including the insurance agency, who bear the losses but it does not affect the fact that a loss exists. Moreover, particularly if federal deposit insurance premiums are not scaled to risk, as net worth becomes smaller and eventually negative, so that a bank has progressively less, if anything, to lose, the bank is progressively encouraged to increase its risk exposure in the hopes of winning big and staying alive.

Thus, the longer an insolvent bank is permitted to operate independently, the larger its overall losses are likely to be. The declaration of insolvency is only a recognition of the loss. Until that time, the loss is only implicit, and possibly hidden—it is not explicit and open.

Because a declaration of insolvency does not really affect the economic value of any bank accounts, it does not, at first approximation, affect the total stock of bank deposits in the system. In the absence of insurance, deposits at the failed bank will be reduced by the amount that net worth is negative. But the deposit losses reduce required reserves and, unless total reserves in the banking system are reduced concurrently or banks increase their excess reserves permanently, will permit an expansion of deposits at other banks. If there is a transfer of funds to banks outside the community, the reduction in deposits at the failed bank may reduce the stock of money and/or liquid wealth in the community and may reasonably be expected to have a greater negative impact on the community than if the bank loss had been caught earlier. But, as there will be little, if any, decline in aggregate deposits or credit, there should be little adverse impact on the banking system or national economy.

If, for whatever reason, the insurance agency guarantees all deposits, losses to depositors do not occur. The entire loss, beyond that borne by the shareholders and uninsured creditors, is borne by the insurance agency and is passed through to surviving banks and/or taxpayers. Losses to the community, other than those it bears for the losses of the insurance agency, will approximate those for the earlier case where the bank was closed when net worth became zero.

So far the analysis has not differed greatly from that of any firm experiencing a decline in the market value of its assets that propels its net worth to zero or less. Banks differ primarily because a very large proportion of their liabilities are effectively due on demand (by containing a put option that is exercisable at par value by the depositors at any time without notice) or are very short-term. Banks invest the funds they raise in assets that, on the whole, have risks of default and/or contract rates that are fixed for terms that are different from those of the deposits. Thus, banks assume both default and interest rate risk. If depositors (and other creditors) doubt the ability of the bank to discharge all their claims timely and in full, many are both motivated and able to withdraw their funds quickly. If they do, banks face the need to sell assets quickly or restore their funding through borrowing. The larger and quicker any withdrawal of funds, the larger any losses a bank may expect on the sale of assets. At some point, the losses from hurried sales may become sufficiently large to wipe out the bank's capital and make the institution insolvent.

Thus, the solvency of individual banks is more fragile than that of most other types of firms. A simultaneous attempt by a large number of depositors to withdraw a large amount of deposits is referred to as a bank run. Because deposit withdrawals may force the bank into insolvency, all of the claims may not be able to be discharged in full, and those depositors who successfully withdraw first—before insolvency—

benefit at the expense of those who are not so quick and attempt to withdraw later.

Bank Runs

In a world without deposit insurance, depositors know that their claims will be paid in full and on time, as long as the market value of the bank's assets is expected to exceed that of its deposits. Depositors also know that banks operate on a fractional reserve system, so that if at any future time the value of the assets declines by more than the value of the deposits, for whatever reason, the banks may not be able to meet all depositor claims in full and on time. Because the cost of transferring deposits quickly to another, presumably safer, bank is minimal, some depositors will withdraw their deposits whenever they perceive that a decline in their bank's assets value is occurring, without waiting for verification that the bank is actually experiencing financial difficulties and that their deposits are in jeopardy. It is far better to be safe than sorry. Wide-scale and/or large deposit withdrawals will be viewed by other depositors as a sign that something is wrong and they are likely to jump on the deposit-withdrawal bandwagon, setting in motion a self-feeding process. Regardless of whether the cause of a deposit run is justified, the bank must redeem its deposits in full and on time or face insolvency.

Fire-Sale Losses

Banks may meet deposit outflows greater than their cash reserves on hand either by selling earning assets (asset management) or by attracting offsetting funding (liability management). At the time of a significant deposit run, it is unlikely that affected banks can—in the absence of explicit or implicit pre-established arrangements with other banks or intervention by regulatory agencies—quickly attract sufficient replenishing funds to offset all their losses. They will be forced to sell some assets. Every earning asset has two market prices—an "equilibrium" market value (EMVA) and an immediate or "fire-sale" market value (FSVA). (Book values have little, if any, economic meaning and will be considered in a later chapter.) The equilibrium price is that price at which the asset can be sold to the highest potential bidder on the market.

But all markets are not so perfectly efficient that the highest potential bidders are known and continuous participants. The identification and location of these bidders may require significant search efforts. Moreover, different securities require different amounts of information to evaluate properly, which is available at different prices and with different speeds. Banks invest in a wide variety of securities and loans, ranging from those traded in active market for which little, if any, additional information is required, to those that are customer-specific, for which there are only thin markets and high costs of information. The longer the search time and the greater the information costs required, the less realistic a current equilibrium market price is likely to be. Equilibrium market prices are the prices that are recorded on a bank's books if it used market value accounting and assumed "reasonable" search time. At this price, a bank is able to discharge all of its fixed claims without loss, as long as the market value of its assets exceeds the market value of its deposits and other liabilities, and requests for conversion are not unexpected.

The fire-sale price is the price that can be obtained almost immediately without significant search. It represents a lower limit on the obtainable price. The amount of search required to increase the selling price of an asset from its fire-sale value to its equilibrium market value is a function of its uniqueness or marketability, the breadth and depth of the market, and the number of net sellers of the same asset. The more marketable (liquid) the asset and the broader the market, the more easily, cheaply, and quickly can the highest bidder be searched out and found.

For very liquid securities traded in very broad markets, e.g., Treasury bills, the fire-sale and equilibrium prices are basically the same. For many bank securities, e.g., customer-specific loans, however, the fire-sale price will be below the equilibrium price, and it will be lower than the equilibrium price by more, the more unique the asset and the narrower the market.

The relationship between the fire-sale market price of a security and its equilibrium market price is shown in Figure 1 for two securities having the same equilibrium market price but different marketability. Security A is more marketable and requires less information than security B. If an immediate sale is required, security B will have a lower fire-sale price than A. As additional search time is permitted, the fire-sale prices of both securities will approach the equilibrium market value asymptotically from below, but security A

Figure 1

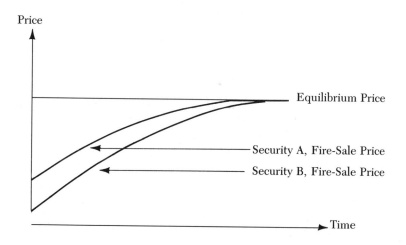

will do so more quickly. The difference between the equilibrium market price of any security and its fire-sale price at any time may be viewed as the liquidity premium for that security. (For a bank that is not experiencing any liquidity strains and can sell its assets at leisure, the fire-sale value of its assets may be considered equal to their equilibrium market value.)

When a bank experiences a significant deposit run, it may be required to sell at least some assets quickly at fire-sale prices. If these prices are below the corresponding equilibrium market prices, the bank suffers losses in its sale of assets that are charged against its net worth; it is said to be experiencing a "fire-sale" or "liquidity" problem.

The severity of a liquidity problem is related to the magnitude of the difference between the equilibrium and fire-sale prices. As long as this loss is no greater than the market value of the bank's capital or market net worth (MNW), the bank is solvent. (These conditions are summarized in Table 1.) Although the bank is solvent and losses are experienced only by shareholders, the run will reduce the bank's deposit size and weaken some bank-customer deposit and loan relationships.

When depositors withdraw funds from a bank, they have three alternatives. They can:

1. Redeposit at other, perceived safer, banks;
2. Purchase perceived safer securities; or
3. Hold currency outside the banking system.

Table 1: Conditions for Bank Liquidity and Solvency*

Liquid and solvent
    EMVA = FSVA > MVD; EMNW = FSNW > 0

Liquidity problem, but solvent
    EMVA > FSVA > MVD; EMNW > FSNW > 0

Liquidity-(fire-sale)-induced solvency problem
    EMVA > MVD > FSVA; EMNW > 0 > FSNW

Fundamental solvency problem
    MVD > EMVA > FSVA; O > EMNW > FSNW

where:

EMVA	=	equilibrium market value of assets
FSVA	=	fire-sale market value of assets
MVD	=	market value of deposits (and credit other than capital)
EMNW	=	equilibrium market value of net worth
FSNW	=	fire-sale value of net worth

*Assuming limited shareholder liability.

Which alternative they choose has important implications for the importance of bank runs on other banks and on levels of economic activity.

Deposit Runs to Other Banks

In the absence of a loss of faith by depositors in all banks, withdrawn deposits will be transferred to another bank, either directly by check or indirectly by a redeposit of currency. Thus, unless reserve ratios at individual banks differ greatly, total deposits in the banking system will remain unchanged. Under these conditions, the bank run is not contagious. To the extent that any economic harm—including financial instability—is suffered from a liquidity problem, it arises from losses to shareholders and the reshuffling of a constant amount of deposits among depositors and banks.

Although small, such shifts are not costless and do produce uncertainties and anxieties. The harm is likely to be more severe in the local markets served by the deposit-losing bank than in regional or national markets, but not very severe even there, because banking services are on the whole interchangeable and, particularly in today's deregulated environment, alternative suppliers are likely.

If the liquidity problem is sufficiently severe, it is possible for the FSVA < MVD even though EMVA > MVD, where MVD represents market value of deposits (and credit other than capital). The bank is fire-sale insolvent (FSNW < 0). The liquidity problem created by the deposit run has been transformed into a solvency problem, although possibly only a temporary one. Thus, if sufficiently severe, bank runs may transform solvent banks into insolvent banks. Whether banks whose FSVA < MVD but EMVA > MVD should be declared insolvent by the regulators is a difficult question, the answer to which may be dictated by public policy. However, in the absence of corrective actions by other banks or by the Federal Reserve in its role as lender of last resort to recycle the bank's funds or purchase the bank's assets, if runs persist, insolvency may have to be declared to protect the remaining depositors.

Appropriate actions by the banking system or the Federal Reserve, which are discussed later in this report, should make this step unnecessary and should minimize damage to the economy. Bank management itself can also take measures to minimize the impact by convincing depositors and the public that whatever reasons ignited the run initially were not correct, and that the bank is solvent in terms of its EMVA being equal to or greater than MVD. If successful, management can halt or even reverse the run and regain some or all of its deposits. Methods by which a bank's management can do so are discussed later in this report.

If corrective actions are not taken in time to prevent a liquidity problem from turning into a solvency problem or if, because depositors do not perceive it to be, a bank's EMVA is less than MVD before a deposit run (so that it was already insolvent), in the absence of federal deposit insurance or in-place subsidy schemes, all of its depositors and creditors cannot be paid in full when due.[1] The bank should be declared insolvent to protect the remaining depositors and creditors. If this is not done quickly and the first depositors to withdraw are paid in full, any run that may develop when depositors eventually perceive the financial state of the bank correctly is likely to increase the bank's losses further, and thereby also increase the losses suffered by the late withdrawers. Unless the funds are redeposited locally, these losses intensify the unfavorable impact of the bank failure on the community by further decreasing the amounts of money and other liquid wealth, further disrupting bank-customer relationships, further raising depositor fears and uncertainties about other banks, and further reducing employment at the insolvent bank. If the bank had been declared insolvent earlier and provision made for depositors and other creditors, depositors would not have been motivated to start or join a run and additional liquidity losses might have been avoided.

Deposit runs may, of course, occur on more than one bank simultaneously or sequentially if depositors at these banks perceive— correctly or not—that these banks are also "tainted," in that the market value of the banks' assets might have or have already declined below the value of their deposits. Multibank runs are most likely to occur if the banks have similar asset portfolios because they: (1) service the same local geographical market area, which is economically depressed; (2) make loans, outside the local market area, to the same customer or industry that is encountering financial difficulties; (3) make loans to the affected bank(s); or (4) have large open positions, such as intraday overdrafts, with these banks.

Thus, financial problems at one bank may be contagious and ignite runs on other banks. The larger the number of affected banks, the more severe the liquidity problem is likely to be, as the FSVAs will be driven down by the larger volume of simultaneous sellers and possibly also a reduction in the breadth and resiliency of the market, and the more likely is the liquidity problem to turn into a solvency problem. In addition, the greater are the number of broken banking connections with the accompanying transfer costs, job changes, and public uncertainty. But as long as deposits are redeposited at some banks and are not withdrawn from all banks, the contagiousness is limited and contained to the troubled banks, and is not transmitted systemwide.

Flight to Quality

The number, size, location, and type of banks perceived to be in financial difficulties are likely to affect the nature of the run. The larger the number and size of the banks in question, and the more they are located in the same market area, the more likely are depositors to be uncertain about the source and extent of the contamination and to question the financial integrity of other banks, and the less likely are depositors to redeposit the withdrawn funds in other banks.

Rather, depositors will either withdraw funds as currency and maintain them in that form or they will purchase more secure securities, such as those of the U.S. Treasury. The latter run is referred to as "a flight to quality." The initial deposit is transferred to the seller of the security, who is now in the position to redeposit or withdraw in currency. Both because the seller surrendered a secure security and because such transactions are likely to occur more frequently among large depositors, who are less likely to be able to conduct their business in currency, the seller is likely to redeposit the funds in his or her bank. Business and other large deposits are the first to participate in a run and to run the most. But they are likely to be the last to be converted permanently into currency in large amounts. If redeposited, funds are not lost to the system, even if the initial withdrawer transfers the deposits to a bank overseas. This bank will now hold the deposit on the original U.S. bank. Thus, a flight to quality is an indirect transfer of funds among banks, i.e., an indirect redeposit.

This is not to argue that a flight to quality with indirect redeposit is completely the same as a direct deposit transfer, or that it does not produce problems beyond those of a direct transfer. By moving funds into nonbank securities, flights to quality initially bid up the prices (reduce the interest yields) of these securities and push down the prices (increase the interest rates) on bank and other perceived "riskier" securities. That is, the flight to quality widens interest rate spreads between bank deposits (and other risky securities) and riskless Treasury securities.

Banks may also become more cautious in their lending. Unless offset by a reverse flow of funds from outside the banking sector, the wider spreads and the more cautious lending posture are likely both to affect (probably reduce) bank income, depending upon the mix of the assets, and to discourage private investments. Neither effect is favorable to the local or national economies, but both are likely to be considerably less important than a decline in total deposits and credit. Nor is such a flight to quality likely to create severe instability in national financial markets.

It is also possible that cautious commercial banks will increase their excess reserves. This would reduce the aggregate deposit-reserve multiplier and precipitate a multiple contraction in bank deposits and credit with more severe fire-sale problems and losses. In this scenario, the Federal Reserve would need to reduce other components in the multiplier under its control, e.g., reserve requirements, to restore the multiplier to its previous value, or, more likely, to inject additional reserves into the banking system to maintain the aggregate level of deposits and credit.

But a significant buildup of excess reserves by the banks is highly unlikely as long as depositors redeposit their funds and sufficient short-term U.S. Treasury securities are available. Banks, as a whole, maintain continuing excess reserves primarily when they believe that their required reserves are insufficient to meet potential deposit losses into currency, as has occurred periodically through U.S. history. But, as is argued in the next section, since the introduction of federal deposit insurance, such net currency drains are unlikely.

Flight to Currency

If a large number of depositors, including the sellers of safe securities, lose faith in all banks or, more likely, all banks readily available to them, they will not redeposit in other banks but will hold their funds in currency outside the banking system. A permanent flight to currency is fundamentally different from a deposit transfer. Net currency outflows drain reserves not only from an individual bank or group of banks, but also from the banking system as a whole. Under a fractional reserve banking system, a net drain of aggregate reserves, *ceteris paribus,* will have to be met by a multiple contraction in aggregate bank assets in order to satisfy legal or voluntary reserve requirements. Moreover, banks are likely to increase their excess reserves to be able to accommodate abrupt deposit losses, thereby reducing the deposit-reserve multiplier and intensifying the multiple contraction in deposits (money) and credit. The resulting larger sale of assets is likely to reduce further the FSVA, increase the severity of liquidity problems, and increase the likelihood that liquidity problems will be transformed into solvency problems. Unlike the effects of the bank runs analyzed earlier, the effects of a net currency outflow are likely to affect banks initially not perceived to have been in financial difficulties as well as those that were so perceived. In the absence of government intervention, the former banks will now have to liquidate assets at possible fire-sale prices and may experience liquidity problems. In addition, these problems may cause depositors to change their perceptions of these banks and to begin to view them with concern. This may ignite a run on previously perceived healthy banks.

As fewer and fewer banks are perceived as healthy, more of the deposit outflow will be in currency that is not redeposited at other banks. This results in further fire-sales at ever lower prices, and both widens the scope and increases the severity of the bank problems. Progressively, more banks experience solvency problems through little or no fault of their own. The initial localized run on one or more banks perceived to have been experiencing financial problems has spread to other healthy banks; the run has become contagious.[2] In contrast to the noncontagious or limited contagious bank run cases, bank management can do little, if anything, to halt a systemwide contagious run. Instability is transmitted from the individual banks to the banking system as a whole. It follows that an aggregate currency drain from the banking system is a prerequisite for a systemwide contagious bank deposit run.

The implications of systemwide contagious bank runs on the stability of the financial system and the economy overall can be severe. It is unlikely that all banks whose FSVA are less than MVD can be declared insolvent at the same time, or, even if they could, whether it would be socially desirable to do so and, if so, whether mergers, sales, or liquidations could be implemented before further losses are incurred. Nevertheless, the number of operating banks may be expected to decline sharply. Bank-customer relations will be broken more frequently and become increasingly more difficult to restore, losses to depositors and other creditors will be larger, aggregate deposits will decline, the remaining value of bank stock will decline further, and more bank employees will be discharged.

The loss of faith in banks is likely to spread to other financial institutions, causing wider-spread liquidations and adding further to selling pressures, driving down security prices and raising interest rates. As progressively more banks are infected and currency withdrawals intensify, the resulting reductions in money supply will depress spending, both in the communities directly affected and in the country overall, and contribute to precipitating or reinforcing an economic recession or depression, as occurred during the Great Depression of the 1930s.

It is accounts of systemwide contagious bank runs that appear to underlie the widespread traumatic—almost psychotic—fears of bank failures and of the severity of their damage on overall economic activity. Such fears remain widespread today. In defending his action in rescuing the Continental Illinois National Bank in May 1984, Comptroller of the Currency C.T. Conover (1984) testified that:

> In our collective judgment [directors of the FDIC, the Chairman of the Federal Reserve Board, and the Secretary of the Treasury], had Continental failed and been treated in a way in which depositors and creditors were not made whole, we could very well have seen a national, if not an international, financial crisis the dimensions of which were difficult to imagine. None of us wanted to find out.

Of course, net currency outflows and thereby systemwide contagious bank runs can be prevented by a central bank able and willing to replenish the loss in aggregate bank reserves, in its role of lender of last resort (LLR), to individual banks through the discount window as well as the economy as a whole through open market operations. The proper scope and implications of such central bank actions are examined in Chapter 5. Suffice it to note that the Fed's failure to fully replenish bank reserves during the large-scale bank failures of the Great Depression of 1930–1933 exacerbated the crisis and led directly to the establishment of the Federal Deposit Insurance Corporation (Friedman and Schwartz, 1963, and Federal Deposit Insurance Corporation, 1984). Because protection of insured deposits, at minimum, is established by statute and thereby is outside the discretion of the FDIC, the existence of the FDIC guarantees should effectively prevent individual bank runs from becoming contagious and spilling over onto other healthy banks. On the one hand, depositors with fully insured deposits (up to $100,000 currently) have little reason to convert their deposits into currency, even at pending or actually insolvent banks.[3] On the other hand, larger depositors cannot carry out their normal operations efficiently using currency.

The only reason fully insured depositors might have to convert to currency would be if they lost faith in the ability of the FDIC to meet its obligations. This might occur if the size of the deposit insurance agencies' funds were perceived to be small or insufficient relative to the potential losses in deposits. (Because the losses to be reimbursed by insurance are only the difference between value of the insured deposits and the prorata share of the proceeds from the fire-sale of the assets, and not the full value of the deposits, this is unlikely to happen in actuality.) To prevent the perception of such a state of affairs and the possibility of a bank run starting a net currency drain, it is desirable to improve the credibility of the FDIC guarantee by transforming the federal deposit insurance fund into a full-faith guarantee of the federal government. (This is discussed in a later chapter.) In such a framework, net currency drains and systemwide contagious bank runs are extremely unlikely and the implications of runs on single or groups of banks on the financial system and the economy are less severe.

Bank failures may also be made more serious than those of other firms as a consequence of inappropriate government actions. One such mistaken policy is to attempt to stem a run by declaring a bank "holiday" and closing a number of banks for all banking business. As long as the holiday is in effect, such action sharply reduces the money supply to the community, freezes loan availability, and encourages currency withdrawals from unaffected nearby banks by depositors who fear that the holiday may spread, thereby lowering levels of economic activity. These results were evident following the recent state-chartered thrift institution holiday in Ohio, as well as the widerspread statewide bank holidays in 1932–1933, which culminated with the national bank holiday in March 1933.

Bank holidays validate what is argued later in this chapter to be otherwise exaggerated fears about the damaging impact of bank failures—they create a self-fulfilling prophecy. As will be discussed later, in pre-Federal Reserve days, banks temporarily suspended conversion from bank notes to specie and later from deposits to currency, but did not close for other business. Depositors maintained access to their funds. Transfers by check and new loan extensions continued to be made. Thus, the adverse effects on the economy were far less severe.

Large Banks

Although all bank runs are widely feared, runs on large banks are particularly feared. Are large banks different? Does the previous analysis not apply to them? While runs on large banks may be more visible, the implications do not differ greatly from those for smaller banks. As long as reserves do not leave the banking system in the form of currency, as is particularly unlikely from runs on larger banks, any run produces only churning—either or both among banks and among securities. But because the flow of funds is larger, the churning will be more serious, particularly from a flight to quality.

In addition, to the extent that most larger banks operate in the same national and international markets and have similar loan portfolios, runs on any one bank may be more likely to set off runs on the others. But the funds must be directly or indirectly transferred to some banks, possibly the "best of the rest" or regional banks. Nevertheless, the degree of public concern and uncertainty is likely to be considerably greater, particularly in foreign countries where knowledge of the U.S. economy is weaker. This may, at least temporarily, depress economic activity. While runs by foreigners to foreign banks again only reshuffle the ownership mix of deposits and do not cause a loss of reserves in the U.S. banking system as a whole, they could exert downward pressure on the dollar exchange rate. (Large banks are also more exposed through electronic clearing with other large domestic and foreign banks. This is discussed later in the chapter.)

Bank Failures in the United States: History and Evidence

It has been argued above that, with the exception of those brought about by fraud, noncontagious or limited contagious bank failures inflict about the same damage on the local or national economies, beyond that already contributed by the forces that brought about the failures, as do the failures of nonbank firms of equal size and relative importance. The main direction of causation is likely to run from the economy to bank failure and not the reverse. Systemwide contagious bank failures do considerably more harm, and the direction of causation between them and the rest of the economy is more likely to be strong in both directions. But systemwide contagious bank failures are likely to be less frequent.

An examination of American history supports these conclusions. Annual data on the number of commercial bank failures from 1865 through 1935 are shown in Table 2. The annual rate of bank failures is also shown in Table 2, although it is apparently overstated for the years 1875 through 1895.[4] The data reveal a number of interesting observations. Until the 1920s, contrary to popular belief, bank failures were relatively infrequent. For the entire 70-year period from 1865 to 1935, the number of bank failures averaged 265 annually; from 1865 to 1919 it averaged only 64; from 1920 through 1929, the annual average jumped to 588; and from 1930 to 1933, to 2,274 (Table 3). Before 1920, there were only nine years in which the number of bank

Table 2: Commercial Bank Failures, Currency Deposit Ratios, and Related Data for the United States, 1864–1940

Year	Number of Commercial Banks[a]	Number of Failures	Commercial Bank Failure Rate	Currency	Total Commercial Bank Deposits	Currency-to-Deposit Ratio	Industr. Production (1913=100)	S&P Index of Common Stocks (1941–43=100)	Long-Term Int. Rate[b]	Business Failure Rate
1864		2					8.35		6.27	
65		6					8.00		7.62	
66		7					9.84		7.95	
67		7		580	700	0.829	10.30		7.87	
68		13		540	730	0.740	10.80		7.80	
69		7		550	730	0.753	11.60		8.13	
1870		2		540	810	0.667	11.70		7.92	0.83
71		7		540	960	0.563	12.30	4.69	7.78	0.64
72		16		550	1060	0.519	14.60	5.03	7.60	0.81
73		37		560	1060	0.528	14.40	4.80	7.76	1.05
74		50		540	1110	0.486	13.90	4.57	7.53	1.04
75	2662	17	0.64	540	1180	0.458	13.50	4.45	7.06	1.28
76	2762	45	1.63	530	1150	0.461	13.40	4.06	6.68	1.42
77	2709	71	2.62	540	1110	0.486	14.60	3.14	6.62	1.39
78	2566	80	3.12	540	1040	0.519	15.50	3.38	6.45	1.58
79	2696	27	1.00	580	1080	0.537	17.50	4.12	5.98	0.95
1880	2726	15	0.55	670	1360	0.493	20.30	5.21	5.60	0.63
81	2798	9	0.32	780	1660	0.470	22.30	6.25	5.19	0.71
82	2943	22	0.75	840	1790	0.469	23.90	5.90	5.24	0.82
83	3205	28	0.87	870	1930	0.451	24.40	5.63	5.23	1.06
84	3477	60	1.73	840	1960	0.429	23.10	4.74	5.15	1.21
85	3704	41	1.11	800	2070	0.386	23.20	4.60	4.89	1.16
86	3700	19	0.51	780	2320	0.336	27.90	5.36	4.55	1.01
87	5486	24	0.44	830	2480	0.335	29.50	5.53	4.65	0.97

Table 2: continued

Year	Number of Commercial Banks[a]	Number of Failures	Commercial Bank Failure Rate	Currency	Total Commercial Bank Deposits	Currency-to-Deposit Ratio	Industr. Production (1913 = 100)	S&P Index of Common Stocks (1941 − 43 = 100)	Long-Term Int. Rate[b]	Business Failure Rate
88	5846	29	0.50	850	2550	0.333	30.60	5.20	4.59	1.03
89	6354	18	0.28	870	2730	0.319	32.60	5.32	4.43	1.03
1890	7078	36	0.51	930	2990	0.311	35.00	5.27	4.55	0.99
91	7630	60	0.79	960	3120	0.308	36.00	5.03	4.71	1.07
92	8279	80	0.96	960	3470	0.277	38.80	5.55	4.53	0.89
93	8462	491	5.80	1000	3260	0.307	34.70	4.78	4.65	1.30
94	8484	83	0.98	930	3350	0.278	33.70	4.39	4.41	1.23
95	8801	110	1.24	910	3520	0.259	39.70	4.53	4.27	1.12
96	11474	141	1.23	890	3460	0.257	36.90	4.23	4.34	1.33
97	11438	139	1.22	920	3720	0.247	39.70	4.45	4.11	1.25
98	11530	63	0.55	1000	4260	0.235	44.70	5.05	4.03	1.11
99	11835	32	0.27	1100	4990	0.220	49.20	6.29	3.85	0.82
1900	12427	35	0.31	1210	5390	0.224	50.60	6.15	3.97	0.92
1	13424	65	0.48	1270	6210	0.205	56.70	7.84	3.25	0.90
2	14488	54	0.31	1340	6830	0.196	63.20	8.42	3.30	0.93
3	15814	52	0.33	1420	7260	0.196	65.40	7.21	3.45	0.94
4	17037	125	0.73	1440	7800	0.185	62.30	7.05	3.60	0.92
5	18152	80	0.44	1500	8740	0.172	73.60	8.99	3.50	0.85
6	19786	53	0.27	1630	9450	0.172	78.90	9.64	4.75	0.77
7	21361	90	0.42	1720	9880	0.174	80.60	7.84	4.87	0.83
8	22531	153	0.68	1760	9680	0.182	68.00	7.78	5.10	1.08
9	23098	78	0.34	1710	10970	0.156	80.20	9.71	4.03	0.87
1910	24514	58	0.24	1740	11600	0.150	85.30	9.35	4.25	0.84
11	25183	85	0.34	1760	12360	0.142	82.20	9.24	4.09	0.88

Table 2: continued

Year	Number of Commercial Banks[a]	Number of Failures	Commercial Bank Failure Rate	Currency	Total Commercial Bank Deposits	Currency-to-Deposit Ratio	Industr. Production (1913 = 100)	S&P Index of Common Stocks (1941 – 43 = 100)	Long-Term Int. Rate[b]	Business Failure Rate
12	25844	78	0.30	1820	13310	0.137	93.70	9.53	4.04	1.00
13	26664	103	0.39	1890	13840	0.137	100.00	8.51	4.74	0.98
14	27236	149	0.55	1910	14480	0.132	94.10	8.08	4.64	1.18
15	27390	152	0.55	1930	15660	0.123	109.30	8.31	4.47	1.33
16	27739	52	0.19	2170	18680	0.116	129.60	9.47	3.48	1.00
1917	28298	49	0.17	2170	22200	0.098	129.70	8.50	4.05	0.80
18	28856	47	0.16	2760	23970	0.115	128.80	7.54	5.48	0.59
19	29147	62	0.21	4020	26990	0.149	113.20	8.78	5.58	0.37
1920	30291	167	0.55	4480	30320	0.148	124.00	7.98	6.11	0.48
21	30456	505	1.66	4040	28810	0.140	100.10	6.86	6.94	1.02
22	30120	366	1.22	3690	30030	0.123	125.90	8.41	5.31	1.20
23	29829	646	2.17	3960	32640	0.121	144.40	8.57	5.01	0.93
24	28988	775	2.67	3960	34620	0.114	137.70	9.05	5.02	1.00
25	28442	618	2.17	3960	38090	0.104	153.00	11.15	3.85	1.00
26	27742	976	3.52	4000	39680	0.101	163.10	12.59	4.40	1.01
27	26650	669	2.51	3980	40750	0.098	164.50	15.34	4.30	1.06
28	25798	498	1.93	3890	42530	0.091	171.80	19.95	4.05	1.09
29	24970	659	2.64	3900	42700	0.091	188.30	26.02	5.27	1.04
1930	23697	1350	5.70	3730	42000	0.089	155.60	21.03	4.40	1.22
31	21654	2293	10.59	4160	38530	0.108	129.70	13.66	3.05	1.33
32	18734	1453	7.76	4920	31130	0.158	100.50	6.93	3.99	1.54
33	14207	4000	28.16	5090	27130	0.188	119.90	8.96	2.60	1.00
34	15348	57	0.37	4630	29730	0.156	129.70	9.84	2.62	0.61

Table 2: continued

Year	Number of Commercial Banks[a]	Number of Failures	Commercial Bank Failure Rate	Currency	Total Commercial Bank Deposits	Currency-to-Deposit Ratio	Industr. Production (1913 = 100)	S&P Index of Common Stocks (1941 – 43 = 100)	Long-Term Int. Rate[b]	Business Failure Rate
35	15488	34	0.22	4800	34270	0.140	149.10	10.60	1.05	0.62
36	15,329	44	0.29	5230	38250	0.137	178.30	15.47	0.61	0.48
37	15,094	59	0.39	5590	40090	0.139	194.50	15.41	0.69	0.46
38	14,867	54	0.36	5550	39960	0.139	152.30	11.49	0.85	0.61
39	14,667	42	0.29	6040	43230	0.140	188.00	12.06	0.57	0.70
1940	14,534	22	0.15	6760	48440	0.140	213.90	11.02	0.41	0.63

[a]Number of commercial banks substantially understated from 1875 through 1895.
[b]Interest rate from 1864 through 1899 is the unadjusted index of yields of American railroads; interest rate from 1900 through 1940 is the one-year corporate bond rate.

Column 1: Bureau of the Census, *Historical Statistics of the United States Through 1970*, Washington, D.C. Series X: 634 + 683
2: *Historical Statistics of the United States Through 1970*, Series X: 741–
3: Column 2—Column 1
4: *Historical Statistics of the United States Through 1970*, Series X: 410
5: *Historical Statistics of the United States Through 1970*, Series X: 411
6: Column 4—Column 5
7: Bureau of the Census, *Long Term Economic Growth, 1860–1965*: A–15
8: *Historical Statistics of the United States Through 1970*, Series X: 495
9: *Historical Statistics of the United States Through 1970*, Series X: 476 through 1899; 487 since 1899
10: *Historical Statistics of the United States Through 1970*: Series V: 24–20

Table 3: Bank and Business Failures, 1865–1935

	Mean	Standard Deviation	Coefficient of Variation
Number of Bank Failures			
1865–1935		262	
1865–1919	64	71	
1920–1933	1,070	966	
1930	2,274	1,062	
Bank Failure Rate			
1875–1935*	1.82	3.88	8.27
1875–1929*	1.02	1.03	1.04
1875–1919*	0.82	0.96	1.12
1920–1933	4.61	6.65	9.60
1930–1933	13.05	8.89	6.06
Business Failure Rate			
1875–1935	1.00	0.24	0.06
1875–1929	1.00	0.22	0.05
1875–1919	1.01	0.23	0.05
1920–1933	1.01	0.26	0.07
1930–1933	1.27	0.19	0.02

*Number of banks substantially underestimated through 1896

failures exceeded 100, and only 1 year (1893) in which the number exceeded 160 (491).

The relatively small number of failures before 1920 did not reflect proportionately fewer banks. The annual rate of bank failures exceeded 2 percent (even when overstated) in only 3 years before 1920, compared with 10 of the 14 years between 1920 and 1933, and exceeded 5 percent only in 1893, a rate exceeded in each of the 4 years from 1930 to 1933. Thus, large-scale bank failures do not appear to have been a normal part of the American banking scene.

Indeed, as can be seen from Table 3, the average annual rate of bank failure for the 1875 to 1919 period was, at most, 0.82 percent— lower than 1.01 percent rate for nonfinancial firm failures. Only between 1920 and 1933 does the rate of bank failure exceed the rate of business failure for any extended period of time. However, the annual rate of bank failure was far more variable than the rate of business failure in all periods. From 1875 to 1919, the standard deviation for bank failures was 0.96, four times the 0.23 for business failures. The difference is even greater for the coefficient of variation, which adjusts for the differences in means between the two series. This statistic is 1.12 for the rate of bank failure, and only 0.05 for the rate of business failure.

For the period 1875 to 1933, the rate of bank failure is only weakly correlated with the rate of business failure. The coefficient of correlation is 0.24. The correlation is considerably greater, however, for the period before 1920—0.59—than for the period after—0.20. To the extent that the rate of business failure indicates the state of aggregate economic activity, this suggests that bank failures and the state of the national economy are intertwined, although not very closely at all times. Between 1875 and 1919, the coefficient of correlation of the annual rate of bank failure with the concurrent annual index of industrial production was −0.42 and with the annual Standard and Poor's index of common stock prices was −0.53. As with business failures, the correlations were considerably poorer between 1920 and 1933. However, in only two of the eight periods of sharp increases in the number of bank failures before the Great Depression (1872–1874, 1876–1878, 1884, 1890–1893, 1895–1897, 1904, 1908, and 1920) did industrial production fail to decline, and in only two did the stock market fail to decline.

Between 1870 and 1919 there were six nonwar-related downturns in industrial production. Each was accompanied by an increase in the number of bank failures. In this period there were also six downturns in the stock market. Again, each was accompanied by an increase in bank failures. Thus, major increases in overall bank failures and major national recessions appear closely related.

It is difficult to obtain a direct measure of systemwide contagious bank failures. It is also difficult to distinguish clearly between systemwide and limited or noncontagious bank runs from descriptive historical accounts. However, as was argued earlier, systemwide contagious bank failures should occur only in periods in which there is an aggregate net currency outflow. Such conditions may be said to exist when (1) currency (including coin) increases relative to total bank deposits and (2) total bank deposits decrease. This condition occurred only three times before the Great Depression—in 1878, 1893, and 1908. In each of these years, bank failures increased sharply to the highest levels of the perspective periods. Each occasion was also marked by a sharp downturn in the stock market, and the last two by a sharp decline in industrial production. Systemwide contagious bank runs may have occurred in these periods. The few number of times that a net currency drain from the banking system occurred in U.S. history suggests that systemwide contagious runs have not occurred frequently. (Kaufman, 1984, 1985 and Tobin, 1984).[5]

Unfortunately, the comparatively poor quality of the data in these periods makes it difficult to identify leads and lags without substantial additional statistical analysis. Thus, it is difficult to identify unilateral directions of causation between bank failures and other economic difficulties. However, in his careful study of U.S. monetary history, Cagan (1965) concluded that financial "panics have not precipitated cyclical downturns; all of them cited here have followed peaks in economic activity." It is also evident that before 1929, bank failures generally did not have a lasting effect on the economy. By far the most severe bank crisis before 1929 was in 1893, when 491 banks failed, 6 times the number of 1892, and 14 times the number in 1890. Industrial production declined 11 percent and the stock market, 14 percent. After declining slightly in 1894, industrial production jumped 18 percent in 1895 to a record level. The stock market, however, remained depressed through 1897. Bank failures dropped sharply to 83 in 1894 before rising again into the one hundreds through 1897, without only small effect on the national economy. The 1908 crisis was similar. The number of bank failures jumped from 63 in 1906 to 90 in 1907 and 153 in 1908. However, this was less than 1 percent of all banks and casts doubt on the contagiousness of the failures in this period. In 1909, the number of bank failures dropped to 78 and to 58 in 1910. Industrial production dropped 16 percent in 1908 but climbed back to its 1907 level in 1909. The stock market dropped 19 percent in 1907, remained stable in 1908, and jumped to above its 1906 peak in 1909.

Bank Failures in the 1920s

The number of bank failures reached a new plateau in the 1920s. Failures averaged about 600 per year, or nearly 10 times the average up to then. Yet no other national economic indicators showed distress. The rate of nonbank failures varied little from its historical average. After falling sharply in 1921, industrial production increased in every year through 1929, except for a slight dip in 1924. The 1929 level was more than 50 percent above the 1920 level. The stock market also rose steadily in this period. Its 1929 value was three times its 1920 value.

Almost all the banks that failed in the 1920s were small banks in rural areas, particularly in the central and western grain areas and the southwest. Almost 90 percent had capital of less than $100,000 (60 percent had capital of $25,000 or less), more than 90 percent had loans and investments of less than $1 million (and 60 percent less than $250,000), 60 percent were located in towns of less than 1,000 in population, and 90 percent were in towns of less than 5,000. The average failed bank was less than one-half the size of all banks. More than 50 percent of banks with loans and investments of less than $150,000 failed, compared with only 3 percent of those with loans and investments over $50 million. (Goldenweiser, 193X, and Benston, 1973).

It is interesting to note that when size, in terms of capital stock, is held constant, more than twice as many state as national banks failed per hundred banks. No national bank with capital in excess of $5 million failed, although 5 percent of state banks in this size group failed. This relationship appears to hold even when account is taken of geographical location. As all national bank shareholders, but only some state bank shareholders, were subject to double liability, this strongly suggests that extended liability provisions might have been effective preventatives of bank failure. Further investigation of this relationship is warranted.

Throughout the 1920s, total bank deposits increased and the ratio of currency to deposits decreased. Thus, it appears that the large number of bank failures neither caused economic or financial hardships at the national level nor ignited ripple effects that toppled other banks outside the same market area. The failures primarily reflected depressed local agricultural conditions brought about by falling farm prices. Most of the small banks were unit banks and were apparently not sufficiently diversified to withstand default on their farm loans, which was their major loan category.

Bank Failures in the 1930s

Things changed abruptly after 1929. The number of bank failures doubled from 659 in 1929 to 1,350 in 1930, almost doubled again in 1931, and, after declining in 1932 to near their 1930 levels, jumped to 4,000 in 1933. In total, almost 9,000 banks failed in these 4 years, 38 percent of all banks. The annual rate of failure was 11 percent in 1932 and 28 percent in 1933. The failures stopped in 1934, even more abruptly than they had started, dropping to only 57.

The bank failures were, of course, accompanied by the most severe economic crisis in U.S. history. Industrial production fell by almost one-half between 1929 and 1932 and the S&P stock index fell by three-quarters. The currency drain from the banking system was also the most severe in U.S. history. Total commercial bank deposits declined by more than one-third, and the ratio of currency to bank deposits doubled from a record low of 9 percent in 1930 to 19 percent in 1933, the highest ratio since 1903. Indeed, although sharp, this rise understates the flight from bank deposits. Postal savings accounts, which were direct liabilities of the federal government, increased six-fold from $165 million to $1,200 million in these three years. If these accounts had been included with currency, the ratio of currency to deposits would have risen by almost 2½ times to 23 percent.[6]

At the same time, banks increased their excess reserves to be in better shape to accommodate the heavy customer demands for currency. This evidence suggests that the public had little faith in almost every bank, and that the wave of bank failures could to a large extent have been the result of extreme liquidity pressures caused by the aggregate multiple contraction in deposits and assets and passed from one bank to another in a domino process. Nevertheless, as in the 1920s, banks that failed tended, on the whole, to be the smaller banks. The proportion of total bank deposits held in banks that failed was considerably less than their proportion of the number of banks. Deposits at failed banks averaged only 2 percent of total deposits in 1930 and 1932, 1 percent in 1931, and 12 percent in 1933. Thus, it is likely that many banks continued to fail primarily because of adverse local business conditions rather than because of spillover from other failed banks outside their market areas.

Not only was the banking, financial, and economic downturn during the early 1930s far more severe than any other downturn in American history, but the subsequent upturn was longer delayed than in any previous crisis. Industrial production did not surpass its 1929 level until 1937. Thus, this period is unique in U.S. history, and the lessons drawn from it are probably not very applicable to other periods, even those of other economic and financial crises, and they should probably not be used to make decisions about financial structure.

The wave of bank failures stopped abruptly in late 1933, for several reasons too complex to be reviewed in detail in this chapter. In brief, all banks were closed by a national banking holiday in early March 1933, shortly after the inauguration of President Roosevelt, and were permitted to reopen only after certification of solvency by the U.S. Treasury or the chartering state.

This strategy apparently restored significant confidence in the banking system. In addition, the Reconstruction Finance Corporation increased its financial aid to banks, the Federal Reserve pursued more active open market and discount window operations, and federal deposit insurance was scheduled to go into effect on January 1, 1934. Total bank deposits started to grow again. The currency-deposit ratio started to decline, but slowly. The slowness of the decline in the currency-deposit ratio as well as the continued build-up of excess reserves by the banks suggests that considerable public doubt lingered about the health of the banking system.

Losses to Depositors

The above analysis suggests that, although wide-scale bank failures appear not to have been a common occurrence in U.S. history and systemwide contagious bank failures occurred even less frequently, bank failures are closely intertwined with national economic conditions, particularly at times of major downturns. However, it is difficult to separate the effects of one on the other. An independent but indirect indication of the importance of bank failures on the economy is the magnitude of the losses experienced at failed banks. Such estimates were made by the FDIC for bank failures in the 76 years from 1865 through 1940. (Federal Deposit Insurance Corporation, 1940).

Although these estimates appear to be the best available, they understate actual losses in a number of ways. Net losses are defined as gross losses minus recoveries. But no provision was made for the fact that many of the recoveries occurred at a later date, in some instances many years after the bank had failed. Thus, the face value of the loss rather than the present discounted value was used. Nor do the estimates include losses, particularly to shareholders, from merging banks or from asset purchases at above-market value to avoid insolvency. Nevertheless, they do provide ballpark estimates.

Looking only at the years before FDIC insurance, 1865–1933, all banks charged off total losses of $12.3 billion. This was equivalent to about 1 percent per year of total bank assets in this period. Of this amount, $7.7 billion, or 63 percent, was charged against the net worth of nonfailed banks (reducing share values); $2.4 billion, or 20 percent, was borne by shareholders at failed banks (including $0.5 billion in assessments through double-liability provisions in amounts up to the par value of the stock in the failed national and some state banks beyond the market value of the shares); and $2.2 billion, or 18 percent, was borne by depositors at failed banks. As a percent of total deposits at all commercial banks, these losses were 0.76, 0.24, and 0.21 percent, respectively, per year.

Thus, on average, depositors lost relatively little. Losses increased substantially during crisis periods, but not to startling levels. During the 12 years identified by the FDIC as crisis years for bank failures (1873, 1875–1878, 1884, 1893, 1930–1933), losses to depositors averaged 0.78 percent. (It is of interest to note that the FDIC did not consider 1908 a crisis year.) Even in the 1930–1933 period, depositor losses were only 0.81 percent. In the noncrisis years, the average loss was only 0.07 percent.

The relatively small losses borne by depositors reflect primarily the fact that the market value of assets at failed banks do not drop to zero, even in crisis years, and the relatively high levels of bank capital in the period. Capital-to-asset ratios at national banks were about 35 percent in 1875, 30 percent in 1890, 20 percent in 1910 before the introduction of the Federal Reserve, and 13 percent in 1930 before the introduction of the FDIC. Losses to depositors are only the difference between the par value of their deposits and the market liquidation value of the assets, less any of the loss that can be charged against net worth (or stockholders under double liability). The high levels of capital permitted relatively high losses on assets before a bank reached insolvency and subjected depositors to losses. Most assets at failed banks were eventually liquidated at relatively close to their equilibrium market values after insolvency. Depositors lost proportionately the most at smaller banks, which could reasonably be expected to have had the least diversified portfolios. Sixty percent of the banks with loans and investments in excess of $1 million, which held 60 percent of assets at banks that failed between 1921 and 1930, paid depositors 80 percent or more of the value of their claims and 80 percent paid 60 percent or more.

Moreover, these data underestimate the recoveries, particularly for the large number of banks that failed in 1929 and 1930, as the cut-off period for these computations was early in 1931 (Goldenweiser, 193X). Even the assets of the large Bank of the United State (New York), whose failure at yearend 1930 was identified by Friedman and Schwartz (1963) as a major ignitor of runs on other banks and the start of the domino effect, were eventually liquidated at near 85 cents on the dollar, and 80 percent of that within two years.

It is highly unlikely that losses of this magnitude can be the primary contributors to national economic crisis. They pale in comparison with losses incurred almost daily on the stock market. However, bank deposits probably were funds that the owners did not intend to put at risk; the owners, therefore, were likely to react more severely to these losses than to equivalent losses on the stock market.

From the introduction of federal deposit insurance in 1934 until the temporary introduction of its modified payout program by the FDIC in 1982, losses to depositors on the relatively few bank failures have been almost nonexistent. Depositor losses at failed banks were eliminated altogether while the FDIC temporarily suspended its modified haircut program after the Continental Illinois failure in mid-1984. All bank losses beyond those that were absorbed by net worth were absorbed by the insurance agency. Neither has there been a currency drain in terms of an increase in the currency-deposit ratio simultaneous with a decline in bank deposits in this period.

Bank Runs

Analyses of recent depository institution failures, including the U.S. National Bank of San Diego (1973), Franklin National Bank (1974), Penn Square Bank (1982), Seattle-First National Bank (1983), and the Continental Illinois National Bank (1984) and personal interviews with senior officials in charge of funding at major banks indicate that the bank runs experienced by these institutions appeared to be, on the whole, similar to those experienced in earlier periods. Runs start with bad news. Such news, particularly about an institution's earnings for a number of quarters, ignites nervousness among uninsured depositors and creditors, e.g., other banks, bank trust funds, money market funds, other nonbank financial institutions and nonfinancial firms, and encourages them to shift their funds as soon as possible to other banks on their approved list until the bank in question is re-evaluated. Those depositors that have or perceive themselves to have fiduciary responsibilities, e.g., pension plans, bank trust departments, and money market funds, are likely to be the first to redirect their funds. The larger the proportion of such deposits, the greater is the vulnerability of the bank. Some of the run is observed on secondary markets when holders of nonmaturing CDs and similar instruments sell them and drive up the interest rate for the bank's funding.

The ability of the bank to handle the run depends on its asset liquidity and the perceived quality of its nonliquid assets. The less liquid its assets—so that the preservation of the existing funding levels becomes more important—and the lower the perceived quality of its nonliquid assets, the more nervous are the depositors and the greater their incentive to switch banks is likely to be. Evidence does not suggest random or casual withdrawals from other banks, but rather deposit-switching for increased perceived safety. There is no evidence in recent periods of systemwide contagious bank runs and instability at individual banks spreading to a large number of other banks, regardless of their financial condition. Nor were any national economic downturns started or intensified by bank failures. Indeed, the increase in the number of bank failures after 1982 occurred during a strong national economic expansion.

In addition, a careful statistical study reported no contagion on the stock market performance of other banks from the failures of the large Franklin National Bank, United States National Bank of San Diego, and the Hamilton National Bank of Chattanooga, which would not have been the case had they ignited deposit runs at other banks. (Aharony and Swary, 1983). A later study by one of the same authors, however, reported stock price contagion from the Continental Bank failure in May 1984 on other large banks, suggesting that other large banks may have been feared to have had similar portfolios. (Swary, 1985). But as noted earlier, there was no currency run.

Historical Interpretations of Bank Failures

Bank failures have long been the subject of scholarly analysis. This section surveys interpretations of the record of U.S. bank failures described in the previous section that have been published in books and leading journals. The analysis focuses primarily on the failures during the Great Depression. Constraints of time did not permit as extensive a search as might have been desirable in a more leisurely setting. Nonetheless, almost all of the books, journal articles, and reports of bank regulatory authorities that have been cited in other studies and have been listed in library card catalogues and computer searches were, at a minimum, scanned.

Recently, a number of re-examinations have been published of the beginnings of the banking crisis of 1929–1930. One study compared the characteristics of the banks that failed in 1930 and the reasons for the failures with those that had failed in the three years before the banking crisis. (White, 1984). The study did not find the differences to be statistically significant and reported that models of bank failure fitted to data for the late 1920s predicted the 1930 failures reasonably well. The study concluded that:

> The 1930 banking crisis, despite its higher rate of bank failures, did not mark a departure from previous experience. . . . The wave of bank failures . . . thus appears to be a part of the economic downturn rather than a major turning point in the depression. . . . The importance of the banking crisis of 1930 in the history of the Great Depression appears to be somewhat inflated.

Similarly, another recent study (Wicker, 1982) that examined the bank failures individually concluded that:

> The evidence examined in this paper points to the conclusion that the initial impact of the banking crisis in 1930 was confined almost entirely to readily identifiable significant local expenditures effects without any clear observable consequence for the economy as a whole . . . [It] left no discernible impact on the central money market, even though the largest banking failure in the United States up to that time was located in that market.

These conclusions are supported by analyses conducted at the time. A session on banking was held at the annual meetings of the American Economic Association on December 29–30, 1931. Two papers were delivered and discussed by four discussants. The participants had information on the banking situation through mid-1931 and impressions through yearend. None of the papers or discussants stressed the existence of systemwide contagious bank failures or identified them as an important cause of the crisis. Professor W.F. Spahr (New York University) (1932), listed 10 causes of the high rate of bank failures since 1920—split regulation, too many banks, too many non-Fed members, lack of loan diversification at small banks, overly restrictive Fed discount eligibility, increased bank investment in longer-term bonds at the expense of shorter-term loans, increased nonbanking activities at unsupervised affiliates, reduced reserves through emphasis on time deposits over demand deposits, high costs at small banks, and poor small bank management. He cited a study by the Comptroller of the Currency that reported that 50 percent of national bank failures were due to depressed local economies, 38 percent to incompetent management, and 9 percent to fraud.

Spahr concluded that bank failures "accompany very closely the rise and fall in commercial failures usually reaching the peak at the same time . . . (and) are not only caused by recessions but contribute to unsound business conditions." His recommendations for lowering the incidence of bank failures included bringing all banks under the Federal Reserve System, liberalizing branching provisions (he noted, as have others, that Canada, which had nationwide branch banking, experienced almost no bank failures in this period), and liberalizing eligibility requirements at the Federal Reserve discount window.

In discussing Spahr's paper, Professor F.A. Bradford (Lehigh) (1932) noted that "if bank failures continue on a wide scale, business concerns, as well as individuals, will be increasingly likely to withdraw their accounts and hold currency or gold." But he did not expand on this or note any resulting systemwide domino or ripple effect. Instead, he supported more permissive branch banking, higher capital requirements, and better management as the most appropriate corrective measures.

Similarly, Professor R.G. Thomas (1935), writing in the October 1935 issue of the *Journal of Business*, concluded that for bank failures through 1931:

> Faulty management rather than external circumstances is the major cause for bank failures. . . . During periods of prolonged depression weak and inefficient management, unable to meet the rigorous requirements of the time, contributes heavily to failure. It follows, therefore, that the most fruitful remedies for bank failure must be sought in the direction of improved management.

Not once in the article did Thomas refer to contagious bank runs.

Thus, through yearend 1931, systemwide contagious bank failures did not appear to have been the primary concern.[7] This may be explained by noting from Table 2 that the currency-deposit ratio increased most sharply after 1931, in 1932 and 1933, and suggests that even in the Great Depression the contagiousness of bank failures was limited regionally until near the bottom. The limited contagious failures also appeared to have come and gone in waves rather than continuously. (Board of Governors, 1934; Wicker, 1982). The model of bank failures discussed earlier that was fitted to data for the 1920s and predicted failures in 1930 reasonably well was far less successful in predicting failures in 1931 and 1932. (White, 1984).

The accounts of bank failures in late 1932 and early 1933, leading to bank holidays in many states and eventually the national bank holiday in March, present pictures of a "classical" systemwide contagious self-perpetuating bank run. The banking system appeared to have been in almost total disarray and despair. Writing in late 1933, Marcus Nadler and Jules Bogen (1933) broke tradition with previous writers and stated unambiguously, "a bank failure is an economic, a financial and a social disaster . . . a series of bank failures is very aptly called an epidemic. Failures are contagious. . . . The collapse of one bank of itself tends to undermine the confidence of the community and start runs on others."

What might have happened in late 1932 that caused depositors to lose faith in all banks at once and set the stage for systemwide contagious bank failures? A reading of history suggests a number of possible factors. On November 8, 1932, Franklin D. Roosevelt over-whelmingly defeated President Herbert Hoover by a 60-to-40 percent popular vote. However, the inauguration was not until March 4, 1933. During this four-month period, the country was nearly leaderless at the height of the most severe economic crisis in its history. The magnitude of the defeat made Hoover almost powerless and hesitant to act, and Roosevelt did not wish to take any actions prior to his inaugu-ration that might enhance the prestige of his predecessor. In addition, there was considerable uncertainty and some fear about Roosevelt's economic and financial policies upon taking office. As a result, confi-dence in the survival of many economic institutions waned, thereby reinforcing tendencies to withdraw currency from banks.

The resulting increase in bank failures led a progressively increasing number of states to impose bank holidays in which banks were generally closed for all banking business, including conversion of deposits into currency, transfers of deposits to third parties, and new loan extensions. These holidays left the community with sharply reduced available money and sharply reduced the levels of business activity in the area. Residents of unaffected states feared similar holi-days and acted to protect themselves by withdrawing currency while they still could. Like systemwide bank failures, bank holidays become contagious and self-feeding. Nevada was the first state to declare a bank holiday, scheduled to last 12 days, on October 31, 1932. Louisiana followed on February 4, 1933, followed shortly by Michigan, Maryland, Ohio, Indiana, and Arkansas. One month later, in the closing minutes of the Hoover Administration, both New York and Illinois suspended convertibility, leaving only 14 states whose banks operated without restrictions. On March 6, newly inaugurated President Roosevelt declared a national bank holiday that closed all banks for at least three days. (Kennedy, 1973).

In contrast, in previous periods of potential net currency outflows and systemwide bank failure contagiousness, the banks themselves—with the mostly tacit approval of the regulators—suspended currency convertibility, but maintained most other banking activities, including third-party deposit transfers and new loan extensions. In addition, clearinghouses in some major communities issued clearinghouse certificates in various denominations that served as currency. Both of these actions served to defuse the currency runs and provided banks with additional search time to sell assets at closer to their equilibrium market value, reducing their losses. This, in turn, reduced pressures to convert deposits to currency and halted the banks runs. At the same time, the continuation of most banking activities and of the major medium of exchange reduced downward pressures on economic activity. (The reasons why such steps were not taken in 1932–1933 are complex and will not be discussed here.)

If it is true that systemwide contagious bank runs were not a frequent occurrence in U.S. history (probably occurring at most only in 1878, 1893, 1908, and 1931–1933 and doing major damage probably only in 1893 and 1931–1933), and that fear of widespread ripple effects did not appear to be of major concern to most students of U.S. banking before 1932, where did the widely held fears originate? It appears to be, in large measure, a lingering aftermath of the extraordinary collapse of the banking system in 1932–33 that so traumatized economists and bankers who lived through it that it colored the entire outlook of many. They wrote about these events in such vivid and graphic terms, and with such flair and emotion, that their analyses were widely accepted as the general rather than the exceptional case. This style is exemplified by the quotes from Nadler and Bogen presented above. Because of the importance and long-lasting effects of the failures, the new analysis replaced the previously held explanations of earlier, less traumatic, rounds of bank failures. In this way it was similar to other analyses of the Great Depression that gave birth to widespread and deeply felt fears, such as permanent high unemployment and stagnation, that survived for many years in this country until challenged, and that played a major role in shaping public policy until then.

In contrast to most U.S. writings, systemwide contagious failures were discussed more frequently in the writings of earlier British economists. Writing in 1802, Henry Thornton (1802, and Humphrey, 1983), among the first students of central banking, noted that:

> If one bank fails, a general run on the neighboring ones is apt to take place, which if not checked at the beginning by a pouring into the circulation a large quantity of gold, leads to very expensive mischief.

In his classic *Lombard Street*, Walter Bagehot (1894) stated that "if any large fraction of (money held by bankers) really was demanded, our banking system and our industrial system, too, would be in great danger . . . in wild periods of alarm, one failure makes many." Bagehot also quoted David Ricardo that "a general panic may seize the country when everyone becomes desirous of possessing himself of . . . precious metals . . .—against such panic banks have no security."

The fact that systemwide contagious bank runs is given greater emphasis in the British than in U.S. literature may not be too surprising, in light of the period in which the British were writing and the smaller number of banks in that country. The public is likely to have entrusted banks less with specie than with currency, and public loss of confidence in the banking system is more likely the smaller the number of banks in the system and the fewer banks that need to be toppled. The fewer the number of banks, the more similar their market areas and the closer their interconnections are both likely to be. Thus, holdings of currency or specie outside the banking system would be more likely. Given the much larger number of banks in the United States and the unit banking structure (meaning that depositors are less likely to know all banks, particularly the more distant banks), and given that the same banks are less likely to serve the same market, the emphasis on noncontagious or limited contagious runs by American writers before 1931 becomes understandable. It is interesting to note that this is not the first paper to question some inherited wisdom about bank failures in the United States. A number of recent studies suggest that free entry banking in the mid-1800s may not have been responsible for the high rate of bank failures in that period. (Rolnick and Weber, 1982, 1983, and 1984).

Implications of Electronic Clearing

It should be noted that, although recent bank runs have been similar to those of earlier years, this does not imply that all future bank runs will necessarily be similar and require similar private and public policy strategies. The progressive decline in banks' capital-to-asset ratios has made them more vulnerable to insolvency from run-induced fire-sales. The increasing importance of electronic fund transfers and of daytime bank clearing overdrafts provides a potential for quicker and larger runs and for larger creditor losses than before, particularly for larger banks. Both the dollar on balance volume and number of large payment clearings have increased rapidly since 1970. In 1970, the daily dollar amount of these transfers were approximately equal to the amount of the banks' aggregate reserve balances at the Federal Reserve. By 1980, these transfer were 26 times as large, so that the average dollar on balance turned over 26 times daily.

Moreover, the dollar amount is very large, approximating $600 billion daily, four times the dollar exposure in check clearing. As interbank transfers are unlikely to flow evenly through the day, this almost necessitates brief overdrafts before final settlement at dayend. A Federal Reserve survey revealed that total daylight overdrafts average some $115 billion daily, and that several hundred banks incurred at least one daylight overdraft per month that exceeded their capital, at times by substantial amounts.

The private and public policies appropriate for dealing with settlement failures (defaults) in such circumstances may be expected to be different. Because of the speed and magnitude of such losses, the time that regulators have for analyzing an institution, estimating the magnitude of any losses, initiating corrective actions, and resolving possible failures is substantially shorter than otherwise. Unlike the check-clearing system or the procedures in effect for clearing on the New York Stock Exchange and most other organized stock and commodity exchanges, neither regulatory rules nor court precedents are in place on most electronic clearing systems for resolving defaults or making indemnifications.

A recent study by the Association of Reserve City Bankers (1983) addressed some of these issues. It noted that the newly established private CashWire network allocates participants' defaults on daily positions proportionately among those banks that had net credit positions with the failed banks. As each bank's maximum debt position is limited to 50 percent of its capital, all payments are in good funds. CHIPS (Clearing House Interbank Payment System) does not yet limit a bank's exposure, but has rules for allocating defaults among participants in such a way, including cancelling that day's transfers, that the defaults will not cause other banks to fail or produce a "gridlock" in which other transfers would not be completed. The study makes recommendations "to limit credit risk by reducing the possibility that failure of one system or participant will cause other systems or participants to fail or sustain unnecessary losses." These include establishing intraday credit limits and on-line real-time monitoring, smoothing the pattern of payments over the day, and providing for emergency collateralized borrowing from the Federal Reserve for amounts in excess of a bank's intraday credit limit. (Association of Reserve City Bankers, 1983; Stevens, 1984; and Smoot, 1985).

These issues were also studied by a Federal Reserve staff committee, which completed its report in early 1985. On the basis of this report, the Board of Governors adopted a policy that requires large-dollar networks using the Fedwire to establish guidelines specifying: (1) individual maximum bilateral net credit limits, (2) sender net debit caps, and (3) procedures for rejecting payments that exceed these limits. The limits for individual institutions are to be established by the banks themselves, based on their creditworthiness and operational controls. The self-evaluations are subject to review by the Federal Reserve. The policy is to become effective March 27, 1986. The Board also recommended similar guidelines for use by individual banks that incur daylight overdrafts on all large-dollar wire networks, effective yearend 1985.

While breakdowns in electronic clearing systems could cause larger losses to the participants and are more likely to threaten their solvency than slower clearing systems, they are unlikely to transform individual bank difficulties into systemwide instability, as long as the Federal Reserve is willing to provide immediate emergency credit to guarantee settlement. The danger, again, is not an aggregate reduction in reserves or deposits, but a reduction in clearing activity supported by the reserves until the system is operating smoothly again. If the curtailment in clearing activity discourages financial transactions and real economic activity, then a temporary injection of additional reserves by the Federal Reserve may be justified.

Nevertheless, further research is required, in particular, on how to reduce incentives for banks to pay on uncollected funds during daytime operating hours, to quickly untangle and reconstruct the transactions in default, and to resolve insolvencies almost instantaneously in order to minimize losses to uninsured depositors and creditors without removing penalties for bank mistakes. The quicker transfer of funds could induce greater potential individual bank instability unless monitoring and failure resolution are accelerated proportionately. (The Federal Reserve Bank of New York has a computer system in operation that prevents U.S. branches and agencies of foreign banks from incurring daylight overdrafts on Fedwire unless they are pre-arranged and fully collateralized.)

Summary

The evidence from most of U.S. history indicates that, contrary to general belief, the adverse effects of bank runs and bank failures on the community have, for the most part, not been much greater than the effects of financial difficulties of most other business firms of comparable relative size and importance in the community, and may often be considerably less. On infrequent occasions, the implications have been more severe, and the instability of individual banks was translated into instability of the banking system as a whole. A run on a bank reflects fears by depositors (and other creditors) that for one reason or another, valid or not, the bank may not be able to redeem all of its deposits in full when due, which for many is on demand. Thus, only the first depositors to withdraw will suffer no harm and many will attempt to be first. To redeem its deposits, the bank is likely to be forced to sell its assets quickly.

The implications of the bank run for both the stability of the banking system and economic activity in the community depends on the type of bank run, the financial condition of the bank, and the reaction of the regulatory authorities. A run on a bank may result in deposit shifts to other banks, a flight to quality in which the deposits are used to buy safer nonbank securities, or a net transfer into currency. The first two types of run generally result in direct or indirect deposit shifts to other banks and, although reflecting fears about the affected banks, indicate faith in the solvency of the banking system as a whole. A run on one bank would not ignite runs on all other banks, even if it resulted in the failure of the bank, although it might do so for some banks considered by depositors to be subject to similar external shocks. Direct redeposits of the withdrawn funds in other banks will primarily reshuffle deposits among banks and have little if any effect on the total volume of bank deposits or credit. Because, particularly in today's environment, most bank services are offered by many providers and are relatively interchangeable, runs are unlikely to cause more economic harm than the failure of nonbank firms of comparable size and importance in the community, even if they lead to bank failures, which need not and in most cases should not be the case. The individual bank's problems will not spill over to the banking system as a whole. Even with direct redeposit, runs are, however, likely to do some economic and social damage by breaking banking connections and producing uncertainty.

If a sufficient number or size or similarity of banks experiences runs, depositors are likely to flee from bank deposits to safer securities. The effects of such behavior depend on whether the sellers of the securities redeposit their proceeds in other banks or store them in the form of currency. By widening the spread between Treasury and other, including bank, securities, a flight to quality with redeposit will have more serious adverse effects on levels of economic activity than direct redeposit. This is likely to depress private investment, reduce bank profits, and increase public uncertainty and concern. But the consequences are not the feared collapse of the banking system. If the sellers of the securities hold the proceeds in currency or if depositors run directly into currency—a run on the banking system as opposed to individual or groups of banks (the third type of run)—a distrust of all banks is indicated. A run on one bank without redeposits at other banks will ignite runs on banks systemwide, and cause banks to increase their excess reserves. The combined effects of a reduction in reserves and in the multiplier will precipitate a multiple contraction in total bank deposits (money) and assets (credit), requiring hasty asset sales at fire-sale prices with potentially large losses. This will both upset the stability of the national financial system and reinforce the adverse impact on economic activity of the shock that set in motion the initial run. Thus, it is important to distinguish between a run on an individual bank or a group of banks and a run on the banking system as a whole. The consequences differ significantly.

By permanently eliminating the need for small depositors to flee into currency, federal deposit insurance has severely reduced the contagiousness of individual bank runs on other banks. Although this conclusion appears also to hold for potential "electronic" deposit runs, this area requires further research.

If a bank is solvent at the time of the run, so that its EMVA exceeds its MVD, its ability to meet the deposit drains in full depends on the magnitude of any losses it may suffer from having to sell assets quickly at fire-sale prices—below their equilibrium market value—to supplement other sources of funds. If any such losses total less than its net worth, the bank can accommodate all depositor claims, and there should be no adverse effects on other banks or on local economic activity. The run should peter out on its own, and the bank should be able to regain its stability, although it will have suffered a cost. If the losses from the quick asset sales are greater than its net worth (EMVA > MVD > FSVA), the bank cannot accommodate all due deposit liabilities in full and is driven into fire-sale insolvency. However, all it needs in order to remain solvent is time. There is little social benefit in declaring a fire-sale insolvent bank economically insolvent. Appropriate private and public policy is to monitor banks sufficiently closely to be aware of their true financial condition on a timely basis, and to assist a bank in gaining the required time either by cooperative action by other banks to recycle the withdrawn funds to the bank through Fed funds and correspondent balances or loan purchases, or through loans from the Federal Reserve in its role as lender of last resort.

If such policies are carried out, bank runs on solvent banks produce few if any problems for regional or national financial stability or for regional or national levels of economic activity. (Timely monitoring and assisting in providing sufficient time to initiate corrective policies may be expected to be more challenging for electronic bank runs.) Bank runs, *per se*, distinct from the problems that caused them, produce adverse effects for regional financial stability and economic activity only if the bank is insolvent through inappropriate actions, either of its own in assuming *ex post* risk or of other banks and the Federal Reserve in failing to reverse fire-sale insolvency.

If at the time of a run the bank is insolvent in the sense that the equilibrium market value of its assets is less than the market value of its deposits and shareholder liability, then clearly all the bank's depositors cannot be satisfied in full and the bank needs either to be declared insolvent or granted financial assistance to provide equal protection to all depositors. Once depositors become aware of the bank's financial plight, they will attempt to withdraw their deposits. Both because a run will lead the bank to sell assets at fire-sale prices and because it is more likely to take larger gambles to recover its solvency, the bank is likely to experience further losses. The sooner the bank is declared insolvent by the regulators and its management changed, the smaller these losses will be and the smaller also will be any adverse effects on the community that would reinforce the initial shock that precipitated the bank's problems. Upon being declared insolvent, the bank may be liquidated, sold, merged, or operated temporarily by the FDIC, depending on circumstances such as state branching statutes, franchise value, minimization of losses on sale of assets, and financial assistance by the regulatory agencies. Losses to uninsured depositors from the shortfall in the market value of assets relative to that of deposits will be shared *pro rata,* in the absence of legal barriers, with the insurance agency absorbing the loss on insured deposits.[8]

U.S. history suggests that runs on individual banks or groups of banks only rarely spread to other banks that are not subject to the same conditions that started the runs, and that most bank runs have been contained by appropriate action, with only minimal and short-lived adverse effects on national financial stability and economic activity. Generally, the instability of individual banks or groups of banks has not translated into instability in the banking system as a whole. The major exception was the run on all banks in late 1932 through early 1933, which caused the banking system to grind to almost a complete halt and substantially reinforced the economic crisis at the time. Although an exception, this event was so traumatic that it has colored analysis of bank runs and failures ever since.

With the introduction of federal deposit insurance and with some sufficient minimum per account coverage and more informed policy by the Federal Reserve as lender of last resort, the conditions necessary for nationwide bank failure contagiousness have been all but eliminated. Transforming deposit insurance into an explicit deposit guarantee up to the insured amount by the federal government would eliminate altogether the possibility of such an event occurring again.

However, even in the absence of such a change, it is time to discard the fears of bank runs based on the experiences of the Great Depression and to adopt more realistic attitudes and policies based on both the long sweep of U.S. history and the new institutions and arrangements now in place. Bank runs indicate actual or perceived depositor concerns. They can be prevented from destabilizing other, untainted banks and economic activity either by validating justified fears by declaring the bank insolvent or by disproving perceived fears through assisting solvent banks experiencing liquidity problems to remain solvent and operating. Both policies can be pursued success-fully without weakening market discipline and withholding punishing economically inefficient banks because of fears of adverse externalities for other banks or the economy as a whole. Indeed, because they are feared, bank runs may intensify market discipline on other banks. But, because they increase uncertainty,, churning, and potential fire-sale difficulties, the social costs of extended bank runs exceed the benefits.

Nevertheless, public policy should not be directed at prevent-ing bank runs or even failures from ever occurring. Given today's safeguards in the form of the FDIC and Federal Reserve and their ability to pursue stabilizing policies, the banking system is likely to operate most efficiently with some churning among individual institu-tions. This should be encouraged. However, some caution should be exercised so that the number and magnitude of bank failures are not sufficiently large to ignite a substantial flight to quality or currency. At what point individual bank runs cumulate to set off such a flight is not known, but in light of the relatively minor economic harm that is likely to be done by flights on individual banks, even large banks, public policy need not err excessively on the side of caution.

[1]Depositors may also not experience losses at insolvent banks if the liability of the shareholders extends beyond the value of their shares. Before 1934, shareholders of national banks and state banks in some states were liable for *pro rata* losses up to the par value of their stock in addition to the market value of their stock. This was referred to as "double liability." It was repealed in 1933 for new shares and in 1937 for old shares. (The authors are indebted to Charles Haywood for the information on repeal.) Double liability undoubtedly strengthened the capital base of banks, increased depos-itor faith in banks, and discouraged runs. Between 1716 and 1844, most Scottish banks had unlimited shareholder liability, which helped to make these banks far stronger than their English counterparts and almost immune to runs. (White, 1984).

[2]Contagious insolvencies are not unique to banking. Whenever a seller cannot meet customer demand for a good because of an actual or perceived shortage, and the customers cannot readily obtain the good in other shops, there is likely to be a run on the remaining shops. Any stock will quickly disappear until replenished, leaving the accounts for all or a substantial portion of their total sales, also with reduced or no profits. While not unique to banking, bank contagion may be expected to be more virile, faster acting, and more encompassing.

[3]Although all insured commercial banks are insured by the FDIC, state-chartered thrift institutions in some states are insured by state insurance agencies. Because many of these agencies are underfunded and the public is aware that, unlike the federal government, the states cannot print money, threatened losses at larger institutions can and do start runs by insured depositors. See, for example, the run on the Home State

Savings Bank in Cincinnati (Ohio), which was insured by the Ohio Deposit Guarantee Fund, in March 1985. The run was started by reports of losses at Home Savings from investment activities that were estimated to be in excess of the $135-million size of the state insurance fund. The inability of the state fund to rescue deposits at Home ignited runs on the other state-insured associations in Ohio, and resulted in the governor declaring a "holiday" and temporarily closing all state-insured institutions until they received federal deposit insurance. The withdrawn funds were on the whole redeposited at federally insured institutions. A similar run occurred shortly afterwards in Maryland. State deposit insurance programs are reviewed in Federal Deposit Insurance Corporation (1983).

[4]While data on bank failures appear reasonably reliable for this entire period, reliable data on the total number of banks go back only to 1896. Reliable data on national banks date to 1865. But data on the number of state-chartered banks from 1875, the first year of a consistent published series, through 1895, appear to underestimate the actual number of these banks and therefore also the total number of banks significantly. In 1896, the first year the new (and presumably reliable) and the old (and presumably unreliable) series overlap, the new series reports some 2,000 more state banks in existence.

[5]James Tobin (1984) has argued that:

> Economywide consequences of failures of large banks have been greatly exaggerated in the rhetoric of the industry, the news media, and the concerned government officials. Words like dominoes, runs and panics conjure up memories of the early 1930s. The analogy thus suggested is false. In the 1980s we do not confront a wholesale run from banks to currency, and if we did the Federal Reserve would now have no trouble supplying the desired currency without curtailing the supply of bank reserves. The runs we have seen are from troubled bank to other banks; these do not destroy the aggregate reserve base. Or they are from bank deposits to market instruments, domestic or foreign. Contrary, evidently, to widespread misunderstandings, such flight cannot destroy any reserves either. The worst they can do is to force some disintermediation, in which banks sell to their erstwhile depositors the market instruments they now prefer. That may be bad for bank shareholders, but it is not a social disaster.

[6]In part, the unusually large magnitude of the drain could also have reflected the fact that local clearinghouses did not issue their own currency in the form of clearinghouse loan certificates, as they had in earlier crises. In 1907, clearinghouses issued $238 million in transferable large-denomination certificates, $23 million in small-denomination certificates that circulated as currency, $12 million in circulating managers' checks, $14 million in cashiers checks, and $47 million in payable-to-bearer manufacturers' paychecks. In sum, these totalled $334 million, equivalent to some 20 percent of regular currency outstanding. (White, 1983; see also Hammond, 1941, and Timberlake, 1984).

[7]One exception to this conclusion is a study by Ralph Young (1932) for the National Industrial Conference Board. Young described contagious bank runs occurring in 1931 as currency withdrawals that led to a vicious cycle of liquidation, bank failures, new withdrawals of cash, new liquidations, and new bank failures. Yet the preface to the study states that "more serious . . . was the fact that banks generally adopted a policy of great caution in making new loans."

[8]An analysis of alternative failure resolutions appears in Edward J. Kane (1985) and in Chapter 4.

CHAPTER 3

Government Deposit Insurance

C ommercial banks, with the Federal Reserve, are the basic operators of the U.S. money and payments system. The American constitutional system recognized the crucial role of money in the economy from the very beginning, and the responsibility of the government for maintaining a sound money system. The Constitution empowered Congress—and only Congress— to "coin money and regulate the value thereof."

Objectives of Federal Deposit Insurance

As liabilities of banks became the major form of money in the economy, it became clear that the government had the responsibility to ensure that the banking system was stable and sound. This responsibility evolved over time, at least partly in response to financial crises that originated in the banking sector or were exacerbated by the nature of the banking system. This history is discussed in the previous chapters of this report, as in the U.S. experience during the Great Depression of the 1930s. The wave of bank failures in the early 1930s led to development of a system of federal deposit insurance to resolve the crisis and prevent any recurrence. Deposit insurance is useful because a fractional reserve banking system is inherently fragile and potentially unstable. This chapter considers the role of government-provided deposit insurance in affecting the riskiness of individual banks and of the banking system as a whole. This chapter introduces the role of deposit insurance in dealing with the problems presented in Chapter 1.

The discussion so far has emphasized the distinction between stability of the monetary system and failures of individual banks. It seems clear that, as a matter of public policy, the soundness of the system is most appropriately viewed as a responsibility of government. But from the earliest discussions of federal deposit insurance in the United States until today, deposit insurance has also been supported as a means of protecting "the small depositor." Such intervention in the market on behalf of a particular segment of the economy has a reasonable economic basis. Decisions as to which banks are safe depositories require information that is costly to obtain and process. It is economical for the government, which must gather such information in connection with its supervisory responsibilities for the financial system, to provide a certification of bank safety, rather than have each small depositor responsible for making the costly analysis.

One image of the Great Depression that persists in the public imagination is that of depositors who lost their life savings in the failure of their banks. This image is, if not a myth, at least an exaggeration. Bank failures were widespread during the Depression, and most failures involved some losses to depositors. But no bank failure represents a 100 percent loss of assets, and in most failures ultimate losses were only a few cents on the dollar.

In any case, once wealth in the form of bank deposits was insured by the government, it appeared reasonable to extend those guarantees to wealth held in similar forms. Even apart from the merits of protecting small savers, savings and loans (S&Ls), and (later) credit unions were provided with federal deposit insurance in the interests of competitive equality. Today, protecting the public against loss of one's life savings is probably more appropriate in the case of pension rights. Failure of a pension fund is more likely to result in a literal loss of a retiree's life savings than is a bank failure.

In any event, accepting the validity of deposit insurance aimed at protecting the small depositor does not require or justify the current deposit insurance coverage of $100,000 per depositor. The depositor with $100,000 has access to other riskless or low-risk assets, and has the opportunity to diversify his holdings to reduce risk. Ironically, the small saver would have more options today if the government had not raised the minimum denomination of Treasury bills. While this analysis accepts the historical and economic justification for one level of protection for individual depositors (not necessarily $100,000), the principal focus of this analysis of deposit insurance is on its relationship to stability of the monetary system rather than to protection of the small depositor.

Alternatives to Federal Deposit Insurance

Federal deposit insurance is not necessary to ensure a stable monetary system. Numerous observers point out that a central bank, willing and able to provide liquidity to the system through open market operations and to individual institutions, can prevent a disastrous decline in the money supply, thus preventing a liquidity crisis from developing. (The role and responsibilities of the central bank are discussed in Chapter 5.) But the fact that the problems described in the preceding chapters of this report can be handled without deposit insurance is not a sufficient argument against deposit insurance. Society logically prefers the cheapest and most reliable means to meet its objectives. Experience in the United States indicates that the central bank may make mistakes in dealing with a crisis, and that deposit insurance may be an efficient and cost-effective means of ensuring a stable financial system.

Some have argued that the benefits of deposit insurance can be achieved through a private-sector system rather than requiring federal deposit insurance. The reports on deposit insurance prepared by the Federal Home Loan Bank Board (1983) and the Federal Deposit Insurance Corporation (FDIC) (1983) each examined the feasibility and desirability of private deposit insurance, and both came to similar rather negative conclusions. There are three primary reasons why federal deposit insurance is preferable to other options, such as private insurance, cooperative arrangements among the depository institutions themselves, or state deposit insurance systems. These relate to:

1. The capacity of the private insurance industry;

2. The credibility of private insurance; and

3. The nature of the insurance contract.

Insurance companies do not believe that they have the financial capacity to underwrite the hundreds of billions of dollars of deposit insurance that is now in force under the federal system. Traditional insurance standards relate company reserves to the total amount of insurance coverage, even though actual losses in a bank failure represent only a small fraction of total insured deposits. On this basis, insurance companies would not be able to step into the shoes of the federal deposit insurance system.

Even if insurance companies were interested in, and capable of, handling deposit insurance in a financial sense, it is unlikely that a private system would have the credibility of a governmental system. The credibility of the federal system is demonstrated by the continued operations of insured savings and loans that are clearly insolvent in economic terms. That may be contrasted with the experience of Home State Savings of Cincinnati, insured by an Ohio system for state-chartered S&Ls. When large losses were suffered as a result of the failure of ESM Government Securities Company, a massive run on Home State Savings developed, forcing the closing of the institution. A similar situation developed in Maryland, where publicity concerning the problems of one or two savings institutions insured by a private system led to a run on other insured institutions.

A better illustration of the limited credibility of such systems is provided by the North Carolina experience, where institutions covered by a private insurance system opted to seek federal insurance in the wake of the Ohio and Maryland problems, without any triggering event or public indication of reason to question the financial capability of the system.

Unless there is ultimately federal insurance or reinsurance for the private insurers, it is unlikely that a private system can provide the credibility necessary to ensure stability of the system. And, of course, federal insurance of private deposit insurers would involve the same problems that those advocating private insurance seek to avoid.

A final problem for private deposit insurance concerns the nature of the insurance contract itself. It must be recognized that federal deposit insurance involves legal arrangements that are unique. It has been pointed out that FDIC losses in bank failures can be limited by the chartering authority's ability to close a bank when its net worth is exhausted (Horvitz, 1980). If insolvent institutions are allowed to remain in operation, the insurer is at risk.

As a matter of public policy, authority to close a bank is unlikely to be granted to a private insurance company. If it had such power, the economic incentives would lead the insurance company to close the bank as early as possible—perhaps when it could still be saved. The chartering agencies that now make such decisions do so in the context of their public responsibilities for the adequacy and quality of banking services (although, in the absence of financial responsibility, these agencies may tend to keep banks open too long—a consideration that argues for giving the FDIC some authority to close failing banks).

It is also clear that a private insurer could not be given the right to cancel coverage when the condition of the insured bank deteriorates. Cancellation is one means by which an insurance company can protect itself from changes in risk, but deposit insurance that can be cancelled when failure threatens would not contribute to stability of the monetary system. The federal deposit insurance system is inextricably bound up with the supervisory system. It will prove exceedingly difficult, and probably impossible, to switch to a system of private deposit insurance while retaining a purely governmental supervisory system.

Recent experience supports this assessment. In addition to the well publicized problems of nonfederally insured thrift institutions in Ohio and Maryland, there have been losses in recent years to depositors in similar institutions in Nebraska and California. The private systems insuring those institutions lacked regulatory capability and financial capability. They had credibility (until put to the test) largely because they were widely (and erroneously) believed to be backed by the state.

The most promising approach to private insurance appears to be a system of industry cross-guarantees, proposed in a series of papers by Bert Ely (1984, 1985). Such a system mobilizes the capital of the banking system behind individual banks, but some fear that a serious failure under such an arrangement could bring down the whole system.

The preceding discussion makes clear that private deposit insurance cannot be viewed as a perfect substitute for federal insurance. Under some circumstances, of course, an imperfect substitute may be acceptable or necessary. A more useful role for private deposit insurance may be to supplement federal insurance. Such coverage for large deposits, or brokered deposits, might be a means to inject additional market discipline, or market pricing, into the system. Prudential Insurance Company has provided such insurance for certificates of deposit (CDs) issued by its Prudential Bank and Trust subsidiary. Such private initiatives should be encouraged, even though this report concludes that they cannot replace federal deposit insurance.

Current Problems of Federal Deposit Insurance

Despite the apparent success of federal deposit insurance since its inception, recent developments have raised serious questions about the soundness of the system and some of its basic operating principles. Deposit insurance, like other types of insurance, is confronted with the problem that the insured may behave differently simply because of the existence of insurance. Just as the automobile owner with theft insurance may be less careful about locking his car than he would be without insurance, so the depositor protected by deposit insurance may be less careful in his choice of bank. As a result, the insured bank may operate less conservatively than it would if its ability to attract and retain depositors depended only on its financial strength and soundness. In the insurance literature, this tendency of insurance to alter behavior is designated by the somewhat misleading term of "moral hazard."

The danger to the insurance system is that, once covered by deposit insurance, the bank will tend to take greater risks in order to earn higher profits. The higher profits are retained by the bank's owners, while the greater risks are borne by the insurance system. It is important to be clear about this mechanism. It does not suggest that a bank loan officer consciously rationalizes making a risky loan on grounds that, if it leads to failure of the bank, the FDIC will suffer a large part of the loss. It is rather the fact that the desire to seek profits always leads to a choice as to the degree of risk the bank will bear. Without deposit insurance, the cost of attracting depositors is a restraint on risk-taking. The bank with the riskier-than-normal portfolio will find its cost of funds increasing, as risk-averse depositors opt for conservative banks.

With deposit insurance, this pressure towards conservatism is missing or reduced. The banker can get away with a riskier portfolio without increasing his cost of funds, and, because his deposit insurance premiums do not change, his risk-taking is subsidized by more conservative banks. In fact, the only way a bank can take advantage of this deposit insurance subsidy is by adopting a riskier-than-normal stance.

Of course, a deposit insuror, like any insurance company, must have some means of limiting its risk exposure. In many forms of insurance, the solution to the problem is found in charging a higher premium to the greater risks. The higher premiums discourage risk-taking, or at least generate the higher income necessary to cover the greater risks. Deposit insurance in the United States has so far not used this approach of variation in explicit premiums (risk-related insurance premiums are discussed in Chapter 9), but rather has relied on direct regulation and capital requirements to inhibit risk-taking by insured banks. That approach was acceptable for many years, but recently has come into conflict with the trend toward deregulation in the economy. Regulation itself generates inefficiencies. For several reasons, reliance on regulation has become less acceptable as a means of ensuring the soundness of the deposit insurance system.

As discussed in Chapter 1, deregulation and other changes in the economy have exposed the banking system to greater risk than in the past. Further, it appears that banker attitudes toward risk have changed. This suggests that some change in the U.S. deposit insurance system is necessary if it is to remain sound in a deregulated, competitive environment. These changes in the economy have been reflected in a change in the nature of the problems facing the FDIC today.

Through the 1960s, the banks that failed in the United States were primarily small institutions. The FDIC has demonstrated its ability to handle such failures efficiently, with no spillover effects on other banks. It has now become clear, however, that even very large banks can fail. In such cases, the FDIC has been concerned that, depending on how the failure is handled, spillover effects may be large. Such fears have given the FDIC a preference for handling threatened failures in ways that protect all creditors and keep the institution open.

Solutions to Deposit Insurance Problems

A deposit insurance system must have some means to limit its risk exposure. This report has noted that the FDIC has done this by regulation—that is, by restricting the ability of insured banks to take risks—rather than through the pricing of deposit insurance. Deposit insurance in the United States has also sought to use the forces of market discipline to restrict bank risk-taking. From its inception, deposit insurance has provided less than 100 percent coverage. The rationale for that system is that large depositors are uninsured, and hence at risk in case of bank failure. These presumably sophisticated depositors have an incentive to choose their banks on the basis of their soundness and financial strength, opting for conservative institutions rather than aggressive ones. Banks seeking to attract such customers would be forced to operate conservatively.

An evaluation of the current extent of market discipline, and consideration of some alternatives, is provided in Chapter 7. At this point, it is sufficient to note that a potential conflict exists between reliance on uninsured depositors to restrain bank risk-taking and the desire to ensure stability of the banking system. Ideally, the need to attract uninsured depositors will lead all institutions to operate conservatively. The problem is that a mistake or bad luck may result in a bank's being perceived as unduly risky. In that situation, uninsured depositors have every incentive to withdraw their funds as soon as possible. Ideally, the need to attract large depositors should have led Continental Illinois to avoid purchasing poor quality loans from Penn Square. But once that mistake was made, the existence of large depositors at risk represented a source of instability—certainly instability for the bank, but perhaps also instability for the system.

Under the current deposit insurance system, the FDIC has a number of options available for handling a failing or failed bank. These options are discussed in detail in Chapter 4. Some of these options protect depositors up to the limits of deposit insurance coverage—$100,000—while other options protect all depositors and even other creditors in full. Some of these options result in closing and liquidating the bank, while others keep the bank open (often after merging the failing bank with a healthy one).

The FDIC generally chooses among its options on the basis of minimizing its direct costs, much as a private insurance company would. Sometimes, however, as noted, its decision is influenced by concern about the effect of its choice of options on spillover effects and the stability of the system. In particular, when very large banks are concerned, the FDIC has feared that imposing losses on uninsured depositors would cause instability in the system. Could the mini-run on Manufacturers Hanover in the aftermath of the Continental Illinois collapse have been contained if Continental had been closed with losses to uninsured depositors?

These comments do not intend to imply that there is necessarily a conflict between cost minimization for the FDIC and the desire to maintain continuity of the failing bank's operations. It is generally the case that the going-concern value of a bank is preserved if the bank is kept open or merged with a healthy bank. In particular, it appears that the solution worked out by the FDIC in the Continental Illinois case may well turn out to be the cheapest option available to the FDIC.

There may be, however, a conflict between short-run and long-run cost minimization. As a result of the way in which Continental was handled, the perception that some banks are too large to allow their depositors to suffer losses has been strengthened. Such a perception raises problems of both equity and efficiency for the insurance system.

The equity problem relates to the fairness of imposing losses on some depositors of failed small banks, while all depositors of large banks are protected in full. Depositors in small banks have suffered losses, and in 1984 the FDIC adopted a policy aimed at increasing its ability and willingness to impose losses on such depositors. The efficiency problem is that acknowledging that some banks are "too large to fail" (in the sense of losses to depositors) means abandoning market discipline as a method of restraining bank risk-taking.

Further, such a policy will lead, over time, to the public's preference for deposits in large banks, resulting in an increase in the concentration of banking resources in the country. This conflicts with the traditional American preference for avoiding concentration of financial power. The equity problem can be overcome by providing 100 percent insurance for all banks but that, of course, means total elimination of market discipline operating through uninsured depositors. These issues are discussed in more detail in subsequent chapters.

Summary

There is a clear public interest in maintaining a stable banking system. Federal deposit insurance is not a necessary means to achieve such stability, but it is a device that has appeared to work well in the United States for 50 years. There is no logical reason to abandon deposit insurance, but there are several reasons to consider significant change in the system at the present time. Some would argue, in fact, that the system as currently designed is not sustainable indefinitely. The deposit insurance system must have some means of limiting its risk exposure—either by restricting risk-taking by insured banks, or by closing banks before net worth becomes significantly negative. Absent limitations on risk-taking, deposit insurance will tend to increase a bank's tendency to take risk.

Regulation is seen by many now as a less desirable means of risk limitation than it has been in the past. One option, long favored by many academic economists, has been for relating insurance premiums to the riskiness of the institution. The deposit insurance system can be structured so as to provide market discipline toward conservatism. The present U.S. system nominally does this by limiting deposit insurance to $100,000, so that uninsured depositors have an incentive to choose sound institutions. However, the FDIC has provided *de facto* deposit insurance of virtually 100 percent. Many observers believe that a greater use of market discipline would be appropriate, perhaps by reducing the amount of insurance coverage or the types of deposits insured. However, such a change increases the risk of instability in the system, as uninsured depositors may tend to withdraw funds quickly when problems (or rumors of problems) materialize.

Another possibility is to supplement federal deposit insurance with private insurance. Recent problems of large banks raise the question of whether some banks are too large to fail. This refers, of course, to closing and liquidating the bank—no bank is too large to fail in the sense of wiping out the investment of its owners. Differences in the handling of failures of large and small banks by the FDIC have received more attention in light of the protection of all depositors (and other creditors) of Continental Illinois.

In 1984, the FDIC implemented a new approach to handling small bank failures by a "modified payoff" that imposes losses on uninsured depositors. Until 1984, most small bank failures were handled by "purchase and assumption" transactions that protected all depositors. Nearly all observers agree that it is inequitable to treat depositors in large banks differently from small bank depositors are treated. This equity problem should be resolved in any revision of the deposit insurance system.

Differing treatment of large and small banks has implications that go beyond simple fairness. If large depositors receive greater insurance protection in large banks, they will tend to use such banks exclusively, which has adverse implications for competition in banking and the traditional American distaste for concentration of financial power.

CHAPTER 4

Alternative Ways To Resolve Insolvencies

T he banking regulatory and deposit insurance system is intended to prevent or minimize the incidence of bank failures. Nevertheless, there will always be some bank failures. When that occurs, the Federal Deposit Insurance Corporation (FDIC) has several means of dealing with the situation. There are also several criteria by which the FDIC decides which method of resolving failure to use. Unfortunately, there are often conflicts among these criteria. The decision is also made more complicated by the fact that the definition of "failure" is somewhat different in banking from what it is in other businesses.

The Concept of "Failure"

"Failure," surprisingly, is not a clearly defined legal term. The law uses such terms as "insolvency" and "bankruptcy," which are similar to what is generally meant by failure, but are not identical. Insolvency generally means the inability of a firm to meet its obligations as they come due. A business firm in such a situation may seek the protection of the bankruptcy laws, which may provide the opportunity to work out a reorganization that may protect creditors, or otherwise provide for an equitable distribution of the firm's wealth among its creditors. The term "economic insolvency" refers to the situation in which the market value of the firm's assets is less than its liabilities (negative net worth).

The meaning of terms such as bankruptcy and insolvency in corporation law and finance does not carry over in precisely the same way to banking. Most firms face the danger of insolvency only as obligations become due. Insolvency is a potentially greater threat to a bank, because the bulk of the bank's liabilities are payable on demand or on short notice. "Economic insolvency" is not fatal to the business firm, because most of its creditors must wait until their obligations come due to take any action, regardless of the condition of the firm. (In some cases, of course, protective covenants in loan agreements do give the creditor the right to take some action under certain conditions.) Economic insolvency is a potentially serious situation for a bank, because knowledge of that condition might well provoke a run on the bank. With deposit insurance, however, insured depositors have no incentive to participate in a run regardless of the financial condition of the bank. Thus an institution relying largely on insured deposits for its funding can continue to operate indefinitely, even though it may be economically insolvent.

Economic insolvency is defined here in terms of market values rather than book values. Because of the high leverage of most depository institutions, a relatively small difference between book and market values of assets can mean economic insolvency on a market value basis. In fact, based on this definition, many savings and loan associations (S&Ls) are insolvent today. Some believe that the same would be true for a number of commercial banks. Nevertheless, because of deposit insurance, these institutions can continue to operate without fear of development of runs (which would threaten solvency in a legal sense) or other actions by creditors.

Banks are not subject to the bankruptcy laws that apply to other firms. Their analogous legal framework is the power of the chartering authority (Comptroller of the Currency or the state banking supervisor) to declare the bank "insolvent" and close it ("insolvent" in this case means negative net worth, but it is not always clear whether this refers to book or market values). In most cases, following such a declaration of insolvency, the FDIC is appointed receiver, and exercises its insurance powers and responsibilities (when a national bank is involved, the law requires that the FDIC be appointed receiver). In some cases, the determination of insolvency leads to the bank being closed and its assets liquidated, although in most cases the FDIC arranges a transaction that keeps the doors of the bank open (although perhaps under a different name and/or ownership).

What does "failure" mean in this context? A banking or nonbanking firm has clearly and unambiguously "failed" if it is liquidated to meet its obligations to creditors. But, if a firm or bank's financial difficulties result in stockholders being completely or largely wiped out, it is reasonable to view it as a failure, even if a reorganization or merger or direct assistance from the FDIC allows the firm to continue in business. Thus failure means a complete (or close to complete) loss to stockholders, combined with a cessation of independent operation or continuance only by virtue of FDIC financial assistance. By this definition, Continental Illinois, First Pennsylvania, and Franklin National Bank failed, even though only the last was formally declared insolvent by its regulator. A bank in difficulty that arranges a merger without FDIC assistance would not be considered to have failed.

There is a tendency for the public and the press to view actions taken by the FDIC that keep failing banks in operation as "bailouts" of the bank. As shall be seen, FDIC actions often protect uninsured depositors or other creditors who are not entitled to such protection as a matter of law, but the FDIC has rarely protected stockholders. Various interested parties may be "bailed out" or protected even if the bank is closed, and some may suffer loss or be totally wiped out even if the bank's doors remain open. It is important to be aware of the distinction between protection of claims and keeping the bank open in analyzing the FDIC's decisions in dealing with failing banks.

Criteria for FDIC Decisions

The FDIC has several options when a bank approaches "failure"—when it becomes unable to continue in business without loss to creditors or assistance from the FDIC. The FDIC must base its decisions of which option to use on several criteria. One criterion is cost minimization—the same criterion that would be used by a private, profit-making insurance company. The Federal Deposit Insurance (FDI) Act has always set cost-minimization as the primary consideration.

But the desire to minimize costs in a particular bank failure case is sometimes outweighed by other considerations. The principal such consideration is concern for the preservation of confidence in the banking system. This issue arises, of course, only in the context of the failure of a large bank, because failures of small banks are not rare occurrences, and do not shake confidence in the banking system. It is possible, of course, that if large bank failures were common, and experience indicated that they did not lead to spillover effects on other banks, then such failures would have no greater effect on public confidence than a number of small failures do today.

The FDIC has also expressed concern with the development of market discipline in deposit markets. As is discussed in Chapter 7, this requires the existence of uninsured depositors who believe that they are at risk. Clearly, market discipline is encouraged by FDIC decisions that impose losses on uninsured depositors on a consistent basis. Finally, at times the FDIC's handling of particular bank failures has been influenced by the liquidity position of the FDIC fund and concern that a large cash outlay by the FDIC might lead to a loss of confidence in the soundness of the deposit insurance system.

The following section of this chapter analyzes the way in which the FDIC applies these criteria to its decisions on handling failed or failing banks.

FDIC Options in Handling Failures

When a bank fails, insured depositors must receive the amount of their deposit up to the insurance limit. The FDIC options are whether protection is also afforded to uninsured depositors and other creditors, and whether the bank remains open.

The Payoff

The most straightforward option for the FDIC is the deposit payoff. Following a declaration of insolvency by the chartering authority, the bank is closed. The FDIC pays off insured depositors and, as receiver, liquidates the bank's assets. As collections are made by the receivership, funds are distributed to uninsured creditors, including proportionate payments to the FDIC for the amount that it has advanced to the insured depositors. The FDIC also has a claim for its receivership expenses and interest on funds advanced. If collections on assets ultimately exceed liabilities, then all creditors will receive the full amount of their claims plus interest, and neither creditors nor the FDIC will suffer any loss.

The Purchase and Assumption Transaction

As an alternative to payoff and liquidation, the FDIC can arrange for an acquisition of the failed bank by another institution. Although usually described as mergers, technically these transactions involve a purchase of assets of the failed bank and an assumption of its liabilities. This purchase and assumption (P&A) is the most common means by which the FDIC deals with failures, because it has several economic advantages over the payoff.

The acquiring bank in a P&A is usually willing to pay a premium for goodwill and other intangible assets. It does so by accepting tangible assets that are less than the amount of the liabilities assumed. The FDIC saves the direct costs of a payoff (preparing checks, etc.), some liquidation expenses, and potential losses. For example, because the acquiring bank usually needs the bank building of the failed bank, the FDIC avoids the problems of having to dispose of real estate that often has little economic use other than as a bank.

In addition to these cost savings, the P&A preserves the going-concern value of the failed bank, which would be lost in liquidation. That is, the bank has a book of continuing business or customer good-will that will contribute to profit in the future. Because entry into banking is restricted, the bank charter itself has economic value. This is even greater when the charter represents entry into a market that the acquiring bank could not otherwise enter (an interstate acquisition, for example).

In some cases, the P&A can be structured to preserve the right to carry forward the failing firm's past losses against future tax liabilities of the acquirer. (Of course, preservation of the tax-loss carryforward, while enabling the FDIC to obtain a higher premium, does not represent a net gain for the U.S. government as a whole.) Further, the FDIC has developed techniques that usually enable it to get a good price for the failed bank. Under the FDIC's interpretation of the law, it is authorized to arrange a P&A when the costs of doing so will be less than those of payoff; as the above considerations indicate, that cost test is usually met.

When a bank fails, or is about to fail, the FDIC seeks bids from other banks, bank holding companies, or individuals that it believes may be interested in acquiring the failing bank. The FDIC has found that the premium it gets is positively correlated with the number of bidders, so it seeks participation from as many eligible bidders as possible. Unfortunately, assembling a sizable number of bidders and giving them the opportunity to review the financial and economic position of the failing bank takes a fair amount of time, particularly for a large bank or when a complicated deal must be worked out. Sometimes, when the failure is a surprise and the bank must be closed quickly (as when a massive defalcation is discovered, for example), that time may not be available. Again, the FDIC has developed techniques for this situation.

The ideal bid from the point of view of the FDIC would be one in which the acquiring bank takes all of the assets of the failing bank. Obviously, some assets of a failed bank are not going to be acceptable to a purchaser at book value (loans in default, for example). Determining just which assets are acceptable, and what price they are worth to the bidder, takes a detailed analysis of the records of the failing bank and, necessarily, a great deal of time.

The FDIC sometimes sidesteps this problem by putting the bidding on a "clean bank" basis. That is, the acquiring bank assumes all the liabilities of the failed bank, and receives cash from the FDIC equal to the liabilities minus the premium that the successful bidder offers. This approach makes it much easier for interested parties to prepare their bids, because they do not have to review the assets of the failed bank. This procedure increases the number of bidders, and greatly shortens the time of the bidding process. Its disadvantage is that it leaves the FDIC to dispose of the assets (frequently the successful bidder will subsequently review the assets of the failed bank and buy some of those assets from the FDIC), and it requires a greater cash outlay by the FDIC. For this reason, the clean bank approach is used only in relatively small bank failures.

The P&A involving a large bank is necessarily more complicated and takes more time to work out. Because there will usually be some disclosure or publicity about the problems of a large bank (either leaks or disclosure required by securities laws), the time it takes to work out the P&A also provides time in which uninsured depositors and other creditors can withdraw their funds. The time delay, in effect, provides greater protection for depositors in large banks than in small.

The success of the FDIC in finding interested bidders willing to offer significant premiums depends on a number of factors. Obviously the value of the franchise of the failed bank is a key factor—its location and the nature of its market and its business. But state law and the structure of the banking industry of the state in which the failure occurs are also important in determining the number of bidders. If state law prohibits branching and holding company operations, then the failed bank's office must be closed. In such a case, a bidder is unlikely to pay much of a premium for acquiring a book of business that it cannot be sure of retaining. This is why payoffs have been much more common in unit banking states (such as Texas) than where branching is allowed.

Arranging a P&A is also more difficult when the failed bank is so large that there are few qualified potential acquirers. The Garn-St Germain Depository Institutions Act of 1982 improved the FDIC's bargaining position by authorizing interstate acquisitions in case of a bank failure. Nevertheless, it is clear that there are fewer potential acquirers of a multibillion-dollar bank than of a $50-million bank. It appears that there were no banks interested and able to bid on an acquisition of Continental Illinois, and that limited the FDIC's options in dealing with that situation.

P&A Versus Payoff

Because of the premiums offered, and the expense savings noted above, the P&A is usually the cheapest solution for the FDIC. On a purely dollars-and-cents basis, then, one would expect that the P&A would be the most commonly used method when failure occurs. The P&A also provides an advantage to the community that experiences a bank failure. With a P&A, the banking office nearly always stays open and in operation, whereas a payoff means closing the bank. Even customers who are protected by deposit insurance from a financial loss in a failure are inconvenienced by the disappearance of their bank, particularly in smaller communities. Further, borrowers face no direct loss of assets if their bank fails, but they may suffer an economic loss if their credit arrangements are disrupted by the closing of their bank.

In comparing the deposit payoff with the P&A, it is important to recognize that the legal position of the failed bank's creditors and the FDIC are not identical under the two approaches. A P&A protects all creditors, who become creditors of the acquiring bank. Any loss is borne entirely by the FDIC. A payoff imposes losses on uninsured creditors unless the liquidation generates sufficient cash to meet all obligations.

An important distinction concerns liabilities not shown on the books of the failing bank or contingent liabilities. Consider the case of an embezzlement that results in an understatement of the true deposits of the bank. When there is any suspicion of such skullduggery (and even when there is not), the acquiring bank is likely to insist on an indemnification from the FDIC, in case a depositor appears after the closing of the transaction with evidence that he does, in fact, have an account with the bank, even though the books of the bank do not so indicate. The acquiring bank will be protected by the indemnification from the cost of this previously unknown liability, and the loss will be borne by the FDIC.

The possible existence of such undisclosed liabilities affects the FDIC's calculation of the relative costs of a payoff versus a P&A transaction. In the case of a P&A, if the undisclosed deposits are in excess of $100,000, they must be honored in full, while only the first $100,000 would be paid immediately with a payoff. If the deposits are all insured, the FDIC would be obligated to cover them, whether it had opted for P&A or payoff. But in the payoff case, the increased loss from the bank failure, represented by newly discovered liabilities, would be shared with the uninsured depositors, while in the P&A case the loss is borne entirely by the FDIC. Because it is difficult to estimate the number and size of deposit accounts that exist but are not on the books, the FDIC tends to prefer the payoff approach when there is significant evidence that the books have been manipulated.

While acknowledging the significant advantages of the P&A approach, some critics have argued that the FDIC has exhibited a bias in favor of the P&A, even when an objective calculation of costs would show the payoff to be cheaper for the FDIC. Cost minimization is not the only consideration for the FDIC. Whenever a large bank has approached failure, the FDIC has feared that imposing losses on uninsured depositors would cause a loss of confidence in the banking system and produce massive runs on banks (as is popularly believed to have happened during the 1930s).

Thus Kane argues that "the insurance agencies show a de facto commitment to minimizing the risks of cumulative failures that surpasses their de jure commitment to safe and sound banking" (p. 2–8). As a result of these concerns, in all cases in which a very large bank has failed or approached failure, the FDIC has used the P&A approach, or has provided direct assistance to the bank to keep it open. Such considerations were important in the cases of Bank of the Commonwealth, Franklin National Bank, First Pennsylvania, and Continental Illinois.

The one possible exception to that policy was the Penn Square National Bank failure. Penn Square was declared insolvent by the Comptroller, and insured depositors were paid off by the FDIC up to the insurance ceiling. Uninsured depositors have so far received only a small percentage of their excess deposits, and it is expected that their losses will be large. Some observers believed that Penn Square represented a change in FDIC policy, particularly because it was followed by the FDIC's adoption of a system of "modified payoff" (discussed below), which also had the effect of imposing losses on uninsured depositors.

It is clear, however, that the handling of Penn Square was in accord with previous FDIC policy. There were allegations of massive fraud in the operations of Penn Squre and, as noted, in such cases the FDIC tends to opt for a payoff to minimize the risk of loss from undisclosed liabilities. Penn Square may also have had substantial liabilities in connection with loans sold to other banks. Further, Oklahoma is a state in which it is particularly difficult to arrange purchase and assumption transactions because, at the time of the failure, it allowed neither branching nor multibank holding companies.

That this was not a shift of policy was apparent from the handling of the next large bank failure to occur, United American Bank of Knoxville. In the face of widespread publicity about the bank's problems, the chairman of the FDIC announced that all depositors would be protected.

In addition to concern with minimizing cost and maintaining stability in the financial system, the FDIC has long had an interest in encouraging the development of market discipline in banking. But if uninsured depositors believe that they will always be protected by a P&A, they have no reason to exercise care in the selection of their bank. A record of frequent payoffs, with losses to uninsured depositors, is probably necessary to generate depositor discipline. But payoffs usually conflict with the cost advantage of the P&A. (The more serious problem—that they conflict with concern over stability of the system—is discussed in Chapter 7.)

Modified Payoff

The "modified payoff," proposed in 1983, and implemented in 1984, is aimed at combining the economies of the P&A with the discipline-encouraging aspects of the payoff. With a modified payoff, the FDIC arranges for another bank to assume only the insured deposits of a failed bank. Uninsured depositors receive an immediate credit for the amount of their claims that the FDIC estimates will ultimately be recovered. The acquiring bank pays a premium, which reduces losses, and the acquired bank's office generally remains open (as a branch of the acquirer). Uninsured depositors suffer a loss that, in economic impact, is somewhat less than in the ordinary payoff, because they have immediate use of some of their uninsured funds.

The modified payoff approach, if followed consistently (or at least frequently) would tend to encourage market discipline. But, by its very nature, market discipline, so far as depositors are concerned, means an increased tendency toward bank runs and instability. Depositors who believe that they are at risk will tend to move their deposits when the bank's problems become known. Even if this does not create problems for the financial system, it does make more difficult the problem of dealing with the individual failing bank. It generally takes a fair amount of time to work out the optimal P&A transaction. If depositors are confident they will be protected, no run will develop and the FDIC will have time to explore all its options. Market discipline after the fact interferes with the FDIC's ability to find the best deal.

Direct Assistance

Payoff and P&A are not the only options available to the FDIC. Under certain circumstances, the FDIC is authorized to make loans to failing banks, or purchase assets from them. Before passage of the Garn-St Germain Act, the FDIC was limited to use of direct assistance, under Section 13(c) of the FDI Act, only where the continued existence of the failing bank was "essential to its community." This was a standard difficult to meet. It appears that it was originally intended to apply to isolated one-bank towns, in which the closing of the bank would be a community disaster.

On several occasions before Garn-St Germain, the FDIC wanted to avoid closing a failing bank, yet found it impossible or unattractive to arrange a P&A. Some of these cases fit reasonably well with the essentiality criterion of Section 13(c). These included the American Bank of Orangeburg, S.C., which had some branches that were the only banks in their communities, and Unity Bank, the only black-owned bank serving the black community of Boston.

While some stretching of the meaning of "essential" is apparent even in these cases, there have been a few other cases in which the FDIC paid little attention to the letter or the intent of the law in providing assistance to failing banks that it wished to keep in operation. These include the Bank of the Commonwealth, in Detroit, First Pennsylvania Bank, in Philadelphia, and Farmers State Bank, in Delaware. It is difficult to argue that these banks were "essential" to their communities, and the FDIC basically relied on the fear of a serious disruption if those large banks were closed.

For various reasons (related at least in part to the size of these banks), a P&A was not practical in those cases. Closing the banks and paying off insured depositors would have involved significant problems for the FDIC (although had that been done in the earlier cases, the market discipline the FDIC has been seeking might have played a role in inhibiting more recent risk-taking by large banks). Garn-St Germain now allows the FDIC to provide assistance to keep a bank in operation when that is the least costly option available to the FDIC, and it provides the FDIC with a broad basis for considering the cost of a disruption of the financial system. That, of course, was the route taken in the Continental Illinois case.

A major criticism of the use of direct assistance is that it may be a means to bail out stockholders and management. When a bank is declared insolvent, as were Franklin National Bank and Penn Square, its stockholders lose their entire investment. Stockholders in banks that received direct assistance, such as Bank of the Commonwealth, First Pennsylvania, or Continental, suffered substantial but not total loss. First Pennsylvania stockholders, in fact, have had a substantial recovery.

The FDIC has tried to protect against enriching stockholders by obtaining some equity participation if the bank should recover successfully as a result of the FDIC assistance. Further, in nearly all such cases, management deemed responsible for the problems was removed as a condition of the assistance, although some retained valuable pension or other deferred compensation benefits. In several cases, holders of subordinated notes have received protection beyond what they might have received in a payoff or P&A. The assistance to Continental Illinois, for example, protected the position of subordinated creditors of the parent holding company.

Evaluation of FDIC Decisions

It is clear that the FDIC has opted to avoid the payoff of a large bank. In most cases, use of the P&A provides cost savings to the FDIC and benefits to the community. In some cases, however, it appears that the FDIC has been overly fearful of a resulting impact on public confidence and has overestimated the fragility of the financial system. Further, it appears that at times the FDIC has been overly concerned with the political consequences of imposing significant losses on customers of the failing bank. This may be particularly the case when public bodies (school districts, for example) or other "deserving" parties are involved.

The desire to avoid payoffs has led to some cases in which FDIC costs were higher than necessary. It is clear that a payoff of U.S.

National Bank of San Diego would almost certainly have been cheaper than the P&A actually arranged. The assistance to Bank of the Commonwealth proved extremely costly. On the other hand, the FDIC loss in its assistance to First Pennsylvania will no doubt prove to be much less than would have resulted from a payoff of that institution. The FDIC has done relatively little research after the fact to determine what the cost of alternative policy decisions would have been. The purpose of such research would not be idle second-guessing, but a search for means to increase the chances that optimal decisions would be made the next time similar circumstances arise.

It is difficult to be very critical of FDIC decisions if one accepts the objective of cost minimization (which is difficult to reject) and the need for concern about stability of the system (a concern that many believe is exaggerated by the FDIC) in a system of less than 100 percent insurance. Some general results of these decisions, even if defensible in the individual case, are subject to question.

One important result of the way in which FDIC decisions have been made is that there is an inequity in the treatment of similar depositors in small banks and large banks. No depositor in a billion-dollar bank has ever suffered a loss in a bank failure. While such failures are infrequent, the volume of uninsured deposits in banks that have failed (or avoided failure only because of FDIC assistance) is many times the volume of such deposits in smaller failed banks. Those who have suffered losses in bank failures are not necessarily less astute, less sophisticated (AT&T has been a loser in bank failures), or less deserving of government protection than those who have avoided loss because of the way the FDIC handled the failure of their bank.

The general conclusion from the way in which policy decisions have been made is that the FDIC considers some banks "too large to fail" or "too large to allow depositors to suffer a loss" (by this report's definition, of course, Continental Illinois did fail). As depositors act on that belief, one result is a concentration of bank assets in those banks viewed as too large to fail. That has adverse implications for efficiency in the allocation of resources and for competition in banking. Such a result is inequitable and undesirable, in this report's view, and is not mitigated by the fact that large banks with large uninsured deposits are currently paying deposit insurance premiums on their total deposits and not just on insured deposits.

It is this consideration that leads some observers to advocate 100 percent insurance of deposits, so that depositors in all banks would be treated equally—all would be fully protected. The U.S. deposit insurance system has always involved less than 100 percent insurance largely because of the presumed advantages of market discipline. However, the evidence is not clear that uninsured depositors are a useful source of market discipline.

A shift to 100 percent deposit insurance would simplify FDIC decisionmaking in handling bank failures. The choice between payoff and P&A could be made on purely economic grounds, without the need to be concerned with the imponderable impact on public confidence, or with the allocation of losses between the FDIC and uninsured deposits. That is, now the FDIC must be concerned with its losses rather than with minimization of total social losses. It is likely that with 100 percent insurance, the P&A would be used almost exclusively—a bank would be liquidated only when its franchise value was zero. Despite the ambiguity of the evidence, one would be reluctant to lose the possibility of market discipline that would result from 100 percent insurance. These issues are discussed fully in Chapter 7.

Bank Failure and FDIC Loss

Any assessment of FDIC policies in handling bank failures must consider the source of losses in bank failures. As the preceding discussion of FDIC options indicates, the amount of loss the FDIC will incur is not determined by the fact of a bank failure, but is a function of the way in which the failing bank is handled. The FDIC suffers a loss only when a bank becomes insolvent—when its liabilities exceed its assets. An FDIC loan to a (barely) solvent bank will ultimately be repaid if the bank remains solvent.

Obviously, that gives the FDIC a strong incentive to maintain the solvency of banks. It attempts to do that now through a system of regulation and supervision designed to restrict risk-taking by insured banks. It can also be done, as noted, by a system of explicit or implicit risk-related insurance premiums that would provide a financial incentive to conservatism. But even if prevention techniques were inadequate, and banks did fail, FDIC losses might still be minimal depending on the procedures followed.

In general, bank net worth does not disappear suddenly. Most failing banks see an erosion of net worth over time, as loans deteriorate or interest rates change. If a failing bank is closed (or merged) when its assets, on a market value basis, approach equality with liabilities (so that net worth is close to zero), the FDIC suffers no significant loss.

This suggests that accurate monitoring or tracking of the financial position of banks is crucial to minimizing FDIC losses. Horvitz (1980) has argued that this is the true function of bank examination. Pyle (1984), elaborating on a model developed by Merton (1977, 1978), concludes that appropriate monitoring of net worth is more important to FDIC loss minimization than is constraining bank risk-taking.

Evidence on FDIC loss experience supports this view. Where the condition of failing banks has been tracked accurately, and appropriate action taken on a timely basis, FDIC losses have been small. This includes the case of Franklin National Bank, the largest bank to be declared insolvent, but on which FDIC losses are expected to be very small.

FDIC losses are much larger when banks are allowed to operate after they become insolvent. There are two situations in which this may occur. The first is fraud, in which case the supervisors may not know the bank is insolvent, because the bank's books do not reflect its true financial position. The second situation involves a decision on public policy grounds to allow the insolvent institutions to continue in operation.

FDIC losses have been large in cases of large-scale fraud. These may include such bank failures as U.S. National Bank and Penn Square. The FDIC has also suffered massive losses in dealing with the problems of a number of large mutual savings banks (a problem faced on a larger scale by the Federal Savings and Loan Insurance Corporation (FSLIC)). On a market value basis, many mutual savings banks became insolvent in 1966 or 1969. They were allowed to continue in operation, in hopes that interest rates would decline and they would once again become solvent (also, the FDIC has no legal authority to close such economically insolvent institutions). Unfortunately, that delay proved costly to the FDIC.

It is not surprising that large losses result when insolvent institutions are allowed to continue in operation. Once insolvent, an institution has every incentive to take great risks in the hopes of getting into the black again. At that point, after all, if risky policies turn out successfully, the bank benefits. If the risks turn out badly, the losses are borne entirely by the FDIC.

Prompt action to close or take over failing institutions as soon as their net worth is depleted can undoubtedly hold FDIC losses to a minimum. Such action is not easy, however. It requires, first of all, a high-quality monitoring effort, including improved means and efforts to detect massive fraud. It also requires the legal power to close institutions on the basis of economic insolvency, rather than waiting for book net worth to become negative. A change to market value accounting, as discussed in Chapter 8, may be essential.

Even so, some sizable losses to the FDIC may still occur. Some banks may experience sudden losses, perhaps from loan losses affecting a major portion of an undiversified portfolio (concentration in energy, farm, or Third World loans, for example). Not all fraud will be detected before large losses result. More important, perhaps, is the recognition that minimization of FDIC costs is not the only legitimate objective of public policy. There are conditions that might cause many institutions to become insolvent at the same time. The economic, social, or political consequences of closing down a major portion of the savings and loan industry when many institutions first became economically insolvent (perhaps in 1966) would have been very serious, even though it is clear that losses would be less today if that had been done.

Another difficult problem with this approach, even with market value accounting, is that the valuation process is not accurate enough to allow the supervisory agency to pinpoint precisely when an institution has zero net worth. If one is to take the drastic action of ending the independent operation of a bank on the basis of an evaluation of the fair market value of its assets and liabilities, one must be sure that all assets are valued correctly. That may be easy for the securities portfolio or mortgage loans, but it is very difficult to value the charter, the good will of customers, and other intangibles.

One means to cover this band of uncertainty is to require that banks have some subordinated liabilities outstanding (presumably subordinated capital notes). In this case, the supervisor can allow the bank to operate until net worth becomes clearly negative, but only up to the amount of subordinated debt. Any loss will be suffered by the subordinated note holders, and not the FDIC.

Proposals for Reform

It is difficult to be very critical of FDIC handling of failing banks, given the criteria established by law and the FDIC's interpretation of them. Some critics would rather see a greater use of the payoff, as a means to stimulate development of market discipline. Some object to direct assistance because of concern that this represents a bailout of those responsible for the bank's problems in the first place. This chapter has discussed the FDIC's attempts to prevent unfair enrichment resulting from such direct assistance.

There have been a few proposals for change, generally involving legislation, that could improve the FDIC's ability to meet its often conflicting criteria. The FDIC from time to time has advocated giving insured deposits a preferred status in failure, rather than their current general creditor status. That would allow general use of the P&A while imposing loss on uninsured depositors (as the modified payoff does). A more elaborate proposal along these lines has been advanced by George Kaufman (1984).

Kaufman's proposal is designed to enable the FDIC to meet its frequently conflicting criteria efficiently and equitably. The basic concept is that of an FDIC "trusteeship" for a (presumably large) bank that becomes insolvent on a market value basis and faces a loss of creditor confidence. The bank would be declared insolvent by the chartering authority (there may be merit in granting the FDIC the power to declare an insured bank insolvent), and turned over to the FDIC for further disposition. The FDIC would operate the bank temporarily, until a decision was made to liquidate it (unlikely, for reasons already discussed), merge it with another bank or bank holding company, or re-establish it as an independent entity.

If, in the opinion of the FDIC and the chartering authority, at the time of FDIC takeover the bank's assets were greater than its nonsubordinated liabilities, operations would continue normally. Depositors would have full access to their funds and could make withdrawals. If the bank had negative net worth when taken over by the FDIC, the value of all uninsured deposits (and other liabilities) would be written down by the appropriate *pro rata* amount. Depositors would have access to their funds, less the "haircut."

Kaufman refers to this mechanism as a "modified trusteeship," analogous to the modified payoff. Indeed, the FDIC has considered this approach as the counterpart to the modified payoff that would be more appropriate for large banks. Present law gives the FDIC authority to establish a Deposit Insurance National Bank, which could take over the operations of a failed institution and, in effect, liquidate its business over time. Broadened powers for the Deposit Insurance National Bank, including the ability to make loans, would make that approach nearly identical to the scheme described here.

Once such a trusteeship were put in place, the FDIC would have the time needed to work out the most economically advantageous arrangement for disposition of the bank. It would not be subject to the time pressures that now exist when a large bank becomes insolvent and faces a run or loss of depositor confidence.

It is important to recognize the significance of the "and" in the preceding sentence. If a solvent bank faces a run, it should be possible to recycle funds to the bank to replace those being withdrawn. That can be done by depositors who recognize the true condition of the bank or, if necessary, by the Federal Reserve. If an insolvent bank does not face a run, then the FDIC has the time to operate as it currently does in working out a resolution of the problem before the bank is declared insolvent. Even in that case, of course, there is pressure to act promptly, because it is in the interest of management and owners to take great risk in the hope of recouping losses, and one can therefore expect the condition of the bank to worsen if supervisory action is delayed.

The principal problem with this approach is the need for the FDIC to evaluate the condition of the bank almost instantaneously, so as to determine the extent of the haircut to be imposed on uninsured creditors. This would be facilitated by market value accounting, but would still be difficult. Uninsured creditors are entitled, after all, to fair treatment and a day in court, if necessary, to argue that the bank's condition was better than the FDIC believed. That could be done by making the haircut provisional, with additional payments made if the FDIC's recoveries were greater than its original estimate. That is the procedure under the modified payoff approach.

The principal objection that can be raised against the modified trusteeship approach goes not to the practical difficulties, which can either be overcome or which turn out to be substantively no different from those that exist under existing procedures, but rather to the extraordinary grant of power to a government agency. The bank involved would, in a very real sense, be nationalized. That term was used in discussions of the Continental case, and in reference to the "phoenix" S&Ls created by the Federal Home Loan Bank Board (FHLBB). (The "phoenix" S&Ls result from mergers of two or more insolvent institutions and are subject to control of their operations by the FHLBB in hopes that a sound institution may rise from the ashes.) It has been used by the FDIC in discussions of its options for handling the problems of economically insolvent mutual savings banks in New

York City. All of those actions, however, fall somewhat short of government operation that the trusteeship involves. (In a few cases in the past, the Comptroller of the Currency has placed national banks in a "conservatorship" that may be similar to the trusteeship discussed here.)

Despite this objection, the advantages of the modified trusteeship approach are very significant and deserve serious consideration. It would inject genuine and productive market discipline. Large depositors would have to choose their banks carefully because, in case of insolvency, they would suffer a loss. As distinct from the present situation, they could not be confident of having sufficient warning so that funds could be withdrawn before FDIC action. More important, they could not be confident that the FDIC's desire to avoid closure and payoff of a large bank would result in protection of all depositors.

This approach would reduce the number of cases in which direct assistance is given to keep a bank in operation, simply because there is not sufficient time to work out the optimal P&A. The FDIC would simply continue to operate the bank until such time as other large banks had an opportunity to review the bank's portfolio and business situation to determine whether they would be interested in making an offer. That does not exist under the pressure of a loss of confidence in a failing bank. While in control of the bank, the FDIC should have the ability to cancel or limit "golden parachutes" for management.

Finally, if it is determined that neither liquidation nor merger is desirable or feasible, it becomes easier to re-establish the bank as a private entity. The bank would have assets equal to its liabilities (as a result of the haircut) and new stock in the now solvent institution could be sold in the market. Probably, in accord with traditional bankruptcy procedures, some of the stock could be given to those who suffered loss in the failure.

Of course, as depositors become aware of their greater exposure to loss, they may respond by withdrawing funds on the first hint of difficulty. The possibility of such reactions may lead bankers to operate in a more conservative manner, so as to avoid the possibility of becoming subject to a run. On the other hand, if these reactions by depositors do take place, the banking system may become less stable than it now is. As later discussion will make clear, it is difficult to design a system that combines market discipline with stability of the system. If one wants to rely on a system of less than 100 percent insurance, so as to maintain market discipline, then the trusteeship approach may be the least disruptive means of doing so.

CHAPTER 5

The Lender of Last Resort

S ince the development of modern banking, the first line of defense against widespread financial crises has fallen to the lender of last resort (LLR). In almost all countries, LLR functions are the responsibility of the central bank. The central bank is able to issue claims that are the "currency of the realm," and trade these claims at their par value at all times. Thus, the LLR can supply liquidity that prevents the value of private bank claims (deposits) from deteriorating due to the bank's actual or perceived inability to convert these claims at par into the currency of the realm.

This chapter describes the objectives and functions of the lender of last resort, reviews the role of last-resort lending in the United States, examines some issues related to LLR operations, analyzes the roles of the LLR in resolving individual bank financial difficulties, and clarifies the relation between last-resort lending and federal deposit insurance.

Objectives and Functions of Last-Resort Lending

The objectives and functions of last-resort lending were identified in the banking literature by the late 1700s. In 1802, Henry Thornton spelled out the underlying objectives a central bank should pursue in performing LLR functions:

1. Control the money supply over the long run, and

2. Provide temporary liquidity promptly to prevent national financial and economic crises caused by liquidity problems.

Thornton argued that, in seeking the second objective, the central bank should not strive to offset initiating shocks to a borrowing bank's liquidity, but should confine itself to preventing those effects from spreading. His reasoning as to why the central bank should not try to rescue insolvent banks remains relevant today:

It is by no means intended to imply that it would become the Bank of England to relieve every distress which the rashness of country banks may bring upon them: the bank, by doing this, might encourage their improvidence. There seems to be a medium at which a public bank should aim in granting aid to inferior establishments, and which it must often find it difficult to be observed. The relief should neither be so prompt and liberal as to exempt those who misconduct their business from all the natural consequences of their fault, nor so scanty and slow as deeply to involve the general interests. These interests, nevertheless, are sure to be pleaded by every distressed person whose affairs are large, however indifferent or even ruinous may be their state.[1]

As argued in Chapter 2, potential damage to the national economy from individual bank failures is not overly great. However, damage from the failure of the central bank to take prompt and/or appropriate action to contain the initial shock can prove severe.

Thornton's principles were reiterated some 70 years later by Walter Bagehot in his classic book *Lombard Street*. But Bagehot added that the LLR should announce publicly its intentions to lend freely to prevent national crises to remove any uncertainties about its actions. He also argued that the funds provided by the LLR should be at a "penalty" rate above the riskless lending rate, both to limit the use of the facility and to mimic the true market price to avoid distributional distortions.

This was the accepted theory of the LLR when the Federal Reserve was established by Congress in 1913. The United States was one of the last major countries to establish a central bank and LLR. Although the First (1791–1811) and Second (1816–1836) Banks of the United States had assumed some of the functions of a central bank, their ability to issue banknotes was limited by their specie reserves. The possibility that their banknotes would lose their convertibility into specie limited their capacity for last-resort lending.

While the Second Bank's excess specie reserves permitted it to engage in last-resort lending, the United States generally functioned without an LLR through its first century. The inflexibility that the absence of an LLR imposed in dealing with financial crises was a major reason for the creation of the Federal Reserve. The LLR function operates through lending to banks at the discount window. Such lending is among the three major functions specifically delineated in the preamble to the Federal Reserve Act:

> To provide for the establishment of Federal Reserve banks, to furnish an elastic currency, *to afford means of rediscounting commercial paper*, to establish a more effective supervision of banking in the United States, and for other purposes.[2]

Contrary to expectations, however, developing the Fed did not end financial panics in the United States. Indeed, less than 20 years after its founding, the United States suffered by far the worst financial and economic crisis in its history (see Chapters 1 and 2).

Until the Depository Institutions Deregulation and Monetary Control Act of 1980, the Federal Reserve's LLR function was restricted primarily to member commercial banks. The Federal Reserve's reluctance to act as LLR to nonmember banks is widely thought to have contributed to both the start and the severity of the banking crisis of 1929-1933. In addition, the Federal Reserve's failure or inability to prevent or moderate the panic by replenishing reserves lost to the banking system through net currency drains led to the creation of the Federal Deposit Insurance Corporation (FDIC) in 1934.

Although federal deposit insurance lessens the urgency of some LLR activities, it does not make them redundant. As discussed in Chapter 2, net currency drains from the banking system are no longer a serious concern. Appropriate use of open market operations by the Federal Reserve can always replenish aggregate reserves. As long as aggregate reserves are stabilized, bank runs essentially reshuffle deposits among banks. The major costs of runs are losses that affected banks suffer in emergency or fire-sale attempts to liquefy their portfolios.

Although monetary and LLR policies can prevent a run both from greatly hurting a bank that experiences it and from destabilizing the banking system as a whole, runs obviously serve little short-run social good. At a minimum, they increase uncertainty and transactions costs. In the long run, however, they are an important source of market discipline. Hence, it is not desirable public policy to prevent runs totally. What is usually desirable is to resolve a run reasonably soon after it starts. If the bank that experiences a run were solvent to start with and financial markets were relatively efficient, banks that gain deposits would quickly and cheaply recycle the funds back to the banks losing deposits.

Real-world markets are less than perfectly efficient, if only because timely information on the credit standing of roughly 40,000 depository institutions is hard to come by. Information and collateral are not costless to collect or transfer, and financing packages take time for would-be rescuers to arrange.

Because of its access to confidential information and unlimited financial resources, the Federal Reserve has a comparative advantage over private institutions in providing quick and low-cost assistance directly to banks experiencing runs. Opening the discount window a bit wider rather than engaging in open market purchases lets the Fed signal to the market its resolve to recycle all or nearly all of the funds to the specific bank or banks whose liabilities have come into question. This potential for signalling is one of the ways that the Federal Reserve's LLR activity can complement the activities of federal deposit insurers. Deposit insurance and last-resort lending each have comparative advantages in confronting different aspects of potential crisis situations.

Issues in Federal Reserve Lending

The conditions for Federal Reserve support as LLR are spelled out in its Regulation A. Credit is made available on four bases:

1. Short-term adjustment credit—to meet temporary bank requirements for funds or to cushion more persistent deposit outflows,

2. Seasonal extended credit—to assist smaller depository institutions on a longer-term basis in meeting regular seasonal needs for funds,

3. Other extended credit—assistance that is not available from regular sources to meet exceptional needs of individual institutions on a longer-term basis, and

4. Emergency credit to others—advances to individuals, partnerships, and nondepository corporations under unusual and exigent circumstances.

All advances are collateralized by securities whose quality is determined to be "acceptable" by the lending Reserve Bank. The basic rate charged is the discount rate, but higher rates either may or must be charged on other extended credit and emergency credit to others, depending on the length of the borrowing and the type of collateral.

The first two types of credit extension are clearly not related to the LLR function. They are intended primarily to mitigate presumed inefficiencies in the funds market for smaller banks, and to avoid abrupt self-reversing noncrisis shocks to financial markets and institutions from temporary or last-minute-of-the-reserve-week adjustment problems of larger banks. This type of lending need not be discussed here. The remainder of the chapter focuses on problems and issues associated with the nonseasonal extended credit facilities.

When Should the Federal Reserve Provide LLR Assistance?

Whenever the Federal Reserve extends credit through the discount window, total bank reserves increase. Other things being equal, this increases total bank deposits and credit. To the extent that the increase does not offset reductions in deposits and credit at borrowing banks, the money stock may increase above the amount targeted by the Federal Reserve for macroeconomic purposes. This would induce greater upward economic and price pressures than otherwise and require offsetting Federal Reserve actions, say, through open market sales, to bring the money supply back to target levels.

For the sake of economic stability, it is important that the Federal Reserve distinguish at all times between its monetary policy and its LLR function. The LLR function should replace liquidity lost as a result of customer demands; it should not force additional liquidity into the system. Nor should the LLR function be sensitive to cyclical swings in either levels of economic activity or monetary policy. The LLR should be willing and able to provide assistance to troubled banks on an equal basis at all times.

Neither the Federal Reserve Act nor the Fed's Regulation A provides useful guidelines as to what kind of bank difficulties deserve LLR assistance. If the function of the LLR is to prevent a financial shock from spreading and destabilizing the rest of the economy, rather than to offset the initial shock, the LLR should adapt assistance to the economic condition of the institutions bearing the brunt of the shock. The LLR should provide direct assistance to institutions that are economically solvent, but are experiencing deposit runs of sufficient magnitude that such rapid asset sales at fire-sale prices could render them fire-sale insolvent. (Definitions of these terms may be found in

Chapter 2.) Little cost attaches to assisting such institutions, and substantial economic and social benefits accrue from maintaining them as going concerns. The major form of assistance involved is a grant of time that allows the bank to restructure its affairs less expensively.

To avoid selling assets at fire-sale prices, troubled institutions require one or both of the following: a recycling of funds from deposit-gaining institutions or access to credit from other parties. In both cases, the resulting loans should be collateralized by the equilibrium market value of the assets pledged rather than by these assets' fire-sale value. If other private banks do not provide such assistance, even though it is in their mutual interest to do so, the second form of assistance could be efficiently provided by the Federal Reserve through its extended credit facility. The Fed should have a comparative advantage over the private sector in evaluating quickly and accurately both the financial state of the troubled institution and the quality of its potential collateral. If permitted to borrow at the cash equivalent of the equilibrium market value of its assets, an economically solvent institution could meet all of its deposit drains without concern for loss, although dollar-for-dollar collateralization would expose the Federal Reserve to the possibility of future loss if the subsequent equilibrium market value of the collateral fell sharply. Thus, the equilibrium market value of collateral offered on these loans should exceed the loan amount by an appropriate percent, to protect the lender against downward movements in the value of the collateral over the life of the loan.

Justifications for LLR lending to an already economically insolvent institution are less clear. The institution's losses have already occurred whether or not they have been officially recognized. Because current asset returns are the best measure of future asset returns, the *ex-ante* value of the assistance provided exceeds that of only an extension in adjustment time. If the Federal Reserve lends the market value of collateral that declined in value subsequent to its acquisition by the bank, the institution's capital shortage is not altered unless the Fed lends at a subsidized interest rate. If depositors are unaware of the bank's insolvency, the bank could continue to redeem its deposits as they come due until it ran out of assets on which it could borrow the equivalent market value. At that time, losses would be imposed on the remaining depositors or on the federal deposit insurance agency.

Because a first-served, first-paid approach treats depositors of an economically insolvent institution differently, it violates the principle of equal treatment of all customers. Justice requires that an institution should be declared insolvent when a capital shortage is discovered and that the failure be resolved on an equitable basis.

If the Federal Reserve lends more than the market value of the assets collateralized (say, the amount of their historical cost or book value), it assumes the risk of bearing *pre-existing* losses in addition to the symmetric risk of unanticipated future gains and losses. Except to avoid fire-sale losses, a bank need not come to the Federal Reserve to borrow the face value of assets that do not decline in value. Unless it prices its loans so as to compensate itself for concomitant losses and risks, the Federal Reserve subsidizes borrowing institutions, which reduces the market discipline being exerted by uninsured creditors, and encourages deposit-institution risk-taking.

Because the Fed should be concerned about preventing a shock to one institution from spreading to others, the appropriate policy is to provide assistance to any economically solvent institutions that are subject to secondary shocks from the bank's insolvency.

Implementing this policy requires the Fed to determine a troubled institution's solvency. This is both legally difficult and financially costly. Determining insolvency is presently the sole responsibility of the agency that chartered the institution. A commercial bank's chartering agency, either the Comptroller of the Currency or its home state, has little incentive to declare a bank legally insolvent. Insolvent banks become a blot on the agency's bureaucratic record, and any losses suffered from continued operation accrue not to the chartering agency but to the uninsured depositors and the deposit insurance agency. This is particularly costly in light of the incentive given to insolvent or near-insolvent institutions to increase their risk exposure in hopes of restoring a positive net asset value.

In contrast, the FDIC has mixed incentives about a bank's being declared insolvent. On the one hand, unlimited lending by the Fed on "good" collateral to pay out any and all remaining uninsured depositors decreases the value of the FDIC's claim. On the other hand, such assistance may afford the FDIC the time necessary to work out a better method of resolving the insolvency.

These conflicting incentives may be minimized by having the Fed lend against all good collateral, regardless of the condition of the bank, but grant such credits only after prior review and approval by the FDIC. In this approach, the FDIC would be required to attach its explicit endorsement of the troubled bank's request for LLR assistance.

Alternatively, the bank could request assistance directly from the FDIC, which, in turn, would obtain the financing from the Fed. In both alternatives, the FDIC would cut off assistance that threatened its own resources, thereby forcing the bank to be declared insolvent. Letting the FDIC intermediate the flow of LLR credit could make it unnecessary for the Fed to examine banks for purposes of determining their financial condition. Fed examiners would be required only to value the quality of the collateral.

When Is LLR Assistance to Insolvent Institutions Justified?

So far, this analysis has focused on the state of an individual bank, without respect to the accompanying state of the economy. It is conceivable that the threat of simultaneous insolvencies at a large number of sizable institutions because of losses on the same or similar loans or on other assets of the threatened institutions might cause systemwide difficulties. This would occur when such insolvencies would break a sufficiently large number of loan relationships, impose sufficiently large losses on uninsured depositors, or induce depositor fears about the solvency of other banks. The ramifications of denying assistance could be systemwide instability and a downturn in national economic activity.

In such instances, the need to forestall a potential crisis could justify providing LLR assistance, even though assistance to a few isolated banks in similar individual circumstances would not be justified. The issue turns on the likelihood of spreading financial panic. The more serious the potential or actual financial panic that could develop from a given shock, the more easily the provision of assistance could be justified. In periods of national crisis, LLR assistance might need to be provided to a large number of solvent institutions in danger of becoming fire-sale insolvent, and even to selected insolvent institutions whose situation would deteriorate further from fire sales. But the Federal Reserve must avoid routinely assisting insolvent institutions whose closing has only a remote chance of igniting a national or regional crisis.

Because the Federal Reserve has responsibility both for monetary policy and for acting as LLR, the two concerns are easy to confuse. If monetary policy were conducted correctly, major financial and economic crises would be unlikely, as would any need to offer LLR assistance to a large number of institutions. Such assistance is almost *prima facie* evidence of poor monetary control. Use of LLR assistance in place of adequate monetary policy is inappropriate. Likewise, if monetary policy is adequate, LLR assistance should not be denied individual or small groups of institutions because of monetary policy considerations. Institutions that could remain solvent by avoiding fire sales should be assisted at the same support level, regardless of the state of the economic activity or monetary policy.

At What Rate Should LLR Assistance Be Provided?

Earlier writers argue convincingly that the LLR should charge an interest rate that is sufficiently high to avoid subsidies, to discourage nonemergency use, and to prevent market distortions. How should this rate be determined? This report argues in Chapter 2 that the major role of the lender of last resort is to recycle funds to banks encountering runs and to mitigate any fire-sale losses they might be forced to incur. In this scenario, the appropriate lending charge would be the equilibrium market interest rate for the assets the bank uses as collateral. It is unlikely that a troubled bank would use only Treasury securities as collateral, because it could sell most of these at or close to equilibrium market prices. For most borrowing, the appropriate interest rate should be higher than the riskless rate on loans of the same duration. The excess may be viewed as an interest rate "penalty."

The Federal Reserve is required by law to set the discount rate administratively "from time to time with a view toward accommodating commerce and business." In recent years, the discount rate has been close to the federal funds rate, although in a few periods the funds rate has significantly exceeded it. (Figure 1). A higher federal funds rate requires administrative rationing of deposit-institution borrowing at the Fed's discount window. Such rationing is particularly severe during economic expansions in which interest rates rise sharply and the Fed proves reluctant to raise the discount rate commensurately.

To the extent that banks that merely need short-term adjustment or seasonal extended credit do not encounter unusually high interest costs in their traditional markets, a discount rate close to the Fed funds rate may not be unreasonable. However, a higher borrowing rate should obtain for troubled banks that apply for nonseasonal extended credit. These banks would encounter significantly stiffer rates in private markets. An inherent subsidy exists whenever the Federal

Figure 1: Short-Term Interest Rates

MONTHLY AVERAGES, EXCEPT FOR DISCOUNT RATE

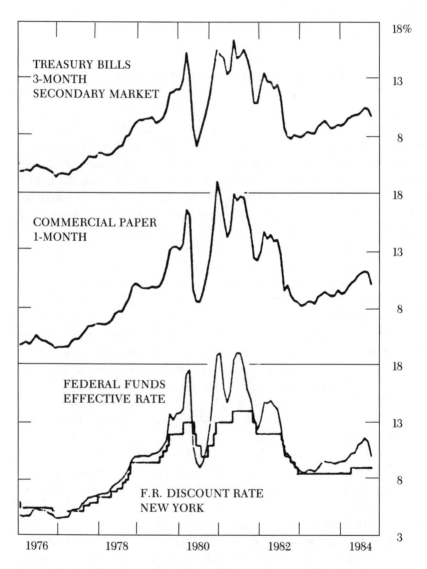

Source: Board of Governor of the Federal Reserve System, *Chart Book.*

Reserve charges a troubled bank only the "basic" or regular discount rate.

Failure to price correctly any guarantee creates incentives for institutions to modify their risk-taking behavior. When the value of a guarantee exceeds its cost, the guaranteed institution is likely to expand its risk exposure. It does so both because the expected costs of failing are reduced and because the net reward for taking additional risks is increased. The cost of subsequent losses is borne largely by the insurance agency and/or the taxpayer.

Access to funds provided by the Federal Reserve in its role as LLR has some of the same properties as deposit-insurance guarantees. If funds were provided in unlimited quantities without surveillance, the borrowing opportunity would have almost the same implications for bank risk behavior as deposit insurance. Consequently, correctly setting the explicit interest cost would be of utmost importance. If restrictive limits on the quantities a bank may borrow exist, they may be interpreted as implicit prices. The larger the role of rationing and implicit prices, the less important the explicit pricing of the restricted guarantee becomes. Efficiency dictates both that Fed officials combine implicit and explicit prices in such a way as to eliminate any subsidy element, and that funds provided through the discount window be priced similarly to deposit-insurance guarantees.

Current regulations require the Federal Reserve to charge interest rates that rise progressively higher than the discount rate, the longer the borrowing bank avails itself of the LLR facility. The interest rate levied equals the basic discount rate for the first 60 days of extended borrowing (first tranche), rises by one-half of a percentage point higher than the basic rate for the next 90 days (second tranche), and increases another half-point higher for terms that extend beyond 150 days (third tranche). However, a bank may be able to borrow adjustment credit at the basic discount rate before its borrowing becomes classified as extended credit and the rate-escalation clock starts ticking. After 150 days, the lending Reserve Bank may also charge a higher rate that takes into account rates on "market sources of funds," but is in no case less than 1 percentage point over its basic rate. This rate schedule does little to price assistance correctly.

A possibly more appropriate way to price LLR assistance would be to base the rate adjustment on the difference between the equilibrium market value of the assets the bank offers as collateral (which is generally related to the dollar amount of borrowing) and the fire-sale price at which the bank would have had to raise its funds otherwise. This difference approximates the equilibrium market value of the assistance to the bank. This assistance could be stated as a percentage spread and the Federal Reserve could charge only a fraction of this amount. In some circumstances, this fraction could even be zero. Although theoretically pleasing, such a system presents a number of practical problems. The Federal Reserve would not only have to estimate the equilibrium market values of the collateral it accepts (EMVA), but also these assets' fire-sale values (FSVA). (The pros and cons of introducing equilibrium market-value accounting are discussed in Chapter 8. Estimating fire-sale values may be expected to be even more difficult.)

An alternative approach would be for the Fed to levy a rate approximately equal to the market rate charged on securities with a similar level of perceived risk of default and duration. Such an interest rate spread may be derived from yields on commercial paper that possess appropriate credit-quality ratings. (The ratings assigned by the major credit rating agencies are summarized in Table 1.)

It is unlikely that a bank perceived to be in financial difficulty and experiencing a run would be able to borrow at an interest rate comparable to that paid by corporations whose capacity for repayment is strong enough to classify them as Moody's Prime-1. It is more likely that they could borrow only at rates applicable to lower-quality but solvent borrowers, such as Moody's Prime-2 or Prime-3. Because either of these rates ought to be more generous than the fire-sale rate, the Fed would not overburden a troubled but solvent bank by charging a rate higher than the basic discount rate. Whenever lending to an insolvent bank is justified, an even higher rate might be levied, both to forestall subsidy extraction and to discourage risky end-game plays. However, as long as the insolvent bank's collateral is good, this rate should lie below the fire-sale rate.

Interest rates on Fed funds, on Prime (P–1) and the highest less-than-prime (P–2) short-term commercial paper, and on one- and three-month Treasury bills for the period from mid-May 1984 through early 1985 are shown in Table 2. (Rates quoted on a discount basis are converted to approximate coupon-rate equivalents.) The overall period is divided into subperiods according to the borrowing tranches on lending to Continental Illinois during and after its May 1984 crisis, which is used as an example of recent Federal Reserve pricing of emergency credit.

Table 1: Definitions of Credit Ratings on Commercial Paper

Rating	Explanation
Moody's	
Prime-1	Superior capacity for repayment
Prime-2	Strong capacity for repayment
Prime-3	Acceptable capacity for repayment
Standard & Poor's	
A	Highest capacity for repayment
A-1 +	
A-1	
A-2	
A-3	
B	Adequate capacity for repayment
C	Doubtful capacity for repayment
D	In or expected to be in default
Fitch's	
F-1	Highest grade
F-2	Very good grade
F-3	Good grade
F-4	Poor grade

The first 4 weeks of Continental's borrowing, which spans the period May 10 through June 6, was classified as adjustment credit; the next 9 weeks, which carried through August 8, as first-tranche extended credit subject to the basic discount rate; the next 13 weeks, running through November 7, as second-tranche extended credit subject to the basic discount rate plus ½ percentage point; and the period thereafter as third-tranche extended credit subject to no less than the discount rate plus 1 percentage point.

The last subperiod represents the period of heaviest borrowing by the Continental Illinois National Bank from the Federal Reserve Bank of Chicago. For much of this subperiod, particularly at the beginning, the Continental was unable to obtain funding at "reasonable" rates from other sources. Because the exact amount of Continental's borrowing from the Federal Reserve Bank of Chicago has not been publicly released, it must be estimated from the published national borrowing figures. For the period after June 6, this estimate allocates

Table 2: Average Interest Rates and Estimated Federal Reserve Borrowing by Continental Illinois National Bank by Extended Borrowing Tranche, May 1984-February 1985

Weeks Ending[a]	Estimated Borrowing[b]	Type of Borrowing	Effective Discount Rate	Fed Funds Rate	One Month			Three Month
					Treasury Bill	Commercial Paper		Treasury Bill[c]
						P-1[c]	P-2[c]	
	(Million $)				(Percent)			
5/16-6/6	2,375[d]	Adjustment	9.00	10.44	9.57	11.61		10.88
6/13-8/8	4,189	Extended First Tranche	9.00	11.25	10.41	12.27		11.12
8/15-11/7	5,995	Extended Second Tranche	9.50	10.92	10.64	11.87	12.21	11.13
11/14-1/2	3,047	Extended Third Tranche	9.65[e]	8.83	8.82	9.41	9.73	8.99
1/9-2/27	888	Extended Third Tranche	9.00	8.45	8.27	8.92	9.23	8.70

a. Reserve periods ending Wednesday. Rates are for Friday of that week.
b. Total nonseasonal extended credit
c. Approximate coupon rate equivalent of discount rate basis
d. Reported as adjustment credit
e. Discount rate reduced from 9 to 8½ percent November 21 and 8 percent on December 24
Sources: Federal Reserve System and Salomon Brothers.

all nonseasonal extended credit on the Fed's books to the Continental. Between May 10 and June 6, only part of the total adjustment credit is so allocated.

Examining Table 2 makes it evident that the Fed underpriced its assistance for the bulk of the interval during which the Continental was borrowing. For the first four weeks before Continental loans were classified as extended borrowing, from May 10 through June 6, the basic discount rate was 9 percent. This rate lies considerably below comparable yields on federal funds, one-month Treasury bills and one-month P-1 commercial paper (the only grade for which data were published for this period). The spread between the discount rate and prime commercial paper averaged more than 250 basis points.

During the first-tranche 60 days of extended borrowing, market rates of interest increased, but the borrowing charge to Continental remained unchanged at 9 percent. This charge averaged more than 200 basis points below the federal funds rate and 300 basis points below the prime commercial-paper rate. The discount rate charged was increased to 9½ percent for the next 90 days. As average market rates remained about constant in this period, the underpricing of the Fed's assistance was only slightly reduced.

Market rates declined sharply in the last weeks of 1984. The applicable discount rate for the third tranche was raised to 10 percent and then lowered to 9½ percent when the basic discount rate was reduced at the end of November. Because the Fed can charge a higher but not lower rate than this for third-tranche borrowing, and because the rate actually charged Continental Bank has not been released publicly, these rates represent the minimum rates that the Fed could have charged. In this period, the applicable discount rate was higher than any one-month rate except the P-2 commercial-paper rate. Thus, the underpricing of LLR assistance fell. Because the appropriate market rate on loans to the Continental was probably closer to the P-2 or P-3 commercial-paper rate and its borrowings extended beyond one month, some subsidy element survived even into this period. It would be difficult to argue that the discount rate charged the Continental Bank was priced correctly for most of the time.

It is interesting to observe that the Continental's borrowings began to decline during the bank's third-tranche period, when the rate charged increased. Without additional information, it is difficult to tell whether imposing a higher rate made the bank search harder for alternative funding sources, or whether the higher rate came just as the Continental's private borrowing capacity recovered so that alternative funding sources opened to it.

Last-Resort Lending and Deposit Insurance

The central bank's willingness to engage in emergency lending reduces search and transactions costs for any bank subject to a deposit run. Without ready access to central bank credit, a bank would have to negotiate credit lines with correspondent private institutions both in advance and after the fact. In the midst of an emergency, loans from wholly private sources tend to be difficult to negotiate and to be available only at premium rates that incorporate substantial allowances for default risk. Having to incur these costs would increase the damage that a deposit run could do to a bank's net worth. By reducing these costs, last-resort lending permits individual banks to operate with both less liquidity and less capital than they would need otherwise.

Troubled banks seeking loans from the Fed may be likened to individuals seeking assistance from hospital emergency-room personnel. Providers of either form of assistance perform simultaneously a first-aid function and a triage function. They assess the overall condition of the patient and take account of competing demands on their own and back-up resources before authorizing treatment.

In both cases, their first job is to identify patients able to recover without treatment. Emergency rooms impose charges that discourage patients from using their services, who either could treat themselves or be treated in nonemergency fashion by their family doctor. When a patient promises to benefit from a specific pattern of assistance, emergency rooms offer treatment designed to limit the degree of injury the patient suffers and to permit the case to pass on to specialists for continuing and definitive treatment. When a patient's prognosis for recovery is nil, their job is to help the victim to face the end realistically and with a minimum of pain.

Last-resort lending helps economically solvent institutions to overcome a shortage of liquidity without suffering fire-sale losses. For a bank that is clearly viable, the central bank seeks to assure depositors that its commitment to the firm is strong enough to ensure the firm's continuing solvency. In borderline cases, central bank lending should seek only to keep the bank going until a more authoritative examination can determine the institution's long-run viability. However, in practice, an economically insolvent bank occasionally gets so deeply in debt to the Fed that it becomes politically embarrassing to close the bank by the time an adverse determination is finally made.

Last-resort lending also benefits deposit insurers. The availability of emergency loans from the central bank acts both as a substitute for, and a supplement to, deposit-insurance reserves. It decreases the insurer's cost of maintaining a given set of deposit guarantees by creating a prior source of federal guarantees that staves off the legal insolvency of otherwise economically insolvent banks.

For individual banks and for the banking system as a whole, the extent of these conjectural guarantees depends on how tightly or loosely the central bank administers its lending facilities. A central theme of this chapter has been that, to keep its lending commitments from becoming a source of unintended subsidies, a central bank must develop strict policies with respect to the explicit interest rate charged, the collateral, loan-to-value ratios, and extent of economic insolvency it is willing to accept from borrowers, especially in situations in which liquidity pressures are not systemwide. The goal of the central bank should be to adjust the sum of the explicit and implicit interest rates it charges individual borrowers to keep borrowing costs from falling below their equilibrium market level.

Deposit-insurance guarantees are valuable because they reduce a bank's funding costs. It should be clear that the value of the guarantees that the FDIC offers to insured banks is conditional on the reinforcing system of liquidity guarantees that market participants expect the Fed to make available. The more generous the terms on which the Fed is perceived to supply last-resort loans, the less effect that guarantees issued by the FDIC have in reducing an insured bank's funding costs. By constituting a first line of defense for banks that experience liquidity pressures, Fed lending makes it easier for the FDIC to make good on its commitments to insured depositors.

Moreover, in the event of shortfall in insurance agency reserves, a March 1982 joint congressional resolution (which put the full faith and credit of the United States behind federal deposit insurance guarantees) may be interpreted as granting Federal Reserve officials the authority to lend directly to the deposit insurance agencies without collateral. To the extent that the central bank is prepared to make emergency loans to deposit insurers on favorable terms, the effective reserves of the deposit insurance system extend well beyond the balances carried explicitly on insurance agency balance sheets.

As government-sponsored corporations, federal deposit insurers may make grants of capital to troubled institutions and may themselves engage in emergency lending. However, they lack the central bank's ability to create their own reserves. In the absence of a true lender of last resort, runs on insured institutions could escalate into fire sales of insurance agency resources. Given perfect information and the absence of countervailing political pressure and benefits from additional time to seek bids for the failing institution from potential acquirers, an insurer's interest in conserving explicit insurance reserves would dispose it to close an institution well before its condition reached economic insolvency.

Because their clients have access to the Federal Reserve's discount window and because the deposit insurance agencies can borrow directly from the Fed themselves, insurers can deal with runs by uninsured depositors more efficiently than they could otherwise. Otherwise, such runs might force banks or deposit insurers to undermine their net worth by selling assets at fire-sale prices. In the current institutional environment, rather than being perfect substitutes, last-resort lending and deposit insurance guarantees supplement each other. They meld into a single federal guarantee, whose continuing credibility presumes predictable and reasonable regulatory reactions to the liquidity and solvency problems that insured institutions encounter.

---

[1]Henry Thornton. 1939. *An Enquiry into the Nature and Effects of the Paper Credit of Great Britain (1802).* (New York; Farrar and Rinehart.)
[2]Board of Governors of the Federal Reserve System. 1983. *The Federal Reserve Act.* (Washington, D.C.), p. 3 (emphasis added).

CHAPTER 6

Risk and the Expansion of Banking Activities

D uring the 1970s and early 1890s, the costs of inflation induced financial and nonfinancial institutions to find ways to avoid binding regulatory constraints. These activities combined with technological innovations in the provision of banking services to cause significant changes in the structure of financial service markets. Thrift institutions now have virtually the same powers as commercial banks (and in a few instances have even broader authority), and nontraditional suppliers, such as insurance companies, brokerage firms, and even merchants, have expanded into the industry. These institutions are pursuing potential scale and scope economies by offering a wide array of services in packages not always legally available from commercial banks (See Kane, 1981, and Eisenbeis, 1985). Moreover, by acquiring nonbank banks and federally insured savings and loan associations (S&Ls), these firms are also seeking to capture deposit insurance subsidies inherent in mispriced deposit insurance. To illustrate these changes, Table 1 compares powers of different categories of institutions competing actively in the provision of financial services.

Banks have responded aggressively to the competitive pressures of these new suppliers and to the promise of achieving cost savings by realizing scale and scope economies. By exploiting new technologically based methods for delivering banking services and through innovative interpretations of existing law and regulations (such as the nonbank-bank device), banks are expanding into new geographic markets and widening their product offerings.

Many states and federal regulatory agencies are also reacting to this push of market forces and are competing to increase the range of permissible services both to ensure the competitive viability of banking firms and to maintain their constituencies. For example, several states have already expanded permissible service offerings, especially in the insurance and real estate areas.

At the federal level, the Federal Deposit Insurance Corporation (FDIC), has put out for public comment proposals that state-

Table 1: Comparison of Products and Powers of Selected Financial and Nonfinancial Institutions

Power/Product	National Bank	State Bank: California	State Bank: Ohio	State Bank: Rhode Island	Bank Holding Company	Federal Savings Bank/ Savings & Loan	State Savings Bank/ Savings & Loan California	State Savings & Loan: Ohio	Unitary Thrift Holding Company	Multiple Thrift Holding Company	Industrial Bank California
Demand Deposit	Yes	Yes	Yes	Yes	Yes	Yes	Yes	Yes[29]	Yes	Yes	No
Savings Deposit	Yes	Yes	Yes	Yes	Yes	Yes	Yes	Yes	Yes	Yes	Yes
Certificate of Deposit	Yes	Yes	Yes	Yes	Yes	Yes	Yes	Yes	Yes	Yes	Yes
Transaction Account (NOW/ATS, etc.)	Yes	Yes	Yes	Yes	Yes	Yes	Yes	Yes	Yes	Yes	Yes
Federal Insurance	Yes	Yes[7]	Yes[7]	Yes[7]	Yes[7]	Yes	Yes[7]	Yes[7]	Yes[7]	Yes[7]	Yes[7]
Commercial Loans	Yes	Yes	Yes	Yes	Yes	Yes[18]	Yes[26]	Yes[29]	Yes	Yes	Yes[38]
Consumer Loans	Yes	Yes	Yes	Yes	Yes	Yes[19]	Yes[27]	Yes[29]	Yes	Yes	Yes[38]
Residential Mortgages	Yes	Yes	Yes	Yes	Yes	Yes	Yes	Yes	Yes	Yes	Yes[39]
Commercial Mortgages	Yes	Yes	Yes	Yes	Yes	Yes[20]	Yes	Yes[29]	Yes	Yes	Yes[39]
Margin Loans	Yes	Yes	Yes	Yes	Yes	No[21]	No	No	Yes	No[33]	Yes
Credit Cards	Yes	Yes	Yes	Yes	Yes	Yes	Yes	Yes	Yes	Yes	Yes
Credit-Related Insurance Agent	Yes	Yes	Yes	Yes	Yes	Yes[22]	Yes[22]	Yes	Yes	Yes	Yes
General Insurance Agent	No[1]	No[8]	No	No	No[13]	Yes[22]	Yes[22]	No[30]	Yes	Yes	Yes
Insurance Underwriter	No	No	No	No	No[13]	No	Yes[22]	No	Yes	No[34]	No
Stock Brokerage	No[2]	No[3]	No	Yes	No	Yes[22]	Yes[22]	Yes[29]	Yes	Yes	No
Discount Stock Broker	Yes	No[9]	Yes	Yes	Yes	Yes[22]	Yes[22]	Yes[29]	Yes	Yes	No[40]
Investment Advisor	Yes	Yes	No	Yes	Yes	Yes[22]	Yes	Yes[29]	Yes	Yes	Yes[41]
Investment in Corporate Securities	No	Yes	No[11]	Yes	Yes[14]	Yes[23]	Yes[23]	Yes[29]	Yes	Yes[35]	Yes
Organization/Operation of Mutual Fund	No	Yes	No[11]	Yes[12]	Yes[15]	No	Yes	Yes	Yes	No[34]	Yes
Real Estate Broker	No[3]	No	No	Yes[12]	No[16]	No[24]	Yes[22]	Yes[22]	Yes	No[36]	No
Real Estate Development	No	Yes[10]	No[11]	Yes[12]	No	Yes[22]	Yes	Yes	Yes	Yes	No

	Industrial Bank Rhode Island	Federal Credit Union	Credit Union Ohio	Credit Union Rhode Island	Merrill Lynch	Dreyfus	Prudential-Bache	Sears	American Express	Kroger Food	Household International
Real Estate Appraisal for Others	No	Yes	Yes	Yes[12]	Yes	Yes	Yes	Yes	Yes	No[34]	No
Data Processing Service for Others	No[4]	Yes	Yes	Yes[12]	Yes[17]	Yes[25]	No	Yes[31]	Yes	Yes[37]	Yes
Travel Agency	No	No	Yes	Yes[12]	No	No	No	Yes[22]	Yes	No[34]	Yes
Leasing Personal Property	Yes[5]	Yes	Yes	Yes	Yes	Yes	Yes	Yes[29]	Yes	Yes	Yes
Retail Sales	No[6]	No	No	Yes[12]	No	No	No	No	Yes	No	No
Manufacturing	No	No	No	Yes[12]	No	No	No	No	Yes	No	No

Source: Banking Expansion Reporter, December 3, 1984, Vol. 3, No. 23.

	Industrial Bank Rhode Island	Federal Credit Union	Credit Union Ohio	Credit Union Rhode Island	Merrill Lynch	Dreyfus	Prudential-Bache	Sears	American Express	Kroger Food	Household International
Demand Deposit	Yes[42]	No	No	Yes	No[51 52]	Yes[55 56]	No	Yes[62]	No[64]	No[69]	Yes[69]
Savings Deposit	Yes	Yes	Yes	Yes	No[52]	Yes[57]	Yes[58]	Yes[62]	No[64]	No[69]	Yes[69]
Certificate of Deposit	Yes	Yes	Yes	Yes	Yes[53]	Yes[57]	Yes[59]	Yes[62 63]	Yes	No[69]	Yes[69]
Transaction Account (NOW/ATS, etc.)	Yes	Yes[43]	Yes	Yes	Yes[54]	Yes[55 56]	Yes[59]	Yes[62]	Yes[65]	No[69]	Yes[69]
Federal Insurance	Yes[7]	Yes	Yes[7]	Yes[7]	Yes[53 61]	Yes[61]	Yes[61]	Yes[61]	No[66]	No[69]	Yes[69]
Commercial Loans	Yes	No[44]	No[47]	Yes[50]	Yes	No	Yes	Yes	Yes	No[69]	Yes
Consumer Loans	Yes	Yes[43]	Yes[45]	Yes[45]	No[52]	Yes[57]	No[60]	Yes	No	No[69]	Yes
Residential Mortgages	Yes	Yes[45]	Yes[45]	Yes[45]	Yes	Yes[57]	No[60]	Yes	No	No[69]	Yes
Commercial Mortgages	Yes	No[44]	No	Yes[50]	Yes	Yes	Yes	Yes	Yes	No[69]	Yes
Margin Loans	Yes	Yes[45]	Yes[45]	No	Yes	Yes	No[59]	No	Yes	No[69]	Yes
Credit Cards	Yes	Yes[45]	Yes[45]	Yes[45]	No[51]	Yes	Yes	Yes	Yes	No[69]	Yes
Credit-Related Insurance Agent	Yes	Yes	Yes[46]	Yes	Yes	No[58]	Yes	Yes	Yes	No[64]	Yes
General Insurance Agent	No	Yes[48]	Yes[48]	No	Yes	No[58]	Yes	Yes	Yes	Yes[69]	Yes
Insurance Underwriter	No	No	No	No	Yes	No[58]	Yes	Yes	Yes	Yes	Yes
Stock Brokerage	Yes	No	No	No	No	No	Yes	No	No	No	No
Discount Stock Broker	Yes	Yes	Yes[48]	No	Yes	Yes	Yes	Yes	No	No	No
Investment Advisor	Yes	No	No	No	Yes	Yes	Yes	Yes	No	No	No

Table 1: continued

	Industrial Bank Rhode Island	Federal Credit Union	Credit Union Ohio	Credit Union Rhode Island	Merrill Lynch	Dreyfus	Prudential-Bache	Sears	American Express	Kroger Food	Household International
Investment in Corporate Securities	Yes	No	Yes[49]	No	Yes	Yes	Yes	Yes	Yes	Yes	Yes
Organization/Operation of Mutual Fund	Yes	No	No	No	Yes	Yes	Yes	Yes	Yes	No[64]	No
Real Estate Broker	Yes	No	No	No	Yes	No	No	Yes	Yes[67]	No	No
Real Estate Development	Yes	No	No	No	Yes	No	Yes	Yes	Yes	Yes	No
Real Estate Appraisal for Others	Yes	No	No	No	Yes	No	No	Yes	No	No	No
Data Processing Service for Others	Yes	Yes[46]	Yes[46]	Yes	No	No	No	Yes	No	No	Yes
Travel Agency	Yes	No	Yes[48]	No	No	No	No	No	Yes	No	No
Leasing Personal Property	Yes	Yes[46]	Yes	Yes	Yes	No	No	No	No	No	Yes
Retail Sales	Yes	No	No	No	No	No	No	Yes	Yes	Yes	Yes
Manufacturing	Yes	No	No	No	No	No	No	No	No	Yes	Yes

[1] National banks located in cities of 5,000 or less population may act as an agent for fire, life, or other insurance.

[2] At least one national bank has received regulatory approval to engage in investment advisory services and discount brokerage operations, thus approaching full service stock brokerage. See, Decision of Comptroller with respect to application of American National Bank of Austin, *American Banker* 4 (Sept. 14, 1983).

[3] National banks located in cities of 5,000 or less population may act as an agent or broker in procuring loans on real estate.

[4] The extent to which national banks may provide data processing services to others is not clear. Compare: *National Retailers Corp. v. Valley National Bank*, 604 F. 2d (9th Cir. 1979), and 12 C.F.R. §7.3500.

[5] National banks may lease personal property when the lease is equivalent to a secured lending arrangement.

[6] Merchandise may be offered in lieu of interest or as an incentive to open an account. See 12 C.F.R. §1204.109-111.

[7] State institutions may apply for federal insurance coverage.

[8] California banks may act as insurance agents in cities and towns of 5,000 or less population.

[9] California banks may underwrite and sell the securities of qualified investment companies.

[10] Investment in real estate development companies is limited to 10 percent of assets.

[11] Legislation is pending in Ohio to permit these activities.

[12] Under Rhode Island law, these activities may be performed by an affiliated corporation.

[13] Insurance activities of bank holding companies under federal law are limited to: (1) underwriting credit-related insurance, (2) acting as an agent for credit-related insurance, (3) insurance agency activities in towns of less than 5,000 if adequate insurance agency facilities are lacking, and (4) engaging in certain other specific insurance activities.

[14] A bank holding company may invest in less than 5 percent of the voting shares of any corporation without prior regulatory approval, and may invest without limit in other corporations engaged in activities closely related to banking.

[15] A bank holding company may sponsor, organize, and manage a closed-end investment company.

[16] A bank holding company may act as the intermediary for the financing of commercial property by arranging for the transfer of title, control, and risk of the real estate project to one or more investors.

[17] Data processing services provided to others is limited to processing banking, financial, and economic data.

[18] Commercial loans are limited to 10 percent of assets.

[19] Consumer loans are limited to 30 percent of assets.

[20] Loans on nonresidential real estate cannot exceed 40 percent of assets.

[21] Loans may be secured by government-backed securities.

[22] These services may be performed through a service corporation.

[23] A federal association may invest in highly rated commercial paper and other corporate debt securities, including convertible bonds. It may also invest in shares of open-end mutual funds that are restricted in their investments to those permitted a federal association directly.

[24] A service corporation may provide brokerage services with respect to property owned by a parent federal association.

[25] Through a service corporation, a federal association may offer data processing services with respect to financial or economic data, or information related to the thrift industry. Customers must be other thrifts or established customers of the federal association.

[26] Commercial loans are limited to 7.5 percent of assets until Jan. 1, 1985, 10 percent thereafter.

[27] Consumer loans are limited to 30 percent of assets.

[28] Investments in corporate commercial paper and debt securities and shares in mutual funds with limited portfolios are permitted.

[29] To the extent permitted a federal association.

[30] Insurance agency activities are permitted by the Ohio Savings and Loan Department, but licenses are not issued to these institutions by the Ohio Insurance Commission.

[31] Data processing services may be provided, through a service corporation, to other financial institutions.

[32] There are no statutory restrictions on the nonthrift activities of unitary holding companies, provided the thrift subsidiary meets the asset test set out in Section 7701(a)(19) of the Internal Revenue Code.

[33] Not permitted, unless authorized by state law for a state-chartered thrift subsidiary.

Table 1: continued

34Multiple holding companies may underwrite credit-related insurance written in connection with an extension of credit made by an insured institution.

35To the extent permitted by federal or state law to insured thrift subsidiaries.

36Unless permitted by state law for an insured thrift subsidiary.

37Data processing services may be provided to other financial institutions.

38Loans must generally be repaid in equal monthly installments over a period not to exceed 120 months.

39Loans secured by real property must be repaid within 8 years 6 months, or be limited to 20 percent of the institution's assets.

40Presently under review by the California Department of Corporations.

41Commencing July 1, 1984.

42In order to accept demand deposits the institution must have deposits in excess of $5 million and paid-in capital of $1 million or more.

43Share draft accounts.

44Commercial loans may be made to businesses that are members of the credit union, but only for amounts up to the amount of shares held. Federal credit unions may make loans to other credit unions or join in participation loans.

45Loans are restricted to members of the credit union.

46Through a service corporation.

47Commercial loans may be made to business members of the credit union.

48Insurance may be made available to members of a credit union on a group basis through a credit union service corporation.

49Investment is permitted in securities approved by the State Division of Credit Unions.

50Rhode Island credit unions must have $10 million or more in assets to engage in commercial lending activities.

51Through a cooperative agreement with Banc One of Ohio, Merrill Lynch customers may access the value of assets in margin accounts and the redemption value of certain shares by either check or credit card.

52Merrill Lynch recently formed a state-chartered bank in New Jersey. The scope of services to be offered by this subsidiary has not yet been determined.

53Merrill Lynch acts as a broker by placing customers' funds in large certificates of deposit offered by insured banks and thrifts. The availability of this insurance may be effectively terminated due to changes in regulations recently proposed by the FDIC and FSLIC. [*Editor's Note:* A federal court has ruled against the proposed regulations of the FDIC and FSLIC; the subject of "brokered deposits" is currently a topic of much interest.]

54Merrill Lynch offers a "Cash Management Account (CMA)" in which funds are automatically transferred from a free credit balance to a money market mutual fund, and are accessible by check or credit card through an arrangement with Banc One.

55Dreyfus recently acquired a "Consumer Bank" in New Jersey. The exact services to be offered by this bank have not yet been determined, but the bank does offer demand deposits and savings deposits.

56Dreyfus offers a "High Yield Checking Service" which permits automatic transfers between money market mutual funds and investors' checking accounts at banks.

57Through Dreyfus Consumer Bank.

58Dreyfus' insurance subsidiary is presently dormant.

59Through Prudential Bank and Trust.

60Under consideration.

61To the extent that the bank or thrift subsidiary is federally insured and to the extent that brokered funds are placed in certificates sold by federally insured institutions.

62Through Allstate Savings and Loan subsidiary.

63Brokered certificates of deposit offered through Dean Witter Reynolds.

64American Express engages in international banking operations, but does not domestically accept demand deposits or savings deposits.

65American Express, through Shearson, offers an "FMA" account which is similar to Merrill Lynch's "CMA Account." See note 54.

66American Express, through Shearson, brokers customers' funds into insured certificates of deposits. The ability to provide federal insurance may be eliminated through new regulations issued by the FDIC and FSLIC. See note 53.

67Commercial customers only.

68Kroger Food and Capital Holding Company have formed a joint venture (Kro-Cap) to provide insurance products and services at locations in Kroger stores. In addition, through a contractual arrangement with the Vanguard Group of Investment Companies, mutual funds, including a money market mutual fund with check writing privileges, are offered at many of these store locations. In at least two stores Kro-Cap leased space to the Home State Savings Association, to provide thrift services at these locations. And Kroger Food leases space in some of its stores directly to banking associations. However, in both cases Kroger Food and Kro-Cap do not provide banking or thrift services directly, but simply rent space to the depository institutions involved.

69Through Valley National Bank or Household Federal Savings and Loan Association.

chartered, insured, nonmember banks be permitted to engage, through bank subsidiaries (state law permitting), in a number of activities, including real estate development, syndication, equity participation, and underwriting. The FDIC has also issued an interpretive ruling reaffirming that the separation between investment and commercial banking mandated by the Glass-Steagall Act of 1933 applies only to Federal Reserve member banks and not to all FDIC-insured banks. The Federal Reserve Board has requested comment on whether to permit bank holding companies to engage in real estate investment activities under Section 4(c)8 of the Bank Holding Company Act, as amended. The Comptroller of the Currency has played a major role in the expansion of both banks and nonbanking firms with liberal policies toward the chartering of special-purpose banks (the so-called nonbank-banks).

The public will benefit from the change in financial service technology and increased competition and from allowing banking organizations to offer new services, if these activities can be provided at lower cost and/or at greater convenience to consumers. Moreover, Chapter 1 concludes that, by limiting portfolio diversification, prohibitions against banks' engaging in certain activities have contributed to increases in risk exposure and in failures. Thus, an important public benefit from expansion of permissible activities may be enhanced bank safety and soundness.

A close analysis reveals that some of the reasons for restricting banking activities, although rooted in concerns about abuses and conflicts of interest, have not proved to be justified, and/or that some of the problems have been made manageable by the imposition of other rules and regulations. (See Flannery, 1985).

In view of the competitive and technological changes taking place in the provision and delivery of financial service, it is appropriate to re-evaluate the existing limitations on the scope of banking activities. This chapter focuses on two broad policy questions. First, how much liberalization of banking powers is warranted to promote efficient and low-cost provision of financial services consistent with maintaining safety and soundness, limiting the potential for conflicts of interest, preventing undue concentration of resources, and protecting the deposit insurance funds? Second, because of their potential ability to limit the risk exposure of the deposit insurance fund, are certain organizational structures (such as bank holding companies, or institutions operating through affiliates) preferable to others for expanding bank activities?

In addressing these issues, this chapter reviews the historical rationale for restricting banking activities, discusses expansion of permissible activities and examines issues concerning organizational structure.

Rationale for Restricting Banking Activities

Banking in the United States has long been heavily regulated. (See Benston, 1983a, 1983b; Di Clemente, 1983; Corrigan, 1983; and Golembe, 1982). In colonial times, fears of governmental intrusion into commerce and concerns about the possible abuse of political and economic power resulting from exclusive franchises granted to banks by state and federal governments were responsible for a general distrust of banking. (Schull, 1984). These fears gave rise to the traditional separation between banking and commerce in the United States. This separation appears to parallel restrictions imposed on the activities of the Bank of England (Schull, 1984), although the precise reasons for the separation remain somewhat unclear.

The need to maintain a sound banking system and stable currency to ensure a smoothly functioning economy resulted in bank safety and soundness regulations; led to the establishment in 1913 of the Federal Reserve, with its lender-of-last-resort function; and resulted in the creation of federal deposit insurance in 1933 to help small banks and to protect deposits and financial wealth of small, unsophisticated depositors. Deposit-rate ceilings, usury ceilings, and tax policy have been imposed to redirect credit flows to socially desirable purposes (primarily housing), and to restrict competition in certain markets. Federal Reserve reserve requirements, and related regulations, have been employed, first to maintain the liquidity and safety of the banking system and, more recently, to facilitate the conduct of monetary policy. Numerous consumer-oriented regulations have been imposed to ensure that banks treat customers in a fair and impartial manner.[1]

Safety and soundness concerns rooted in the "real bills" doctrine also led Senator Carter Glass to conclude that banks' involvement in securities activities was too risky, because of the inherent liquidity problems in funding long-term credit with short-term deposits. (See

Kelly, 1985; Flannery, 1985; or Golembe, 1982). Concern about risk and the problems of conflicts of interest that were said to have occurred in the late 1920s and early 1930s, as well as the pressures from securities firms to limit competition, resulted in the Glass-Steagall Act of 1933 separating what had been an almost continuous association between commercial and investment banking in this country.

Many of these same issues arose in 1956, when Congress passed the Bank Holding Company Act. Largely in response to concerns about "bigness" and concentration of power, about unfair competition through possible preferential treatment of subsidiaries, and about safety and soundness, the 1956 act provided for the separation between banking and commerce. (Natter, 1978). The act prohibited the ownership of nonbanking companies and required divestiture within two years. Certain nonbanking activities, however, were specifically permitted, and these included owning and managing bank holding-company property, providing services to subsidiary banks, operating a safe-deposit company, and liquidating property acquired by subsidiary banks. The only activities permitted to bank holding companies besides the owning and managing of banks were those activities of a "financial or fiduciary, or insurance nature," that were "so closely related to the business of banking or of managing or controlling banks as to be a proper incident thereto" (Section 4(c)6 of the Bank Holding Company Act of 1956).

This separation was reaffirmed in the 1970 amendments to the Bank Holding Company Act of 1956. These amendments provided that permissible activities should be "so closely related to banking or managing or controlling banks as to be a proper incident thereto." Furthermore, the performance of these activities by an affiliate of a bank holding company had to "reasonably be expected to produce benefits to the public, such as greater convenience, increased competition, or gains in efficiency, that outweigh possible adverse effects, such as undue concentration of resources, decreased or unfair competition, conflicts of interests or unsound banking practices." Thus, in 1956 and again in 1970, the rationale for restricting banking activities and maintaining the separation between banking and commerce was primarily to ensure safety and soundness and to prevent concentration of power and conflicts of interest.

In addition, because of the unique role that bank liabilities play as money, the presumed importance of banks to the conduct of monetary policy, and the role banks serve as a source of liquidity to the economy as a whole, Corrigan (1983) argues the banks are special and should remain separate from commerce. Careful review of the issues, however, suggests these arguments are not valid. (See Aspinwall, 1983).

It is the access to government guarantees and federal deposit insurance, more than the functions performed by banks (and any other institutions having access to such guarantees), that makes banks special today. Such guarantees carry with them potential subsidies and incentives for increased risk-taking, especially if the price for those guarantees is not set properly for certain institutions. Thus, there is the danger that incentives may be created for the insured institutions to take on more risk, which is then shifted to the insurance agency (and the taxpayers). For this important reason, federal deposit insurance also carries with it the responsibility to ensure that the insuring agency, and ultimately the taxpayer, is not placed at undue risk.

When underpriced deposit insurance exists, the associated subsidy also carries with it an inherent competitive advantage (just as burdensome regulations carry inherent disadvantages. (See Eisenbeis, 1985). The ability to issue low-cost, risk-free deposits in bank subsidiaries, for example, allows institutions to fund financial activities (such as consumer and commercial lending) that would otherwise have to be funded at higher rates, thereby freeing resources in the rest of the company to be employed in other activities.

Regulation restricts arbitrage possibilities and reduces returns of regulated firms relative to unregulated firms engaged in similar activities. (See Kane, 1981). Unless all competitors have the same subsidies and regulatory burdens, some will be at a competitive advantage relative to others, which helps explain why competitive equity has arisen as a potential criterion for expanding the activities of banks and thrifts. Finally, subsidies that arise from mispriced deposit insurance also create incentives for previously uninsured institutions to attempt to capture these subsidies, which is precisely the reason that the nonbank-bank issue has become of great policy importance. By forming nonbank-banks, nonbanking organizations have found a way to issue federally insured liabilities through subsidiaries and potentially to capture some of the subsidies associated with such guarantees.

Over the longer run, appropriate modifications in deposit insurance pricing (including capital and subordinated debenture requirements) to eliminate the subsidy in the existing flat-rate premium system would reduce the importance of risk as a consideration in evaluating new banking activity expansion. Institutions that chose to expand their activities would be charged premiums and be required to maintain capital in accordance with the risks posed to the insurance fund.

However, absent revisions in the deposit insurance premium structure, risks inherent in product expansion must be given careful consideration for three reasons. First, even if new activities are individually less risky than current ones, their combination with banking may facilitate greater risk-taking by insured firms. Second, new activities, especially during the start-up period, may involve operations risk not fully understood by bankers as they enter the business or by the deposit insurance agencies in monitoring and assessing their risk exposure. Finally, allowing nontraditional firms into the banking business increases the chance that the deposit insurance agencies would be exposed to uncontrolled affiliate risks. Also, the agencies might be required to rescue (especially under the existing set of failure resolution policies) an increasingly wide array of firms whose primary activities are essentially unrelated to the reasons that deposit insurance was put in place. This certainly suggests the need for regulations and/or other governmental involvement to protect the insurance funds from undue risk, and it will result in an increase in government influence in the economy. Although necessary from the government's perspective, such involvement might be costly and undesirable from the point of view of the affected businesses and public at large, especially if the economy is to function efficiently.

Criteria for New Activities

As the provisions of the 1970 amendments to the Bank Holding Company Act illustrate, five considerations have most commonly been balanced in framing restrictions on the activities of insured institutions in the U.S. These are: economic efficiency; risk; conflicts of interest; concentration of power; and competitive equity. These issues continue to be relevant today, although some have declined significantly in importance relative to others, and some other considerations may be more important. The reasons for this conclusion and alternative ways of weighing them are discussed below.

Economic Efficiency

The public has much to gain from activities that improve the efficiency of the financial system. Lower costs to consumers for financial services due to increased competition and lower production costs due to potential scale and scope economies translate into more efficient use of resources and potential reductions in the use of real resources in facilitating the exchange of goods and services. In addition, increased diversification, both geographically and in services provided, may result in increased safety and soundness and a more stable financial system. Therefore, efficiency considerations are an important base against which other policy concerns should be assessed.

Also, decisions to grant new powers might give greater weight to those activities that offer obvious synergies with existing activities— those, for example, that offer potential scale and scope economies or that could potentially reduce risk. However, it should be noted that investors and managers are probably better equipped than are regulators to judge the potential returns and benefits from engaging in particular activities.

Risk

Although there are important reasons to be concerned about the potential risk exposure of the deposit insurance fund, there are both theoretical and practical difficulties with the use of risk as a basis for decisions on the permissibility or impermissibility of new activities. For example, from the perspective of the insurance agency, it is not the riskiness of an activity, per se, that is relevant (as is suggested in most policy discussions of new activities), but rather, what happens to the insurance agency's risk exposure in the entire organization when a new activity is added to the firm's existing complement of activities. The change in the risk exposure of the insurance fund may be increased or decreased, depending on the correlation of the cash flows of the new activity with those of activities already being engaged in and on whether the new activity permits the organization to achieve an increased level of efficiency with an increased level of both risk and return. A negative correlation of the cash flows of the new activity with that of the insured firm may reduce the overall riskiness of the resulting firm, even though the variability of cash flows of the activity may be greater than the variability of cash flows of the firm before adding the activity. (See Boyd, Hanweck, and Pithyachartyakul, 1980).

The net effect on the riskiness of the firm and whether adding a new activity will increase the overall riskiness of the firm depends upon the variability of the cash flows of the activity, the covariance of the cash flows of the activity with that of the firm, and the proportion of resources devoted to the activity relative to those devoted to the rest of the firm's activities. This suggests that the risk elements of particular activities are firm-specific and not easily generalized to make judgments that certain activities should be permissible for banks and others should not.

Although it may be difficult to generalize about the riskiness of particular activities, concerns about risk (especially during the transition to risk-based premiums and/or capital requirements) have led many to argue for limiting banking diversification to financial activities.[2] The U.S. Treasury Department's recent proposals to expand the array of activities for banking organizations, for example, would restrict banking organizations to "financial activities."[3] The Treasury indicates a number of activities that would qualify as financial activities, including: investment advice; leasing; extensions of credit; real estate development and brokerage; data processing; underwriting or acting as broker for the sale of insurance; underwriting and dealing in revenue bonds; and sponsoring and managing an investment company. Banks already have substantial expertise in operating many of these activities, and the prospects for synergies tend to be greater than for many other activities.

Moreover, some of these activities promise to be relatively low-risk. (See, for example, the analysis in Arthur Young, 1983; and the following tables: Wall and Eisenbeis, 1984, Table 1; Heggestad, 1975, Tables 1 and 2; and Cole, 1985, Tables 1, 2, and 6). Indeed, the data indicate that certain activities already permissible to commercial banks, such as personal credit, small business investment corporations, and business credit activities (see Eisenbeis, 1984) may be more risky than some of those activities under consideration, such as life insurance, insurance brokerage, and certain real estate brokerage activities. More importantly, there clearly are very low-risk nonfinancial activities, particularly in the communications area, for example, that might be attractive to banking organizations because such activities offer potential scope and scale economies. Thus, there is very little justification for limiting activities to financial activities.

The main issue the insurance agency faces as new activities are added to banking organization portfolios is the feasibility of assessing and monitoring the risks to which it is exposed. These, then, should probably be the most important criteria to be applied when deciding on the permissibility of particular activities.

Conflicts of Interest

Legitimate concerns arise from potential conflicts of interest. The problem relates less to the danger that an organization may abuse one class of customer or part of the organization to favor another than to the existence of incentives for cross-subsidizing from one part of the organization to another because of the subsidy from mispriced deposit insurance.

Six different policies have historically been pursued to limit the potential for real and alleged conflicts of interest. These policies include: (1) outright prohibition of certain activities, such as the co-mingling of commercial and investment banking; (2) public disclosure of important events that affect earnings and operations is required for all firms and, in banking, insider transactions must be reviewed by the board of directors and reported; (3) regulation and limitations on permissible behavior, such as national bank requirements that commissions earned in the sale of credit life insurance accrue to the bank and not the bank oficer acting as an insurance agent; (4) restriction of exchanges of information and personnel, and requirements that certain activities be carried out in separate affiliates or departments; (5) promotion of competition; and (6) imposition of penalties and remedies when abuses may be shown to take place.

These options are not mutually exclusive. Most extreme, of course, have been outright prohibitions, which have probably been applied too stringently. The alleged conflicts involving bank securities activities, for example, although egregious in a few particular cases, did not appear to be widespread among banks, nor were they peculiar to banks. Rather, the abuses resulted from unregulated activities in securities markets, generally, that other policies have arguably eliminated. (See Flannery, 1985; Kelly, 1985; and Golembe, 1982). Furthermore, there is reason to believe that the separation of commercial and investment banking was due more to Senator Glass's belief in the faulty real bills doctrine and to demands by securities underwriters than to evidence of conflicts of interest. (See Flannery, 1985).

Concentration of Power

As previously shown, potential problems of concentration of power have been dealt with in two ways: The comingling of commercial banking with commerce or with investment banking has been prohibited; and the antitrust laws have been applied to banking and to bank holding companies. In certain respects, these approaches have worked reasonably well. The experience under the Bank Holding Company Act, as described in Appendix B, suggests, for example, that concentration has not increased appreciably in permissible nonbanking activities or in banking, generally.

At the same time, it has proven difficult to implement the concentration-of-power criteria where the Federal Reserve has had discretionary authority. Economic theory, the empirical literature, and legislative and judicial deliberations have provided little guidance to help decisionmakers balance what types of combinations or levels of concentration are dangerous, or what increments of concentration are unacceptable (for discussions of the problems, see Eisenbeis and Glassman, 1978; Rhoades, 1979; Glassman, 1981; Rhoades and Rutz, 1984; Rose, 1978; and Esty and Caves, 1983). Even the legislative debate suggests several interpretations of what the exact fears were. (See U.S. Congress, House, 1969a, U.S. Congress, Report, 1969b, and U.S. Congress Hearings, 1970).

Competitive Equity

As suggested earlier, competitive equity issues have arisen in the debate over expanding the powers of insured financial institutions primarily because of differential regulatory treatment and the hidden subsidies associated with mispriced deposit insurance. Elimination of these two incentives should alleviate concerns about competitive inequities associated with expansion of banking institutions' powers. Policies to promote competition aggressively and to do away with protective regulation designed to restrict competition will let the efficient providers of services prosper and result in increased benefits to the public. In this respect, policies to promote competition are designed to accommodate the drive to realize cost savings and efficiencies and are an integral part of the efficiency objective set forth above.

Organizational Issues in New Banking Activities

To achieve the efficiency and other benefits of product expansion while also insulating bank subsidiaries and other insured subsidiaries from risk-taking and abuses by other parts of the organization, the Treasury and others (see Chase and Waage, 1983) have suggested that new activities be permitted only in separately chartered subsidiaries.[4] In effect, bank holding companies would be divided into a regulated component, which would fall under the jurisdiction of the banking agencies and would consist of those subsidiaries taking insured deposits, and an unregulated component, which would consist of nonbank subsidiaries. Financial transactions between these two components would be strictly limited by Section 23 A-type restrictions, and safeguards would be imposed to limit conflicts of interest and other problems.

In this way the risk to the deposit insurance fund would be limited, and the nonbank subsidiaries would be free to operate without the burdensome regulations affecting insured depository institutions. Proponents claim that restricting new activities to separate affiliates and subsidiaries would also promote competitive equity, because subsidiaries would be separately capitalized and presumably would be funded similarly to independent firms. Finally, equity in regulation would be facilitated by permitting regulation by function.

If, however, banking organizations (and other conglomerates) operate as consolidated entities seeking a single profit objective, they could not be insulated from risk-taking in their less regulated subsidiaries without severely limiting the economic gains that might follow from the new activities. (See Eisenbeis, 1983).

To clarify the issues raised by these policy alternatives, it would be useful to discuss why U.S. banks formed bank holding companies and how the holding companies behave. (Appendix B compares independent firms with bank holding company subsidiaries, regarding risk transference among affiliates and operating performance.) The chapter concludes with a summary of the key issues associated with the alternative ways to permit product expansion.

Incentives for Bank Holding Company Formation

Banks formed bank holding companies to avoid regulation. (See Eisenbeis, 1985, 1980, and Kane, 1981). Prior to 1956, avoiding state and federal limitations on branching was the prime motive for banks to form bank holding companies. (See Savage, 1978, and Fischer and Golembe, 1976).[5] Similarly, by operating through nonbank subsidiaries, lending could be carried out more easily across the nation.

More recently, not only geographic diversification restrictions, but also limits on product expansion, limitations, deposit-rate ceilings, reserve requirements, tax considerations, and capital adequacy and related regulatory requirements provided significant economic incentives for banks to restructure their operations under the umbrella of a holding company. (See Eisenbeis, 1983a and 1983b, and Eisenbeis, 1985). For example, in the 1970s, because of increased competition (with the open market and with unregulated institutions) for funds and because of binding deposit-rate ceilings, banks were less flexible than their competitors in adjusting to periods of inflation-induced high interest rates.

The need to meet the competition and to blunt the effects of disintermediation led banks to seek a less regulated (hence, less costly) environment by adopting the bank holding company form. By shifting certain funding operations from bank subsidiaries into a parent holding company or a nonbank subsidiary, management could fund lending, provided it was carried out in nonbank subsidiaries, free of deposit-rate ceilings and reserve requirements. Name association and the sharing of facilities and operations permitted a company to retain many of the advertising and operational benefits that had previously been available within the bank. The effect was that parent companies and nonbank subsidiaries began to assume an increasingly important role in funding the expansion of banking and nonbanking activities, especially during tight money periods (when interest rates are high).

Tax considerations provided another important set of incentives to form bank holding companies and were probably the most important factor in the formation of the majority of the nation's small bank holding companies. (See Eisenbeis, 1983b and 1985). Forming a holding company was an attractive way to acquire a bank because the bank holding company could repay acquisition debt with tax-deductible dividends from subsidiary banks. This allowed individuals to avoid the double tax on bank income and dividends.

Additional tax benefits accrued to larger banking organizations from the favorable treatment of income earned abroad in foreign subsidiaries. The United States does not tax income earned in foreign subsidiaries until it is repatriated, whereas income earned in foreign branches is taxed as repatriated income.

Bank holding companies could also avoid certain local city and state taxes, thereby minimizing the total tax liabilities of the consolidated firms.

Early regulatory and supervisory policies reinforced and unintentionally encouraged certain banking activities in other parts of the company rather than within bank subsidiaries. For example, regulations implementing the 1970 Amendments to the Bank Holding Company Act of 1956 were designed to compartmentalize bank holding companies into a regulated component, consisting of the bank subsidiaries and a less regulated component, consisting of the parent companies and nonbank subsidiaries. The object was to isolate insured bank subsidiaries and to protect them from risk-taking and abuse, thereby limiting risks to the deposit insurance system flowing from the rest of the organization, which was to be permitted to operate in a relatively unsupervised manner.

At the same time, parent companies were to be sources of strength to bank affiliates, and there was an attempt by the Fed to permit any benefits from bank holding company affiliation to be passed downstream to bank subsidiaries.[6] For this reason, the practice known as double leveraging, in which the parent company issues debt that is passed on to subsidiary banks through the purchase of equity, was not only permitted but also encouraged, because the financial strength of the holding company was presumably being relied upon to issue the debt. As long as bank affiliates were isolated by laws and regulations, the banking industry believed that the courts would uphold the limited liability of the parent holding company in its affiliates and subsidiaries and that, in the event of a financial problem, the corporate veil would not be pierced to draw on the resources of other parts of the organization. Thus, no harm would come to subsidiary banks.

The practical effect, however, was that holding companies leveraged themselves beyond what their bank subsidiaries would have been permitted had the debt been issued at the bank level. Moreover, the debt-servicing requirements of the parent companies imposed quasi-fixed-dividend requirements on subsidiary banks rather than the variable dividends expected from equity. Thus, the long-term fixed-debt-servicing requirements of the parents changed the duration of the banks' liabilities, and hence, increased their exposure to interest-rate risk. Recently, the Federal Reserve has revised its bank holding company capital policies. Capital adequacy is evaluated on a consolidated-entity basis, and double leveraging is now discouraged.

The initial regulatory policy toward double leveraging and financial structure would clearly have been appropriate if subsidiaries operated as independent affiliates and holding companies functioned as passive investors (in effect, as mutual funds) exercising no management, operational, or financial influence over the rest of the organization. The evolution of bank holding companies, however, suggests they have tended to function as devices for conducting traditional banking and funding activities that, but for the existence of regulatory constraints, would have been conducted within bank subsidiaries. (See Eisenbeis, 1985, 1983b). This history implies that bank holding companies are more likely to operate as integrated (or partially integrated) entities than as collections of independently operated firms generating income in the form of dividends and debt payments. This conclusion is confirmed by a review of the evidence on how bank holding companies actually operate and has important implications, both for policies that authorize new activities and for deposit-insurance pricing.

Operating Policies of Bank Holding Companies

Surveys of how bank holding companies have organized their activities reveal a wide range of organizational structures, conditioned in part by corporate cultures, sizes, and types of business.[7] For example, some smaller one-bank holding companies consist of shell parent companies formed for tax purposes, whose primary assets are single subsidiary banks. Strover (1978) indicates that approximately 55 percent of all one-bank holding companies have single subsidiaries. Such companies have no significant value or purpose separate from that of the subsidiary banks, although debt servicing requirements may impose significant constraints on bank operating policies. Therefore, it makes little sense to look at its financial structure on other than a consolidated basis.

Although companies with multiple subsidiaries tend to grant differing degrees of autonomy to their affiliates and subsidiaries, bank holding companies tend to operate more as integrated firms than as collections of independent affiliates. Parent companies exercise substantial control over operations, organizational structure, financial, and managerial philosophy, as well as determine specific functions such as securities and federal funds management, asset and liability management, capitalization, loan mix, correspondent relationships, loan participations, selection of senior management, and budgets. Holding company nonbank subsidiaries appear even more integrated and tightly controlled than bank subsidiaries. (See Lawrence, 1974).

Murray (1978) discusses a number of reasons for this integration. In addition to the regulatory incentives, certain technological changes, such as the introduction of computers and electronic accounting, make it more economical to centralize some activities to take advantages of operational efficiencies. Also, the 1973 recession exposed weaknesses in many bank holding company subsidiaries and heightened the need to exercise more control over costs, risk-taking, and internal operating policies.

Centralization was also necessitated by the enactment, during the 1970s, of new legislation (such as the Community Reinvestment Act, the Truth-in-Lending Act, and the Financial Institutions Regulatory Reform Act) and the imposition of additional reporting requirements. These new requirements carried stiff penalties, in the form of fines and vulnerability to class action suits, for noncompliance. Some companies, in seeking to attract new affiliates, promote the benefits of centralization as an inducement for the managements of independent firms to support their being acquired by larger firms.

Studies of the comparative operating performance of affiliated and unaffiliated bank and nonbank subsidiaries reveal important differences in portfolio composition, risk, and profitability. (See Curry, 1978, for a review and summary of the studies). These studies, together with those of the post-acquisition operating policies of bank affiliates, suggest that banking subsidiaries do not operate similarly to independent firms. In particular, affiliated banks tend to choose more risky loan and investment strategies, to be less liquid, and to make higher proportions of loans than they did as independent companies. Both earnings and expenses increase after acquisition, but profits are unaffected. Affiliated banks tend to be more highly leveraged than independent banks.

In the nonbank area, the limited number of studies of performance in mortgage banking, consumer finance, and equipment leasing suggest that bank holding company subsidiaries appear to be less profitable and more highly leveraged than independent firms are. Consumer finance subsidiaries also have higher expenses and lower growth rates than do independent firms. In the case of mortgage banking, affiliated firms tend to have real estate loans outstanding at about the same level as that of independent companies but to experience slower growth rates.

The studies of both operating policies and performance indicate that bank holding company affiliates do not operate as though they were separate affiliates. Instead, the association involves sharing of management, funding, operations, and reputation, presumably in an attempt to take advantage of possible synergies. The results of the studies also suggest that when activities of bank holding company parents, affiliates, and other subsidiaries are determined or strongly influenced by centralized policies and may be supported by even an implicit association with insured subsidiary banks, it may be very difficult to insulate affiliated banks from risk-taking by nonbank subsidiaries or from the public's perception that the safety of depositors' funds is affected by what goes on in the less regulated parts of the organization.

Moreover, the fact that most of the nation's largest bank holding companies are dominated by their banking subsidiaries, both in terms of management and resources, may make this association appear especially strong in the eyes of the market. This conclusion is strengthened by the recent Continental Illinois failure, in which the debts of the holding company were also guaranteed by the government.

Chase and Brown (1984) describe other factors that would serve to link the subsidiaries of a bank holding company together from both the institution's and customer's perspective. Most of the benefits of expanding bank services are seen as arising from the existence of scope economies due to unused capacity in the: (1) delivery of financial services (such as branches), (2) the production of services (such as excess computer capacity), (3) marketing capacity, and (4) borrowing capacity.

Allowing the consumer to purchase services from one source promises lower costs to both the individual and to society as a whole. In discussing why consumers might prefer to purchase products from a supermarket of finance rather than a specialty house, Chase and Brown point out that bundling reduces the information and search costs the consumer might otherwise incur, especially in purchasing complex goods and services. Sears and other major retailers, for example, incur some of the shopping and related transactions costs for customers, and for fees that are usually embedded in the prices of the products, place their reputations behind the products.

In financial services, the reputation of the financial institution is one of the links between services supplied by insured and uninsured subsidiaries that may justify the provision of multiple services. The need to maintain reputation, and to market and trade on that reputation, serves to link the affiliates and subsidiaries of a holding company together from both the public's and management's perspectives. The need to guard the health of affiliates and subsidiaries will induce an organization to come to the rescue of a troubled subsidiary.

Perhaps the clearest example of this reputation-driven incentive was provided during 1974 and 1975 in the way many major banking organizations responded to the Real Estate Investment Trust (REIT) problem. As some bank-sponsored and advised REITs began to experience difficulties, bank subsidiaries of holding companies provided loans and revolving credit, attempting to prevent the bankruptcy of REITs. (See Sinkey, 1979 and Hamilton, 1978). Bank holding companies incurred substantial further risks to protect and support REITs to which the companies were not linked by ownership or affiliate relationships. McConnell and Marcias (1975) have suggested that these rescue efforts went "far beyond the normal bounds of the traditional conservative American banking industry." This is not to suggest that the industry's response was inappropriate or irrational. In fact, financial support from the banking system probably saved the REIT industry from a collapse that would not only have seriously damaged the banking industry's reputation, but would also have been even more costly to the public and to the stability of financial markets. This experience suggests that banking organizations would have been even more likely to stand behind their subsidiaries and affiliates when they encountered trouble.

Additional evidence of this reputation motive has been provided by the experience of some financially troubled subsidiaries. For example, United California Bank assumed the debts of its Swiss affiliate, United California Bank of Basel, to prevent the affiliate's failure from large losses from speculating in commodity futures.[8] Similarly, in more than one instance involving major U.S. money-center banks and foreign joint venture partners, the U.S. banks were motivated to provide funds to save troubled entities in amounts far in excess of what was required by the proportionate ownership interest of the U.S. banks.

Policy Alternatives

Three general alternatives have been proposed as ways to permit banking organizations to take on expanded powers while preventing undue risks to the deposit insurance fund and avoiding other problems that may be associated with the expansion. The alternatives include: (1) requring that new activities be carried out in independently operated subsidiaries of bank holding companies that operate as passive mutual funds receiving only dividends from otherwise independent affiliates and subsidiaries; (2) permitting all new activity expansion to take place within a bank (or permitting a holding company to engage in any activity permissible for a bank); and (3) requiring new activities to be engaged in only by separately incorporated affiliates with certain restrictions on financial and other sharing of resources and management among subsidiaries and affiliates. The first two of these policy options are polar opposites and the third represents an intermediate ground. Because the consequences of the first and third options differ mainly in degree rather than in direction, they will be considered together.

Permitting New Activities in Separately Incorporated Affiliates and Subsidiaries

The main arguments for permitting new activities in separately incoiporated subsidiaries rest on the behalf that segmenting new activities: (1) would protect bank affiliates from undue risk-taking and potential abuse, thereby protecting the deposit insurance funds; (2) would protect the public from conflicts of interest and related problems; and (3) would allow the parent organizations to engage in new ventures in an unregulated environment.

Existing and potential regulations and other policies are cited as adequate to provide needed protections:

1. Section 23A of the Federal Reserve Act already limits the extent to which a bank can make loans and purchase assets as a means of channeling resources to its parent and nonbank subsidiaries.[9] Loans to any single subsidiary are limited to 10 percent of capital and surplus, with an aggregate limitation of 20 percent on all such loans.

2. There are restrictions on dividend payments by subsidiary banks. Federal regulatory approval must be obtained whenever dividends are paid out of capital and surplus or whenever payments exceed net profits for the previous three years. Although such approvals are routinely given, there is a regulatory check on the payments.

3. The agencies have cease-and-desist powers to stop any unsafe and unsound banking practice, and they have the authority to modify capital-adequacy standards in response to increased risk exposure for banks. The standards were modi-

fied recently, when minimum primary capital requirements were raised to 5.5 percent of assets.

4. Numerous reports are required by statute and the banking agencies on intercompany transfers of funds and assets.

5. The agencies have employed their authority to require that nonbanking subsidiaries affirmatively disclose to the public that liabilities are not federally insured and that they are not liabilities of bank subsidiaries. These restrictions were imposed in the late 1970s on bank holding company issues of small denomination notes.

6. The Federal Reserve has the authority to prohibit resource sharing and name identification of a nonbank subsidiary with a bank subsidiary. Numerous examples of such restrictions exist. In New Hampshire, for example, common housing and marketing of liabilities between bank subsidiaries and stock thrift institutions were prohibited as a condition for bank holding company affiliation. Recently, the Federal Reserve restricted activities of nonbank-bank affiliates of bank holding companies. Because these restrictions waste many of the advantages of affiliation, however, most have been rescinded or soon will be.

7. Anti-tying provisions of Section 106 of the Bank Holding Company Act of 1956 prohibit tied sales, reciprocity agreements, or exclusive-dealing contracts that serve to limit alleged abuses of customers. In hearings on the tying issues in connection with bank holding company insurance activities, the Comptroller of the Currency testified that no evidence of abuses had been uncovered by National Bank Examiners. (See Heinman, 1979).

8. Under corporate law, affiliates and subsidiaries are separate legal entities, which limits the extent that a bank subsidiary, the parent, or other affiliate can be held liable for the debts of a troubled or failing affiliate. This corporate veil would permit a holding company to walk away from a troubled situation without posing undue risks on its subsidiary banks. (See Chase, 1972, 1971, and Chase and Brown, 1983).

Additional arguments for this approach are that it would promote competitive equity between regulated and less regulated competitors. The advantages to leverage that banking organizations might have, for example, would be restricted, because under the separate-affiliate approach, capital would be segmented among the bank and nonbank affiliates; presumably, the affiliates would be capitalized similarly to unaffiliated firms. In addition, equality in regulation and regulatory burdens would be facilitated since it would be possible to apply uniform rules, regulations, and enforcement to all institutions.

Duplicative and overlapping responsibilities could be eliminated, because the separate-affiliates approach would permit regulation by function rather than by dividing regulatory responsibilities among different agencies, as is done now. Currently, for example, the banking agencies have authority to enforce the securities laws with respect to banks, whereas the Securities and Exchange Commission (SEC) is responsible for enforcing the laws with respect to bank holding companies. This resulted in conflict among the agencies over appropriate disclosure of information on the financial condition of banks, because the banking agencies felt the disclosure increased the potential for runs (for a discussion of general issues, see Peterson, 1985).

The separate-affiliates approach is, however, subject to numerous problems. For example, the incentives for bank holding company formation, together with the fact that banking organizations tend to operate more as integrated firms than as collections of truly independent companies, suggest there are important reasons to question the feasibility and practicality of policies designed to force compartmentalization.

First, because of built-in profit incentives within banking organizations and the way they respond to binding regulations, and because of the reputation considerations, policies designed to force separation are likely to be self-defeating. Attempts to segment the institution into regulated and less regulated segments can put it into a suboptimal operating and competitive position. This reduces profits and encourages the organization to shift activities from the more heavily regulated subsidiaries to less regulated subsidiaries, because from the point of view of the consolidated entity, it is total firm profits, and not necessarily the profits of individual (and often wholly owned) subsidiaries, that are being maximized.

Furthermore, shareholders and management are indifferent as to where within the entity a particular function is being conducted as long as its contributions to total profits is optimized. For a bank holding company that owns at least 80 percent of a subsidiary, dividends that are upstreamed are tax deductible. This fact, together with the company's ability to file a consolidated tax return, means that only the interests of the shareholders of the parent company matter in determining company behavior.

In addition, those customers desiring packages of services can be served by coordinated cross-selling strategies. This can often be made transparent to the customer by judicious employment of technology.

Another problem with this general policy is that more heavily regulated affiliates, especially subsidiary banks, will shrink relative to the less regulated affiliates as more functions are shifted to avoid regulatory constraints. Operational and other dependencies among the subsidiaries are likely to increase, especially if customer relationships are better served by providing packages of coordinated products offered now by different subsidiaries. Shifting of banking services into other parts of the organization reshuffle function-related or customer-related activities, and may raise costs because new coordination efforts are required. The need for coordination to maintain customer relationships means that affiliates and subsidiaries must be tightly controlled.

Because of these structural changes, the entire holding company is likely to become more integrated, and it becomes increasingly unlikely that the parent company will walk away from a troubled subsidiary that is offering services that the public views as being intimately intertwined with those of the rest of the organization. The effect will be to increase the risks to the insuring agency.

Moreover, there is some evidence that the existence of Section 23A-type protections and bank examinations cannot prevent problems in nonbanking affiliates from being transmitted to other parts of a banking organization. The failure of Hamilton Bankshares, for example, indicates that without monitoring and supervision of *both* the banking and nonbanking activities, the existence of prohibitions on resource transfers become difficult to prevent in desperate situations. Monitoring is especially important in affecting the ability to detect fraud and related problems. A complex system of subsidiaries and affiliates, some of which are neither supervised nor examined, makes it that much easier for dishonest bankers to engage in fraudulent and self-dealing practices. For this reason, along with the separate-affiliates approach goes the need for the insurance agency to increase risk-monitoring and regulation to enforce complete separation.

The shifting of activities to nonbank subsidiaries may pose special policy problems for the insurance agency when a parent company or its nonbank subsidiary issues uninsured liabilities that are close substitutes for the insured liabilities of subsidiary banks. The failure of Beverly Hills Bancorp, for example, provides graphic evidence of the problems the public can have in separating the liabilities and risk-exposure of bank subsidiaries from those of the rest of the organization. In that case, a run on the liabilities of the holding company was transferred to the bank subsidiary. This problem has been dealt with by requiring that bank holding company liabilities, such as subordinated notes, be clearly stamped to indicate they are uninsured and by prohibiting affiliates from using names that suggest association with subsidiary banks.

If a large proportion of financial liabilities move from insured to uninsured status, the benefits of deposit insurance may be lost for certain classes of creditors, unless the government chooses to extend guarantees to such claims. As the cases of Continental and Midland Bank demonstrate, the pressures on the insurance agency to extend coverage can be very great.

If activity shifting is prohibited by regulation, as would clearly be the intent if a company were forced to operate as a collection of independent affiliates, then it is clear that profits will be reduced as certain packages of service are excluded. Over the long run, the resulting competitive disadvantage would mean that less regulated firms would be expected to capture a larger and larger portion of the financial service business relative to banking organizations.

Imposing limitations on resource sharing, on common management, on common advertising and name association, on cross-selling of customers, and on internal funds transfers would effectively reduce and/or eliminate the benefits of subsidiary operations. What would remain would be the benefits to the shareholders of the parent company of risk-reducing diversification resulting from any imperfect correlation of returns between the bank and nonbank affiliates. Finance theory, however, suggests that because of the ability of individual shareholders to diversify on their own, the diversification potential of mutual fund-type ownership of affiliates under a holding company structure may be of little value to shareholders. (See Copeland and Weston, 1983).

Finally, to the extent that there are economies of scale and scope in bank and nonbank activities, the separate-affiliates approach would place small banks at a cost, and hence competitive, disadvantage if their operations were not sufficiently large to achieve an efficient scale of operations. Research suggests these benefits are realized at a relatively small size, but not small enough to prevent well over half the nation's institutions from being unable to take advantage of the new powers. (See Humphrey, 1985, for a summary of the economies of scale and scope evidence). Thus, proposals to permit smaller banks to conduct nonbanking activities in bank subsidiaries, as opposed to incurring the costs of forming a bank holding company, may not adequately address the cost disadvantages that are at issue.

Permitting New Activities Within a Consolidated Entity

There are two essentially equivalent ways to permit banking organizations to engage in new activities as alternatives to the separate-affiliates approach. The first would reorient regulatory and supervisory policies away from the subsidiary bank to concentrate instead on the holding company as a single decisionmaking entity. The second alternative would involve creating a set of incentives to induce holding companies to fold their activities back into subsidiary banks. The key to evaluating the alternatives is that both are geared to structuring regulation and supervisory activities to the mode that most companies would prefer to operate—the consolidated entity. The second alternative also seeks to remove those unnecessary barriers that have induced the organizations to adopt different forms.

Under the consolidated entity approach, there would be no need to be concerned, for safety and soundness reasons, with the financial relationships among subsidiaries or with the subsidiaries ability to maintain their independence. For regulatory, reporting, examination, and supervisory purposes, the firm would be viewed as analogous to a branch system, with its subsidiaries representing ways for the firm to organize its internal accounting and control systems. If regulated in this manner, the organization could evolve—in a deregulated environment—into the functional equivalent of a bank. Alternatively, banks could be given powers and authorities that would make them functionally the same as holding companies.

This policy would have several benefits. First, the approach focuses the attention of both the institution and the supervisor on the net risk exposure of the institution as a whole. This exposure should be the ultimate concern of the federal insurance agencies, because the consolidated entity is also the ultimate source of return, and hence risk, to shareholders and other creditors (as the problems in Continental demonstrate).

The trend in bank holding company supervision has for some time been toward treating a holding company as a consolidated entity. For example, multibank holding companies are considered identical to branch systems for purposes of analyzing the competitive effects of proposed mergers and acquisitions. Similarly, the recent revisions in Section 23A proposed by the Fed also move a considerable way in this direction. The revisions remove virtually all the restrictions on interbank movement of funds within a bank holding company and essentially treats the organization as a single entity for funds-management purposes. The Federal Reserve has instituted a bank holding company surveillance and computer-based monitoring system that focuses almost exclusively on the holding company as a consolidated organization. The Chairmen of the FDIC and the Comptroller of the Currency have argued that, because of complicated two-way relationships between a holding company and its subsidiaries, it is impossible to assess the riskiness and financial condition of banking subsidiaries without information on the entire entity. Recently, the banking agencies' capital-adequacy guidelines have been applied equally to banks and to consolidated bank holding companies.

A second benefit of the consolidated-entity approach is that it eliminates the need for regulations instituted to force separation to avoid risk shifting. Substantial portions of existing regulations could be dropped. For example, there would be no need for Section 23A limitations or regulations; and supervisory conventions, rules, and reporting requirements pertaining to intercompany transfers of funds and tax liabilities could be eliminated. Reporting burdens could be substantially reduced, because only consolidated-entity data would need to be collected. Reducing regulatory burdens would also increase the flexibility of banking organizations to adjust to changing economic conditions and would reduce the incentives for less regulated firms to enter into the business.

Finally, for monetary control purposes, the consolidated entity should be subject to the same reserve requirements as a similarly sized bank. For example, there would be no need to innovate different types of intra institutional fund transfers and investments to avoid constraints related to reserve requirements. This would eliminate the need to trace the sources and uses of intrafirm transactions to determine their regulatory status and would reduce the associated reporting burdens.

As is the case with the separate subsidiaries approach, the consolidated entity approach also has some drawbacks. For example, some would see the refocusing of regulation as an extension of regulation to parts of banking organizations that were not regulated before. This might place banking organizations at a competitive disadvantage to the extent they compete with less regulated firms. However, with only minor exceptions, the activities presently authorized to bank holding companies are permissible to banks. Clearly, the ability of the holding company to use the organizational form to avoid regulation would be reduced, but this would be offset by reductions in other regulations and related costs.

Some transitional legal problems would also arise. For example, although subsidiaries might be operated as part of a single entity, they would remain legally separate because the minority shareholders and debtors would have interests and claims on subsidiary firm assets and earnings. Determining the ownership and phsyical location of assets in the event of failure (especially when foreign branches are involved), and liquidation, may prove difficult.

Conclusions and Recommendations

The review of the rationale for restricting banking activities suggests that the traditional concerns for economic efficiency, safety and soundness, concentration of power, and conflicts of interest continue to be valid. Public policies to balance these concerns against economic efficiency objectives have at times resulted in distortions and have created perverse incentives because activity restrictions (and other constraints) have been imposed differentially and because deposit insurance has been mispriced.

Several policies should be implemented to rebalance the system.

First, the repricing of deposit insurance and/or instituting risk-related capital standards, together with policies to promote competition, would create the flexibility to expand the permissible activities of banking organizations.

Second, although the analysis suggests that, because risk is firm-specific, concerns about preventing undue risks to the insurance funds and concentration of governmental and economic power imply that insured banking organizations should be restricted to engaging in those activities whose risks can be assessed and easily monitored. This policy would be especially important during the transition to a new deposit insurance pricing scheme.

Third, potential conflicts of interest and concentration of resources are adequately addressed by existing laws and regulations. Outright prohibition of certain activities should be employed only in the face of substantial evidence that the potential conflicts are so great that the only way to control them would be to completely divorce insured activities from other activities.

Fourth, the evidence indicates that banking organizations tend to operate as consolidated entities, rather than as collections of independent affiliates. Therefore, it is difficult to insulate insured components of a banking organization from the effects of risk-taking in the rest of the entity without imposing regulations that take away the potential benefits (aside from normal profits) of engaging in the activity. For this reason, risk regulation (and risk-based insurance premiums) must be imposed on the consolidated entity. Moreover, with properly priced deposit insurance, the regulators should be indifferent as to organizational structure, although monitoring and supervisory costs should be lower in less complex organizations.[10]

Fifth, during the transition to a new insurance pricing system, new activities should be permitted in only the regulated portions of the organization so that they can be properly monitored to prevent imposing undue risks on the insurance funds.

---

[1]Benston (1983a), for example, lists seven different kinds of regulations: (1) entry; (2) expansion; (3) contraction, including mergers; (4) prices paid for funds; (5) rates earned on loans; (6) supervision of management; and (7) customer relations.

[2]Corrigan (1983) argues for limiting banking diversification and maintaining the traditional separation between banking and commerce on other grounds—namely, the desire to maintain the impartiality of the credit decision. Such an argument, however, is not unique to commercial banks and suggests that all credit granting activities should be separated from commercial activities. Moreover, Corrigan's concern is essentially unrelated to risk or to protecting the interests of the insurance agency. We would argue that the best protection for the borrower is providing ample competitive alternatives, rather than precluding entry of potential suppliers.

[3]The Treasury proposal recognizes that in particular cases, it may not always be clear whether a particular activity is financial in nature. It has attempted to deal with cases not specifically considered in its recommendations by stipulating that the Federal Reserve shall define other activities that may also qualify. Additional guidelines (such as the incidental powers clause in the National Banking Act of 1864) should be provided, however, to aid in the determination of what related activities would qualify.

[4]The Reagan Administration proposed legislation (S. 1609) provided for expansion of banking powers but only within separate affiliates. Similar legislation, S. 2181, was introduced by Senator Garn in 1983.

[5]Prior to the McFadden Act of 1927, which gave national banks the authority to engage in securities activities, national banks formed state-chartered subsidiaries through which to engage in securities activities. (See Golembe, 1982).

[6]Section 23A of the Federal Reserve Act's limitations on transactions are essentially one-way: A bank is not permitted to engage in transactions with other parts of the organization that might be detrimental to the bank, but no similar prohibitions apply to protecting the nonbank subsidiaries from abuse by bank affiliates (see Rose and Talley, 1978).

[7]See, for example, Fischer (1961), Lawrence (1971, 1974), Weiss (1969), Jesser and Fisher (1973), Stodden (1975), Whalen (1982a, 1982b), and Murray (1978). For a review of the earlier literature, see Rose (1978).

[8]See Chase and Brown (1983). They note that American Express was motivated to back the claims against American Express Warehousing, Ltd., in the famous salad oil scandal.

[9]See Rose and Talley (1978) for a detailed discussion of Section 23A of the Federal Reserve Act.

[10]Presumably these costs would be passed on to the firm in the form of charges for examination.

Appendix A.

Administration of Section 4(c)(8) of the Bank Holding Company Act of 1956

Table 2 lists the activities that have been approved or denied by the Federal Reserve Board for bank holding companies. In general, these activities are either those that have traditionally been carried out by banks directly (activities such as consumer financing, mortgage financing, factoring, and leasing) or those that are services banks must carry out in conducting their own business (activities such as data processing, bookkeeping, courier service, consulting for unaffiliated banks, and loan servicing).

In view of the criteria the Federal Reserve Board was required to weigh, a brief review of the evidence on the effects of bank holding company product expansion under existing law is in order better to assess the potential tradeoffs between the benefits to the public of relaxing the restrictions on banking organizations' activities against the safety and soundness risks to the Federal Deposit Insurance fund, and other concerns that were expressed in the legislation about concentration of resources, unfair competition, and conflicts of interest. Of particular interest is the extent to which the existing expansion has resulted in benefits to the public (as the present criteria require) and/or benefits to the institution (and hence to shareholders and customers) in the form of increased competition and efficiency.

The discussion of existing research has been divided into six areas. These include the effects on:

1. The operating performance of nonbank subsidiaries;

2. The cost efficiency of subsidiaries;

3. The risk implications of new activities;

4. The competitive implications of new activities;

5. The consequences for concentration of economic power and potential for conflicts of interest; and

6. The convience and needs of the public.

Two points should be emphasized. First, research on these issues with respect to nonbank activities has been extremely limited. The main reason for the paucity of work lies in the lack of available data

Table 2: Domestic Nonbank Activities Approved and Denied by the Board of Governors (as of February 1, 1984)

Activities Approved by Regulation
 1. Extensions of credit
      Mortgage banking
      Finance companies: consumer, sales, and commercial
      Credit cards
      Factoring
 2. Industrial bank, Morris Plan bank, industrial loan company
 3. Servicing loans and other extensions of credit
 4. Trust company
 5. Investment or financial advising
 6. Full-payout leasing of personal or real property
 7. Investments in community welfare projects
 8. Providing bookkeeping or data processing services
 9. Acting as insurance agent or broker primarily in connection with credit extensions
10. Underwriting credit life and credit accident and health insurance related to consumer loans
11. Providing courier services
12. Management consulting to all depository institutions
13. Sale and issuance of money orders with a face value of not more than $1,000, and travelers checks, and retailing of savings bonds
14. Performing appraisals of real estate
15. Discount brokerage firm
16. Underwriting and dealing in certain federal, state, and municipal securities
17. Acting as a futures commission merchant regarding foreign exchange, U.S. government securities, certain money market instruments, and options on those instruments
18. Arranging equity financing with institutional lenders for commercial and industrial income-producing properties
19. Offering informational, advisory, and transactional foreign exchange services

Activities Approved by Order
 1. Operating a "pool reserve plan" for loss reserves of banks for loans to small businesses
 2. Operating a thrift institution in Rhode Island
 3. Buying and selling gold and silver bullion and silver coin
 4. Operating a guaranty savings bank in New Hampshire
 5. Operating an Article XII New York investment company
 6. Acting as a futures commission merchant to cover gold and silver bullion and coins
 7. Retail check authorization and check guarantee
 8. Providing consumer-oriented financial managment courses

Table 2: continued

9. Executing unsolicited purchases and sales of securities as agent for the customer (limited securities brokerage)
10. Engaging in commercial banking activities through branches located in Nassau and Luxembourg of a limited-purpose Delaware bank
11. Operating a distressed S&L in the same state
12. Acquiring a distressed S&L in another state

Activities Denied by the Board

1. Insurance premium funding ("equity funding")—combined sales of mutual funds and insurance
2. Underwriting general life insurance not related to credit extension
3. Real estate brokerage
4. Land investment and development
5. Real estate syndication
6. General managment consulting
7. Property management services generally
8. Armored car services
9. Sale of level-term credit life insurance
10. Underwriting mortgage guaranty insurance
11. Computer output microfilm services
12. Operating a travel agency
13. Operating a savings and loan association (except in certain states or unless the S&L is distressed)
14. Underwriting property and casualty insurance
15. Underwriting home loan life insurance
16. Real estate advisory activities
17. Offering investment notes with transactional features

Source: Savage (1985), pp. 190–91.

on the nonbank activities of bank holding companies and data on independent firms to use for comparative purposes. The concern for the reporting burden by the regulatory agencies and the Bank Examination Council, the Paper Work Reduction Act, and the costs of collecting and placing these data in usable form have been the main barriers to research in this area.

Second, the requirement of the Bank Holding Company Act that approved activities be " . . . so closely related to banking or managing or controlling banks as to be a proper incident thereto" means that most of the activities engaged in are not really nonbank activities. Rather, they are essentially bank activities conducted in nonbank affiliates and subsidiaries; less than a handful of approved activities were not permitted to bank holding company bank subsidiaries.

Operating Performance

Nowhere have the problems of data availability acted to limit research on the effects of bank holding company affiliation more than in the area of assessing the impacts on operating performance. (See Curry, 1978). In fact, of the more than 30 activities that have been approved by the Federal Reserve Board, only three—mortgage banking, consumer finance, and equipment leasing—have been studied. Fortunately, these activities account for the bulk of bank holding company expansion to date, at least when measured in terms of the number of offices established. (Whitehead, 1983). The studies suggest that when compared to independent firms, bank holding company subsidiaries appear to be less profitable and more highly leveraged. In the case of consumer finance, the two available studies also suggest that affiliated companies have higher expenses and grow faster than independent firms. The one study of mortgage banking suggests that affiliated companies grow more slowly than independent companies and have about the same level of real estate loans outstanding as independent companies.

Three important cautions should be followed when interpreting these studies; the cautions apply equally to the other areas under consideration. First, all of the studies used relatively old data (the most recent data, used in the study of equipment leasing, were for 1977). For the most part, the acquired subsidiaries had only been part of bank holding companies for short periods of time; moreover, the time period studied included several years of severe economic recessions.

Second, by comparing affiliated and unaffiliated firms, the studies implicity assumed that the reported accounting data adequately captured economic performance of the affiliated subsidiary. It is well known, however, that numerous ways exist to transfer funds within a holding company organization besides upstreaming of dividends, and these transfers, together with the tax treatment of consolidated income, tend to distort reported accounting data. This suggests the studies may have been comparing noncomparable firms.

Third, the studies do not capture any synergies that may exist between the bank affiliates and nonbank affiliates within the holding company organization and thus may tend to underestimate the efficiency of nonbank expansion.

Cost Efficiencies

Only one study of nonbank activity costs has been performed. That study examined consumer finance subsidiaries and failed to find significant cost differences between bank holding company subsidiaries and independent consumer finance firms. (Rhoades and Boczar, 1977). In banking, however, Burke (1978) discovered cost efficiencies.

Safety and Soundness

Rose (1978) reviewed a total of six studies that examined the risk implications of nonbank expansion by banking organizations. The results of these studies are somewhat mixed. Those studies that have analyzed the comparative riskiness of affiliated and unaffiliated subsidiaries have suggested that leverage of affiliated nonbank firms increases with expansion relative to independent firms, at least in consumer finance and mortgage banking area; this is interpreted as implying that risk has increased.

Other studies looking at the overall risk implications of potential new activities, however, suggest that the variability of an organization's earnings might be reduced by nonbank expansion. In fact, banking consistently shows up as being among the more risky of activities. A recent set of studies suggests that several of the activities presently under consideration as permissible new activities, including life insurance, security brokerage, and thrift institutions, have cash flows that are negatively correlated with those of banking and hold the possibility of risk-reducing diversification benefits. (Wall and Eisenbeis, 1984, Heggestad, 1975, Eiseman, 1976, Meinster and Johnson, 1974, Boyd, 1980, and Cole, 1985). These studies also suggest that bank holding companies, as a result of their nonbank activities, may be less risky than commercial banks alone.

Competition

One significant benefit of bank holding company nonbank expansion that would be expected would be enhanced competition. This results because anticompetitive acquisitions are proscribed by the antitrust laws, and because, to the extent that synergies exist and that the bank holding company device provides an effective method to circumvent anticompetitive interstate and intrastate banking restrictions, bank holding companies would be expected to be positive, competitive forces in the markets they enter.

Again, however, the existing research is sparse. (Rhoades, 1978). The studies suggest that bank holding company affiliation may have had slight pro-competitive effects in consumer finance and, at best, neutral effects in mortgage banking. The more rapid growth of bank holding company consumer-finance subsidiaries suggests pro-competitive pricing policies. In mortgage banking, the subsidiaries are more highly leveraged and less profitable, which provides little reason to believe that the holding companies have had any effect on competition.

The evidence is also mixed in the banking area. Most of the research has failed to identify significant or systematic competitive effects of bank holding company bank expansion except when foothold acquisitions are involved.

Finally, a recent study of bank holding company credit insurance underwriting indicates that lower prices have resulted, and that competition has been enhanced. Here it is important that the Federal Reserve Board requires, as a condition of approval, that insurance be offered at rates below the legal maximum prevailing in the state.

Concentration of Resources

Nonbank expansion has not contributed significantly to increasing bank holding companies' control over aggregate financial resources.[11] Nonbank resources of bank holding companies account for less than 7 to 9 percent of bank holding company resources (including nondomestic subsidiaries). This proportion has not changed significantly since 1977, and most of the increase is due to internal growth, because few major acquisitions have taken place.

Significant consolidation has taken place in the consumer-finance industry, but bank holding companies have not played a major role in that consolidation. The picture is more mixed in mortgage banking and factoring. Bank holding companies now account for more than 40 percent of the top 100 mortgage servicers but, in general, have not made significant acquisitions. Nor are banking organizations in a position to dominate the industry. The one industry that does appear to be dominated by bank holding companies is factoring. In 1977, they controlled over 56 percent of the receivables and 17 of the top 20 firms.

The nonbank expansion of bank holding companies has been counterbalanced by the entry and growth of numerous nonbank organizations into the financial service industry. Not only have the alternative suppliers to banking organizations increased in number, but they have made significant inroads into many traditional banking markets, including consumer finance, long-term business lending and deposit-type services. (Rosenblum and Pavel, 1985).

Convenience and Needs

In acting on proposed nonbank activities, the Federal Reserve is required by the Bank Holding Company Act to consider the effects on the convenience and needs of the public and to make findings that the public benefits in terms of effects on competition, efficiency, and convenience outweigh any anticompetitive effects. Studies of Federal Reserve Board decisions suggest that there were no instances in which applications were approved and the Board determined that public benefits of nonbank acquisitions outweighed serious anticompetitive effects, undue increases in concentration of resources, or adverse effects on safety and soundness.

The substantial difficulties of measuring and specifying public benefits explain why few studies exist on the topic. (Cyrnak, 1978). Those studies that have examined the performance-related aspects of the public benefits test suggest that the chief benefits that accrued to the public have been in the form of increased availability of credit, mainly through loans and municipal finance.

In the insurance area, benefits undoubtedly have arisen because of the Federal Reserve Board's requirement that bank holding companies' underwriting fees reduce insurance costs to the customers. These benefits are counterbalanced by evidence of somewhat greater leverage and poorer operating performance by bank holding company affiliates.

Summary and Observations on Research

The lack of a large body of research on the public benefits of nonbank activities by bank holding companies makes it especially difficult to render unambiguous conclusions about the overall effects of expanding bank holding company powers. It is especially hazardous when those studies are not free from methodological problems, when they concentrate on a period of great economic stress, and when they examine bank holding company nonbank expansion that is not mature. The bottom line on the evidence to date suggests that the movement's overall effects on public benefits has been essentially neutral. Both slight benefits and slight costs appear to have resulted, but neither is large enough to be significant for public policy purposes. Equally important, there does seem to be some evidence of increased riskiness when leverage ratios are examined; risk-reduction possibilities do seem present for some activities when the correlations of cash flows are examined. The evidence also suggests that unless new activities that might be authorized differ significantly from those that have already been permitted, little effect on operations can be expected. For a discussion of evidence on those activities presently under consideration, see Appendix B.

---

[11]See Glassman and Eisenbeis (1978).

Appendix B.

Review of Frequently Mentioned New Activities

The activities most frequently cited as ones that banking organizations might find most attractive can be conveniently divided into five categories: (1) securities activities, including underwriting, brokerage, and mutual funds; (2) insurance, including underwriting of both general life insurance and property and casualty insurance and brokerage of property and casualty insurance; (3) electronic communications and data processing, including telecommunications and cable television; (4) real estate brokerage and development; and (5) miscellaneous activities, including non-full-payout leasing, management consulting, and travel agency activities (Arthur Young & Company, 1983).

In the cases of investment activities, insurance, and many of the miscellaneous activity categories (and to a lesser extent the electronic communications area), banking organizations and/or bank holding companies have already engaged in many of the activities domestically or abroad. For example, general insurance activities, including underwriting, have long been permitted to national banks. The only restriction has been that the activity may be carried out only in towns with populations of less than 5,000. No mention in the National Banking Act is made of limits on the volume or scope of the activity in proportion to the total business the bank conducts.

The Garn-St Germain Depository Institutions Act of 1982 imposes differential limits on insurance activities of bank holding companies based on whether the companies have more or less than $50 million in resources. Such restrictions seem to be imposed as measures to protect the interests of the insurance industry rather than to be based on the traditional concerns about concentation of resources, risk-taking, or other abuses. Certainly, too, the fact that U.S. banks may conduct investment banking activities abroad that are prohibited domestically, suggest that the risks associated with such activities are of much less concern than other potential problems.

Attractiveness of Particular Activities

Studies about the nature of the benefits associated with product expansion and to whom—shareholders or customers—the benefits might accrue, have been limited. Recently, Arthur Young & Company (1983) reviewed 13 activities (see Table 3) with regard to profitability, existing market structure, risk, and barriers to entry, in an attempt to assess the attractiveness for entry by small, medium, and large banks. Only aggregated results are presented and no attempt is made to identify or quantify the extent or nature of the sources of benefits flowing from the various activities. Table 4 summarizes the ranking of the attractiveness of the different services.

The study attempts to evaluate the extent of synergies and potential scope economies that are associated with each activity, taking into account differences that may exist for different sized banks. Among the factors considered are: customer-base transferability; distribution system complementarity; bank image; product synergies; skill similarities; personnel policy similarities; risk; and defensive motivation for entry. The highest-ranked activities for banks of all sizes are discount brokerage, real estate equity, insurance brokerage, and real estate brokerage. For large banks, additional attractive activities are securities brokerage, mutual funds, and non-full payout leasing. Among the least attractive are telecommunications and insurance underwriting. A number of additional activities, including data processing, futures brokerage, management consulting, mutual funds, and non-full payout leasing, are ranked as unattractive for community banks.

Table 3: Activities That Are as Potentially Attractive for Entry by Banking Organizations

---

Securities Underwriting
Securities Brokerage
Mutual Funds
Commodities and Futures Brokerage
Insurance Underwriting
Insurance Brokerage
Travel Agency
Telecommunications
Data Processing
Real Estate Brokerage
Real Estate Equity
Non-Full Payout Leasing
Management Consulting (including Tax Advisory Services)

Table 4:

High Attractiveness

Securities Brokerage
Discount Brokerage
Securities Underwriting
Real Estate Equity
Insurance Brokerage
Data Processing
Futures Brokerage

Medium Attractiveness

Real Estate Brokerage
Management Consulting
Mutual Funds
Telecommunications

Low Attractiveness

Travel Agency
Non-Full Payout Leasing
Insurance Underwriting

The study attempts to combine the attractiveness of the markets with the ability of banks to enter them. Among the most attractive activities for banks of all sizes are real estate equity, insurance brokerage, and securities brokerage; insurance underwriting, telecommunications, management consulting, travel agency, and insurance underwriting are among the least attractive. This study, however, does not consider some of the issues that are most likely to be of public policy concern. These issues include risks to the insurance funds, potential for conflicts of interest, and concentration of resources.

Riskiness of New Activities

Relatively little work has been done on the riskiness of particular nonbank activities currently being considered. Heggestad (1975) examined the riskiness of activities that were mentioned as potential laundry list candidates prior to passage of the 1970 Amendments. By looking at the correllations of profits of banking with those of industry aggregate information, he attempted to identify activities that would reduce the variability of cash flows to the consolidated company. Wall and Eisenbeis (1984) updated Heggestad's results applying the same methodology. They also looked at several activities that are currently under consideration and found that there were potential risk-reducing benefits for life insurance, thrift institutions (other than failing thrifts), and securities brokerage.

These and other aggregate studies suggest that there are potential risk-reducing benefits from diversification; however, a number of recent studies suggest that the diversification benefits depend upon many firm-specific factors. (See Eisemann, 1976, Johnson and Meinster, 1974, 1979, and Strover, 1982). Therefore, activities that may be risk-reducing for some firms may be risk-increasing for others. This result suggests that it is difficult, and potentially misleading, to make judgments about risk based on industry aggregates. Case-by-case analysis may be required for assessing the risk implications of activity expansion.

Further support for this contention is found in work by Cole (1985), who attempted to evaluate the potential risk-reducing benefits of expansion by nonbank firms into the commercial banking business by acquiring nonbank banks. Cole found that, for his very small sample, expansion into banking reduced the variability of earnings for some firms and not for others. Even when risk was increased, however, the increases were not large. More important, Cole found that it was not possible to generalize on the basis of industry classifications, that certain types of combinations were potentially better than others.

These risk studies are clearly limited by the nature of the data, the small samples, the difficulty in breaking out firm-specific considerations, and methodological problems. Despite these problems, however, the results do not suggest that risks associated with activity expansion, at least into financially related activities, should be a major policy concern.

CHAPTER 7

Market Discipline

T he design of the U.S. deposit insurance system has always contemplated a role for market discipline. The system has consistently provided less than 100 percent insurance on deposits, and nondeposit liabilities have never been insured. As a result, some large depositors and other creditors are always potentially at risk in the event of bank failure.

This chapter focuses on the mechanisms by which market discipline works. In particular, it examines the roles of changes in liability costs (which include returns on equity and debt) and changes in the availability of funds, including capital, to signal to managers and shareholders the market's assessment of the riskiness of the institution. (Risk-related deposit insurance premiums are an additional means to introduce market discipline into the system, and are discussed in Chapter 9.)

The research evidence on how market discipline affects depository institutions is reviewed and the potential for enhancing that discipline is explored. The chapter also discusses existing impediments to making market discipline work effectively, including possible conflicts between the interests of the insurance agencies and uninsured creditors and the differential impacts of market discipline on small and large organizations. Finally, it reviews policy issues concerning the objectives of deposit insurance and their implications for introducing more risk into the financial system. Before addressing these issues, however, it is necessary first to define market discipline and to describe how it works.

Market Discipline and Deposit Insurance

In principle, banks should compete for uninsured liabilities on the basis of their demonstrated financial strength and soundness. If some creditors are at risk, it is believed, they will select among competing banks on the basis of capital ratios and other measures of financial strength, and the resulting discipline will be a force for conservatism. Uninsured creditors should demand higher rates of return on funds placed with an institution that they perceive to be more risky than others. When faced with higher costs in response to the market's signal that it is perceived to be too risky, the institution can either pay the higher rates and/or cut back on risky activities to reduce its overall exposure, or else face the loss of funds as they mature. Thus both prices and quantities of available funds will adjust to differences in risk.

The importance of changes in the cost of funds in constraining bank risk-taking depends upon how well the market is able to monitor bank risk and how quickly perceived changes become reflected in required rates of return. The more costly that information and monitoring are, the more difficult it is for depositors and debtholders accurately to assess and price their risk exposure. Faced with the lack of information and uncertainty about their estimates of bank risk, depositors and debtholders may simply choose to withdraw their funds if they perceive that bank risk has increased to an undesirable level, regardless of the rates the bank offers. Uncertainties about future repayment of principal, and the embarrassment of having left funds with a troubled institution that subsequently failed, may outweigh any gains that might result from higher rates, especially for large depositors and other liability holders (such as corporate treasurers, suppliers of federal funds, and institutional investors).

If many liability holders decide to move their funds to other institutions in response to unfavorable performance or because of bad news, a run may result. Runs and systemwide panics, which are discussed in Chapter 2, represent the extreme form of market discipline that is exercised principally through precipitous declines in the availability of funds to banks. Such discipline is seen by some observers more as *ex post* punishment for excessive risk-taking rather than as a deterrent, because the signals to management to assume different risk return tradeoffs may come too late for it to respond, once the run actually begins. But one bank's punishment can serve as a deterrent to excessive risk-taking by other banks, and should surely provide an incentive to ensure adequate liquidity to meet unforeseen withdrawals of funds.

Market discipline, when exercised through the threat of a run, only has credibility if in fact some runs on individual institutions are allowed to follow their course, and if uninsured liability holders have reason to select their bank carefully because they believe that they are at risk. However, as described in Chapter 4, the Federal Deposit Insurance Corporation (FDIC) has handled most bank failures, particularly failures of large banks, so as to provide *de facto* insurance protection for large depositors. As a result, large depositors do not necessarily view themselves as being at risk. If that is the case, they have no incentive to do the type of screening in their choice of bank that can provide useful market discipline. Rather than select their bank carefully at the outset, large depositors may rely on their ability to withdraw funds quickly once the bank does get into trouble. In this case, the existence of uninsured depositors increases the possibility of bank runs.

The analysis in Chapter 2 indicates that bank runs are not necessarily contagious, and runs have rarely, if ever, caused the demise of an economically solvent bank. Nevertheless, runs may impose some costs on the system, and because of the weight given to avoiding these costs, it has proved politically difficult for the regulators to let a liquidity problem run its course.[1] To let liquidity problems run their course increases the likelihood that failure will occur. Furthermore, sales of assets to pay off uninsured liability holders, especially when capital losses occur, only increase the cost to the insurance agency and equity holders if the institution actually fails. For these reasons, some advocates of increased market discipline believe that such discipline cannot come from uninsured depositors.

Alternative Sources of Market Discipline

It must be noted that the present system, in which deposits are insured 100 percent up to $100,000 per account and uninsured after that, is not the only possible design to rely on market discipline as a supplement to regulation and supervision to limit risk-taking. There are means to enhance market discipline from other than uninsured depositors, and these are discussed below.

Stockholders

Stockholders are an important potential source of market discipline. Stockholders risk losing their investment in case of bank failure because their claims to the bank's assets rank lowest in priority in case of failure. Thus, if the operations of an economically insolvent bank are halted, the stockholders are the first to lose. Even when direct assistance from the FDIC keeps the bank in operation, the stockholders may be completely wiped out or suffer large losses. The desire of stockholders to avoid such losses is one force making for conservative operation of banks.

On the other hand, under the current system of limited liability, stockholders cannot lose more than their initial investment, yet if the bank is extremely successful, all the gains accrue to the stockholders.[2] The opportunity for large rewards, combined with a truncation of potential losses, may lead stockholders to prefer relatively risky firms. The existence of deposit insurance, in fact, may encourage that attitude. Especially during the 1950s, bank stocks were viewed as particularly "safe" investments, and, through a "clientele effect," may have attracted particularly risk-averse stockholders. That is less likely to be the case today in light of the costs that have been imposed on shareholders of Midland Bank and Continental.

The evidence reviewed in the next section provides only tenuous support for the view that stockholders of banks are a significant force for conservative operation. Of course, that result may be attributable to the nature of stockholders' limited liability and the high leverage prevailing in banking. For many years, national bank stockholders were subject to double liability, whereby owners of a bank that failed were required to make an additional payment if necessary to protect creditors. That payment was related to the par value of their stock. Evidence from the 1920s suggests that such payments were partly responsible for holding losses to depositors to a very small amount, despite a large number of bank failures. Although there may be little support today for the idea for reinstituting double liability, consideration of that concept is helpful in emphasizing the fact that the stockholder should be the ultimate party at risk, and the party with the basic responsibility to creditors.

It has long been recognized (see Peltzman, 1970) that the institution of federal deposit insurance has allowed a substitution of deposit insurance for equity capital as a protection for depositors. In analyzing risk in the banking system, capital plays a key role. Although a full discussion of the problem of bank capital is beyond the scope of this project, some aspects of bank capital must be discussed. Increases in bank capital would have several beneficial effects on the soundness of the banking system.

Increased bank capital could eliminate what this report calls the "deposit insurance subsidy"—the fact that flat-rate deposit insurance is underpriced for those institutions that operate in a risky manner. Bank owners with a substantial amount of their own funds at risk will have more incentive to operate conservatively—a market discipline effect. Moreover, in case of mistake, adverse economic conditions, or bad luck, a larger capital cushion protects the deposit insurance fund. Finally, a larger capital cushion lowers the cost of monitoring the real value of capital, so institutions that drift into financial difficulties can be closed when the market value of net worth goes to zero.

The supervisory agencies have taken several steps in recent years to increase bank capital requirements. Recent legislation has given the agencies, for the first time, the authority to specify mandatory capital standards, and they have done so. Primary (equity) capital of the largest banks, which was as low as 4 percent of assets a few years ago, must be raised to 5½ percent and the ratios for other banks will not be permitted to fall below 5½ percent.

There is considerable dispute about the desirability and feasibility of a significant further increase in capital requirements. Bank capital, of course, does not use up physical resources. Additional funds channeled into bank capital are still available to other seekers of funds. This is different from the physical capital of a manufacturing firm—the labor and materials used to build a steel plant are no longer available to anyone else.

If there were no imperfections in capital markets, and no restrictions on bank investments, there would be no social cost to a substantial increase in bank capital requirements. Bank stockholders would provide funds that would be invested at market rates, and rates of return on equity would be unaffected. But with the imperfections in the equity markets and regulations that exist, together with the present tax structure, many observers believe that increased capital requirements would reduce bank returns. In other words, raising additional capital would represent a substantial dilution of existing shareholders' returns.

The role of stockholders is clearly an important one in considering bank risk. But stockholders have a further role. Stockholders are represented by boards of directors, and directors may comprise an additional source of restraint on risk-taking.

Directors

In addition to representing stockholders, and being stockholders themselves, directors have an additional stake in the soundness of their institution. First, their position as directors—which can be both profitable and prestigious—is at stake should the bank fail. This should lead directors to restrain any tendency toward excessive risk-taking by management. Second, directors are personally responsible for the safety of the institution. Allowing excessively risky policies or investments can result in lawsuits against directors. Directors have not always been mindful or aware of their responsibilities in the past, but recent actions by the FDIC and Federal Savings and Loan Insurance Corporation (FSLIC) against directors should increase the efforts of directors in curbing risk-taking. The practice of the Comptroller of the Currency of not giving examination reports to each director personally works against this goal. The directors of Penn Square Bank, for example, testified that one copy of the examination report was given to the bank's president for them to see; they saw the report only at the bank at a rushed meeting of the board of directors.

Management

Management has much at stake when a bank fails. If a bank is closed and liquidated, with a payoff of insured depositors, all bank employees lose their jobs. If a purchase and assumption is arranged by the FDIC, it is unlikely that top management will keep their positions with the succeeding bank. Even if direct assistance from the FDIC keeps the failing bank open and operating, the FDIC usually insists that some top management be replaced.

It is logical to believe that managements concerned with protecting jobs—their own and those of others—will tend to operate the bank in a conservative manner. The extent to which management can be viewed as a source of restraint against risk-taking depends on compensation arrangements and the personal attitude of managers. "Golden parachutes" and liberal pension benefits that survive economic failure of the bank (such as in the case of Continental) can tend to offset such tendencies toward conservatism. If executive salaries are tied to short-run profits, there is some incentive toward risk-taking. Salaries tied to the size of the organization may produce incentives toward growth that may be reflected in riskier-than-normal operations.

The net effect of these conflicting incentives is difficult to assess. It turns on the extent to which the bank is controlled by management, as well as the form of management compensation. Several studies have compared the performance of stock and mutual thrift institutions. The mutuals are generally believed to be controlled by management (they have no stockholders), and the studies have found that mutual thrift institutions tend to be more conservative in their operations than comparable stockholder-owned institutions. This suggests that management can be a force toward conservatism. Again, this can be enhanced by actions of the supervisory agencies to hold managers personally responsible for failures under some circumstances.

Subordinated Debtholders

Holders of subordinated debt are a particularly attractive source of market discipline because, as distinct from depositors, debtholders cannot withdraw their funds on demand when bad news surfaces. As distinct from stockholders, they do not share in the increased profits that may arise from increased risk-taking; therefore, they have every incentive to prefer safe, conservatively managed banks. Unfortunately, the amount of subordinated debt outstanding at the present time is not sufficient to amount to a significant source of market discipline. There are feasible and attractive means to increase market discipline emanating from holders of subordinated debt, particularly short-term subordinated debt. This proposal is described in Section IV of this chapter.

Empirical Evidence on the Working of Market Discipline

Gilbert (1983) reviews the evidence on the extent to which market discipline is exercised in the major markets for bank funds, which include: large certificates of deposit (CDs), interbank deposits and federal funds, and equity and subordinated debt.[3] Gilbert's emphasis is on: (1) the amount of funds raised in each market as an indicator of the extent to which banks of different sizes are exposed to discipline, (2) the efficiency of the market in reacting to changes in firm-specific risk, and (3) the responsiveness of institutions to market signals that undesired changes in risk have occurred. The evidence on market discipline arising from each of these funding sources is discussed below.

Large Certificates of Deposit

Available data on the distribution of funds raised in CD markets indicate that such funds are more significant for large than for small banks. About 70 percent of total uninsured deposits are in banks larger than $1 billion. This represents a much larger proportion of total deposits for these institutions than for smaller banks, and suggests that discipline exercised in the CD markets is likely to be more important and effective for large than for small banks.

FDIC surveys of large depositors of failed banks during the 1970s do not support the idea that CD customers are concerned about risk when they place their funds. Convenience and availability of service and credit seem to be a more important determinant than risk in affecting where corporate treasurers placed funds. The lack of concern for risk, however, is consistent with the view of the respondents that the government would step in and bail out any large, troubled institution. Thus, corporate treasurers acted as if they were purchasing riskless securities.

A different conclusion emerged from interviews with institutional investors. They were much more concerned with the risk of issuing banks, and more sophisticated than corporate treasurers in their analyses of bank risk. Discussions conducted in connection with this Report of officials of both a large Midwest and a New York money center bank confirm that there seems to be a tiering in these markets. It was asserted that institutional investors with fiduciary responsibility were the first to withdraw funds at the hint of financial difficulties. Overall, the interviews indicated that there was a segmentation in the CD market with respect to its potential for exercising market discipline, with institutional investors being the most concerned about risk exposure.

Some empirical support for the responsiveness of the CD market to differences in perceived risk appeared after the failure of Franklin National Bank. A tiering in the pricing of CDs developed, and about a 25-basis-point-higher spread was required from regional banks over money center banks. This pricing differential, however, was related more to size than to risk. Crane (1976) found a similar preference for placing funds in larger banks during the latter half of 1974. Rates were inversely related to size, and there was little evidence to suggest that rates were affected by risk or financial condition of the issuer, where several different factors were included to capture different dimensions of risk.

Again, because the government handled the Franklin National problem by keeping the discount window open, which gave the uninsured depositors the option to withdraw their funds, the pricing behavior and Crane's results might be expected. Large depositors may simply have concluded that the Federal Reserve would not let large banks that failed be paid out—thus the preference for size.

The FDIC's payout of Penn Square, however, came as a surprise to the market. One likely consequence might have been to decrease the market's perception of the advantage of size, and to refocus attention on risk. Although Penn Square was the largest bank to be paid out, it was still substantially smaller than the major money center banks. Thus, Penn Square might only change the perception of what are large and small banks, rather than change the market's basic assumption that the large money center banks would not be permitted to fail and lead to losses to large depositors. The FDIC's analysis of spreads on CDs over Treasury bills following the Penn Square failure, however, failed to reveal a tiering in the market similar to that following the failure of Franklin National.

In the case of Continental, a 100-basis-point penalty was imposed on the bank for four months following the failure. Moreover, there was some evidence that uninsured deposits were reduced. It might be argued that 100 basis points is not a large spread, given the potential risk exposure, but when compared with net interest margins of major banks, 100 basis points is a significant penalty. Furthermore, the potential spread may have been much larger. Interviews with funding officers suggest that when an institution begins to experience funding problems, it attempts to limit the visible spread that appears in the market. The institution will keep borrowing as long as the spread remains within a narrow range. If the range diverges beyond self-imposed limits, the institution becomes concerned that an adverse signal will be sent to the market, and it responds by shifting funding to other markets with less visible rates, or it begins to contract in size as loans are allowed to run off. The implication is that the visible spread would have been much larger if the institution attempted to borrow in quantities as large as those borrowed before the problems appeared.

Interbank and Other Money Markets

Strover and Miller (1983) studied the response of commercial paper, federal funds, and bankers' acceptance markets around the time that Franklin National began to experience substantial difficulties. Using the spread between the rates in these markets and the Treasury bill rate as a risk proxy, they observed that Franklin's failure appeared to have been anticipated. The risk premiums did widen. However, they did not persist for very long. The authors do not reveal the size of the premiums nor do they attempt to relate the premiums to expected losses. With respect to the pattern of the individual rates, the Fed funds rate did not peak until the failure occurred. Rates in all three markets (federal fund, commercial paper, and bankers' acceptance) declined shortly thereafter. The authors concluded that the short-term money markets did react to the announcement of adverse information about Franklin National, but that reaction did not persist following the failure and subsequent sale to European American.

The subsequent failures of Herstatt and Banco Ambrosiano, and the recurring credit-quality problems in less developed countries, have resulted in a similar divergence of rates in the Eurodollar and interbank Eurodeposit markets. As a result, Gilbert (1983) suggests that these markets might be a source of market discipline for the multinational banks that rely on them for funding. He also argues, however, that these markets are inefficient because they tend to allocate funds by rationing the supply of funds to individual banks rather than on the basis of changes in price.[4,5]

Gilbert also suggests that these markets are unable to distinguish between systematic and firm-specific risk. These problems, and problems in interpreting accounting information across countries, result in market tiering based on whether the bank is private or public, on the availability of government support, and on country-risk considerations.

Equity and Debt Markets

Several studies have investigated the responsiveness of the debt and equity markets to differences in risk.[6] One group of studies focuses on required returns when a financial institution has relatively greater leverage (a lower capital), higher loan loss experience, or other indications of higher risk than its peers. In general, the results indicate both that debt and equity markets do require higher returns in such instances, and that these markets are also reasonably efficient in identifying problem situations well in advance.[7]

The second group of studies examines market response in specific instances where adverse information is released. Here, the evidence is mixed. For example, Johnson and Weber (1977), using an event study methodology, looked at the market reaction to the release of the bank regulatory agencies problem bank lists in the mid 1970s. The authors found no significant negative market reaction, suggesting that the lists did not contain new information not already considered by the market.

On the other hand, studying the same event but using less standard methods and more narrowly defined controls, Murphy (1979) found a significant negative reaction. It should be noted that information on loan quality was not publicly available. This was likely the principal information contained in the disclosure of the problem bank information, and it is known that the volume of classified assets is a critical determinant of examiner ratings. Since those studies, extensive additional information on both asset quality and interest rate exposure has been made available to the markets. So, even if Murphy's conclusions were correct, a similar study today might be less likely to discover abnormal returns in response to such disclosures.

Contrary to Gilbert's characterization of the operation of foreign money markets, the studies of debt and equity market efficiency imply a certain selectivity in processing information, and they imply that investors can distinguish between firm-specific and systematic risk. For example, there was little evidence from either the events surrounding the Franklin National failure or from the disclosure of the problem bank lists that investors revised upward their views of the riskiness of other banks because of the problems that were exposed in a few.[8]

Responsiveness of Banks to Market Discipline

There is now a fair body of evidence showing that markets do recognize and impose higher debt and equity costs on more risky institutions. The studies of capital market efficiency indicate that problems are identified and signals sent as long as a year before failure. The public policy case for increase reliance on market discipline to control risk-taking, however, also requires a demonstration that these signals are recognized and reacted to by bank managers. Unfortunately, there is little evidence on exactly how institutions respond— either in terms of portfolio allocation or in risk preferences—to a repricing of their securities by the markets. The only such study is by Gendreau and Humphrey (1980). They tested whether the market penalizes increased leverage by requiring higher returns on debt and equity, and whether institutions respond to such a signal by reducing leverage. They also examined whether the market regulated both the absolute risk of the industry and relative bank risk within the industry.

Examining the period between 1970 and 1975, they found that the market did constrain the average leverage position of the largest banks, but they could not find support for the hypothesis that the market exerted relatively more influence on the more risky banks compared with the less risky banks in their large-bank sample. It is possible, for example, that one reason Gendreau and Humphrey did not find evidence that the market effectively distinguished between relatively more and less risky banks was because of the deposit insurance subsidy and the system of implicit guarantees that were in place. Furthermore, there were few significant bank failures until 1973–1974.

Further work needs to be done on this important issue, perhaps by studying the relationship between changes in market risk premiums and portfolio changes of banks that remained going concerns. Additionally, one could look at the relationship between serious problem banks that were later taken off the problem bank list and portfolio changes in relation to changes in the market value of the firm. Finally, the results of the Gendreau and Humphrey studies should be updated to look at more recent periods.

Conclusions and Limitations in Interpreting the Research

Existing research suggests four important observations and conclusions about the potential for market discipline as an effective tool to control bank risk-taking.

1. Equity and debt markets appear to be more efficient at evaluating risk and better able to separate systematic and firm-specific risk than are the short-term money markets.

2. By virtue of maturity and higher transaction costs, equity and longer-term debt markets are less subject to rumor and flights of funds than are the short-term purchased money markets.

3. Access to debt and equity markets is essentially limited to large money center and regional banks. These markets operate reasonably efficiently, but for only about 1 percent of the nation's institutions (albeit, this would cover about 75 percent of the banking resources in the nation). While over-the-counter markets exist as well and presumably provide a source of market discipline for the issues of less frequently traded firms, the potential for market discipline is not uniform across the banking system. Other institutional, structural, or regulatory changes are needed if market discipline from this source is to play an important role in controlling the risk exposure of smaller banks.

4. Finally, there is little evidence on the most important issue for policy purposes, and that is, the responsiveness of portfolio behavior and risk-taking to market signals that an institution is too risky.

There are also several important caveats to these observations. The empirical evidence on market behavior may have been affected both by creditors' belief that the federal government would prevent losses by uninsured creditors as institutions failed, and by the deposit insurance subsidy. Certainly, it was widely argued, over most of the period covered by the research studies, that at least the largest institutions were *de facto* 100 percent insured. This might explain the lack of concern by short-term uinsured depositors about risk. The payout of Penn Square might have served to change the public's perception, but the FDIC's actions were the result of concern about undisclosed losses and could be interpreted as being consistent with longstanding policies in purchase and assumption cases. Furthermore, the subsequent resolution of the Continental problem confirmed that uninsured creditors would be protected if a major money center bank failed.

The efficiency of markets, especially short-term money markets, improved over the period of the 1970–1980s because of the significant expansion of information available. For example, it was not until 1971 that the Reports of Income on individual banks were released to the public. In this regard, proposals to increase and improve further disclosure can have important beneficial effects. Additionally, the growth of importance of money brokerage activity in insured amounts would serve to limit observed risk premiums on uninsured deposits; the most risky institutions would not need to offer significantly greater rates than the safest firms if insured deposits could be substituted for uninsured deposits.

Finally, there is a fundamental statistical problem with much of the empirical work. The work of Gendreau and Humphrey indicates that most tests of the effect of leverage on required returns implicitly assume only one-way causation, and ignore the feedback effects that higher returns have on desired leverage. Consequently, much of the existing work is suspect. Hence, a simultaneous equation framework would seem to be the preferred methodology.

Means to Increase Market Discipline

The research suggests that the sources of market discipline may not be strong enough now to allow a significant reduction of direct supervision by the insurance agencies without exposing the insurance system to an unacceptable degree of risk. The remainder of this chapter examines a number of options for reaching the desirable goal of increasing market discipline.

Under present arrangements, the restraint on risk-taking by owners and management is rather limited. However, a number of observers have suggested increasing personal liability for directors and management of failed banks in order to discourage risk-taking from these sources. For example, Mayer (1965) proposed that bankers involved in bank failures be barred from working for other banks for a period of time.

An equally revolutionary (or reactionary) option would be a return to double liability on bank stocks. Not only was double liability a factor in keeping depositors' losses low, but the exposure to double liability apparently led stockholders to prefer well-capitalized institutions, providing a market force toward higher capital. The FDIC took a related approach to the failure of Continental Illinois, requiring contributions of additional capital from stockholders of the failed institution who wanted a chance to participate in a recovery of the new Continental.

Changing Insurance Coverage

More likely approaches to market discipline involve some change in the nature or extent of existing deposit-insurance coverage. Options include reducing the amount of coverage to less than $100,000 per account, requiring co-insurance, and limiting deposit insurance to transaction accounts.

The current $100,000 insurance coverage provides virtually 100 percent coverage to all but large corporate accounts. The depositor with $1 million can divide it among 10 or more banks. There are transaction costs and some inconvenience involved in such an arrangement, but those costs may be lower than the costs of analyzing the financial condition of a bank in which an uninsured deposit is to be made. That is probably not feasible for multimillion-dollar accounts, and is unlikely to be convenient for checking accounts.

The transaction costs involved in splitting funds are often reduced by the use of money brokers, who have the capability of dividing large amounts of funds into a number of insured accounts. The money brokers' transaction costs are low enough that even a significant reduction in the amount of insurance coverage is unlikely to increase the volume of uninsured deposits. Reducing legal insurance limits to $50,000, or even less, for example, would still provide the money brokers with the ability to divide deposits into fully insured amounts (although it might limit the total amount of funds that brokers could deliver to weak institutions). Reducing the insurance coverage might even benefit the brokers, by increasing the demand for their services.

Some observers believe that a change in insurance coverage would probably be effective in increasing market discipline from uninsured depositors, especially in the absence of risk-related premiums, only if the change were accompanied by restrictions on the operations of deposit brokers. The FDIC and the FSLIC have attempted to restrict or eliminate the deposit brokers in order to impede the flow of funds to risky institutions. The agencies would like to treat all funds brought to a bank by a broker as a single deposit, subject to the $100,000 insurance limit. If the agencies succeeded, the deposit insurance coverage were significantly reduced, then a substantial proportion of deposits might become uninsured. Market discipline emanating from uninsured depositors might then become significant, provided *de facto* 100 percent coverage were not provided by the FDIC in resolving failures.

Elimination of money brokers would not achieve this objective, however. Institutions could still seek large amounts of insured deposits by using their own employees to solicit out-of-area funds and placing advertisements in major newspapers, as is currently done. Furthermore, brokers play a useful social function in reducing transaction costs and, ideally, in channeling funds to where they are most needed (i.e., earn the highest return).

Requiring Coinsurance An alternative means of increasing depositors' sensitivity to risk is by subjecting insured depositors to modest losses in cases of failure. The depositor with under $100,000 would be assured of receiving only 95 or 97 cents on the dollar. This coinsurance would be analogous to provisions in medical insurance policies requiring that the insured bear some of the cost so that he will avoid unnecessary procedures and charges. It is difficult to believe that depositors would become more sensitive to the riskiness of their banks, or would be more willing to make the effort to distinguish safe banks from risky banks, when only a small percentage of their funds were at risk. If the coinsurance were significantly larger (say, 20 percent), however, such a system might lead to deposit instability and runs when bad news was revealed.

Even if the volume of uninsured deposits in the system were significantly increased, it is not clear that effective and beneficial market discipline would increase. An increase in market discipline would depend on two additional factors: First, uninsured depositors would have to feel that they were at risk; and, second, they would have to have the means of distinguishing between sound and unsound banks.

The FDIC has handled most bank failures, particularly those involving large banks, by arranging assistance or purchase-and-assumption (P&A) transactions that have protected all depositors. If uninsured depositors believed that pattern would continue, then a reduction in the $100,000 insurance ceiling would have little effect on their choice of banks and might even be perverse. Furthermore, even if uninsured depositors believed that they were at risk, market discipline would serve a useful role only if these depositors had the ability to determine which banks warranted confidence. If uninsured depositors could make such determinations, banks would compete for uninsured deposits by operating in a sound manner. If the depositors could not determine bank soundness, their effects on market discipline would be, at best, random and nonproductive. At worst, depositors might simply restrict themselves to the largest banks on the ground that such banks would be less likely to be allowed to fail. The result would be an increase in concentration of financial power and a reduction of competition in banking markets. This issue is related to the quality and quantity of information available.

It is hard to predict how a larger role for uninsured depositors would affect the stability of a banking system, although experience in a much earlier period suggests the system would be stable. Perhaps with more uninsured depositors, the chances would increase for runs on banks in financial difficulty. But if a bank were solvent, it should be able to stay in operation by using the Federal Reserve discount window or by obtaining a direct loan from the FDIC. (If the bank were insolvent, of course, it should be closed or assisted, and the run would probably not increase the ultimate loss.)

The recent difficulties of Ohio and Maryland savings and loan associations that were not insured by the FSLIC illustrate how uninsured depositors may be expected to act. In those states, runs on weak institutions led to runs on other non-federally insured thrifts, but it is not clear at this point whether any economically solvent institutions were endangered by such runs.

Limiting Coverage to Transaction Accounts Reducing insurance coverage increases market discipline, in part, by increasing the risk of runs. This results because a large proportion of uninsured depositors can withdraw their funds at the first indication of trouble. One way to reduce the likelihood of runs would be to insure all demand (transaction) deposits and to leave time deposits uninsured. When bad news is revealed, demand depositors would have no incentive to run, and time depositors would not have the option of withdrawing their funds immediately.

There are public policy justifications for limiting deposit insurance coverage to transaction accounts. There are benefits to the general public (externalities, in economic jargon) when everyone uses checking accounts. But many people would be less willing to use bank deposits in the absence of insurance. Government insurance of transaction accounts can be justified on the ground of governmental responsibility for protecting the integrity of the monetary system. There is less justification for insuring wealth in the form of time deposits, because even consumers of modest means have access to safe investment outlets (government securities, for example).

Some fear that 100 percent deposit insurance would increase the vulnerability of the system to fraud. If 100 percent insurance were combined with an end to interest-rate controls on demand deposits, the banker who was intent on fraud could raise large amounts of funds rapidly. Benston (1984) has argued that 100 percent insurance, therefore, would require some interest rate ceiling. Such controls would be less intrusive if 100 percent insurance and the ceilings were limited to transaction accounts. Because there are substantial costs involved in servicing transaction accounts, a ceiling tied to the Treasury bill rate would be unlikely to affect legitimate operations. The difficulty of specifying a meaningful ceiling on time deposits without unduly restricting operations would be another reason to avoid 100 percent insurance of time deposits.

Limiting deposit insurance to transaction accounts would probably have been more workable when such deposits were non-interest-earning. Now that interest is paid on negotiable orders of withdrawal (NOW), money market deposit accounts (MMDA), and Super-NOW accounts, those seeking deposit insurance can continue to earn interest on funds held in transaction accounts. The result of eliminating insurance on time deposits might simply be the elimination of longer-maturity time deposits, at least for all but the soundest banks. This would be a form of market discipline, in that sound banks would be able to obtain time deposits at lower cost than weaker banks. But the shortening of the maturity of liabilities for most banks would not generally be viewed as a desirable change. Furthermore, such a change might be ineffective if banks were allowed to buy CDs back from the holders (perhaps through merchant bank subsidiaries abroad).

Private Insurance

Increased market discipline coming from uninsured depositors might be only a marginal improvement over the present system. Market discipline, in a somewhat different form, could come from private insurers of deposits. Private insurance companies would not insure all comers at a uniform rate. Insurance would be available only to banks that met the insurers' standards, or would be available to other banks only at higher premiums. Premiums set by this market system (because insurance companies would compete for business, premiums would reflect a market assessment of relative riskiness), would be a form of discipline, in that riskier institutions would face the penalty of higher insurance premiums.

The principal reason private insurance probably could not replace federal insurance is that it is hard to imagine a private system having the necessary credibility to assure stability. The question of who would insure the insurers is an important one. Credibility would not be a problem if a federal guarantee backed up the private insurance system, but it is difficult to see what advantage that arrangement would have over direct federal deposit insurance. Either risky banks or risky private insurance companies would be receiving a subsidy for risk-taking, which is much like what exists under the present system.

The experience of the troubled savings and loan associations in Ohio and Maryland has generated useful information on the operation of private deposit insurance under pressure. The insurance systems in those states had neither federal nor state guarantees although the systems were, in some sense, state-sponsored, and many depositors believed that the states had financial responsibilities. In the absence of such guarantees, the financial difficulties of an individual institution can generate doubts as to the soundness of the insurance system (even if, in fact, the insurance system is sound).

An interesting proposal for private deposit insurance involves a system of cross-guarantees of bank liabilities by other banks. Ely (1984, 1985) has developed a system under which all banks would be required to obtain the guarantees of other banks to support all deposits. Other proposals would call for a bank's CDs to be backed by the letter of credit of another bank, just as many issues of commercial paper are now.

The principal rationale for such systems is that bankers should be knowledgeable about the riskiness of other banks and should be able to make what is essentially a credit judgment. Banks often (but not always) make such judgments in establishing correspondent relationships and in setting federal funds lines. Because the charge would presumably vary with the risk, a form of market discipline would be created.

The principal disadvantage, of course, is that cross-guarantees do not bring any new capital or backing for bank liabilities into the system. Cross-guarantees would be similar in that respect to the guaranty systems in use in most states to cover the failures of casualty insurance companies on an *ex post* basis, whereby surviving firms chip in to cover the losses to customers of the failed firm. Some view such a system as dangerously increasing the interconnections among banks so that isolated failures might lead to systemic problems. That is, the failure of a single bank might cause the failure of the banks that guaranteed the first bank's deposits.

The basis for the cross-guarantee system is the view that the current aggregate level of capital in the banking system is more than adequate to protect bank creditors. Individual banks might be subject to risks that could swamp their capital, but, in Ely's view, the solution would be simply to harness the existing capital of the system to support the obligations of the failing institution. Those observers who agree with this report that the aggregate level of bank capital is inadequate (which is especially relevant to the current situation for S&Ls) do not find the Ely proposal attractive.

Subordinated Debt

There is a final potential source of market discipline, which could avoid the problems of the other proposals. This proposal would involve a much increased role for subordinated debt in the capital structure of insured banks. The use of subordinated debt by banks has grown considerably over the past 20 years, but the traditional supervisory approach has been to view debt capital as less desirable than equity. This view neglects the important characteristics of subordinated debt with respect to market discipline.

Holders of capital notes can be put at risk in the case of a bank failure even with a purchase and assumption. Because of their subordinated position, they are at greater risk in a failure than are uninsured depositors or the FDIC. More important, because holders of capital notes do not share in any increased profits that result from high-risk operations, they have no incentive to invest in risky institutions (as common stockholders might).

In choosing among available issues of subordinated notes, investors buy riskier issues only at a significantly higher interest rates. The higher interest cost represents a market discipline on risky institutions. Moreover, noteholders can be expected to insist on covenants in their indentures that restrict the ability of the banks to engage in risky activities. Such restrictions could play a more important role in the future if governmental regulation were reduced. Finally, like stockholders, holders of subordinated debt cannot contribute to a run by pulling out their funds prior to maturity.

Market discipline from subordinated creditors is not important now because debt capital is a relatively small source of funds for banks, and banks engaged in risky activities can simply avoid selling such securities. But banks could be required to maintain relatively short-term subordinated debt at a significant level (or as a certain proportion of equity).

Although the supervisory agencies have traditionally preferred that debt capital have a long maturity (so that the required retirement is far off), market discipline would be enhanced by a short maturity that forced the bank into the market on a frequent basis. (Even greater market pressure could be obtained if a small percentage of the issue could be redeemed at the option of the holder.)

Subordinated debt fits well with the proper functioning of a deposit insurance system for other reasons. For example, subordinated debt could help the FDIC close a bank promptly when its net worth approaches zero. It is, of course, difficult to determine the precise moment at which net worth becomes zero, so failing banks generally continue to suffer losses before they are finally closed. Moreover, when equity is small, the insurance agency must expend more effort and resources on timely monitoring to determine when institutions become insolvent.

Subordinated debt could provide the ideal cushion between losses to stockholders and losses to the FDIC. Consider the bank whose net worth declined to 1 percent of assets. The bank would still be solvent, and its principal supervisor would be likely to be reluctant to close the bank (in fact, he might not have the legal authority to do so). If this bank had subordinated debt equal to, say, 4 percent of assets, its net worth could be allowed to decline below zero. At that point, the bank would be insolvent and could be closed. Even if its losses had brought net worth to, say, a negative 2 percent or 3 percent of assets, the loss would be borne entirely by the holders of the subordinated debt (and the stockholders), and the FDIC would suffer no loss at all. Subordinated debt could thus provide the ideal margin of error for determination of when a bank should be closed. The buyers of the subordinated debt would probably have imposed covenants that would give them some rights to close or take over the bank under such circumstances. Private regulation could take over some of the role of governmental regulation.

If all insured banks were required to have subordinated notes equal to, say 3 to 5 percent of deposits, the need to meet the market could have a significant effect in influencing decisions. For banks, of course, a capital requirement that could be met with debt would be less onerous than an equity requirement because of the tax deductibility of interest payments. This approach has been endorsed by the FDIC and by the Administration's Cabinet Council on Economic Affairs. There are, however, some uncertainties about its workability.

Some analysts and investment bankers question whether the market could absorb the very large increase in the volume of bank capital notes that would result from such a requirement. They fear that rates would become prohibitively high. In order to best protect the FDIC, the notes would have to allow for wide discretion by the FDIC in arranging purchases and assumptions in cases of insolvency, without the need for approval by the holders of the notes. This would make the notes less attractive than those currently issued, which include various provisions to protect noteholders in case of insolvency. Holders of subordinated notes have, in fact, come out virtually as well as insured deposits in most P&A transactions and most cases of direct FDIC assistance. Capital notes without such protection might, indeed, require interest rates significantly above those now observed.

This matter of designing an instrument with appropriate protective covenants is an important one that must be resolved successfully if a subordinated debt requirement is to play a useful role in encouraging market discipline. For the most part, the interests of investors and the interests of the FDIC with respect to protective covenants coincide. Both would want to restrict such things as risk-taking and excessive leverage. Their interests might diverge, however, if the FDIC sought to protect itself by taking action that might be inimical to the interests of noteholders. That would be most likely to occur when the condition of a bank was such that liquidation or restructuring could be expected to result in total or near-total loss to the noteholders. It should be possible, however, to construct language that would prevent the noteholders from tying the hands of the FDIC, without severely weakening the marketability of the notes.

Other analysts fear that, although large banks might be able to sell subordinated notes in sufficient volume, small banks might be unable to do so. Small banks clearly would not be able to tap the national financial markets, but they might be able to sell capital notes over the counter to customers or locally by other means.

A more difficult problem might arise for medium-sized banks—those too large to sell sufficient capital notes locally, but not large enough to have access to the national markets. Useful modifications to consider would be to invoke the requirement only for banks above a certain size; only when capital ratios fell below a certain proportion of assets; or on a permissive basis for smaller institutions.

Although some observers doubt the ability of the financial markets to absorb a large additional volume of bank securities, such issues would not represent a net absorption of funds from the market, because whatever funds banks raised would be available for bank investment. If other banks were allowed (or required) to invest in the issues, the demand for funds would create its own supply. Such a system, in fact, would be very similar to Ely's cross-guarantee insurance system.

In any case, these questions about the ability of the securities markets to absorb a large volume of new issues of bank subordinated debt, and the accessibility of the market to smaller institutions, deserve additional research. The advantages of greater use of subordinated debt, both as a protection to the insurance system and as a source of market discipline, seem convincing. Effort should be made to determine whether there would be practical difficulties in making greater use of this instrument.

The Role of Disclosure

The availability of information concerning the operation of financial institutions influences the effectiveness of market discipline, and the costs and benefits of increased disclosure differ depending on the importance and form of market discipline. Insured depositors have no need for financial disclosure.

Depository institutions historically have been treated differently from other corporations with respect to legal requirements for disclosure of financial information. One of the first forms of financial regulation enacted in several states was a requirement that banks publish periodically a Report of Condition. This was intended as a form of market discipline, in that depositors or noteholders (whose bank liabilities were not government-insured) would be provided with information useful in making informed judgments as to the soundness of individual banks.

As regulation and supervision of banks developed in the United States, particularly after the advent of deposit insurance, the role of disclosure declined. Traditionally, supervisory officials (and bankers) believed that they could more easily deal with problems in the absence of publicity. There is no doubt that secrecy has enabled the supervisors to work out a number of problems in a manner that avoided loss to the public—problems that could have resulted in bank failures had depositors been aware of the problems.

Despite this benefit, it is doubtful that the public has been well served over time by the supervisory penchant for secrecy. It would be unrealistic to assume that with greater disclosure all market reactions would be correct, with depositors withdrawing funds only from institutions that would inevitably fail, but leaving funds in those that could be saved. The real question is whether, in the long run, market discipline fortified with good information could be more effective in reducing failures by restraining excessive risk-taking than are the efforts of the supervisors in handling secretly the problems of which they become aware. The costs of depositors' mistakes—withdrawing funds from sound banks on the appearance of bad news—are relatively small. The Federal Reserve can lend on good collateral and prevent the dumping of assets at fire-sale prices. And such mistakes might be less likely with good disclosure than without it.

The supervisor's historical preference for secrecy was bolstered by the introduction of deposit insurance. From the point of view of insured depositors, disclosure is irrelevant. The choice among institutions is not influenced by financial information, because the depositors are relying on deposit insurance. Uninsured depositors might have an interest in being informed, but as long as failures are handled through means that protect all depositors, they have no need for information. It is necessary to analyze separately the effect of increased disclosure on insured depositors, other creditors, and stockholders.

Disclosure and Insured Depositors

Additional disclosure is not necessary to be helpful in protecting insured depositors, but the converse of that conclusion is also important: If all depositors were insured, disclosure would not be destabilizing. That is, the principal reason for restricting disclosure is concern that the release of adverse information would lead to runs, and the runs would preclude, or make more difficult, actions that might save the troubled institutions. If all depositors were insured, such a run would not develop. One benefit of 100 percent deposit insurance would be to make clear that banks could be treated exactly like other firms in setting disclosure requirements. It must be emphasized that in banking, as distinct from other industries, many regulations have restricted the ability of the firms to make disclosures on a voluntary basis. Many of those who oppose additional disclosure requirements, or who believe they would be ineffective, support removal of existing restrictions on disclosure.

Disclosure and Uninsured Creditors

If the FDIC followed a consistent policy of arranging mergers of failing institutions with healthy ones, then disclosure would not be helpful, and might be harmful, to uninsured creditors. If disclosure led to a run, there might not be sufficient time to work out a purchase and assumption. Hence, the uninsured creditors might be better off if adverse information were not revealed.

But this analysis ignores the potential benefits of market discipline. Market discipline from uninsured depositors could only be effective if some depositors believed that they were at risk, and if they considered risk in choosing among institutions. They would be able to make helpful choices (i.e., choices that provided incentives for banks to operate in a conservative manner) only if they had sufficient information.

There is reason to believe that accurate disclosure of risk would tend to discourage risk-taking. Assume that a bank was controlled by a group that preferred a riskier posture than the majority of competing institutions. A riskier portfolio should lead to proportionally higher expected returns. If that portfolio had to be financed with uninsured deposits, the bank would have to offer uninsured depositors expected returns that were more than proportional to the increased risk, because most uninsured depositors would presumably be averse to risk. The excess return promised to the uninsured depositors would absorb the excess returns expected from the riskier-than-normal portfolio, and hence there would be little incentive to operate in a riskier-than-normal manner.

Because good information would be necessary for this effective market discipline, it would be reasonable to regard disclosure as promoting stability in the overall financial system. These considerations suggest that the conservatively run firm would have an incentive to disclose evidence of that. Some argue that these incentives would be strong enough to assure adequate disclosure even in the absence of disclosure requirements. They would argue, of course, that regulatory restrictions on disclosure should be removed. (See Benston, 1984).

Disclosure would have a different effect in individual cases. Once an investment decision turned out badly, disclosure of that outcome could have a destabilizing effect as uninsured depositors withdrew funds in fear of failure. In this situation, disclosure could increase losses. Of course, the fear of such an outcome would affect a bank's decision to make risky investments.

In the absence of thorough disclosure, market participants would still make judgments. Because the judgments would be based on less than full information, they would be less useful in constraining risk-taking. In the absence of information, depositors might have a preference for very large institutions (and thus sound banks would have an incentive to disclose).

Although disclosure could contribute to market discipline in conjunction with uninsured depositors being at risk, disclosure would not contribute if there were no creditors who believed themselves to be at risk. If uninsured depositors believed that they would be protected by a P&A in case of failure, market discipline would not be effective, and disclosure would not contribute towards it. However, in such cases disclosure could do no harm (though it might be costly), so there would be little reason to treat depository institutions differently from other businesses.

Disclosure and Stockholders

Information is most important to stockholders. Stockholders make choices among alternative investments based on their assessments of expected returns and risks. From the point of view of effective market discipline, market prices should reflect the true risk-return position of the institution. If two banks had equal earnings, but one were viewed as riskier, the riskier stock would sell at a lower price, because the typical investor is believed to be averse to risk. This would tend to pressure those in control to adopt a conservative operating philosophy. But this force could be effective only if market prices reflected full and accurate information. The evidence suggests that this is now the case.

Disclosure of adverse information to equity holders of a bank with no uninsured depositors could have no destabilizing effects on the institution. Stockholders might sell their stock, and the stock price might decline, but this would not affect the finances of the bank itself. This supports the argument that if there were no uninsured depositors, banks should be subject to the disclosure rules that apply to corporations generally. In fact, it could be argued that banks should be subject to a stricter requirement for disclosure because the disclosure might provide a public benefit in reducing incentives toward excessive risk-taking. Disclosure decisions by other corporations are based on the best interests of stockholders (taking account, of course, of the effect of disclosure on providers of funds). In dealing with insured banks, however, one might seek disclosure that would tend to restrain risk-taking that goes beyond the desires of stockholders.

Information to Be Disclosed

Although a detailed analysis of the information that should be disclosed by banks is beyond the scope of this report, there are some specifics that should be addressed in terms of the effectiveness of market discipline. The basic principle is that financial information useful for evaluating the true economic condition of the banks must be available.

Market discipline is advanced as an alternative (or complement) to supervision as a means of inhibiting risk-taking by banks. It appears reasonable, in that context, to argue that whatever information the supervisory agency finds necessary for performing its function would be equally relevant to market participants, and should therefore be disclosed. There are two issues involved here. First, one reason for nondisclosure is that providing information is costly. This consideration makes one reluctant to seek additional disclosure. But if information must be provided to the supervisors, the additional costs of making it available to the public are minimal. Second, much information generated in the supervisory process is treated as confidential and the bank is prohibited from disclosing it. This is generally true of the examination report, for example.

Some specifics are fairly easy to deal with in this context, whereas others are controversial. For example, although information on the volume of past-due and nonperforming loans obviously should be disclosed, it is less clear whether data on loans classified by examiners should be made public. These two types of data can be distinguished by the fact that the former is objective, while the latter relies on subjective judgments by examiners. A similar issue concerns disclosure of the supervisory agency's summary "CAMEL" rating of the bank. This report is not prepared to recommend that this information be routinely published, but it would not prohibit any bank that chooses to do so from disclosing this information.

An easier judgment concerns the disclosure of legal actions taken by supervisory agencies against institutions (the FDIC has recently begun to disclose such actions) or of agreements between the agencies and institutions. The market-discipline rationale for such disclosure was summarized in a 1982 statement by Comptroller of the Currency C.T. Conover: "If you knew that information about problems would be disclosed, maybe you would act to avoid them."

Conclusions

With respect to uninsured depositors and creditors, disclosure and market discipline are two-edged swords. When effective, market discipline might cut the tendency of those controlling institutions to engage in excessively risky operations. But disclosure of adverse information could lead to runs or deposit outflows that might worsen the problem. As long as such runs were not permitted to spread to the system, however, they could serve as important deterrents to excessive risk-taking by other banks.

On balance, market discipline could be useful in constraining risk. Some information would be necessary to make market discipline effective. Some would favor additional disclosure requirements; others believe that incentives already exist for banks to make appropriate disclosures.

One approach that would be consistent with this analysis would be to adopt a policy of 100 percent deposit insurance coverage. This would allow market discipline to operate through stockholders, management, and subordinated creditors. An increased capital requirement in the form of subordinated debt could provide the vehicle for greatly increased market discipline and could also provide a substantial cushion for the FDIC. A higher capital requirement would reduce the deposit-insurance subsidy that is the principal structural flaw in the present system. If this left institutions with a tendency toward risk-taking beyond what was considered socially optimal, risk-taking could be discouraged by regulation and supervision, as at present, or through a system of risk-related insurance premiums. This policy would minimize the danger of runs, provide full protection to the public, and allow the insurance agency to adopt optimal procedures for handling failures when they occur.

---

[1]Benston (1984) argues that any benefits from having certain proportions of deposits uninsured will be lost if in fact the regulators act to prevent these depositors from experiencing losses.

[2]See Black and Scholes (1973), Jensen and Meckling (1976), and Galai and Masulis (1976) for discussions of the role of limited liability and the incentives it creates for increased leverage.

[3]This section draws heavily on a recent survey by Gilbert (1983).

[4]Again, conversations with funding officers of major money center banks tend to confirm these conclusions, but with very important distinctions. When troubled firms initially experience funding difficulties, they begin to turn abroad because the foreign markets tend to be somewhat less informed than domestic markets. Moreover, funding officers tend to operate on self-imposed quantity limits based on infrequent risk evaluations, rather than on the basis of price. If it becomes noticed, however, that an institution has begun to shift funding to foreign sources, this becomes a signal that all may not be well. Thus, too great a reliance on foreign sources, especially if the proceeds are used to fund domestic operations, becomes a negative signal to the market.

[5]The same interviews with funding officers suggest that their own decisions to place funds operate on a quantity basis. They establish funding limits for individual institutions. Also, if traders pick up rumors of potential difficulties within a particular institution, they simply make no more funds available until the rumors can be checked out. The result may be a drying up of funding for particular institutions for two or three days. In such circumstance, access to temporary sources of liquidity become critical in affecting potential ability to weather an adverse market reaction. Continental, in the end, had used up its backup liquidity sources, whereas Manufacturers Hanover was able to survive because it had ample temporary funding sources.

[6]See for example, Peighley (1977), Jacobs, Beighley, and Boyd, (1975), Beighley, Boyd, and Jacobs (1975), Fraser and McCormack (1978), Herzig-Marx (1977), Murphy (1979), Pettway (1980, 1976a, 1976b), Pettway and Sinkey (1980), and Shick (1978).

[7]A few studies, notably Pettway (1976b), failed to find a significant relationship.

[8]See Pettway (1976a), Fraser and McCormack (1978), and Murphy (1979).

CHAPTER 8

Market-Value Reporting

Accountants and economists both view the market value of a firm as the capitalized value of the firm's uncertain future profits. However, mainstream practitioners of the two professions disagree sharply in their approach to measuring profitability and to selecting an appropriate discount rate. Whereas the concepts implemented by contemporary accountants emphasize historical costs of a specific and concrete nature, economic analysis focuses on opportunity costs that are abstract in character and not directly observable.

Accountants seek to establish information systems that can deter the misuse of corporate resources, assist in coordinating the activity of firms' employees, and conform to record-keeping and tax-paying requirements established by outside authorities. (Benston, 1982). This leads accountants to concern themselves primarily with cataloging resources that are tangible in nature and with registering obligations, expenditures, and receipts that occur in explicit and verifiable market transactions. Most other types of values and transactions may be described as unbookable under generally accepted accounting principles. In contrast, economists see no essential difference between sources of value that are bookable or unbookable, tangible or intangible, explicit or implicit.

Given the use an economist wants to make of information on cash flows, market-value accounting of total returns furnishes the appropriate measure of the performance of a firm, and historical-cost accounting values provide misleading measures of the magnitude, timing, and origins of firm income. The following examples illustrate how interest volatility distorts accounting measures of bank earnings and net worth, when financial assets are carried at historical cost, and when records of implicit forms of income and expenses are not recorded with economic sensitivity.

On a bank's continuing holdings of loans and investments, historical-cost accounting records interest income only. It does this even at times when fluctuations in interest rates subsequent to acquisition induce substantial amounts of observable (though unrealized) appreciation or depreciation in the value of these assets. Such unrealized capital gains and losses are reported, but not at the time they occur. Rather they are impounded into above-market or below-market accounting returns that the misvalued assets generate throughout the period in which they remain in the bank's possession. To illustrate, we may suppose that the yield on a 10-year $100 bond purchased at par rises from 10.0 to 10.5 percent. If an institution marks its portfolio to market, it books an immediate capital loss equal to the decline in the market price of the bond. This price decline occurs to permit the bond to earn the market yield of 10.5 percent over its remaining life. If the institution continues to record the bond at par, it effectively amortizes the bond's decline in market value by recording future returns on this investment at the below-market rate of 10 percent. The difference between the 10.5 market interest rate and the coupon rate of 10 percent reflects the gradual realization of the unrecorded capital loss.

Changes in market interest rates similarly distort liability values. Recording core deposits and outstanding certificates of deposit (CDs) at par neglects interest-induced gains and losses that, when properly conceived, serve to reduce the net impact of parallel fluctuations in the market value of bank assets. A related distortion occurs because implicit interest that banks pay to depositors in the form of advantageously priced account services is typically recorded as non-interest operating expense. If core deposits were valued at market, implicit interest expense would have to be allocated across account types to permit an accurate comparison of total returns received by accountholders with market rates of interest on other types of funding.

Financial analysts seek to bridge the gap between accounting reports and economic values. They routinely estimate unrealized charges against a bank's reported capital position, using (among other data) differences between market and accounting yields. Their detective work helps to explain why empirical evidence supports the hypothesis that eventually (i.e., after making allowance for recognition lags) stock markets penetrate the veil of historical-cost accounting to estimate total returns. (Hagerman, 1975; Sachs and Kyle, 1985). Now that call-reporting procedures require banks to disclose the amount of market-price depreciation in selected assets, financial analysts and bank regulators should soon be able to produce more timely estimates of the market value of bank capital accounts.

Pros and Cons of Mandating Greater Disclosure

Benston (1979) emphasizes the difficulty of establishing that *mandated* publication of accounting data ever proves of net benefit to society. A key point in his argument is that, in competitive securities markets, managers face strong incentives to disclose and communicate useful information to investors. Benston also stresses the inappropriateness of expecting mandated disclosures to prevent determinedly dishonest managers from making false and misleading financial reports to the public.

What makes the situation of insured deposit institutions different is that the penalties they most need to worry about are not determined in competitive markets. The penalties these institutions face are set by regulators whose information system focuses on judgments by examiners whose rapid average turnover ensures uneven skills and experience. An examiner's job is the difficult one of ferreting out evidence on managerial dishonesty or incompetence and on the extent to which deposit-institution managers succeed in exploiting deposit-insurance subsidies to risk-taking. To the extent that all managers can increase the flow of expected subsidies if they make it hard for examiners to monitor their behavior, a common industry interest develops in limiting voluntary public disclosure and in negotiating additional private disclosures with important stockholders and uninsured creditors.

Moreover, because regulatory agency heads typically have short horizons, agencies may naturally favor reporting systems that retard the release of information that is unpleasant enough to compel the agencies to take unpopular actions. However, by suppressing clues that could help auditors and financial analysts to detect fraud and mismanagement, disclosure limitations make it possible for dishonest and incompetent deposit institution managers to survive longer than they could otherwise. In an era in which interest-rate volatility and specific classes of loan losses have differentially undermined the net worth of different deposit institutions, the distribution of the benefits from nondisclosure may well have become skewed toward high-flying and loosely managed firms.

Whatever information managers choose to disclose selectively and to whom, financial institutions ought to use market-value records in their internal information systems. Such information should help managers to see their operations as savvy regulators and stockholders ought to see them and to reassess traditional portfolio practices whose effectiveness may have been undermined by the surge in interest-rate volatility created by the October 6, 1979, shift in Federal Reserve procedures and priorities for monetary control.

Probably the chief example of a maladapted portfolio practice is that of buying and holding long-term securities as a liquidity reserve. Although many bankers object that the potentially deleterious effects that market-value reporting would have on returns earned on long-term bonds over short accounting periods would force their banks to seek liquidity only in short-term securities, it is hard to treat this as a logical drawback of market-value accounting. When examined carefully, portfolio policies that seem undesirable under market-value accounting ought to be undesirable under historical cost accounting, as well. A bank that would buy fewer intermediate or long-term government bonds if it had to account for them at market value ought to hold fewer of these securities even under the current system. Permitting bankers to control the time at which capital gains and losses are recognized lets them defer some taxes, but permitting bankers to time the recognition of important classes of losses cannot markedly reduce the risks to which a bank's capital (and therefore its stock price) is ultimately exposed. Moreover, a bank's use of market-value accounting for purposes of internal information and external reporting would not affect its tax liabilities, which must be computed from historical-cost records.

Whether timely information on total returns (where total returns are given by earnings statements that adjust explicit income for changes in portfolios' market values) is too sensitive to disclose to various groups of outsiders is a more controversial issue. It is fair to say that, during most of the last 20 years, the banking industry has determinedly resisted proposals by the Securities and Exchange Commission (SEC) and the Financial Accounting Standards Board (FASB) to require more meaningful accounting for bank balance sheets and earnings statements. Besides trying to reduce regulatory interference in deposit-institution operations, industry resistance to market-value reporting reflects concern about the technical difficulty of estimating meaningful market prices for nontraded assets and liabilities (including intangibles).

Current fears about disclosing unrealized losses are aggravated by the accumulation of unfavorable shocks that the industry has had to weather, although this is primarily a problem of managing the transition from one reporting system to another. As Figures 1 and 2 show for bank holding companies whose conditions are tracked by the Compustat data service (identified in Table 1), since 1973 these shocks have driven the market values of capital accounts at the average reporting bank cumulatively well below book values. At savings and loan associations and mutual savings banks, the decline is even sharper. (Kane, 1985).

No matter how much individual managers might want to move their institutions toward market-value accounting in the long run, large unrealized losses on investments and problem loans predispose the managers at this time to let sleeping dogs lie. Threatening times seem poor occasions either to inform regulators about the true size of

Figure 1: Ratio of Aggregate Stock Market Value of Compustat Bank Holding Companies to the Aggregate Book Value of Their Capital Accounts, 1973-1983 (Quarterly)

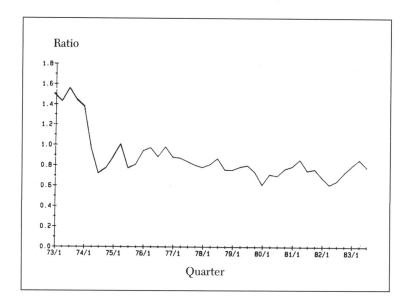

Figure 2: Aggregate Stock Market Value of Compustat Bank Holding Companies and the Aggregate Book Value of Their Capital Accounts. 1973-1983 (Quarterly)

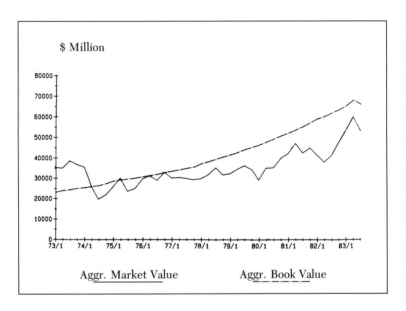

market-value losses or to put to an additional empirical test academic economists' beloved hypothesis that deposit and stock markets have already discounted whatever unpublicized information is unfavorable to their banks. Maintaining traditional standards of secrecy appears instead to be the very soul of managerial discretion.

However, waiting for banks to find a propitious time in the interest-rate cycle to make the transition to market-value accounting may bear more than a minor resemblance to waiting for a myopic homeowner to find an ideal time to insulate his attic. In the summer, it is too hot to work under the roof; in the winter, it is too cold. During the fall and winter, he sees no need for insulation at all.

Transitional and continuing costs might be minimized by taking a permissive approach, authorizing individual institutions to switch to market-value accounting at their own option. Supporters of this

Table 1: Bank Holiday Companies Whose Portfolios Are Tracked by the Compustat Tape, As of August 18, 1983

Company	Ticker-Tape Symbol
Affiliated Bankshares Colo.	AFBK
Allied Bancshares Inc.	ALBN
American Fletcher Corp.	AFLT
American Security Corp.	ASEC
Ameritrust Corp.	AMTR
Amsouth Bancorporation	ASO
Arizona Bancwest Corp.	AZBW
Atlantic Bancorp.	ABAN
Banc One Corp.	BONE
Bancal Tri-State Corp.	BNC
Banco Popular de Puerto Rico	BPOP
Bancohio Corp.	BOHI
Bancorp Hawaii Inc.	BNHI
Bank of Boston Corp.	BKB
Bank of Commonwealth-Detroit	BDET
Bank New England Corp.	BKNE
Bank of New York Co. Inc.	BK
Bank of Virginia Co.	BKV
Bankamerica Corp.	BAC
Bankers Trust New York Corp.	BT
Banks of Iowa	BIOW
Barnett Banks of Florida	BBF
Baybanks Inc.	BBNK
CBT Corp.	CBCT
Centerre Bancorporation	CTBC
Central Bancorporation Inc.	CBAN
Centran Corp.	CENB
Chartercorp.	CHCP
Chase Manhattan Corp.	CMB
Chemical New York Corp.	CHL
Citicorp.	FNC
Citizens & Southern Ga. Corp.	CSGA
Colorado Natl Bankshares	COLC
Comerica Inc.	CMCA
Commerce Bancshares Inc.	CBSH
Commerce Union Corp.	COMU
Continental Bancorp-Pa.	CBRP
Continental Illinois Corp.	CIL
Corestates Financial Corp.	CSFN
Crocker National Corp.	CKN
Cullen/Frost Bankers Inc.	CFBI

Table 1: continued

Company	Ticker-Tape Symbol
Deposit Guaranty Corp.	DEPS
Dominion Bankshares Corp.	DMBK
Equimark Corp.	EQK
Equitable Bancorporation	EBNC
Fidelcor	FICR
Fidelity Union Bancorp.	FDU
First & Merchants	FMCH
First Alabama Bancshares Inc.	FABC
First Atlanta Corp.	FAC
First Bank System Inc.	FBKS
First Chicago Corp.	FNB
First City Bancorp. (Texas)	FBT
First Empire State Corp.	FEMP
First Florida Banks Inc.	FFBK
First Hawaiian Inc.	FHWN
First Interstate Bancorp.	I
First Kentucky National	FKYN
First Maryland Bancorp.	FMDB
First Natl Cincinnati Corp.	FNAC
First Natl State Bancorp.	FNS
First Oklahoma Bancorp.	FOKL
First Pennsylvania Corp.	FPA
First Security Corp-Del	FSCO
First Tennessee Natl Corp.	FTEN
First Union Corp. (N.C.)	FUNC
First Virginia Banks Inc.	FVB
First Wisconsin Corp.	FWB
Flagship Banks	FLAG
Fleet Financial Group Inc.	FLT
Florida Natl Banks of Fla.	FNBF
General Bancshares	GBS
Greater Jersey Bancorp.	GJBC
Harris Bankcorp Inc.	HBC
Hartford National Corp.	HNAT
Heritage Bancorp.	HRTG
Huntington Bancshares	HBAN
Indiana National Corp.	INAT
Industrial Valley Bk & Trust	IBKT
Interfirst Corp.	IFC
Intrawest Finl Corp.	INTW
Irving Bank Corp.	V
Key Banks Inc.	KEY
Liberty National Corp.	LIBN
Lincoln First Banks	LFBK

Table 1: continued

Company	Ticker-Tape Symbol
Manufacturers Hanover Corp.	MHC
Manufacturers National Corp.	MNTL
Marine Corp.	MCRP
Marine Midland Banks	MM
Marshall & ILSLEY Corp.	MRIS
Maryland National Corp.	MDNT
Mellon National Corp.	MEL
Mercantile Bancorporation	MTRC
Mercantile Texas Corp.	MTD
Michigan National Corp.	MNCO
Midlantic Banks Inc.	MIDL
Moore Financial Group Inc.	MFGI
Morgan (J.P.) & Co.	JPM
NCNB Corp.	NCB
NBD Bancorp Inc.	NBD
National City Corp.	NCTY
Norstar Bancorp. Inc.	NOR
Northern Trust Corp.	NTRS
Northwestern Financial Corp.	NWFN
Norwest Corp.	NOB
Old Kent Financial Corp.	OKEN
PNC Financial Corp.	PNCF
RIHT Financial Corp.	RIHT
Rainier Bancorporation	RBAN
Republic New York Corp.	RNB
Republicbank Corp.	RPT
Riggs Natl Corp Wash DC	RIGS
Security Pacific Corp.	SPC
Shawmut Corp.	SHAS
Society Corp.	SOCI
South Carolina Natl Corp.	SCNC
Southeast Banking Corp.	STB
Southwest Bancshares	SWB
State Street Boston Corp.	STBK
Sun Banks Inc.	SU
Sunwest Finl Services Inc.	SFSI
Texas American Bancshares	TXA
Texas Commerce Bancshares	TCB
Third National Corp.	TDAT
Trust Company of Georgia	TRGA
Union Natl Corp-Pennsylvania	UNBC
Union Planters Corp.	UPCM
United Banks of Colorado	UBKS
United Jersey Banks	UJB

Table 1: continued

Company	Ticker-Tape Symbol
United Missouri Bancshares	UMSB
US Bancorp.	USBC
US Trust Corp.	USTC
United Virginia Bankshares	UVBK
Valley National Corp Arizona	VNCP
Virginia Natl Bankshares	VNAT
Wachovia Corp.	WB
Wells Fargo & Co.	WFC
Zions Utah Bancorp.	ZION

Source: Standard & Poor's Compustat Services, Inc. Investors Management Sciences, Inc., Bank Compustat. Denver: Aug. 19, 1983.

approach would draw a careful distinction between market-value accounting and required addendum reporting of changes in the market value of selected assets. Market-value accounting implies a double-entry system of market-value records. Market-value reporting focuses on requiring market-value reports of material facts at least to regulators. A voluntary approach would leave managers free to choose whether and when market-value accounting should take hold at their institutions, and would grant a breathing space in which firms for which the transition seems particularly difficult could restructure their balance sheets to smooth the passage. However, if strong institutions find it advantageous to use market-value accounting to signal their financial vigor to depositors and subordinated debtholders, weaker firms would probably feel market pressure to adopt it, too.

An additional fear is that, where a bank's survival is threatened, market-value accounting might tend to deteriorate into fire-sale accounting. At an institution's most perilous moments, accountants' and examiners' disposition to protect themselves against hind-sighted criticism could lead them to pressure the bank into understating the current going-concern values of problem loans and investments. Whereas the clients of financial analysts are apt to criticize them as severely for undervaluing as for overvaluing a bank's stock, regulators and accountants are apt to suffer more from overstating a bank's financial condition than for understating it. Even though auditors who place their own interests ahead of their clients' interests are apt to lose business in the long run, their first concern is to minimize their own liability to civil action in the event of client-bank failures. This makes auditors reluctant to assign sufficient value to concessions and operational adjustments made by troubled borrowers during the work-out process. Any banker who decides to implement the principle of honest accounting for hidden losses is bound to open up new fronts of warfare with fainthearted auditors and examiners.

The other side of the picture is that the degree to which bank stock prices and deposit flows are sensitive to bad news is heightened by the absence of reliable data both on the dollar size of particular shocks and on individual institutions' capacity to absorb unfavorable shocks of different sizes and types. The lack of adequate regular disclosure of the value of unrealized charges against bank capital makes it reasonable for uninsured depositors and non-insider stockholders to seek private disclosures, demand informational risk premiums, and be prepared to run for cover at the first signs of heavy weather.

In not facing up to this problem, industry strategists suffer from what we might term the cosmetics fallacy. The knowledge that wearing thick pancake make-up hides a wearer's facial blemishes from direct view doesn't justify the hypothesis that intelligent observers must assume that the wearer's unseen blemishes are minimal. Wearing heavy make-up signals one's unwillingness to show an untouched-up face to the world. Depositors and investors assume that an institution resorts to make-up precisely because some aspects of its complexion are ugly enough to conceal. Although trade association efforts to sidetrack regulatory proposals that would make banks disclose their hidden losses are beginning to slacken, past efforts deepened the suspicion that a bad complexion may be an industry-wide phenomenon rather than an isolated problem.

By making it easier for the Federal Savings and Loan Insurance Corporation (FSLIC) insurance fund to slip under water (Kane, 1985), cosmetic accounting has hurt deposit institutions in an even subtler way. It has exposed them to a greater risk of having to pay *ex post* for the excesses of their highest-flying competitors. To rebuild FSLIC reserves that have been devastated by past S&L failures, federally insured S&Ls have been asked to pay supplementary assessments of 1/32 of 1 percent of their deposits each quarter in 1985. If additional failures should render S&L resources too small a tax base, Congress is likely to merge the FSLIC into the Federal Deposit Insurance Corporation (FDIC). This means that the S&L insolvencies threaten to spill over onto the books of the commercial-banking industry.

Market sensitivity to the extent of cosmetic accounting leads Kane (1983), among others, to conclude that the short-term interests of all but the nation's weakest deposit institutions and the long-term interests of the industry as a whole now lie in the direction of regular and adequate disclosure of the income and balance-sheet consequences of favorable and unfavorable economic events. If informational risk associated with growing and unresolved insolvencies is depressing the stock prices of strong and weak banks alike, the major beneficiaries of shifting to market-value accounting may turn out to be executives who hold stock option positions in healthy banks. To paraphrase Franklin Roosevelt, except at the weakest institutions, managers may have nothing to fear so much as the fear of market-value accounting.

To protect themselves against being stung directly or indirectly by unobservable bad investments of the types that have recently come to light at the industry's worst problem banks, suppliers of capital and of uninsured deposits may currently penalize many well-capitalized banks by exacting informational risk premiums that drive a bank's stock price lower and its CD rates higher. Even in times that are less troubled than the present, because a bank's power to shop for more flexible auditors gives it some leverage in debating its asset values with squeamish accountants, investors' and creditors' fear of surprises leads them to discount bank stock and uninsured bank debt to compensate them for the industry's insistence on maintaining the right to report capital gains and losses in its own way and in its own time. Along with the market's need to correct for bankers' tendency to overstate their own earnings, the opportunity cost paid for deposit-insurance authorities' ability to postpone the resolution of their own insolvency problems helps to explain the traditionally low price-earning multiples observed for bank stock.

It is unlikely that it currently serves the self-interest of soundly managed banks to assist their loosely managed competitors to cover up the extent of their relative weakness. In a free society it is hard to see why a bank should not be given the right to disclose any valid information relating to its economic condition that the bank's managers deem useful to stockholders and uninsured creditors.

Nor is it reasonable to maintain that disclosing the unvarnished truth about problem institutions could provoke a financial panic that might engulf the banking system as whole. Such an argument overlooks the recent willingness of the Fed to act as lender of last resort to failing banks and S&Ls and of the FDIC and FSLIC to husband their explicit deposit insurance reserves by assisting troubled firms on generous terms. Institutions depend, not on customer confidence that accounting reports will alert the public to serious problems before the value of their deposit holdings can be jeopardized, but on customer confidence in the Fed and state and federal deposit insurers to resolve economic insolvencies in ways that keep insured creditors whole and (to eliminate the threat of contagious runs) typically rescue uninsured ones, as well.

The industry's fight against applying principles of current-value accounting to such obvious losses as those in Third World loans and low-interest mortgages has mixed benefits. Because book-value accounting encourages regulators to postpone actions that could resolve major economic insolvencies at thrift institutions and problem banks before they become major, it makes the investing public more suspicious of the entire industry.

Benefits and Costs of Market-Value Reports

Bankers need to recognize that if they don't take action to limit unintended subsidies to deposit-institution risk-bearing, regulators will do it for them. By substituting market for regulatory discipline, market-value accounting and even regulatory disclosure lessen the industry's exposure to arbitrary changes in the burden of regulation. Because market-value accounting threatens to expose regulators as well as bankers to more effective outside criticism, it would force agency heads to make the criteria used by bank examiners less subjective and to develop procedures for reducing variation in the toughness of examinations both from one examiner to another and across different stages of the business cycle. Evidence exists that variation among banks in the ratio of substandard loans to total loans is significantly affected by variation in examining agencies' methods and individual examiners' biases. (Benston and Marlin, 1974).

Market-Value Accounting as a Form of Risk-Rated Premium

An important source of many regulatory difficulties is that a deposit institution's managers have more and better information about the riskiness of their firm's operations than its insurers and customers have. In 1938, generally accepted accounting principles and regulator-imposed accounting rules made it easier to keep outsiders in the dark by authorizing deposit institutions to employ what is misleadingly called intrinsic-value accounting. Intrinsic-value accounting permits assets whose scheduled cash flows are relatively current to be carried on the lender's books at historical cost, even when the borrower's economic prospects have deteriorated sharply. Contemporary accounting principles relieve managers who report book values (and absolve their outside accountants as well) from legal liability for communicating less than their best estimate of the value of an institution's portfolio. Legal authority to use book-value accounting to cover up adverse information gives a financial institution manager (especially an unscrupulous one) too much discretion over the extent to which current problems show up on an institution's income statement and balance sheet.

At least with respect to the particular subset of individual deposit institutions for which valuing intangibles and nontraded assets raises few problems in implementation (a class that should include most thrifts), instituting market-value accounting for loans and investments can be justified as an administratively cheap scheme for raising a firm's implicit regulatory premium on deposit insurance in a risk-sensitive way. This is because the opportunity cost of having to report the market value of these assets tends to rise with an institution's exposure to capital losses.

The most attractive aspect of adopting a market-value approach is that by better focusing traditional capital requirements and other implicit premiums, it would make regulatory discipline more effective. Using market values would permit market forces to help bureaucrats conduct their ongoing assessments of institutions' risk exposures and develop appropriate penalties for overly aggressive risk-takers. (Kane, 1983).

Deposit-institution regulators increase an institution's capital requirements with their assessment of the level of the institution's risk exposure. This means that capital requirements are intended to function as risk-rated implicit premiums designed to choke off the subsidy to risk-taking inherent in the risk-insensitive structure of the explicit premiums deposit insurers are required to charge.

At the same time, the traditional approach to financial accounting gives bank regulators and bank managers considerable discretion over what items are and are not currently recorded as capital. The root problem is that accountants designate several important sources of value as unbookable. These sources include loan commitments, credit guarantees, opportunities to engage in fee-for-service business, and unrealized increases and decreases in the market value of assets and liabilities. By undertaking carefully selected transactions, the manipulative manager may lessen the impact of capital requirements by systematically overstating the value of his or her firm's capital account. This is accomplished by deferring unbooked losses and realizing unbooked capital gains. For example, the manipulative manager might arrange sale-and-leaseback transactions or sell fee-for-service business to an affiliated or subsidiary firm.

In a world where declines in market value were not obscured by book-value (i.e., historical-cost) accounting, deposit-institution managers who contemplated aggressively pursuing unregulated risks would know that they would have to defend their risk-taking strategies against more timely criticism from regulators and financial analysts and would have to offer correspondingly higher interest rates more quickly to any depositors who perceived themselves to be truly uninsured. This means that, when risky strategies went awry, managers would face quicker and more extensive damage to their careers and to the stock prices and deposit flows of the institutions they manage.

Managerial discretion over the release of unfavorable information puts the burden of valuing deposit institutions on financial analysts and weakens political controls that would otherwise limit institutions' and insurers' risk exposure. Such discretion may also delay the effect of market discipline. Losing the right to touch up and string out the unfolding implications of unfavorable news should make managers more responsive to the interests of insurers and uninsured depositors when their institutions are facing potentially injurious developments. This increased sensitivity establishes incentives for deposit-institution managers to modify and to bond their behavior in helpful ways. The May 1984 crisis at Continental Illinois can be interpreted as a growing and belated recognition that the bank's unrealized losses may have exceeded its capital. Even in the face of explicit FDIC guarantees of all Continental Illinois liabilities, depositor reaction was severe. In particular, responding to their exposure to hindsighted criticism under prudent-man rules, institutional investors insisted on substantially reducing their positions in the bank.

If private parties are to bear more of the risk inherent in *de jure* and *de facto* failures, we must expect regulators, deposit-institution investors, and uninsured depositors to ask managers to give—and accountants to attest to—a best-efforts estimate of the risk exposure and changing market value of the assets and liabilities that deposit institutions hold on their books. To protect the interests of federal taxpayers and healthy institutions in the insurance pools, deposit insurers need to press for reliable information on the value of unrealized losses and gains at financial institutions, information of the sort that conscientious deposit-institution managers should be assembling and analyzing in the course of operating their firms.

Technical Difficulties of Market-Value Accounting

In an era of interest volatility, to produce estimates that would be more accurate than historical costs, accountants need only to insist that deterioration in borrowers' repayment capacity be recognized on the books as quickly as management becomes aware of it and to supplement their traditional auditing skills with solid competence in financial asset appraisal. Much as in real-estate appraisal, to value an asset that does not trade, an analyst must rely heavily on projections of a borrower's earning capacity and on current yields and prices in secondary markets for comparable investments.

For an institution as a whole, as long as unbiased appraisal techniques are employed, errors in valuing the individual assets in its portfolio should tend to cancel one another out. Of course, establishing that in a specific case a particular accountant did, in fact, employ unbiased appraisal techniques can be a difficult and litigious problem. The required reorientation of professional effort and legal burdens of proof helps to explain accountants' reluctance to support a switch to market-value accounting for financial institutions.

To estimate the value of fixed assets, mortgages, and directly placed loans (such as those to troubled farmers, energy firms, and less-developed countries), the major problem is to assess the reliability of lender projections of future cash flows and to obtain appropriate estimates of market discount rates to use as inputs into present-value formulas. Practical use of these formulas has been trivialized by software that preprograms the necessary calculations onto floppy discs or hardwires them into the circuits of hand-held calculators. Obtaining reliable numbers to key into the calculations is where skill must be exercised.

If federal deposit insurers wanted to develop rather than to conceal such information, they could expand the set of transactions observed in secondary markets. Specifically, they could request their liquidation divisions to arrange for periodic auctions of assets chosen for their inherent comparability to the most important classes of hard-to-value instruments currently being held by troubled institutions.

Until very recently, neither banking regulators nor the deposit-institution industry has *wanted* to publicize such base-line values. Although some tentative administrative steps have incurred in the direction of greater disclosure, backsliding continues to occur with respect to risks that are politically protected. On the plus side, authorities have required banks to report their positions in troubled foreign loans and required S&Ls to report gaps between the interest sensitivity of their assets and liabilities. In 1982 and 1983, the Federal Home Loan Bank Board (FHLBB) explored very seriously a proposal to require FSLIC-insured S&Ls to adopt market-value accounting. (U.S. Federal Home Loan Bank Board, 1982 and 1983). In 1984, the SEC (which has continually pressed for improved disclosure) and the Office of the Comptroller of the Currency pointedly forced several large institutions to restate their 1983-1984 profits in a less self-serving manner. However, authorities have encouraged cosmetic accounting by permitting problem loans to less-developed countries to be carried at book value and by promising to take a "flexible" approach to valuing distressed farm loans at banks located in agricultural regions.

Liabilities such as contingent guarantees, intangible assets, and reputational values pose more difficult valuation problems. Such problems might be resolved most expeditiously and most equitably by assigning to a self-regulatory industry board the tasks of identifying currently unbookable sources of value and determining valuation principles and procedures.

Opponents of disclosing market values cite two drawbacks: First, the costs of providing market appraisals might exceed the benefits; and, second, outside parties might dangerously misinterpret the accounting reports that result. One cost is that, to the extent that estimating market values is inherently less objective and reproducible than the process of recording historical acquisition costs, opportunities for exaggerating or concealing economic income are expanded. Because auditors and government examiners would have to check reported figures more carefully than ever, the projected cost and complexity of outside audits and governmental monitoring would increase.

One offsetting benefit is that making public any changes in bank portfolio values creates incentives for managers to adopt policies that make the true value of income fluctuations smaller. Other offsetting benefits are ethically more defensible standards for truth-telling in accounting, improved decisionmaking at any firm whose internal information system does not already employ market-value data, and a potential reduction in the size of informational risk allowances that market participants demand to compensate them for the uncertain cosmetic nature of bank accounting reports.

The issue of misinterpretation focuses on the likelihood of increased fluctuations in reported earnings under market-value accounting. Economic analysis suggests that, if it weren't for the blunting of incentives by the deposit-insurance subsidy, many deposit institutions would have moved to market-value accounting soon after increased interest volatility significantly impaired the ability of historical-cost accounting to track bank portfolio values and economic profits.

Finally, it should be noted that the net costs of producing market-value estimates would be less than their direct costs, because similar analysis is already being performed by others. By simplifying the tasks of financial analysis and of deposit-institution examination, market-value accounting promises to free up resources employed elsewhere in the financial industry.

Regulatory Benefits

On the regulatory side, if federal taxpayers were well-informed, political pressure would have led Congress to insist that deposit insurers require market-value reports long ago. Such information would help regulators to discover and to resolve problems more quickly and generate popular pressure on authorities to make more timely and better focused interventions.

Because legal insolvency differs from economic insolvency, a market-value reporting system would not take the failure decision out of governmental hands. As long as deposit-insurance agencies remained free to offer capital assistance to failing clients, market-value accounting would merely curtail rather than eliminate regulatory discretion as to whether and when to close an economically insolvent institution. However, by forcing more timely and more explicit forms of intervention, market-value accounting would reduce an insolvent institution's opportunities for pursuing go-for-broke strategies.

Spokespersons for financial institutions whose portfolio book values mask market-value insolvency promote the sunny, though dangerously false, view that unrealized losses are less harmful to society than realized ones. However, the main difference between the two types of losses lies in the incentives they generate. In realizing a loss, the institution publicly acknowledges its effect and takes out of its portfolio the continuing risks associated with the investment that generated the loss. When past net losses remain unrealized, the effect remains hidden and the investments that generated the losses stay in the portfolio to grow or decline in the future. Because unanticipated gains tend to accrue in greater proportion to stockholders, whereas unanticipated losses tend to accrue disproportionately to government guarantors, it is inappropriate for regulators to employ an accounting scheme that neglects the effect that unrealized losses have on an institution's capital position and risk-taking incentives.

Accounting standards that make it possible for individual deposit institutions to disguise insolvency and risk-taking beyond all recognition without violating the law make a mockery of existing capital requirements. Until these standards are changed, merely raising or restructuring deposit-institution capital requirements cannot solve deposit insurance problems.

Disclosure of Administrative Actions

Public embarrassment can reinforce the career risk to which subsidy-maximizing managers are exposed. For this reason, some critics of FDIC policies have urged that periodic bank examination ratings be made public.

In a precedent-setting case, the FDIC in February 1985 released the names of persons it had fined in connection with the failure of a small Tennessee bank and publicly identified the money brokers who had placed funds in the bank before it failed. In May 1985, the FDIC announced that henceforth it would release each week the names of banks and bank employees against whom it has obtained cease-and-desist orders, removals of directors and officers, or civil penalties. It will also disclose the termination of FDIC insurance at any bank. Although these disclosures do not occur until FDIC enforcement proceedings have been concluded, the FDIC has threatened to open its administrative hearings to the public and has reserved the right to expand its disclosures to include notice even as to the initial bringing of charges against an insured institution.

When agency actions are well-founded, general or selective disclosure of regulatory sanctions is a weapon that promises to increase the penalties that uninsured creditors impose on banks that engage in unsound banking practices. The problem is that agency criticisms are not always well-founded. Bankers fear that capital markets may over-react to negative publicity generated by adverse, but ill-conceived, criticisms of their business policies. This fear makes the threat of disclosure a device that strengthens the capacity of federal regulators to persuade banks to adopt the practices and balance-sheet structures they recommend.

Nevertheless, overreaction should not be the market's typical response. Regulatory reversals won in appellate courts and ordinary citizens' experience with the arbitrariness of government bureaucracy provide evidence that regulators frequently make mistakes. Although it is costly to defend managerial practices against regulatory attack, bankers should not assume that their customers are unwilling to listen sympathetically. Because of such explanations, Ohio's six uninsured S&Ls prospered in the aftermath of the state-imposed 1985 banking holiday that undermined confidence in roughly 70 S&Ls whose de-posits had previously been insured by a state-sponsored fund. Pub-licity over unfounded regulatory criticism can even redound to a bank's net advantage by calling regional and national attention to creative and tough ways in which it has conducted its affairs.

Moreover, bankers and uninsured creditors should recognize that disclosure is a two-edged sword. When regulatory actions must be debated in the open, regulators have a strong incentive to double-check the theories, facts, and circumstances on which their objections are based. As regulators come to appreciate the bureaucratic penalties that the political system imposes on agencies that act high-handedly, the frequency of arbitrary action should fall.

Switching to Market-Value Accounting

This section discusses the feasibility of valuing the capital of different kinds of banks (as well as the contribution to capital generated by any particular subportfolio) as the net difference between the market value of *all* of its assets and liabilities. Market-value accounting is feasible as long as data on scheduled cash flows and on related timing options conferred on various classes of customers can be combined with interest rates and asset prices from secondary markets for com-parable instruments. As the computerization movement matures, and as investment banking firms extend the range of instruments whose cash flows they strip and package for resale in derivative instruments, such as collateralized mortgage obligations and collateralized automobile receipts, the task of appraising the market value of institutional portfolios will become progressively easier and more precise. Where comparable secondary markets for nontraded assets have not yet developed, regulators could facilitate the use of market-value accounting by arranging periodic auctions of instruments selected to produce data suitable for appraising other categories of assets and liabilities.

Top managers of many large depository institutions and insurance companies regularly review market-value records. To assist them, at least one firm (BARRA of Berkeley, California) has developed a bond valuation service. In its promotional literature, the firm claims that its model isolates the important characteristics of 15,000 government and corporate bonds and 60,000 Government National Mortgage Association (GNMA) pools and estimates daily market values for these characteristics. Extrapolating the daily values assigned to analogous characteristics for private placements and bank loans allows any institution's portfolio to be revalued daily. Although these estimates must be recognized as accurate only to within a few cents on the dollar, it is clear that in an era of volatile interest rates, on average such figures would more closely approximate the true value of a representative deposit institution than would measures of the firm's traditional book value.

Large banks are distinguished from small banks primarily by the complexity of their affairs, by their higher percentage of uninsured and interbank liabilities, and, in the event of their insolvency, by the FDIC's greater difficulty in locating and negotiating with suitable acquirers. For large and small banks alike, the internal advantages of assembling market-value information are great. The problem comes in deciding how much of this information to report to what parties and whether to install a full-fledged market-value accounting system. To specialized institutions, the prospective costs of installing a market-value accounting system consist of the trouble of establishing and maintaining a system for tracking changes in the market value of only a few assets and liabilities. Apart from the trouble of re-educating managers and re-orienting their activities, the transitional and continuing costs of adopting a market-value accounting system are more a function of portfolio diversity than of institutional size. To insurers, market-value reporting promises to prove most beneficial for the firms that currently profess to fear it the most.

To take account of transitional costs that can be traced to differences in the size and complexity of different institutions, the switch to market-value reporting could be phased in gradually. One approach would be to set different phase-in deadlines for different kinds of banks, based on the extent to which market-value reports are already used for internal purposes. On this criterion, money-market banks and those with a large correspondent business could be required to make the change first, followed by other large banks (particularly those whose holding companies are publicly held). Managing the speed of transition is essentially a matter of reading and responding to political counterpressures. Decisionmakers must balance the benefits from improving the flow of information to insurers and uninsured creditors against the temporary disruptions that installing the new system might cause managers and stockholders in various institutions.

The most serious technical problem concerns the difficulty of identifying and appraising intangible assets and off-balance-sheet sources of value. Cosmetically minded bank managements would have an incentive to acknowledge and to overestimate all positive sources of value (such as opportunities to earn fee income) and to neglect and underestimate negative sources of value (such as standby guarantees and loan commitments).

To counter these biases, even if only selective market-value reporting were established, objective standards would have to be established. Because financial market opportunities are changing so fast, it seems appropriate to assign the proactive task of standards-setting to a banking industry self-regulatory board rather than to inherently less well-informed parties at the Financial Accounting Standards Board or the federal agencies. Such an institution's interest in minimizing inequities in the *distribution* of net deposit-insurance benefits should make instituting market-value reporting more palatable politically.

The board's task would be to enunciate general principles, to determine what items should be reported or disclosed, and to act as either an appeals board or an arbiter in settling disputes between institutions, their accountants, and their insurers. Representation on this board should include financial institution managers, practicing and academic accountants, experts in asset appraisal, regulators, and academic economists.

Summary

Deposit-insurance reform should aim not at preventing future bank failures, *per se*, but at preventing the taxation or subsidization of bank risk-taking at all times. Given that federal deposit insurance systematically subsidizes any form of risk-taking that the FDIC does not administratively penalize, to control risk-taking over the long run it is necessary to unblock opportunities for banks (including very large banks) to fail. Economic analysis suggests that it is possible to reduce *de facto* bank failures in the long run by making it more likely in the short run that market forces will punish stockholders and managers for risk-taking that goes awry.

Permitting or mandating market-value reporting is a relatively low-cost way of improving market discipline. Currently, market incentives for and against voluntarily disclosing changes in market values vary with the size and other characteristics of individual banks. For widely held institutions, stock prices already provide ongoing market-value estimates of firms' net worth. Moreover, even at privately held corporations and mutual firms, important depositors and creditors are often able to force the firms to disclose parallel information to them. The rapid turnover of those who head regulatory agencies, however, disposes them to prefer reporting systems that can delay the release of unpleasant news until after their term of duty has expired. Given that the burden of financing the deposit-insurance subsidy falls disproportionately on federal taxpayers and conservatively managed deposit institutions, the public has an important stake in the disclosure issue.

An accounting presentation is deceptive if it leads its audience to form an erroneous impression of important values. Regardless of whether bankers or regulators actually intend to deceive anyone, many have been less than forthright in acknowledging the effect that off-balance-sheet items have on the adequacy of bank capital and in writing down the value of impaired assets. Even if this lack of candor does not generally fool the marginal investor, it may fool some bank managers and lead a few of them to believe that they can sometimes con a few uninsured creditors and even bank regulators, if only for a while. To the extent that intrinsic-value accounting leads to taxpayer, regulator, and managerial confusion, market-value reporting represents a promising way to lessen unintended deposit-insurance subsidies to risk-taking and to increase the safety and soundness of the banking system.

CHAPTER 9

Risk-Related Premiums

Technically, deposit insurance is not insurance at all. It is a financial guarantee. Rather than insure a bank or thrift against a particular set of hazards, federal last-resort lending and deposit insurance guarantee the ability of an insured institution's customers to redeem their deposits. Agency funds are at risk only because monitoring difficulties and political conflict frequently prevent an insurer from closing troubled institutions before their net worth is exhausted.

Every accountholder's guarantee is a contingent obligation of the deposit–insurance agency. The agency promises to cover the first $100,000 of an accountholder's losses in the event that an insured institution becomes insolvent. A guarantor's credit stands behind, rather than with, the credit of the guaranteed party. A guarantee occasions no payouts until and unless the guaranteed party fails to meet its obligations under the guaranteed contract. The value of a guarantee depends both on the risk of this contingency and on the perceived willingness and ability of the guarantor to make good on its explicit and implicit guarantees. For an insured institution, the guarantees offered its customers are a source of value to stockholders. Credible guarantees permit the institution to finance its operations at a lower cost or with a higher degree of leverage than it otherwise could. Whether a guarantee is also a net source of value depends on the fees the guarantor collects in exchange for its services.

Because a guarantor may renege on its contractual obligation, the credibility of a guarantee forms an important part of its value. The value of a guarantee decreases with any increase in the current credit standing of the issuer of the guaranteed obligation and with any increase in the guarantor's ability to monitor and to protect itself against subsequent deterioration in the issuer's credit standing. At the same time, the value increases with any increase in the credibility and financial strength of the guarantor.

Little can be learned about the value of a guarantee by analyzing the cash flows it has required the guarantor to make in the past. The market value of a credible guarantee may be estimated from the perspective of either the benefits it confers on the issuer of guaranteed debt (whom we portray in contradistinction to the depositor as the guaranteed party) or the costs it visits on the guarantor. Guarantee benefits may be identified as the capitalized value of the annual interest savings (net of guarantor fees) that the guarantee enables the guaranteed party to achieve. Guarantee costs may be measured as the risk-adjusted present value of a fund of reserves sufficient probabilistically both to cover the insurer's monitoring effort and to meet the cash flows that would be demanded if the guaranteed party should fail to deliver as promised. The risk adjustment serves to give the guarantor a margin for forecasting error. In a competitive equilibrium, the two perspectives would give the same value.

If monitoring cost nothing, and deposit insurers were empowered to close institutions before they could become economically insolvent, the value of agency guarantees would be zero. Insurers would not need to hold any reserve funds at all and insolvency risk would fall entirely on the institutions' stockholders. Nor would any social benefits accrue from assigning the task of monitoring to a government agency. If monitoring cost nothing, the duplicate monitoring efforts of individual depositors would not waste resources.

Free guarantees to insured institutions are valuable, however, when monitoring is costly and the response system is imperfect. The value is clearest where perfect guarantees are extended to every dollar of a bank's nonequity liabilities. In this case, a bank's funding cost would be unaffected by increases or decreases in its risk of failure. Depositors would have no incentive either to monitor or to respond to adjustments in the bank's risk-taking posture. Bank risk-taking would not be disciplined in markets for deposits, or markets for other debt, because the costs of bank risk-taking would fall entirely on the guarantor. Whether a bank's managers consciously recognize their insulation from market discipline, profit opportunities shape up differently under the guarantee. If risk-taking is to be disciplined at all, the task falls to the guarantor.

More generally, it is instructive to contemplate the following rhetorical questions: Why do banks carefully investigate the financial conditions of their loan applicants, and why do banks worry systematically about how potential borrowers plan to use the proceeds of bank loans, when, as depositors, only the largest few of these same borrowers bother to investigate the financial conditions of their banks or to inquire what their banks intend to do with their money? The key to understanding this asymmetry turns out to be a greater asymmetry. This greater asymmetry is essentially that the bank puts its net worth at risk in its loans, whereas all but the largest accountholders perceive the value of their federally insured deposits to be perfectly protected against loss.

Modern financial theory conceives of the return on any financial instrument as the sum of the interest rate that would be charged for an equivalent risk-free loan and a series of allowances for the *undiversifiable* risks inherent in the given asset. Financial equilibrium is reached when the market price for bearing every relevant type of undiversifiable risk is the same for every asset to which this type of risk applies. The basic tenet of modern theoretical finance is that, once anticipated returns are adjusted for risk, prospective yields should be the same on all investments. Given this perspective, the more undiversifiable risk an asset possesses, the greater the *ex ante* return it must offer to compensate potential investors. Hence, differences in the anticipated rates of return on different assets reflect perceived differences in the pattern of risks to which the assets expose well-diversified investors.

This conception merely maintains that when financial markets are in equilibrium, the law of one price holds so that arbitrage opportunities cannot exist. Arbitrage opportunities exist when investors can buy and sell equivalent claims at unequal prices in a way that produces riskless profit. Whenever the law of one price is violated in financial markets, a clever investor (i.e., an arbitrageur) can book a profit without risking any wealth by carefully borrowing funds in cheap markets and relending them in dearer ones. Unless deposit-insurance premiums are effectively risk-rated, the law of one price is effectively violated, creating opportunities for arbitrageurs.

Portfolio theory and practice postulate a positive relation between the perceived risk and the anticipated return on individual investments. In the absence of a credible guarantee, the interest rate offered to creditors of a deposit institution would have to rise with the institution's leverage and with the riskiness of the net interest income the institution could earn on the assets and liabilities in its portfolio. This hypothetical funding interest rate (which is a function of an institution's portfolio composition and organizational structure) can be called the institution's warranted rate of return, represented symbolically by R_W. To compensate lenders for the increasingly imperfect collectability of their claims, R_W must rise in proportion to the degree to which a bank's capital is exposed to various risks. In particular, R_W should be sensitive to the institution's leverage, asset quality, and duration gap. This sensitivity exists because rational creditors must demand compensation for the increasing chance that the bank will not be able to repay the creditors' claims in full.

The gross benefits of a credible guarantee can be seen by comparing R_W with the interest cost of funds to an institution whose deposits are fully and perfectly guaranteed. In perfect markets, a completely guaranteed institution could borrow unlimited amounts at the riskless or Treasury interest rate, R_T, independent of both the institution's degree of leverage and the riskiness of the portfolio the institution holds. In this conception, the interest-rate differential R_W-R_T represents the warranted risk premium the firm earns by placing into a leveraged portfolio of risky assets the funds it raises via guaranteed obligations. If the firm's funds were invested in riskless assets of the same average life as its equity and nonequity liabilities, the firm's capital would not be exposed to risk. R_W would equal R_T, and the prospective (or *ex ante*) gross benefits of the guarantee would be zero.

To find the *net* benefits of a guarantee requires subtracting all forms of annualized per-dollar fees (or premiums) that the guarantor collects in exchange for its monitoring and backstopping services. The symbol R_G denotes the equivalent dollar value of all forms of annualized fees. In assessing net benefits, it makes no difference whether R_G is collected in a nonpecuniary form (i.e., implicitly) or in the coin of the realm (i.e., explicitly).

Moreover, if R_G is levied explicitly, it does not matter whether the guarantor's bill is collected in advance (*ex ante*) or tied to the states of the world that actually emerge at the end of any guarantee period (*ex post*). What does matter is whether managers perceive that an institution's effective fee for guarantee services is linked appropriately to the riskiness it imposes on the insurance fund. To eliminate taxes and subsidies, the level of R_G must respond appropriately to changes in R_W.

Clearly, the guaranteed institution's annual profits per dollar of guaranteed liabilities equals the difference between the warranted risk premium and the per annum guarantee fee: $(R_W$-$R_T)$-R_G. For any *given* R_W, unless R_G equals the *ex ante* risk premium R_W-R_T, the guaranteed institution is effectively taxed or subsidized. When R_G

exceeds the warranted risk premium, deposit insurance represents an additional form of taxation, and clients should look for ways of leaving the federal deposit-insurance system.

Given the structure of explicit and implicit deposit insurance premiums in the United States today, the pressure runs the other way. Many nondepository financial institutions have been seeking to acquire insured subsidiaries. This indicates that most deposit institutions receive *ex ante subsidies* from their guarantors (i.e., that R_G is smaller than R_W-R_T). The capitalized value of deposit-insurance subsidies is, in principle, a capital asset. It belongs on the asset side of insured balance sheets and on the liability side of insurer balance sheets.

In the special case where R_G is fixed independently of R_W (i.e., is not itself risk-rated), the insurer creates incentives for its clients to undertake adverse selections of risks that are designed to expand the risks of the clients' operations while shifting the burden of supporting these risks onto the guarantors. Although many bankers may not consciously consider their insured status in deciding how much risk to take into their portfolios, federal insurance greatly reduces creditors' resistance to increases in their institution's risk exposure.

From an *ex ante* point of view, the absence of creditors' insistence on appropriate risk premiums makes the risks taken by a bank appear to bank managers to be both more profitable and less risky for the bank than they are for society as a whole. With a flat schedule of insurance premiums, the manager of an insured firm can maximize the value of the subsidy stockholders receive by pushing stockholder-contributed capital as close to zero as permitted by regulators and any creditors who perceive themselves to be less than fully insured, while energetically pursuing various kinds of business risks in asset, funding, locational, and other business choices. The attractiveness of this value-maximizing strategy to an individual manager declines with the amount of capital the firm possesses and with the manager's willingness to tolerate the career risks associated with leading a firm into failure.

The principal reason that a deposit institution would voluntarily maintain a capital account is to buffer business risks. Increases in capital lower a firm's warranted financing rate, R_W, by making more credible the firm's capacity to absorb the risks inherent in its operations. When guarantees are perfect and guarantee fees are not risk-rated in any way, capital may be decreased even to zero without affecting the cost of deposits. For this reason, a deposit-insurance contract that underprices portfolio risks establishes incentives for a deposit institution's manager to lower capital ratios and to take other risks that increase the institution's warranted funding rate.

Of course, in responding to these incentives, managers no more intend for their firms to fail than a family that is perfectly insured against losses from theft would intend for its household goods to be stolen. Nonetheless, if insured households that installed burglar alarms and sturdy locks were offered no compensating reduction in their insurance premiums, their natural interest in installing alarm systems and heavy-duty locks would be economically attenuated.

Although the FDIC tries, through examination and supervision, to ration inadvertent and voluntary risk-taking by the firms it insures, many forms of risk-taking by deposit institutions are easy for their managers to conceal and hard for the insurer to diversify against. To arbitrage an underpriced guarantor, managerial risk-taking must increase the chance of a complete collapse of the firm. To protect itself against such arbitrage, a rational guarantor must not only erect a monitoring system, but also negotiate a set of clearly defined takeover rights. When a guaranteed firm loses enough of its bets, the guarantor must gain the option to take over the firm, wiping out stockholder equity and firing some managerial employees in the process. In such cases, losses that exceed stockholder capital accrue to the guarantor.

However, because of external or contractual restraints, a guarantor may permit an economically insolvent institution to continue to operate autonomously. In such a case, the guarantor allows the firm's managers to retain their jobs and permits the firm's stockholders to retain a valuable claim (reflecting the possibility that future states of the world could generate enough earnings to restore the firm to solvency) that the guarantor would have preferred to demand for itself. As long as the firm can control its risk exposure, while letting the guarantor supply guarantees that contribute to the firm's stock-market value, the bulk of its stockholders may expect to receive a disproportionately large share of the upper tail of the distribution of prospective returns, leaving the guarantor a disproportionately large portion of the distribution's lower tail.

This basic asymmetry in stockholder-guarantor sharing of unanticipated gains and losses is created by stockholders' limited liability for the guaranteed firm's losses. Whereas a government guarantor's liability is potentially unlimited, stockholder liability cannot exceed the value of the firm's accumulated capital. The asymmetry is increased by informational advantages that deposit-institution managers have over the insurer, which make it difficult to monitor and respond adequately to an insured's behavior, and is reduced by the size of the firm's capital account.

Along with legal and political constraints on deposit insurers' rights to close or sell off economically insolvent institutions, these asymmetries constitute the heart of the problem of pricing deposit insurance. Stockholders who select a diversified portfolio of other assets that serves to insulate their wealth against the risk that the firm might fail can lock in a sure return. Such stockholders effectively arbitrage the price of risk-bearing services between markets for loanable funds and the market for guarantee services.

The annualized value of deposit insurance to stockholders of an individual institution may be measured *ex post* (i.e., at the end of the period of insurance coverage), as well as *ex ante*. *Ex post* measurement centers on observed changes in the net value of the continuing guarantee. For expositional convenience, F_G represents the discounted present value of the expected flow of future net taxes or subsidies from federal deposit guarantees. In any year, t, the *ex post* flow of benefits to an institution from its deposit insurance guarantee is the sum of two components: an interest component and a capital-gains component. Over any accounting period, the interest component records the average interest cost to the federal government of supporting (i.e., financing) the capitalized value of the guarantee the institution receives. To a first approximation, this implicit interest cost may be conceived as the product of the average interest rate on federal agency debt, i_t, times the intra-year average market value of the guarantee the institution enjoyed: $i_t F_{G,t}$. The capital-gains component represents the change in the value of FG over year t (i.e., $F_{G,t} - F_{G,t-1}$), reflecting changes in the value of the guarantor's risk exposure in the firm. When managerial decisions or environmental change reduce the value of the guarantor's risk exposure, the change in F_G can be negative. If the decline in F_G were greater than the interest component, the flow of benefits in a given period might actually be negative.

Implicit and Explicit FDIC Premiums

The principal business of every insurer and every guarantor is to price and manage its net exposure to risk. To be able to price and to control its risk position, an insurer must identify all relevant forms of risk and operate an information system that tracks in timely fashion all changes in the risks it insures.

In the United States, the fees that deposit insurers exact for the risk-bearing services embodied in their guarantees differ along two dimensions: whether they are received *ex post* or *ex ante*; and whether they are levied in explicit or implicit fashion. The FDIC's *explicit* premium is paid as an annual *ex ante* assessment of $\frac{1}{12}$ of 1 percent of assessable deposits. This premium is subject to an *ex post* partial rebate that varies from year to year. Each year's rebate is based on the FDIC's annual loss experience and operating expense. During years when the FDIC's budgetary costs of resolving insolvencies are high (as they were from 1982 through 1984), rebates tend to be small.

The FDIC's *implicit premium* takes the form of capital require-ments and other forms of regulatory interference with insured institutions' operations. Partly to restrict insured institutions' ability to arbitrage deposit insurance guarantees, state and federal bank reg-ulators restrict and monitor institutions' competitive activities in many ways. Most importantly, they set geographic limits on office locations, prohibit banks from engaging in various types of financial activities, compel them to hold reserves of various types, and impose interest-rate ceilings on various loans and deposits. Individual restrictions aim either to reduce an institution's risk or to insulate its profits from the threat of competitive entry. However, these restrictions reduce a firm's opportunities for diversification and impose economically waste-ful barriers against entry by outside competitors into the particular markets in which deposit institutions operate.

To enforce their regulations, authorities monitor bank opera-tions by periodic reports and field examinations and stand ready to penalize undesirable behavior as they discover it. Sanctions include issuing cease-and-desist orders against specific practices, removing bank officers who engage in particular violations, and levying mone-tary fines. From the point of view of the insurer, these actions serve two purposes: to investigate the nature of the risks that banks are taking at any time and to develop and enforce penalties meant to control the kinds of risk-taking that deposit–insurance guarantees encourage and that remain underpriced as long as the explicit pre-mium is flat.

From an institution's point of view, the implicit insurance premiums appear as compliance costs in the form of anticipated profits the institution is prevented from earning because of regulatory restrictions on its activities and balance-sheet positions. The compliance costs include reporting and examination costs as well as the direct costs of conforming to the rules that these monitoring costs are incurred to enforce.

Federal interference in the operations of an insured institution is designed to escalate when examiners' assessments identify increases in the degree of risk that the institution's operations impose on federal insurance reserves. For the prospect of these penalties to serve as effective disincentives to counter the price incentives that encourage institutions to take excessive risks, examiners' judgments about the relevance or irrelevance of various kinds of risks and the adequacy of the institutions' capital to absorb them must be well-founded.

As a practical matter, authorities' ability to impose risk-rated implicit premiums on undesirable forms of risk-taking is limited in three ways:

1. By inadequacies in the regulatory information systems. (These inadequacies reflect inherent difficulties in monitoring insured institution's voluntary risk-taking and reflect regulatory lags in keeping up with changes in monitoring technology. Regulatory lags explain why regulatory information systems have lagged notably in efficiency and scope behind the information systems operated by well-managed large banks.)

2. By differential administrative lags in recognizing the implications of emerging forms of risks. (These lags are worse in bureaucratic than in profit-oriented organizations.)

3. By political protections against insurer-instigated sanctions for particular classes of risk-taking.

These restraints prevent deposit insurers from eliminating *ex ante* subsidies to risk-taking. The principal counterincentives to risk-taking lie in the size of a firm's accumulated capital and in managerial aversion to the career risk an executive suffers from having led an institution that fails. As a firm approaches economic insolvency, the force of both counterincentives declines.

Setting Appropriate Explicit Premiums

Opponents and proponents of risk-rated deposit insurance agree that, under the current information system, an institution's portfolio risk is *hard to measure* and *hard to price ex ante.* They also agree that if authorities had an information and insolvency-response system that was good enough to let them take over and dispose of insured institutions before private equity could be exhausted, deposit insurance funds would have monitoring costs to recover but would have no risk exposure to price from even the riskiest and most dishonest client.

The properties of such a system and the costs of installing and operating it are matters of speculation. Empirical evidence shows that large claims on deposit-insurance reserves have resulted mainly from two sources: managerial fraud; and desperately risky endgame plays made by client banks that were allowed to remain in operation long after they became economically insolvent. Hence, experience confirms the theoretical hypothesis that information risk, bureaucratic lags, and political restraints on closing economically insolvent institutions underlie the imperfect controllability that, together with stockholders' limited liability, creates risk-management and pricing problems for deposit insurers.

These problems do not differ essentially according to whether explicit or implicit pricing is employed. Because bureaucratically imposed *ex ante implicit* premiums have failed to control risk-taking in a changing environment, it is unlikely that, without additional reforms in insolvency resolution and information collection, bureaucratically imposed *ex ante explicit* premiums would offer much chance for improvement.

It is inherently difficult for teams of individual regulators to set appropriate *ex ante* premiums, even for such conceptually straightforward risks as those due to fraud, variations in asset quality, and asset-liability mismatching. However, when viewed as a problem to be solved by financial markets rather than by bureaucrats, the task falls well within the capabilities of financial technology.

Although fraud is particularly difficult to predict actuarially and even to uncover after the fact, fidelity insurance companies sell insurance against fraud. Bonding companies' profit margins have come under considerable pressure recently, but the market for bonding services is too strong not to be served. At the same time, bond markets and bank loan officers make and price parallel assessments of corporations' warranted financing rates every day. To make risk-rated premiums work would require an information system rich enough to let markets help observers both to make adequate assessments of institutions' risk exposure and to price the levels of risk assessed.

In principle, an institution's premium would be risk-rated if it captured the aggregate value of the different kinds of risk exposures that the institution's operations and portfolio positions imposed on the FDIC insurance fund. Each component of the aggregate premium could be interpreted as the product of the amount of the specific type of risk imposed on the fund and the market price for bearing risk of this specific type. The process of setting prices and quantities for specific risks could be approached either by surveys of expert opinion or by statistical analysis of empirical data.

Empirical analysis of call report information conducted by government and academic economists has begun to focus beyond the determinants of bank problems and failures (Sinkey, 1979; Bovenzi, Marino, and McFadden, 1983, who conduct an excellent literature review; Short, O'Driscoll, and Berger, 1985) to the determinants of insurers' losses in failures. (Avery, Hanweck, and Kwast, 1985; Barth, Brumbaugh, Sauerhaft, and Wang, 1985). Relying on the statistical technique of probit analysis, the latter authors show that information generated by reporting requirements added to the call report during the past few years can (when appropriately weighted) function as important predictors of individual failures and the explicit costs of insolvency resolution. Their research suggests that this information might be used, along with interest rates on what is perceived to be uninsured deposits and debt, to calculate expected losses and risk-rated insurance premiums. Another line of academic research suggests the possibility of double checking the adequacy of such premiums by using principles of option pricing. (McCulloch, 1985; Pyle, 1983).

Recent experience strongly suggests that insolvent institutions undertaking risky endgame plays can be identified by continually monitoring information on the interest rates insured institutions offer for brokered and other insured deposits and by monitoring institutions' net interest margins and the comparative growth rates of institutions' portfolios.

With an adequate and well-defined information system for monitoring client risk-taking, an agency's *ex ante* pricing decisions could be tested in the market place in either of two ways. First, they could be tested *ex post* in secondary markets by requiring private reinsurance of selected portions of federal deposit-insurance guarantees. Reinsurance transactions transfer the liability for the coverages in question to a third party, who is said to reinsure the risk. Alternatively, FDIC pricing could be tested *ex ante* in primary markets by fostering competition among alternative government and private providers to write guarantees. Although a private guarantor might be more or less well-diversified than would the FDIC against the risks in question and might lack the infinitely deep pockets of a federal guarantor, unless the private guarantor attached nearly the same value to deposit-insurance contracts as the issuing agency did, at least as a first approximation, the contract might be regarded as mispriced.

Reliance on private guarantors would push insolvency possibilities through an additional level, thereby underscoring the need for improved methods of insolvency resolution. Unless financial haircuts for uninsured creditors and private guarantors could be assured, predictable political responses to the threatened insolvency of an important guarantor could undo most of the benefits of private competition. In recent years, maintaining the perfection of the *de facto* guarantees provided by federal deposit insurance has imposed large implicit costs on federal taxpayers. Underpricing federal deposit insurance has made it easier for federal agencies to keep the true costs of the nation's soft-hearted insolvency-resolution policies from appearing in their budgets. However, these costs show up implicitly in the growing value of aggregate deposit-insurance guarantees and in increasing public doubts about the adequacy of accumulated insurance reserves.

Market checks on federal deposit-insurance fees are important precisely because political goals and constraints frequently encourage agencies to underprice their services. For example, tradeoffs between maintaining the economic strength of federal insurance agencies and responding to political and bureaucratic pressures help to explain why widespread *de facto* insolvencies at thrift institutions in the early 1980s led deposit insurers to lower their standards for capital adequacy rather than to enforce their agencies' narrow economic interest. By reducing the net-worth-to-assets ratio used as a threshold in identifying problem institutions, insurers reduced their caseloads to a size that their overworked supervisory staffs and explicit insurance reserves could handle. So far, taxpayers have perceived the benefits of this maneuver far more clearly than they have perceived the costs.

Risk-Rated Premiums, Market-Value Accounting, and Self-Regulation

What are needed are a better information system and a better system for adjusting implicit and explicit insurance premiums in response to the information produced. One strategy for assembling an information base from which a reliable process of risk-rating could be developed would be to permit deposit insurers to vary their coverages and fee structures. This could generate information on just how valuable managers of different institutions and their customers found different kinds and patterns of coverage. In the aggregate, clients' willingness and unwillingness to pay different prices for different kinds of coverage in different portfolio circumstances would signal how coverages might usefully be adjusted (through deductible and co-insurance provisions in the underlying guarantee contract) and whether premiums ought to be raised or lowered.

To assist deposit-insurance administrators in designing differential patterns of coverage and in interpreting market responses, a self-regulatory commission could be empowered to negotiate changes in information requirements, coverage structure, and pricing. The purpose of this commission would be to call public attention to inappropriate insurer behavior and to give the banking industry a voice in the development and evolution of premium and coverage structures meant to curtail distributional inequities and limit deposit insurers' exposure to adverse actions by insured institutions.

Even if its powers were carefully circumscribed by those of federal deposit insurers, the commission could provide a forum for identifying and analyzing the consequences of emerging opportunities for risk-taking. Such opportunities would be generated by technological changes and evolving customer needs and would arise as innovative banks and nonbank competitors discovered loopholes in existing regulations. The system would work because conservatively run banks effectively backstop the insurance funds: Any banks that fail to exploit unregulated risks are forced to underwrite *de facto* the insurance funds' exposure to aggressive risk-taking by the insured institutions with which they compete. Conservatively run institutions would therefore have a strong incentive to act as whistle-blowers for the insurance agencies.

As to improving the quality of information flows to deposit insurers, an advantage of requiring deposit institutions to report their incomes and balance sheets on a market-value basis would be the role the resulting information could play in setting risk-rated premiums. Market-value reporting would make the existing system of bureaucratically determined implicit premiums more effective and could also serve as a basis for collecting risk-related insurance fees by *ex post* assessment. Market-value reporting would do these things by making it easier for regulators to assess an institution's true exposure to traditional and nontraditional forms of risk. Disclosing market-value information to the market at large would make the same benefits available to an institution's uninsured creditors, as well.

Market-value reporting would increase the risk-sensitivity of existing implicit premiums by permitting capital requirements and oher balance-sheet restrictions to be redefined in a more meaningful, market-value sense. In a regulatory environment in which declines in market value formally passed through to an institution's net worth account, deposit institution managers who contemplated aggressively pursuing unregulated risks would have to prepare themselves to rebuild their capital as soon as losses occurred and to defend their risk-taking strategies against more timely criticism from regulators.

If market-value accounting were established and the resulting information were regularly disclosed, the criticism of private financial analysts ought to become more timely, as well. Having to record losses as they occurred would force an institution with deteriorating economic solvency to pay appropriately higher interest rates sooner to uninsured creditors. Having to worry about how regulators and uninsured creditors would respond to unfavorable news that could not automatically be suppressed or retouched would establish incentives for deposit institution managers to modify and to bond their behavior in ways that would reduce their ability to extract deposit-insurance subsidies to risk-bearing.

In principle, market-value reporting would also create opportunities for collecting or rebating a portion of an institution's risk-based premium on an *ex post* basis. However, a considerable expenditure of energy, ingenuity, and managerial tenacity and resourcefulness would be required to render such a system operational. If the industry could be persuaded to report to regulators the market value of *all* components of deposit institutions' expanded balance sheets, including intangibles and sources of value that current accounting principles designate as off-balance-sheet items, the value of federal guarantee services to any widely held firm could, theoretically, be calculated straightforwardly from the value that the stock market placed on the equity of the firm. In principle, a firm's stock value, S, would equal the market value of bookable and unbookable assets other than federal insurance guarantees, $A + A'$, minus the market value of bookable and unbookable nonequity liabilities, $L + L'$. If (and only if) every other off-balance-sheet source of value were accounted for, the value of a firm's explicit and conjectural federal guarantees net of discounted future premiums, F_G, could be calculated as:

$$F_G = S - (A + A') + (L + L').$$

Because F_G would be calculated as a residual, it would include the net measurement error in the accounting scheme. For some types of firms, this error might be considerable, especially in such a scheme's first few years of operation. For this reason, the margin of error embodied in calculated values would need to be investigated statistically and taken explicitly into account in estimating guarantee costs. A self-regulatory body could conduct such research without greatly threatening mainstream industry interests in the process.

The annual cost of providing a guarantee whose value is F_G may be written as $C(F_G)$. This cost may be defined as the interest cost of supporting the guarantee's average value during the year, $i_t F_G(t)$, plus the change in the market value that occurs from year end to year end:

$$C(F_G) = i_t F_G(t) + F_G(t) - F_G(t\text{-}1).$$

Because the change in value could easily be negative, the *ex post* annual cost would not always be positive. To supplement *ex ante* premiums, a fraction of the estimated *ex post* cost could be collected from each institution each year. For different types of risks, this fraction could vary with the perceived precision of market-value estimates.

This method of establishing an *ex post* settling-up for the cost of maintaining federal guarantees would be hard to implement and would be directly applicable only to publicly held institutions. Those institutions, however, control a substantial portion of industry assets, and the acknowledged difficulties of liquidating any of the nation's largest institutions grant these firms broader *de facto* guarantees than smaller institutions enjoy. Different *de facto* guarantees pose problems of equity that an *ex post* settlement scheme could eliminate by price differentials. Moreover, it is possible that values assigned to different risks in the process of applying the scheme to publicly held institutions could be used to estimate the current market prices of different kinds of risks. In principle, disaggregated prices found in this manner could be adapted by statistical methods to interpolate a set of market-based fees that could be levied on closely held institutions.

Extended Stockholder Liability as a Risk-Based Premium

To give *ex post* settlement greater *ex ante* force at failing firms, it would be useful to extend the liability of stockholders in insured institutions. The liability of stockholders in every financial institution that enjoyed implicit federal guarantees of its uninsured debt could be extended to two (or more) times the par value of their stockholdings, as was the liability of stockholders in national banks until the late 1930s. Deposit insurers could levy quarterly or annual charges on individual institutions, designed to recover all or at least a large fraction of the *ex post* value of the guarantee services received. Moreover, these charges could be collected even from bankrupt firms.

When increased implicit premiums take the form of higher capital requirements, they usually demand increased reliance on either uninsured debt or stockholder capital. However, except that they impose different constraints on stockholder liquidity and default possibilities, regulatory requests for more-capital are formally equivalent to extending the liability of existing bank stockholders. Viewed from this perspective, the cost of bonded (i.e., collateralized or externally insured) methods of extending stockholders' liability would increase with the cost of insolvency to bank stockholders. The effect would be all the greater if the extended-liability multiplier or the degree of bonding could be increased administratively as a bank's riskiness increased. In any case, permitting bank stockholders to opt for bonded forms of extended liability instead of issuing subordinated debt might ease the burden of meeting higher capital requirements, especially for small banks. However it might be accomplished, extending stockholder liability would simultaneously reduce one of the asymmetries that makes the deposit insurance subsidy so hard to control and would generate additional implicit private capital for the banking system.

When reinforced by a well-bonded system of extended stockholder liability, an *ex post* settling-up scheme for assessing the value of insurance services after they had been received would not mean merely collecting from a bank's stockholders after the bank fails. The knowledge that stockholders would have to put up additional funds in the event of failure would exercise market discipline by increasing the stockholders' *ex ante* cost for bearing failure risk. As long as stockholders' extended liability were adequately bonded, it would lower the *ex ante* benefits stockholders could anticipate from institutional risk-taking. This would provide a mechanism for preventing the *ex ante* expectation of deposit-insurance premiums from being driven below the market returns that insured institutions could anticipate earning on risky projects.

CHAPTER 10

Supervision and Examination

Supervision refers to the oversight of banking organizations and their activities to ensure that they are operated in a safe, sound, and law-abiding manner. The state and federal agencies that charter banks, and the agencies that insure their deposits are charged with their supervision. Other activities may be regulated by agencies (such as the Department of Justice) that enforce laws (such as the antitrust laws) that apply to other institutions as well as to banks.

Examination is a means for supervisors to obtain information. Examiners visit banks for the purpose of reviewing their records and procedures, interviewing their managers, determining whether the banking laws are being complied with, and evaluating the banks' condition and performance. The examiners report their findings to the banks' senior officers and boards of directors, as well as to their superiors. The examination reports are not permitted to be made available to the public.

Banks must file a large number of reports, including quarterly Reports of Condition, quarterly Reports of Income and Dividends, and periodic (generally annual) reports on trust department activities, international operations, foreign exchange activities, executive officers' and principal shareholders' stock ownership and indebtedness to the bank and its correspondents, past due loans, and foreign country lending exposure. These reports include a great deal of detail, including memorandum items, such as average amounts of daily loans and deposits, that reveal the presence of inflated year-end numbers (window dressing). Bank holding companies with stock subject to the federal securities acts also are required to file statements with the SEC, including such data as loans outstanding by foreign country or major area and loans that are nonperforming.

The Reports of Condition and Income are publicly available individually and in aggregates published by the Federal Deposit Insurance Corporation (FDIC) under the title, *Bank Operating Statis-*

tics. A quarterly compilation, *The Uniform Bank Performance Report* (UBPR), has been available since 1982. It presents ratios for each insured commercial bank and compares each bank's ratios with those of peer groups and states. The Security and Exchange Commission's (SEC) mandated reports are also publicly available.

Thus, field examinations are not the only means for supervisors to obtain the information needed to do their jobs. Nor have examinations been as effective as might be expected for obtaining information that can only be obtained in the field.

Reasons for Supervision and Examination

Before deposit insurance was enacted, a major reason for supervising banks was to protect depositors. A bank failure could result in the loss of depositors' funds, in the failure of other banks, and in financial distress caused by a multiple contraction of the money supply. As is discussed in Chapters 1 and 2, these are no longer serious problems, however. Now, it is the deposit-insurance agencies and the taxpayers that have reason to be concerned about bank safety, because they bear the costs of bank failures. Uninsured depositors also may be protected by supervision, although (as is discussed in Chapter 7) there is reason to want these depositors to be concerned about the bank safety. Should it be the lender of last resort (see Chapter 5), the Federal Reserve also might have an interest in bank supervision, a concern that is addressed in Chapter 11.

Another reason for bank supervision is to provide a means of enforcing certain laws. Previously, the principal laws to be enforced were those (such as non-interest-bearing reserve requirements) that imposed taxes and those (such as antibranching laws, interest rate ceilings, and constraints on the services and products that banks could offer) that limited competition. Recently, laws designed to protect consumers and trace the movement of funds related to currency "laundering" have become important.

Field examination is a form of supervision that is almost unique to banking. Examiners usually make regular visits to other types of enterprises only when questions of public health or safety are involved, as they are in meat-packing companies, restaurants, nursing homes, and nuclear power plants. Some types of examinations (such as tax audits or narcotics busts) are conducted when there are particular reasons to suspect wrongdoing or to prevent certain actions from taking place. But banks are periodically visited by field examiners, even when they are believed to be conducting their affairs properly. The fact that banks handle large sums of money and credit is not the only reason, because small-loan and mortgage companies, as well as department stores, handle large sums of money and credit but are not regularly examined.

It is useful to understand why field examinations have been imposed on banks. If the reasons were once meaningful but are no longer so, this expensive form of supervision should be modified or discontinued. Banks may have been singled out for field examinations in the early days of banking because they were the suppliers of the nation's money supply—banknotes. State and federal laws generally required banks to hold marketable assets, such as specie and bonds, equal to at least a specified portion of the notes issued, to assure the banks' ability to convert notes into specie. Because these assets could be stolen very readily or otherwise misappropriated without the knowledge of the holders of the notes, physical checks by a government agency might have been considered more efficient than duplicative checks by many noteholders. However, demands for conversion of bank notes to specie by holders and competitors appeared to have been an effective means of keeping banknote issuers honest. In any event, only the Federal Reserve now issues currency; therefore, inspection for convertibility is no longer an issue.

Another reason for on-site examinations is that the principal assets in which banks invest—loans to companies and individuals—do not have readily ascertainable market values. Therefore, examination of the documents may be necessary to determine that assets are good. Perhaps also important was the experience that the failure of one bank resulted in the loss of confidence in others, with resulting externalities. But deposit insurance has invalidated justification for field examinations.

Today, it is the moral hazard of deposit insurance that makes some form of examination or supervision desirable. This conclusion is supported by the experiences of the state deposit insurance plans that preceded federal deposit insurance. The beginnings of effective bank examination can be traced to the New York State deposit insurance plan established in 1825. That plan, and those established by Vermont in 1831, Indiana in 1834, Ohio in 1845, and Iowa in 1858, included provisions for bank supervision and examination and were successful. The 1836 Michigan plan was wiped out by the panic of 1838 before it could get established. Eight additional state plans were adopted between 1908 and 1918. Compulsory deposit insurance was enacted by Oklahoma in 1908, Nebraska in 1909, Mississippi in 1915, South Dakota in 1916, and North Dakota in 1917; voluntary plans were established in Kansas in 1909, Texas in 1910, and Washington in 1917. In its review of these plans, the FDIC concluded that, "For the most part . . . examinations were perfunctory. Except in Mississippi, inadequate time was allowed for making examinations." (FDIC, 1952, p. 67). Mississippi experienced relatively few failures, and its plan lasted the longest, terminating in 1930. The other states' plans became bankrupt.

A comparison of the failure rates of national banks and state-chartered banks during the 1920s provides additional evidence supporting the hypothesis that effective supervision and examination reduce failures. It was generally acknowledged that the Office of the Comptroller of the Currency (OCC) supervised and examined national banks more closely than did most state supervisors. After comparing the failure rates, Benston (1973, p. 36) concluded:

> Accounting for differences in region, size of town, size of bank, and numbers of banks, the national banks experienced a significantly lower rate of failure than did state banks . . . although other factors may have been responsible for the national banks' lower failure rate.

Thus, the experiences of state-sponsored insurance plans and the comparisons of failure rates support (although they do not demonstrate) the conclusion that some form of field examination and supervision is necessary and desirable. The remaining questions are the extent to which present practices are effective and whether alternatives would be preferable.

The Method and Cost of Field Examinations

Sound national banks with assets of $300 million and above are examined by the Office of the Comptroller of the Currency every 12 months; smaller banks are examined every 18 months. State-chartered commercial and mutual savings banks are examined about every 18 months by the Federal Reserve if they are Fed members, by the FDIC if they are insured nonmembers, and by some state banking departments. The state and federal examinations may be concurrently or jointly conducted; in a few states, the federal authorities accept state examinations, and vice versa. The Federal Home Loan Bank Board examines institutions that are insured by the Federal Savings and Loan Insurance Corporation (FSLIC), at least once annually, and requires that the institutions' financial statements be attested to by certified public accountants (CPAs). State-chartered savings and loans are also examined by some state banking departments. When a bank or thrift is determined to be a problem, it usually is examined more often, particularly if it is large.[1]

The principal purpose of the usual field examination remains to evaluate a bank's loan portfolio and management. The examiners look at the documentation, collateral, and payment records of most large loans and a sample of small loans. The loans are classified as good, substandard, doubtful, or loss. The bank's internal control system and managerial practices are reviewed and evaluated, the amounts of recorded assets, liabilities, and off-balance-sheet accounts (such as security and loan commitments and guarantees) are verified, and the bank's compliance with federal and (for state examiners) state laws is determined. Emphasis is placed on laws that prohibit or restrict dealings between the bank and its officers, directors, and stockholders, and that limit loans to individual and related borrowers. Separate "compliance" examinations are conducted to verify that consumer protection laws (principally the Equal Credit Opportunity Act and the Fair Housing Act) are being followed. The examiners' findings usually are discussed with management and given to the board of directors for comment.

Bank holding companies are inspected, rather than examined (because a fee would have to be charged were the practice labeled examination), by the Federal Reserve. Several states also examine bank holding companies. Because holding companies can include national and state-chartered banks, units (such as consumer finance companies) that are regulated by state agencies, and units (such as mortgage banking companies) that are not regulated, there can be problems of coordination and completeness of supervision and examination.

The banking supervisors use the bank's required reports and the examination report to determine the extent to which the bank is complying with regulations or must be specially supervised (is a problem). Numerical ratings from one to five are given in five categories of performance: capital, assets, management, earnings, and liquidity. The ratings are known by the acronym, CAMEL. An overall CAMEL rating is made; a bank given a one or two is considered to be no problem. A rating of three calls for watching by the Federal Reserve, consideration for formal administrative action by the OCC, and closer scrutiny by the FDIC. A bank rated four or five is designated as a problem or a serious problem. The most important aspect of this determination is the extent to which the bank has adequate capital, which is measured as the book value of equity, plus loan-loss reserves, and minus loans specified as losses and a portion of those criticized as doubtful and substandard.[2] The key variable determined by the examiners is the amount of substandard loans.

The costs of examinations are borne by the supervisory agencies and by the banks. The Bush Task Group (1984, p. 29) reports that "the federal financial regulatory agencies spent $237 million on examinations alone in 1982, with the three bank agencies accounting for $173 million of this total. Of course this figure significantly understates the total cost of examinations, as it does not include the expenditures of state regulatory agencies or the expenses of the firms subject to examination." The latter cost has not been estimated, but it is considered to be substantial. Examiners must be provided with space, records, special computer runs, and management time. Banks must keep records that they otherwise would not maintain. The only federal agency to charge banks a direct fee for examinations is the Office of the Comptroller of the Currency. Some states also charge for their examinations. The FDIC and the FSLIC charge indirectly for examinations by making annual assessments against all deposits at insured institutions, regardless of whether (in the case of banks) the institutions are examined by other agencies. The total cost of examinations and other aspects of bank regulation has not been estimated.[3]

Evaluation of Field Examinations

Two general questions can be raised about field examinations: First, are they useful supervisory tools; and second, are they the most cost-effective approach available?

The usefulness of bank examinations can be evaluated from four perspectives: the usefulness of examiners' identifications of substandard loans for predicting loan losses; the comparative abilities of statistical models and of examiners to predict bank failures; the examiners' record in uncovering fraud; and the examiners' record in discovering and dealing with excessive risk-taking. The value of consumer compliance examinations also merits review.

Prediction of Loan Losses

The evaluation of loans, which is a major purpose of field examinations, presumably cannot be achieved by alternative methods. The classification of loans as loss or doubtful is important, but those classifications are neither difficult to determine nor useful for preventing failures, because by the time loans deteriorate to those points, the classifications affect only the banks' books. Substandard loans, however, are those that the bankers might be able to do something about and that the supervisors should see as early warnings about the financial conditions of the banks.

The first, and perhaps the only, published study to examine the extent to which loans that became losses were previously identified as substandard was conducted by Wu (1969). He sampled 33 national banks and examined 162 charged-off loans. Of these, only 42 were above the examiners' cut-off points and, therefore, could have been subjected to criticism. Five had been classified as "loss," leaving 37 that could have been identified as substandard. Of these, 28 (77 percent) had been so identified, indicating that the examiners were fairly successful in predicting loan losses. It is remarkable, though, that the supervisory agencies (who are the only ones with access to the data) have not published more current and larger scale studies so that the general validity of this finding could be determined.

A later and much more comprehensive (though more aggregative) study used two models in comparing the predictions of net loan charge-offs in each of three years, 1972 through 1974, at 501 banks, which were grouped by size into three classes. (Graham and Humphrey, 1978). One model used only the net charge-offs in the previous year and the change in loans during the year—publicly available data. The other model used these data plus the loan amounts classified by the examiners. The researchers found that the addition of the examiner-determined data added very little to the predictive ability of the second model—indeed, the model without the examination data predicted somewhat better.

Examiners' and Statistical Models' Predictions of Failures

An important limitation of statistical models is that they do not incorporate nonquantitative data, particularly when these data are derived from current conditions that were not present in the past. Furthermore, statistical models must use the data that are reported, even though these data might be fraudulent or otherwise misstated. Consequently, field examinations should provide supervisors with better predictions of failure than the statistical models, even though field examinations are more expensive.

Published studies reveal that the examiners' ability to identify banks that are likely to fail is far from perfect. Among the 56 bank failures that occurred between January 1959 and April 1971, fully 59 percent were rated as "no problem" at the examinations just prior to their failures. (Benston, 1973, Table XIII, p. 43). For the 73 banks that failed in fiscal years 1981, 1982, and 1983, 63 percent of the banks received ratings of "probably no problem" (CAMEL numbers one, two, and three) and 34 percent received ratings of "definitely no problem" (CAMEL numbers one and two) in the year prior to failure. Two years before failure, the examiners rated 78 percent of the banks that failed as "probably no problem," and 57 percent as "definitely no problem." (Bovenzi, Marino, and McFadden, 1983, Table 6).[4,5]

Statistical early-warning models have been available for use by the supervisory agencies since the mid-1970s. The models appear to be used primarily as a means of aiding the examiners in writing up their reports rather than for evaluating banks and deciding which institutions should be examined more intensively or more often.[6] This is unfortunate, because the models alone appear to do as well as examinations in identifying problem banks. Furthermore, the models tend not to identify banks as problems that are not problems.

Sinkey and Pettway (1980) used two simple models to predict large bank failures. One model is a multiple discriminant analysis (MDA) that uses only two ratios measured with financial accounting data. Operating expenses as a percentage of total income and investments as a percentage of total assets of 33 banks that failed over the period from 1970 to 1975 were compared statistically to the ratios of similar nonfailed banks. The coefficients developed from the model were applied to data from the 16 banks that failed in 1976. Sinkey and Pettway report that "the . . . model correctly identified 15 of the 16 banks as future failures one year prior to failure and 14 of the 16 two years prior." (p. 144). This accounting-screen model was then applied to earlier data from six of the nine largest banks that failed through December 1976 (U.S. National, Franklin National, Security National, American City Bank & Trust, Hamilton National, and International

City Bank & Trust).[7] The model predicted the failure of three banks four years in advance and that of the other three banks three years in advance. The model also predicted the banks' classification as "problems" by the examiners between 51 and 103 weeks (66 weeks, on average) before the actual beginning examination date.

Sinkey and Pettway also used stock market data to predict failures by comparing the stock price returns of the failed banks with those of nonfailed banks, adjusted for expected changes in stock prices generally. This market screen identified the banks as problems between 7 and 140 weeks (53 weeks, on average) before the beginning date of the examination from which this assessment was drawn. The models were also tested on a sample of six very large nonfailed large banks with actively traded stocks.[8] The market screen identified none of these banks as problems during the test period. The accounting screen, though, flagged four of the six banks as potential failures in one year (1976). However, when only the operating-expense ratio was used, the model misidentified only one bank in 1974 and in 1975 and none in 1976. With respect to the earlier sample of 33 banks, the accounting-screen MDA model misclassified as failures the following percentages of nonfailed banks: one year before failure, 18 percent; two years before failure, 25 percent; three years before failure, 23 percent; and four years before failure, 24 percent.

Bovenzi, Marino, and McFadden (1983) reviewed and updated a large body of similar research. They used bank call-report data from one year before failure in a MDA model, with which they correctly predicted 64 percent of the 73 failures that occurred between fiscal years 1980 through 1983. Adding data available only from examination reports increased the success rate merely to 67 percent. In comparison, CAMEL ratings three, four, and five (watch, problem, and serious problem) predicted 66 percent of the failures; ratings four and five predicted only 37 percent of the failures. For data available two years before the failures, the model with only call-report data correctly predicted 50 percent of the failures; compared to 58 percent when examination data were added; 43 percent were predicted with CAMEL ratings three, four, and five, and 22 percent with ratings four and five.

Based on these results, the more costly field examinations have only a slight advantage over the statistical model in predicting failures, and evaluations by the banking supervisors (as reflected by the CAMEL ratings they assign to banks) are not as effective as the statistical model in using examination and publicly available data. This record is unfortunate, considering that the majority of bank failures are due to fraud and malfeasance, for which statistical models should not have a comparative advantage.

Fraud and Malfeasance

Fraud is the principal contributor to bank failures. A study of 105 bank and savings and loan failures between January 1980 and June 1983 by the U.S. House of Representatives Subcommittee on Commerce, Consumer, and Monetary Affairs of the Committee on Government Operations (1984c, p. 5) found that "criminal activity by insiders was a major contributing factor in roughly one-half of the bank failures and one-quarter of the savings and loan failures," at a cost to the insurance funds perhaps in excess of $1 billion. From its analysis, the subcommittee concluded (p. 5):

> Despite such enormous losses, neither the banking nor the criminal justice systems impose effective sanctions or punishment to deter white-collar bank fraud. The few insiders who are singled out for civil sanctions by the banking agencies are usually either fined de minimus amounts or simply urged to resign. The few who are criminally prosecuted usually serve little, if any, time in prison for thefts that often cost millions of dollars.

The subcommittee identified several problems with the supervisory agencies' handling of fraud. One was their not keeping track of insider crimes and criminals. The report (pp. 3–4), concluded from a hearing held in 1983:

> The results of this hearing were disturbing. The FDIC, OCC, FHLBB, and the Federal Reserve were unable to provide the subcommittee,[sic] with information on criminal activities by insiders because they lacked systems for (1) compiling data on the numbers and types of criminal referrals they make to the Justice Department, (2) tracking the ultimate disposition of these referrals, and (3) maintaining records on civil enforcement actions taken against individuals who were the subject of these referrals. Worse, the agencies' indifferent attitude toward keeping useful records on criminal misconduct reflected a deeper—and much more fundamental—lack of interest in dealing with insider abuse in a meaningful way.

Furthermore, "the subcommittee's investigation reveals that a substantial portion of all insider abuse and criminal misconduct that does exist does not get detected or reported by the banking agencies in a timely fashion." (p. 52). Five major factors are identified as keeping examiners from detecting frauds (p. 52):

> (1) inadequate training for examiners in "white-collar crime," (2) revision in the examination process [that deemphasized audits for fraud], (3) the failure of examiners to pursue the "paper trail" of questionable loan transactions outside the institution being examined, (4) time pressures and manpower cutbacks on examining staff, and (5) the high turnover rate among experienced examiners in several of the agencies.

The subcomittee additionally pointed to supervisory delays.

There also is evidence that the examiners have been not very assiduous in checking loans for evidence of fraud. A strong concern for fraud is required, because the evidence thereof is unlikely to be obvious. As Gregory Jones, First Assistant U.S. Attorney for the Northern District of Illinois, told the subcommittee (p. 27):

> One of the most common forms involves the issuance of loans by officers or directors of a financial institution to companies in which they have a concealed financial interest or to individuals who are willing to pay kickbacks to obtain loans. Other forms may involve the receipt of a financial institution of phony or stolen collateral as security for loans. Finally, they may involve the issuance of loans to nominee borrowers who immediately turn the loan proceeds over to others who could not borrow directly from that financial institution.

Although it is difficult to trace the disposition of loans, a long-standing aspect of bank examination is the checking of collateral. Yet, there is evidence that this is done mechanically and, therefore, ineffectively. For example, the massive insider frauds that resulted in the failure of the Ranchlander National Bank of Melvin, Texas (which had been purchased a year and a half previously by a woman with no banking experience who was the common-law wife of a person who had been convicted of bank fraud and embezzlement), could have been discovered had the examiners physically checked collateral. As described by the subcommittee (p. 57):

> [The president of the bank] told Federal prosecutors that she had been "closely questioned" by OCC examiners during bank

examinations in 1981 and 1982 about out-of-territory loans and loans which exceeded the legal lending limit. At that time, the bank was actually carrying many fictitious cattle loans with no collateral, but the examiners did not follow up their questions by independently verifying whether the cattle actually existed. The FBI informed the subcommittee staff informally in this case that the examiners could have uncovered these fraudulent loans with "one or two phone calls" to the purported borrowers.

Several conclusions can be drawn from this record. One is that it is not as bad as it might be. Considering the speed with which insiders can steal or misappropriate large sums from banks, it is remarkable that more banks haven't been looted. Thus, although they are not perfect, the supervisory authorities may have prevented many frauds.

An alternative explanation is that banks tend to be owned and managed by people who find honesty to be a better policy, and that the frauds that are seen are not uncovered by the authorities but are discovered when the looted banks collapse. If this alternative explanation is correct, changes in bankers' attitudes and increased incentives towards excessive risk-taking as a consequence of underpriced deposit insurance do not bode well for the future.

Excessively Risky Banking

The major concern of bank examiners is reviewing loans and operating procedures, presumably to determine whether bankers made excessively risky credits and/or violated laws, particularly laws that constrain insider lending. This expensive procedure is undertaken because it is believed that some bankers deliberately or incompetently conduct their affairs in ways that risk the failure of their institutions. Doubts about the efficacy of bank examinations are supported, however, by the 1982 failure of Penn Square Bank, which resulted in the loss of hundreds of millions of dollars to uninsured depositors, the deposit-insurance agencies, and shareholders, and the related failures (or near failures or considerable losses) of banks that purchased over $2 billion in loans from Penn Square. These banks included Continental Illinois, Seafirst, Michigan National and Chase Manhattan, among others. Penn Square was able to write and sell very large loans to persons who had little prospect of repaying them, and who pledged grossly inadequate collateral. Furthermore, the bank's control procedures and loan documentation were missing or seriously incomplete.

The Comptroller of the Currency, C.T. Conover, testified that Penn Square "failed despite OCC's supervision, in significant part, because bank management acted imprudently and abandoned their compliance with our remedial directives. If the bank had fully implemented the terms of the agreement, its conditions would not have deteriorated so rapidly and, very probably, would have improved." (Conover, 1983, p. 13). Instead, Conover complained, the bank originated approximately $800 million in loans between the September 1981 and April 1982 examinations (the latter examination revealed sufficient losses to demonstrate insolvency), despite a downturn in the oil exploration industry in which these loans were concentrated. But the OCC examiners had previously found Penn Square in violation of prudent banking practices. Conover stated that a special examination, conducted from January 5 through February 27, 1981, "disclosed deterioration in the bank's overall condition [including] inadequate capital, poor asset quality, ineffective loan administration, inadequate staffing and policy development, weak internal controls, deficient liquidity, and imprudent asset and liability management practices." (Conover, 1983, p. 32). The OCC was mollified, however, by the assurance of bank management that things would be corrected, and by the appointment of a new president who, it turned out, did not have the authority to make the changes demanded by the supervisor. The September 1981 examination noted "improvements . . . [in] asset-liability management and control," corrections of previously noted violations of law, and "a desire by the new management to improve the condition of the bank and to comply with the terms of the agreement." (Conover, 1983, p. 35).

The OCC's failure to examine and monitor closely the operations of Penn Square is not understandable, for at least five reasons. First, there was reason to be concerned about the probity or competence of the bank's key officers. Penn Square's principal and controlling stockholder and chief executive officer, William "Beep" Jennings, was an unindicted co-conspirator of the 1972 Four Seasons Nursing Centers fraud (then the largest criminal securities fraud in U.S. history). His protégé, the officer in charge of over $2 billion in oil-and-gas lending, Bill Patterson, had no credit experience before he was hired by Jennings in 1977.

Second, Patterson's lending practices were so bizarre that it is difficult to understand how they could have escaped notice by examiners who were in the bank for several months. An example is the following description of a $2 million transaction consumated in December 1981:

> In a single afternoon Patterson heard their proposal, agreed to lend the money, and did so. It was a handshake, slap-on-the-back proceeding, culminating in a trip by Patterson to the cashier's window. He returned with a check for a million six hundred thousand dollars, the initial draw against a two-million-dollar line of credit. The oilman asked about the mortgage documents. "Patterson said, 'Don't worry. We'll do those later.' He knew me, as it happened, but did my corporation exist? Was I an officer? The fact is that the answer to both questions was no. He didn't care. He knew who I was. That was his only saving grace. I'm a reputable person, supposedly. But I could have just as easily been Willie Sutton." (Singer, 1985, p. 71).

Third, the documentation and control practices for loans were found by the examiners to be severely inadequate. These practices are described as follows:

> Lending money in the absence of a formal loan application; asking a customer, for the sake of expediency, to sign several blank notes; lending additional funds to meet interest payments; looking a customer in the eye but not looking closely at his financial statement; neglecting to update reservoir-engineering reports; failing to require borrowers to have the mortgaged oil-and-gas-production income sent directly to the bank each month; advancing interest payments to upstream banks on behalf of customers who had not yet sent the interest payments to Penn Square. . . . (Singer, 1985, p. 71).

Fourth, Patterson's actions when loans were classified during the April-May 1981 examination should have alerted the examiners that they were dealing with a serious-problem bank. As it is reported by Singer (1985, p. 78):

> [When the examiner, persisted in classifying a loan,] Patterson would cavalierly reply, "Go ahead. Classify the loan. We'll just sell it." Patterson moved out of Penn Square and into the hands of upstream banks eight and a half million dollars of loans that the examiners had declared *losses.*

From the congressional testimony, it does not appear that the OCC notified the upstream banks or the examiners of those banks of Penn Square's practice of selling examiner-identified loss loans.

Fifth, Penn Square originated $800 million in loans between the OCC's September 1981 examination and the April 1982 examination, after having originated about that amount between the May 1981 and the September 1981 examinations. Comptroller Conover did not state why the OCC believed that any small bank could write that volume of loans and still maintain control.

It is difficult to understand why the examiners didn't carefully check out some of the borrowers who were very deeply in debt to Penn Square or to those banks that purchased its loans and participations. In particular, Mahan and Rowsey, Inc., a small oil-and-gas producer consisting of one well and two partners, went from an initial $2 million oil and gas production loan and a $2 million line of credit for lease acquisitions in early 1981 to a $60 million debt by the end of 1981, a debt that the company had no possible way of repaying. (Singer, 1985, pp. 72–75).

A reading of the 1982 congressional hearings on the Penn Square failure and of the later report by Singer (1985) leads to the conclusion that the banks that purchased Penn Square's loans were guilty of very poor credit-granting practices. The public and other banks, which made their own errors, paid a substantial part of the cost when Penn Square and Continental failed. Preventing such situations is a major reason for bank examination, which presumably is directed towards the discovery, correction, and stopping of such practices when they threaten bank solvency. There is reason to believe that the examinations of Penn Square Bank, and possibly those of Continental and the other upstream banks that purchased loans originated by Penn Square, were seriously deficient in this regard, which leads to concerns about the efficacy of examination practices in less egregious situations.

Summary

Examinations are evaluated with respect to four criteria. First, loan losses were fairly well predicted by examiners in a 1969 study of 37 loans, but a 1978 study found that predictions of net loan charge-offs at 501 banks were not improved by the addition of classified loan data. Second, statistical models using only publicly available data did about as well or better in predicting failures as did examiners' predictions, as measured by the designation of banks as problems. Third, fraud is not well tracked or discovered by examinations, a comprehensive study by a congressional committee revealed. Fourth, excessive risk-taking by the Penn Square Bank was not prevented, and perhaps not discovered, by the examination process.

The results of the evaluation are not supportive of examinations, as presently conducted, as a means of preventing or mitigating the effects of costly bank failures. However, it might not be worthwhile to reduce failures and frauds below the levels presently experienced if the resources that would be required would exceed the savings that could be expected. Moreover, examinations are only one aspect of supervision.

Consumer Protection Compliance Examinations

The usefulness of these examinations depends, first, on whether the laws that are being enforced are necessary for protecting consumers from abuse by bankers. Some research has been done on this subject, particularly on invidious discrimination against females (prohibited by The Equal Credit Opportunity Act) and on redlining— the practice of not making mortgage loans in older, urban neighborhoods (the subject of the Home Mortgage Disclosure Act and the Community Reinvestment Act). Because these practices do not affect the safety and soundness of banks and the financial system, they are not analyzed in depth here. However, the empircal evidence (reviewed by Benston, 1983, pp. 237–239) provides no support for the belief that banks were practicing invidious discrimination when the laws were enacted.

The effectiveness of examinations directed towards evaluating and enforcing laws relating to consumer protection and criminal activity has not been studied. With respect to consumer protection, a question that should be raised is why, if field examinations are considered to be important, such examinations are not conducted on the premises of other suppliers of credit, such as department stores, gasoline retailers, and mortgage and consumer cash lenders? These companies issue much more consumer credit than do banks.

Supervisory Use of Examination or Early Warning Reports

Once it has been determined that a particular bank or thrift presents more than a very small probability of failure, the supervisors have to determine how and when to act. The first stage is a discussion with the offending bank's managers and a report to the directors. The supervisors usually elicit bank promises of actions to correct deficiencies and/or cease certain activities. If the supervisors believe that the bank is in dire risk of failing unless something is done or stops being done, a cease-and-desist order can be obtained from a court, after a hearing. If necessary, an immediate temporary order can be issued. Additional capital investments by equity holders can be demanded. More extreme actions include removal of bank officers and directors, cancellation of deposit insurance, and seizure and closing or merger of the bank.

Expeditious Actions by Banking Supervisors

There is reason to believe that the supervisors often fail to use their powers expeditiously to correct potentially dangerous or deteriorating situations. With respect to insider abuse, the House Subcommittee on Commerce, Consumer, and Monetary Affairs of the Committee on Government Operations (1984c, p. 15) determined that "the agencies fail to take timely enforcement action against individuals because (1) they impose too many layers of internal review for the consideration of most types of enforcement actions, and (2) because they disperse responsibility for taking action against insider abuse among too many individuals, rather than assigning primary responsibility to a single, designated official at the regional level."

In a number of very expensive failures, the supervisory authorities failed to take decisive action to stop extremely abusive banking practices, even after the examiners or others had reported them. Four such examples are the United States National Bank of San Diego, the Metropolitan Bank & Trust Company, the United American Bank and affiliates, and the Penn Square Bank.

The failure of the United States National Bank of San Diego (USNB) in 1973 was the first very large insolvency clearly due to fraud. Sinkey (1979, p. 219) reports the claim, published in the Boston *Sunday Globe*, that the Comptroller had substantial information about C. Arnhold Smith's misuse of USNB resources for more than 10 years before the bank was closed.

The 1982 failure of the Metropolitan Bank & Trust Company of Tampa, Florida, cost the FDIC at least $10 million. This failure was notable because the Federal Reserve had had many years to observe the increasingly self-serving lending practices of its president, Don Regar, and Allen Z. Wolfson, whom the House subcommittee described as "the mastermind behind the fraud that ultimately destroyed the bank." (1984c, p. 70). The subcommittee reported that the bank had been involved in very questionable loans and activities since its founding in 1974, and that the problems accelerated in 1978 when Wolfson, who was convicted of bribing a bank officer in that year, became increasingly and publicly involved in the bank's affairs. The June 1980 examination severely criticized the quality and legality of the bank's lending practices but did not give rise to a full investigation. "[I]f the Federal Reserve had conducted a full investigation," the subcommittee said, "it would have walked right into the very activity for which Allen Wolfson has plead guilty to and for which Regar is now awaiting trial." (pp. 73–74).

The 1983 failure of the United American Bank (UAB) of Knoxville, Tennessee, and six related banks was the most costly failure for the FDIC: The total loss is expected to be $219,701,000. (Committee on Government Operations, 1983, p. 3). The bank and related institutions were owned or controlled by the Butcher family, who made and transferred loans among the various units as they wished. It is admitted by FDIC Chairman William M. Isaac that:

> UAB for years operated on the fringe of soundness. It eschewed caution in favor of leverage, reasonable conservatism in favor of aggressiveness, and diversification in favor of real estate concentration and loans to insiders or quasi-insiders and their interests. . . . UAB was a bank bordering on being out of control, both in an operational sense and in credit administration. (Quoted from Hearings, Committee on Government Operations, 1983, p. 4).

After reviewing the record of the failures, the Committee on Government Operations Report (1983, p. 6) concluded the following:

> The FDIC's failure to take strong administrative and enforcement action against the UAB Knoxville principals years before the bank's February 1983 insolvency represents a case of extreme neglect. This conclusion is inescapable given the FDIC's specific knowledge over 6 years of the abusive practices taking place at UAB Knoxville and of senior management's repeated failure to correct these abuses; its doubts concerning the accuracy of the bank's books and records; and its thorough

understanding of the relationship, historically, between insider abuses and bank insolvencies.

The 1982 Penn Square Bank failure shows a similar, if shorter, record of supervisory inaction. Despite the pattern of abuses and violations of law, the OCC relied on jawboning and believed promises by the bank's officers and directors.

Supervisors' Failure to Act Expeditiously

Three reasons appear to explain the supervisors' reluctance to move quickly against insiders who might be looting or grossly mismanaging a bank. One is concern for the civil liberties of bank officers and owners and a reluctance to deprive them of their livelihood or investment without due process. For example, the Federal Reserve is quoted as maintaining that it could not oppose the establishment or control of a bank by a person unless he or she had actually been found guilty of a crime. (Committee on Government Operations, 1984c, pp. 46–47).

The second reason is that the supervisors (the Federal Reserve in particular) view the discovery and prevention of criminal misconduct as beyond their abilities or responsibility. (Ibid., pp. 108–109). Consequently, perhaps, they refer almost every possible violation of law to the Department of Justice, which does not have the resources to investigate them all. As a result, serious violations are not punished.

Third, the supervisory authorities appear almost never to believe that they are dealing with dishonest bankers who willfully attempt to deceive them. Comptroller Conover's explanation for the OCC's lack of action towards Penn Square provides an important insight into why the supervisory authorities have been fooled by wrongdoers. Conover avers: "If Penn Square had ever *openly* refused to cooperate with our supervisory efforts, OCC would have taken stronger action." (Conover, 1983, pp. 13–14, emphasis added). When the bank's chief executive officer (CEO) and controlling stockholder promised to correct the violations found in the examinations and to impose the suggested controls, the supervisors believed him. They even believed that a respected banker who was brought in as president, Eldon Beller, actually had control of the bank's lending. They also neglected the possibility that Beller might not forthrightly admit that Patterson still controlled the bank's oil-and-gas lending (80 percent of its originations) because, had he said otherwise, he was likely to lose a job that paid him twice what his previous position paid, plus stock benefits.

The flaw in the supervisors' approach towards misbehavior is shown in the following admission by Comptroller Conover:

> [O]ur experience with Penn Square demonstrates that the agency's supervisory effectiveness is to some extent limited by the responsiveness (or unresponsiveness) of a bank's management and board to our efforts. Over the long term, OCC will usually detect and overcome management resistance. However, in the short term, our supervisory efforts can be defeated by a bank management that promises one thing and does another.
>
> . . . . .
>
> In the final analysis, the agency's ability to affect the condition of a bank depends upon the execution of our directives by the officers and directors of the bank. It is not desirable for the regulator to substitute for bank management. . . . The bank supervisory system could not operate under a presumption of management dishonesty. (Conover, 1983, pp. 15–17).

Thus, the supervisory effort is directed towards honest, though perhaps confused or insufficiently competent, bankers. Yet there is considerable evidence that dishonest bankers exist, and that they can wreak considerable havoc on the insurance funds. Furthermore, the Comptroller's confidence in the effectiveness of a board of directors for effecting change is based on the assumption that they can take independent action. The possibility that a controlling stockholder or powerful CEO might control a board of directors seems to be overlooked, because the Comptroller follows the policy of giving a single copy of the examination report to the CEO, when then gives it to his or her board for their approval. In short, the supervisors operate as if there were no dishonest and devious bankers.

The FHLBB supervisory record is not better. It was studied with respect to the relatively large number (19) of savings and loan associations in Illinois that required FSLIC financial assistance from 1963 through 1968. (These represented 75 percent of the total losses suffered by the FSLIC over this period.) Bartell (1969, p. 419) concludes: "In contrast with the generally high quality of examinations, supervisory performance in the handling of failed associations leaves much to be desired." Indeed, from the description he gives prior to this statement, he is much too kind. More recent evidence is presented in the House Committee on Government Operations' (1984a) report on the 1984 failure of the Empire Savings and Loan of Mesquite, Texas. The committee found that the Bank Board did not act for some time after the examiners revealed very questionable lending practices, by which time many millions more of FSLIC-insured deposits were borrowed, loaned out, and lost.

It should be noted, however, that dishonest bankers have been a rarity in most supervisors' experience. As the Comptroller points out, bankers and boards of directors generally follow the supervisors' advice and admonitions. The supervisors thus have the very difficult problem of determining which few bankers are lying when they promise to correct a potentially dangerous situation. As is discussed next, legal impediments also constrain the insurance agencies from acting in time to prevent losses to the insurance funds.

Limitations on Supervisors' Ability to Act Expeditiously

Among the structural or legal factors that may prevent banking supervisors from acting to prevent banks from becoming problems and to prevent problems from becoming failures are the divided authority over regulated institutions and the lack of power to enforce supervisory commands.

Divided Supervisory Authority and Responsibility

Two types of divided authority should be delineated: (1) authority to close institutions versus responsibility for deposit insurance; and (2) authority and responsibility over different parts of the same banking organization. Both types can have seriously dysfunctional consequences.

The first concern stems from the fact that the agencies with the greatest interest in preventing or mitigating the costs of failures—the FDIC and the FSLIC—do not have the authority to close a bank before its capital becomes negative, with some exceptions. The FDIC can recommend that the Comptroller of the Currency close nationally chartered banks, and both insurance agencies can ask state authorities to close their institutions. But there are incentives for the OCC and the state agencies to delay closings. One incentive is the chartering agencies' natural allegiance to and sympathy with *its* institutions. Another incentive, which is particularly relevant for state agencies, is the fact that generally a federal agency, depositors, and taxpayers invisibly assume the costs of delaying a closing, whereas a state's citizens visibly bear costs when an institution is closed. Related to that incentive is the cost to a state banking supervisor of closing an institution where the owners and managers enjoy local regard and/or political power. Therefore, the state chartering authorities have incentives to delay, perhaps in the hope that conditions (e.g., the level of market interest rates) will change for the better.[9]

However, an argument against giving the insurance agency the sole power to close an institution is the fact that it is a monopoly supplier of deposit insurance. As the failure of the (state-sponsored) privately insured Home State Savings of Cincinnati and the runs on similarly insured Maryland savings and loan associations recently demonstrated, federal insurance dominates all other types of insurance, because the federal government is unlikely to default on its insurance pledge, if the Sense-of-Congress resolution passed in 1982 can be believed. Absent competition from other insurers, the FDIC and FSLIC (or any supplier of insurance) tends to be overly conservative. At the same time, deposit insurance that is not priced to account for risks gives some bankers incentives to find means of taking risks that the supervisors have not effectively constrained. Thus, conservative bankers tend to be overregulated, whereas those who prefer risks are insufficiently regulated. Some methods of dealing with this situation are suggested in Chapters 7 and 11.

The second concern refers to bank holding companies and related financial institutions, where the subsidiaries and affiliates are chartered by state and federal agencies and even foreign countries. Complicating the situation is the Federal Reserve's supervision of bank holding companies and state-chartered member banks. Thus a bank holding company and its bank subsidiaries can be inspected or examined by three federal agencies and one or more state agencies (if it has subsidiaries in states that allow them). When these agencies do not coordinate their examinations and supervision, the costs to the bank holding company can be unnecessarily high, and an excessively risky situation may not be discovered.

It is difficult to determine how serious the problem is. Shull (1980) studied this aspect of holding company failures. He concluded that "the extent of actual conflict among federal banking agencies in holding company supervision, while difficult to quantify, is important, time consuming, and diverting in problem cases." (p. 119). The Bush Task Group (1984) emphasized this concern, but it only provided descriptions of the delays and problems that it said might result.[10]

The failure of the United American Bank and other Butcher-owned financial institutions would seem to provide the best example of the need for coordination among supervisors or for a single supervisor of a related group of financial institutions. A former FDIC examiner testified as follows in hearings before the Congress:

> The UAB system was fragmented and examined by different agencies, different field officers and different state agencies. The FDIC could not get along with the Comptroller's office; there were political issues involved at the state level, too. Memo after memo went into the FDIC offices pointing out the frustration of field examiners in evaluating stock and participation loans. It was always felt if a major coordinated effort was ever made to examine the entire system there would be major revelations that constituted abuse. It took almost six years to orchestrate such a move. (Committee on Government Operations, 1984c, p. 66).

Yet, the Committee's earlier report on the UAB failure did not mention lack of interagency cooperation as a serious problem, except to note that although the Federal Reserve routinely made its reports available to the FDIC, the FDIC refused to make its reports and actions routinely available to the Fed, and the FHLBB had little or no knowledge of the extensive business dealings between the Butcher banks and savings and loan associations. (Committee on Government Operations, 1983, pp. 10–11).

Supervisory Power

Prior to the enactment of the Financial Institutions Supervisory Act of 1966, the supervisory authorities could enforce their will only with moral suasion, with the granting or withholding of regulatory favors, and with a very blunt and devastating instrument—the termination of insurance and/or banks' independent operations. Since 1966, the authorities have been able to use immediate temporary and/or delayed permanent specific cease-and-desist orders to make institutions change their ways or to remove incompetent or dishonest officers or directors. The law was modified in 1978 to make it easier for the supervisors to remove the directors or officers of insured banks. This law (P.L. 95-630, 12 U.S.C. §1818(e)) now authorizes removal when three conditions occur: (1) the officer or director has committed (a) any violation of law, regulation, or final cease and desist order, *or* (b) engaged or participated in any unsatisfactory or unsound practice in connection with the bank, *or* (c) committed a breach of fiduciary duty, *and* (2) the agency has determined that the bank has (a) suffered or will probably suffer substantial financial damage, *or* (b) the interest of depositors could be seriously prejudiced, *or* (c) the person has received financial gain by reason of the violation or breach of duty, *and* (3) the violation of law or breach of fiduciary duty is one (a) involving personal dishonesty, *or* (b) which demonstrates a willful or continuing disregard for the safety and soundness of the bank. Thus, if an agency wished to remove an offending person, it would appear to have the authority to do so. Congressional criticism of the agencies has been based, in large measure, on the supervisors' failure to remove officers who appeared clearly to have been those against whom the law was directed. To the dismay and disbelief of the Congressmen, the Comptroller interpreted the "or's" in the law as "and's."

The regulatory agencies can order institutions to raise additional equity capital. However, they have not been very successful in this regard for reasons that have not been explained, as is discussed in Chapter 9.

Restrictive regulations, though, have been employed to make failures less likely. These have included limits on charters, ceilings on deposit interest, and limits on the products and services that could be offered to the public. These restrictions were effective until the high nominal interest rates of the late 1970s and improvements in technology made it desirable and economically feasible for other suppliers to enter the banks' and thrift institutions' markets. At the same time, the thrifts' specialized portfolios made them particularly vulnerable to the devastating effect of interest-rate increases and volatility. Regional economic misfortunes have also been responsible for the failures of banks that specialized in loans to the affected industries (see Bovenzi and Nejezchleb, 1985), in part because restrictions on interstate branching have prevented the development of more diversified banks. Prohibitions against banks and thrifts offering a wider range of products and services also limited their opportunities for diversification and for profits that could have been earned as a consequence of comparative advantages. Thus supervisory and statutory restrictions at best forestalled failures, while making adjustments to change more difficult.

Considering the propensity of regulators towards conservatism, it does not appear that additional supervisory restrictions on the assets in which banks could invest or on the services they could offer would be helpful in reducing failures and payments from the deposit insurance funds. Nor do the supervisors appear to need additional powers to remove offending officers and directors. However, from the evidence on the effectiveness of statistical models for predicting bank insolvencies and problems, it would seem desirable for the supervisors to receive much more timely information for use in such models. In addition, improvements in the supervisors' ability and willingness to expeditiously close institutions that are close to insolvency would be desirable, particularly if their power to act arbitrarily were constrained.

Alternatives to Field Examinations and Close Supervision

Deposit insurance carries with it the requirement that banks with insured deposits be regulated in some way. Imposition of risk-related insurance premiums and *ex post* settling up (which makes shareholders additionally responsible for the cost of insolvency, as discussed in Chapter 9) reduce considerably the need for regulations to limit excessive risk-taking. But, because these means of reducing moral hazards are imperfect, changes in the regulations and in the approach taken by supervisors would decrease the bank supervisors' needs for field examinations and close supervision.

A required level of capital (or capital standard) could absorb most losses that a bank might incur under situations other than a massive general economic collapse (such as occurred in the Great Depression). The capital could consist of equity or subordinated debentures that would not come due during the period when losses where expected.[11] A diversification requirement would enable a bank's portfolio of assets and liabilities to reduce the effect of most expected losses to the amount that would be covered by the bank's capital.

Supervisors should be prepared to act swiftly to remove officers and directors who endanger the deposit insurance fund and to close an institution before it becomes completely insolvent. The authorities should recognize that, while the overwhelming majority of bankers are honest and competent, there are a few "bad actors" who can do great damage unless they are stopped quickly and effectively. Determining which people are dishonest or grossly incompetent, and which can correct a bad situation if given time and guidance, is not an easy task; some errors are inevitable.

If the authorities could be certain that the two regulatory requirements were continuously met, there would be no need for further regulation. The functions of supervision and examination, then, would be giving banks an incentive to fulfill the requirements (because their failure to do so would be revealed) and informing the authorities as quickly as feasible about those few bankers who chose to take excessive risks or commit fraud.

Statistical analysis of bank financial data, preferably enhanced by relevant market data, could substitute for a large number of field examinations. The specific numbers analyzed could be derived from theoretical and empirical studies of the factors that predict bank failures and financial distress. Such studies have been done and the models are available. If necessary, banks could be required to report some of the required numbers on a monthly or even weekly basis. Increasingly inexpensive communications equipment is likely to make early or real-time transmission of data desirable. The transmitted data might include deposits (including total deposits, large deposits, and brokered deposits); repos bought and sold; futures and options contracts and other contingent liabilities; total loans and large loans; interest and other income; and operating and other expenses (monthly only). Data on loans by industry might be reported, depending on the value and cost of the data. Banks might be required to schedule their own loans. This exercise would provide a timely report of substandard loans to both the banks' managers and to the supervisory authorities. Estimates of maturity gaps or durations and other analyses might be required quarterly.

The numbers could be reported via communication devices in computer readable form. They could be analyzed with data on regional and industry economic activity, and in conjunction with the ability of individual banks to absorb losses, as measured by their realistically measured noninsured liabilities and equity. The supervisory authorities thus would have very early warnings of potential problems and could more effectively target their limited examination and supervisory resources.

Field examinations would be used for four purposes. One would be to audit the numbers reported by banks. Those that were found to misreport significant numbers would be subject to immediate and extensive examinations. The cost of the examinations could be charged to the banks so that they, rather than banks that reported correctly, would pay the expense. The banks might be fined additionally as a means of giving them a further incentive not to misreport. The second purpose would be to uncover fraud. Specially trained auditors should be able to discover most frauds. The third would be to determine whether specific laws had been broken, because lawbreakers would be unlikely to report their transgressions voluntarily. The fourth would be to determine whether reported numbers were correct and to guard against the troubled institution's temptation to "bet the bank." This goal would be accomplished by sending examiners when the statistical and economic analysis indicated that a bank was coming close to using up its capital.

[1]See Chapter 5 of Golembe and Holland (1983) for a good description of examination practices.

[2]Sinkey (1979) compared 21 items on the examination reports of 143 commercial banks on the FDIC's March 31, 1974, problem list with those on the reports of 163 randomly chosen nonproblem banks. He reported that "[t]he most significant variable and the most important discriminator between the groups . . . was the net capital ratio [total capital accounts plus valuation reserves plus nonbook sound banking values less criticized loans (loss, doubtful, and substandard) divided by average gross assets]." (Sinkey, 1979, p. 55).

[3]Darnell (1982) estimated the costs of complying with government regulations by the United Bank of Denver. He found that the direct and indirect compliance costs amounted to 33.2 percent of the bank's before-tax net income.

[4]The two-years-before-failure sample excluded 13 banks on which the researchers did not have data. Some of these data were published only in Benston. (1984, p. 10).

[5]Similar studies do not appear to have been made of FHLBB examinations.

[6]See Altman and Sametz (1977) and Flannery and Guttentag (1980) for descriptions and critiques of those systems. Altman (1983) describes the models applied to a wide variety of industries and companies. An early warning model was developed by Altman (1977 and 1983) for the FHLBB but was not implemented by the Board.

[7]American Bank and Trust, N.Y., American Bank & Trust, Orangeburg, and Northern Ohio Bank, Cleveland, were excluded because there was insufficient trading volume in their shares for the stock market tests that were made.

[8]The six are: J.P. Morgan; First National Boston Corp.; National Detroit Corp.; Wachovia Corp.; First International Bankshares, Dallas; and Wells Fargo.

[9]See Chapter 5 for a discussion of alternative means of closing insolvent banks.

[10]See Chapter 7 for a more complete discussion.

[11]Short-term debentures also are valuable in providing the supervisors with market signals about the financial condition of the issuing institutions, as is discussed in Chapter 7.

CHAPTER 11

Centralization or Decentralization of Regulation, Supervision, and Examination

Commercial banks can be chartered by the Office of the Comptroller of the Currency (OCC) or by each of the 50 states. National banks must be members of the Federal Reserve System and must be insured by the Federal Deposit Insurance Corporation (FDIC). State-chartered banks may be Federal Reserve members; the larger ones are members, but most are not. Almost all banks obtain deposit insurance from the FDIC, in part because all but five states require depository institutions to have federal insurance. (In 1985, two of these states, Ohio and Maryland, required most of their state-chartered institutions to obtain federal insurance.) National banks can be supervised by three agencies, the OCC, the Federal Reserve Board, and the FDIC. But unless the banks require assistance from the FDIC or the Fed, only the OCC actually conducts field examinations and supervises the banks. State-chartered banks are examined and supervised by the Fed if they are members and by the FDIC if they are nonmembers. They also may be examined and supervised by their state banking supervisors, either separately, concurrently, or jointly with the federal examiners. As of December 31, 1983, there were 14,463 banks in the United States with total assets of $2,342 billion. The OCC was responsible for 33 percent of the banks and 60 percent of the assets; the Fed, for 7 percent of the banks and 18 percent of the assets; and the FDIC, for 60 percent of the banks and 22 percent of the assets. The states could supervise 67 percent of the banks and 40 percent of the assets.

The Fed is also responsible for regulating, supervising, and inspecting bank holding companies, which had 87 percent of total commercial bank assets as of December 31, 1983. Additionally, the states can regulate and supervise holding companies. Federal Reserve Board regulations, such as Regulations Q and Z, also apply to all insured commercial banks.

Savings and loans associations (S&Ls) can be chartered by the Federal Home Loan Bank Board (FHLBB) or by the states. Unlike commercial banks, about 75 percent of the savings and loan associations are mutuals. The deposits of S&Ls, except for those of some S&Ls in five states, are insured by the Federal Savings and Loan Insurance Corporations (FSLIC). Mutual savings banks (MSBs) that are state-chartered have deposit insurance with the FDIC; those few that are federally chartered by the FHLBB may, if they wish, have FSLIC insurance rather than FDIC insurance. Federally chartered and some state-chartered mutual thrifts may convert to stock companies. As of December 31, 1983, there were 3,040 S&Ls and 436 MSBs, holding total assets of $754 and $234 billion, respectively. Thrift-holding companies are regulated by the FHLBB. As of December 31, 1983, they held 21 percent of total S&L assets.[1]

Concerns About the Present System

The present dual (or, more accurately, multiple) system of regulation, supervision and examination has been criticized many times[2] for being (1) inadequate; (2) too costly; and (3) inequitable.[3]

Inadequate Regulation, Supervision, and Examination

Two types of inadequacy usually are delineated. One is the result of agencies' finding it difficult to cooperate with other agencies that are responsible for parts of the same banking organization. Problems have occurred, for example, because only the chartering agency has the authority to close a bank before its capital is completely depleted. Because the FDIC is not a chartering agency, and the FHLBB does not charter all insured S&Ls, the authority is divided, which can result in losses to the deposit insurers. Also, holding companies with units chartered by different agencies and operations in different states can be inadequately regulated when the several regulators fail to pool information and coordinate their actions.

The lack of cooperation might be overcome by merging the supervisory agencies or by making a single agency responsible for an entire banking organization.

The other type of inadequacy is said to result from regulatory laxity, as alternative regulators compete for the bottom. Such claims were made by Bremer (1935), who wrote: "competition for banks and resources has necessitated repeated relaxations of the banking laws." (p. 95). After describing a number of regulatory changes, he concluded: "It is evident that these changes in the national statutes—made in order to enable national banks to meet the competition of state institutions—resulted in lowering the level of banking operations generally, and gradually undermined the soundness and safety of the banking system." (p. 98). This concern was reiterated in 1974 by then chairman of the Federal Reserve Board Arthur Burns, who asserted: "Even viewed in the most favorable light, the present system is conducive to subtle competition among regulatory authorities, sometimes to relax constraints, sometimes to delay corrective measures." (quoted in Sinkey, 1979, p. 21).

The validity of these concerns (which is crucial to suggested changes in the provision of deposit insurance) can be seen by the following complete list of relaxations in the banking laws, adapted from Bremer. (Chapter VI "Responsibility for" Bank Failures pp. 95–112).

reducing minimum capital requirements for national banks (1900);

changing the amount that could be lent to one borrower to 10 percent of capital and surplus rather than 10 percent of just-paid-in capital (1906);

for other than central reserve city banks, loans on improved farm land, if the land was in the bank's Federal Reserve district, did not exceed 50 percent of actual value, and was for no more than five years;

providing authority to offer trust services, on a limited scale (1913);

permitting national banks not in central reserve cities to make loans of no more than one-year maturity on other real estate within 100 miles of the bank (1916);

widening the location of real estate loans to include the entire reserve district and extending the maximum maturity to five years, although limiting the aggregate to not more than 50 percent of savings deposits. (1927).

permitting national banks in central reserve cities to make real estate loans (1927);

granting authority to issue bankers' acceptances (no date given); and granting the right to engage in security-market operations (which had previously been conducted in state-chartered affiliates). (1927).

Bremer also stated, as evidence of low standards for chartering, that "management was directly responsible for 60 percent of these [national bank] failures." (p. 99). However, this is about the same percentage as is reported for failures in the post-World-War-II period, after more than a decade of very restricted chartering. He doesn't mention that national banks first were permitted to branch only in their home cities in 1927, and were not given branching rights equal to those enjoyed by state-chartered banks until 1933. But, as the analysis of bank failures in the 1920s and early 1930s (Benston, 1973) revealed, and as Bremer later concluded, unit banking was a (if not the) principal regulation-related cause of the failures.

With regard to more modern concerns, Sinkey (1979, p. 23) stated that:

> Although Burns (1974) did not give any examples of "subtle competition in laxity," several come to mind. Most notably was the competition (which at times was not very subtle) between the Federal Reserve and the Office of the Comptroller of the Currency during the period November 16, 1961, to November 15, 1966, which marked the reign of James J. Saxon as Comptroller. Comptroller Saxon believed that a little competition among the banking agencies would benefit the public in the long run.

Saxon removed the extreme restrictions on charters that had characterized the post-Great-Depression period. In just 4 years, 1962 through 1965, he approved charters for 514 national banks, twice the number chartered in the previous 12 years. Contrary to the predictions of Saxon's detractors, neither the newly chartered banks nor their competitors failed in greater proportions than other banks. He also interpreted the National Bank Act to permit national banks to lease equipment, engage in certain insurance activities, underwrite municipal-revenue bonds, and offer data processing and travel agency services. It is difficult to see how the provision of these services reduced the financial soundness of the national banks, although other suppliers of these services argued that it did.

The development of NOW accounts as a means of paying individuals interest on checking accounts is a state-chartered savings bank initiative that benefited consumers without endangering banks. NOW accounts were accepted first by state authorities. Federal authorities grudgingly permitted banks to offer NOW accounts, with the Congress initially limiting these accounts to banks in the states where they were established, and later permitting them to be offered by all banks.

Evidence on banks' changing regulators also speaks against the assertion of competition for the bottom. Although several large state banks switched to national charters during the Saxon years, between 1960 and 1978, only 5.9 percent of the state-chartered banks changed regulators. During the same 18-year period, 6.3 percent of the national banks became nonmembers, primarily to avoid the implicit tax on required non-interest-bearing reserves. A detailed study of these and other changes revealed that "some, but not many, bankers abuse the forum shopping principle of choice." (Miller, 1980c, p. 492).

The weaknesses of supervision and examination delineated in Chapter 10 are unrelated to differences among agencies. No evidence or even assertions were found charging that fraud was not searched for, dishonest people were not prosecuted, excessively risky banking practices were not stopped, or examination resources were not used effectively for fear that the banks supervised would move to other agencies or complain to higher authorities.

However, competition among regulators, like competition generally, can yield considerable benefits to banks and to the general public. The dual banking system, under which banks can be chartered by either the states or the federal government, has been cited frequently as having mitigated the tendency of regulators to stifle innovation and restrict new entrants. The extension of federal charters to mutual savings banks in December 1980 resulted in the states' granting savings banks additional powers to serve their customers. Concern about the establishment by securities brokers of nonbank banks (that take advantage of the legal definition of a bank as an institution that both takes deposits and makes commercial loans) led the Federal Reserve in December 1983 to allow nonbanking subsidiaries of bank holding companies the following additional powers: issuing money orders; arranging equity financing for real estate; underwriting and dealing in government and specified money-market obligations; providing foreign-exchange advisory services; and performing as futures-commission agents. (Kane, 1984, p. 770). Delaware and South Dakota enacted legislation that permitted out-of-state bank holding companies to conduct less-restricted credit-card operations and to offer insurance. As Kane (1984, p. 767) pointed out:

> Competition between overlapping federal and state regulators looks in the short run like wasteful duplication, but leads in the long run to better-adapted regulatory rules. When the opportunity cost of an exclusionary rule rises, pressures develop to soften the rule. It is unlikely that laws meant to hold deposit institutions out of brokerage and insurance activities and brokers and insurance companies out of deposit-institution markets can stand up indefinitely against opportunities to reduce product costs created by scope economies. While it is natural for lobbyists from an invaded industry to fight a rearguard political action to delay change, American politics and ideology favor innovation over regulation in many ways. In one way or another, low-cost schemes for producing and distributing products are able to push aside high-cost ones. This is partly because reregulation is a competitive process that responds to *economic* as well as political forces.

The Costs of Regulation

Two costs of the present regulatory structure may be delineated: agency resources, and costs imposed on the regulated banks and holding companies. The agency costs may be further described as those relating to the existence of several federal agencies and those relating to the overlap between federal and state supervisors.

If the federal regulatory agencies were merged, some resources might be saved, but greater additional costs probably would be incurred. If all banks in a region were examined by a single agency, there might be savings from lower travel costs and centralized computer facilities. However, travel is a very small portion of examination costs, and the agencies now use the FDIC's computer facilities because its tapes include data on all insured banks. There also might be diseconomies of scale, because managing a larger number of examiners is likely to necessitate more formal and costly procedures.

A greater cost from merging the agencies probably would result from the difficulty of combining organizations that had long histories of somewhat different operating procedures. The six-year experience of the Federal Financial Institutions Examination Council in carrying out its mandate to prescribe uniform federal examination principles, standards, report forms, and training is informative. The Council's efforts were studied by the General Accounting Office (1984), which found that little progress was made. The reasons were detailed in the report, which concluded: "There are many barriers to achieving uniformity, such as the reluctance of the participating agencies to reach compromises and coordinate the use of their powers in managing their programs." (p. 77). It is possible, though, that a merger of the agencies would give sufficient power to the chief administrator to "knock heads together." However, experience from other mergers of similar organizations (i.e., the New York Central and Pennsylvania Railroads) provides reason for concern about the effectiveness with which long-standing bureaucracies can be combined.

Thus, it is doubtful that a merger of the several federal agencies would result in administrative savings, although a greater uniformity in regulation and supervision would be likely. Nonetheless, the present regulators have considerable experience with the institutions they regulate, the benefits of which would be at least partially lost if the agencies were reorganized and the personnel were forced to be responsible for all institutions within their geographically determined areas. Those who believe that the agencies tend to be too protective of their constituents, however, would consider this loss of concern to be a benefit.

State chartered federally insured institutions are examined and supervised by the state chartering agencies as well as by the Federal Reserve, the FDIC, or the FSLIC. This dual supervision often (but not always) results in multiple on-site examinations. However, federal and state supervisors can and often do rely on each other's reports. Many state agencies do not expend the resources to examine banks, and the FDIC and the Federal Reserve alternate with state examiners in a few states where the state agency is considered to be very competent. (This practice is called divided examinations.) Joint examinations also are conducted. In a study of the manpower costs of examination, Miller (1980b, Vol. I p. 129) found that divided examinations required "roughly 35% less examiner manhours for the FDIC and 25% less total examiner manhours than the next most efficient program, joint examination." Miller (1980a) also attempted to measure the cost to state-chartered banks of double supervision. From "a representative nationwide sample of 1,585 chief executive officers of national, state member and state nonmember banks" (p. 379), he learned that the banks' chief executive officers (particularly those of smaller banks) tended to find double supervision "quite costly," but not sufficiently so to induce them to change charters, especially when only national and state-member banks at that time were required to hold non-interest-bearing reserves.[5]

Considering that federal deposit insurance protects most depositors and that the insurance agencies bear most of the costs of failures, the states' interest in the safety and soundness of banks is questionable. As the chartering agencies, the state agencies bear some responsibility for banks. But, the states also charter a much larger number of other corporations, for which they presumably are equivalently responsible. Therefore, it seems evident that the state's interest in bank supervision and examination is a vestige of the pre-federal-deposit-insurance period and is no longer relevant but can be costly to banks under multiple supervision and examination.

Inequitable Regulation, Supervision, and Examination

The regulation, supervision, and examination of financial institutions by several federal and state agencies can be inequitable to the extent that the agencies impose different burdens and benefits on suppliers of essentially the same products and services. Some regulations were intended to be inequitable. These include laws and regulations (such as state antibranching laws, and controls on interest rates) that were designed to restrict competition. Laws and regulations (such as the Glass-Steagall Act's prohibition against most securities transactions by commercial banks, and the congeneric product limitation of the Bank Holding Company Act) that limit the products banks can offer were intended to be inequitable, but also may serve to reduce (or increase) the risks banks can take. Laws and regulations (such as the Equal Credit Opportunity Act) that were designed to protect consumers are inequitable if they are enforced by field compliance examinations only of banks and not of other suppliers of similar credit (as is the situation). Whether or not the inequity was planned is unclear.

Other laws and regulations presumably were intended to enhance the safety and soundness of banks and the banking system. Constraints on depository institutions' assets, liabilities, and operations in the name of protecting the deposit insurance fund are inequitable if they are imposed unequally or improperly (e.g., without a demonstrated relationship between the regulations and risk). From this viewpoint, it is inequitable to impose, as state and federal agencies have done, different limitations on the same products and services that different suppliers can offer and in which they can invest. These inequitable limitations are imposed (principally by the FHLBB and the bank supervisory agencies) and include differences in the treatment of securities services and investment. The Glass-Steagall Act prohibits only Federal Reserve member banks from underwriting and dealing in corporate securities (however, the FDIC has not yet permitted nonmember insured banks to offer securities services). Some states permit state-chartered savings banks and thrifts to invest in corporate securities. Branching is another example. Federally chartered thrifts may branch within and, to a limited extent, across state lines, although federally chartered banks are prevented by the McFadden Act from branching, except as permitted by state law. Direct investments provide a further example. Some states permit state-chartered thrifts to invest without limit in real estate and equities. In 1985, the FHLBB adopted regulations that permit such investments by FSLIC-insured S&Ls, but limited the investments to the greater of 10 percent of total assets or twice capital. Bank holding companies are constrained to financially congeneric activities as defined by the Federal Reserve, whereas one-thrift S&L holding companies are permitted to do almost anything.

Combining the agencies would not eliminate most of the differences, because they are imposed by laws, although the laws probably would be equally applied if the federal agencies were merged. A single federal agency, however, would be more likely to eliminate differences by reducing the powers of the regulated institutions. For example, the FHLBB's restraints on direct investments appear to be based less on its concern about risks to the FSLIC and more on the Bank Board's concern about competition between the state-chartered S&Ls, which were permitted to make direct investments, and federally chartered SLAs (S&Ls, which were not). Because even a unitary regulatory agency would not have control over nondepository enterprises, the result probably would be greater inequity between the regulated and the unregulated providers of financial services. Furthermore, liberalizing change has tended to have come from one or another agency rather than from all; thus, combining the agencies is likely to reduce the possibilities for change.

Field examinations conducted by different agencies tend to be similar in scope. However, national banks are charged for examinations on a *per-diem* basis, whereas thrifts and state-chartered banks may not pay explicit fees, depending on the practice of their state supervisors. Not charging or undercharging banks for the agencies' cost of examinations is a source of inequity, because the fees are a form of risk-related premium that charges banks and thrifts with some of the cost of monitoring the risks they impose on the insurance funds. Similarly inequitable is the failure of some regulators to impose constraints or equity-capital requirements necessary to protect the deposit insurance funds.

With respect to federal deposit insurance, the principal inequities are: (1) the provision of different coverage for the same types of deposits; and (2) the imposition of different costs for the same insurance. The first inequity occurs when the deposit accounts exceeding the *de jure* insured amount held in giant banks and thrifts are, *de facto*, 100 percent insured with great certainty, whereas deposits in smaller banks and thrifts have no certainty of being 100 percent insured. But this is not a function of there being different regulators, because the FDIC and the FSLIC have not acted differently (possibly because the FSLIC is rarely faced with thrifts holding uninsured deposits).

The second inequity has four sources that should be considered separately: (1) Deposit insurance premiums are charged for all domestic deposits, even though deposits over $100,000 per account may not be insured; (2) Deposit insurance premiums are not charged for deposits in foreign branches, even though these deposits are, *de facto*, insured; (3) Explicit deposit insurance premiums are not charged according to the risk imposed on the insurance fund, resulting in cross subsidization; and (4) Implicit premiums, in the form of the costs of examination and of restrictive regulations, are only partially charged according to the risks imposed by the insured institution. Only the last two sources are related to dual- or multi-agency regulation.

Federally subsidized deposit insurance reduces opportunities for state- and self-regulation. State-provided and privately sponsored insurance plans cannot compete with federally provided plans as long as the federal agencies do not charge for the presumed absolute guarantee of the federal government. Although members of the public benefit from knowing that their deposits are safe without their having to do much, if any, investigation, the costs of the guarantee should be recognized. In addition to the incentives towards risk-taking, federally provided deposit insurance tends to reduce the benefits from innovation and diverse operations that might have developed under a more heterogeneous deposit insurance system.

Conclusions

Incomplete cooperation among agencies appears responsible primarily for some difficulties in the expeditious closing of insured institutions that have become insolvent and for failing to control fraudulent transfers between units of a banking organization supervised by different agencies. A significant legal problem is that the insurance agency must get permission from the chartering agency to close an insolvent institution.

Laxity in supervision and examination has not occurred as a result of competition among agencies. Charges to that effect in the 1930s and the 1960s have not been borne out by the experience. Nor are the recently documented weaknesses in examination and supervision related to attempts by the different agencies to keep their constituents or attract other institutions. Indeed, there is reason to believe that competition between, or at least differences in the approaches of, different agencies has led to changes in laws and regulations and permitted innovations that have benefited the public.

The present system of regulation has several disadvantages and advantages. Although it might seem that having multiple regulators would be operationally inefficient, that does not appear to be the case. It is doubtful that the federal regulators could benefit from the economies of scale that might be achieved if the agencies were merged; indeed, diseconomies seem to be more likely. In any event, the cost of merging the agencies probably would be great. Supervision by state agencies, though, often duplicates that provided by federal supervisors. Some resources could be saved by eliminating this duplication. However, greater costs of the present system are the incomplete sharing of information among the supervisors and the difficulty faced by the deposit insurance agencies in closing an institution before its economic equity reaches zero or less.

The present system imposes costs on the regulated institutions in two principal regards. First, holding companies that have state-chartered and nationally chartered subsidiaries are regulated by several agencies, as are state-chartered banks where state supervisors are active regulators. Second, the different bank supervisors and savings and loan supervisors charge differentially for examinations, have different capital-adequacy rules, and impose regulations that are inconsistently restrictive. However, although combining the agencies might result in a consistent set of charges and regulations being imposed, there is reason to believe that these regulations would be less liberal than the controls on nonregulated suppliers of financial services. Furthermore, the present system of multiple supervisors makes change and adaptation to market conditions more expiditious. When not all institutions are affected, experiments are potentially less costly and alternatives can be tried. Furthermore, it should be noted that some inequities reflect political preferences. Different laws and regulators have been established to benefit some groups and further some goals (e.g., home building and housing, large or small banks, and local or nonlocal control).

Finally, there are inequities in the coverage and charge for deposit insurance. Only at giant banks are all deposits *de facto* insured. Premiums are charged on all domestic deposits, whether covered or not, and not on foreign-branch deposits, even though these are *de facto* covered. The premiums charged and equity capital required do not reflect the risks imposed on the deposit-insurance funds, which benefits some depository institutions and penalizes others.

Proposed Changes in the Present Structure

Pursuant to the Garn-St Germain Act requirement for studies of deposit insurance, the FDIC and the FHLBB (along with the National Credit Union Administration) prepared fairly extensive background reports with recommendations. A task group, led by Vice President George Bush and including the heads of all of the federal agencies that regulate providers of financial services, also developed a plan to reorganize the regulatory structure. As the reports note, theirs are the latest in a long chain of such plans. The following is a partial list of post-Great Depression studies with brief descriptions of their proposals:

1937—Brookings Institution Study for a Senate Committee (recommended abolishing the OCC and making the FDIC predominant);

1949—Hoover Commission in 1949 (transferring the FDIC to the Department of the Treasury);

1956—President Eisenhower's Reorganization Plan No. 2 (separating the FSLIC from the FHLBB);

1961—Commission on Money and Credit (transferring the FDIC and the OCC to the Federal Reserve System and insuring mutual savings bank deposits by the FSLIC);

1971—Hunt Commission (President's Commission on Financial Structure and Regulation) (establishing a Federal Deposit Guarantee Administration to administer the insurance funds, which would remain separate; transferring the FDIC and the Federal Reserve's regulatory functions to a new agency, the State Banks Administration; and transferring the OCC and the regulation of federal mutual savings banks to a new agency, the National Banks Administration); and

1975—FINE (Financial Institutions and the Nation's Economy) Study (consolidating all federal banking regulatory agencies).

The FHLBB has called essentially for a continuance of the *status quo*. The Bush Task Group has recommended extensive restructuring, and the FDIC has proposed consolidating the federal agencies' examination functions. These and other proposals, are described and evaluated in the following section.

The FHLBB's Proposals

The FHLBB recommended continuation of the present regulatory system. Its study concluded that, although there are inefficiencies and inconsistencies in the present arrangements, "consolidation of the insurance agencies should not be initiated without first rationalizing the functions of the financial regulators." (Federal Home Loan Bank Board, 1983, p. 166). The rationalization would be desirable because banks and thrifts now have similar functions and powers and yet are regulated differently. However, the FHLBB found that there would be costs from combining the agencies, such as a reduction in valuable competition between regulators, but that the savings in operations costs would be slight. Having the chartering agency and the insurance fund within the same organization (as they are in the FSLIC and the FHLBB) would permit the expeditious closing of failing institutions. (The present chairman of the FHLBB, Edwin J. Gray, very strongly opposes a consolidation of the federal supervisory agencies and insurance funds. This view is also expressed by the National Credit Union Administration.) Inequities would be reduced with risk-related insurance premiums.

The Bush Task Group's Proposals

The group's recommendations that pertain to the supervisory structure are outlined in Table 1. In brief, the group would give the Federal Reserve Board primary responsibility for supervising and examining banks, with the following exceptions. The OCC (trans-formed into the Federal Banking Agency) would supervise and examine national banks, except for large bank holding companies, and banks with international operations. The FDIC would examine and deal with troubled banks only. The FHLBB would continue to supervise and examine thrifts and other depository institutions that held a large (undefined) percentage of their assets in mortgages. The Federal Reserve Board would continue to supervise bank holding companies, except that the OCC would have primary responsibility for national bank holding companies. At its discretion the Fed could delegate its examination responsibilities to states that applied for the privilege. The insurance funds would not be merged. Risk-related insurance premiums were recommended.

The Working Group of the Cabinet Council on Economic Affairs supported the recommendations as follows: "We recommend legislating the regulatory recommendations in the *Blueprint for Reform: The Report of the Vice President's Task Group on Regulation of Financial Services* because the division of responsibilities among the various agencies has created inefficiencies and potential gaps in effec-tive supervision." (Healey, 1985, p. 72). No other discussion was included in the 75-page (plus three appendixes) report.

The FDIC's Proposals

With respect to the organization of bank supervision, the FDIC recommended that it should have sole responsibility to insure deposits and to examine banks. It would be empowered to "require reports from, take enforcement actions against, and conduct examina-tions of all federally insured banks and thrifts and their affiliates." (Federal Deposit Insurance Corporation, 1983, p. VI-1). Accordingly, the FDIC proposed a merger of the FDIC and FSLIC insurance

Table 1: Bush Task Group Recommendations

The following proposed changes in the regulatory structure are pertinent to deposit insurance:

1. Office of the Comptroller of the Currency:

   a. National banks and their holding companies would be regulated and examined by a new agency, the Federal Banking Agency (FBA), essentially just a new name for the Office of the Comptroller of the Currency (OCC).
   b. The FBA, in conjunction with the Federal Reserve Board (FRB), would be responsible for determining the permissible activities of bank holding companies; however, the FRB would have the right of veto. The FBA and the FRB also must agree on common capital and reporting requirements and on interpretations of the Bank Holding Company Act.
   c. The FBA would be supported with fees assessed against national banks.

2. Federal Reserve Board:

   a. *All* nonproblem state banks would be regulated and examined by the Federal Reserve Board, except as noted in 3.
   b. For these banks, the FRB would be responsible for consumer protection, civil rights, environmental protection, branching, trust powers, etc.
   c. "International class" holding companies would be regulated by the FRB. These institutions include (i) any U.S. banking organization engaged in a full domestic banking business in a foreign country, (ii) domestic organizations with more than 0.5% of total aggregate holding company assets ($12.5 billion), and (iii) all bank holding companies under foreign ownership. The 35 of the 50 domestic "international class" institutions that are national banks would continue to be subject to dual regulation.
   d. No mention is made about fees assessed against the regulated banks.

3. States:

   a. Upon state application, the FRB (in consultation with the FBA and the Federal Deposit Insurance Corporation (FDIC)) could certify states to take responsibility for examination and supervision of state-chartered banks and their holding companies.
   b. Holding companies must be regulated no less stringently by states than by the FBA and FRB. The FRB can veto state decisions that it believes are inconsistent with federal law or regulations.
   c. No mention is made about how the states will pay for the examinations and supervision they undertake.

Table 1: continued

4. Federal Deposit Insurance Corporation:

   a. Risk-based insurance premiums are suggested, but would not be required.
   b. The FDIC would have not have any supervisory authority over such matters as are given in 2b above.
   c. Examinations would be limited to "troubled" insured institutions plus a sample of non-troubled institutions; the examinations would be done in conjunction with the primary supervisor.
   d. Enforcement authority would be limited to revoking insurance or raising premiums, if a system of risk-based insurance were in effect. Other enforcement action would be requested of the primary supervisor, but could be taken independently by the FDIC if necessary.
   e. No mention is made of fees that might be assessed against insured banks for examinations.

5. Federal Home Loan Bank Board:

   All current savings and loan associations and commercial banks that so elect may be regulated by the Federal Home Loan Bank Board if they qualify by means of an undefined "portfolio test." Savings and loan associations that fail the test must obtain bank charters and FDIC insurance.

6. Holding Companies:

   The possibility of inadequate regulation stemming from having several regulators in charge of a holding company is largely eliminated by giving authority to the FRB or the OCC (or the FBA).

7. Deposit Insurance Funds Generally:

   a. The deposit insurance agencies and funds would remain separate.
   b. Common minimum capital requirements and accounting standards would be required, to be implemented over a seven-year period. However, each agency would retain authority to vary the standards for individual institutions and at times of industry-wide financial difficulties.
   c. Risk-related insurance premiums would be authorized, but not be required.

funds. However, it recommended "removing the FDIC from the applications process and all other regulation function not directly related to safety and soundness." For this purpose, the FDIC favored "establishing a separate agency for chartering and regulating all federal banks, thrifts, and holding companies." (P. VI-1). These recommendations were based on the fact that thrifts now have, at least, the same powers as commercial banks, and similar institutions should be treated similarly. A unified agency also would offer the advantage of facilitating the mergers that are likely to be necessary and desirable between thrifts and commercial banks. Furthermore, a larger insurance fund could be more diversified and less expensive to operate, although the merger of the funds would necessitate commercial banks' subsidizing S&Ls. While recognizing that eliminating the FHLBB would remove the bias of S&Ls towards the housing industry, the FDIC considered this a small price (or none at all) to pay for the advantages of uniform regulation of institutions with similar functions and objectives.

The FDIC also recommended the institution of risk-related deposit insurance premiums to reduce, somewhat, the subsidization of risky banks by conservative banks. The inequity of providing almost certain *de facto* 100 percent insurance only for very large banks would be eliminated by making explicit a modified payout system for uninsured deposits, whereby these deposits would receive only their pro-rata share of an insolvent bank's net assets.

Evaluation of Possible Changes

Leaving the Present System in Place

Not changing the structure of the present system would have the advantage of saving the costs and other trauma that change usually entails. From past experience, it is the most likely outcome. The present system is not nearly so complex as it often is described in charts that show crisscrossed lines connecting all the agencies to most of the banks. In practice, only one federal agency examines each bank, and the states may forgo supervising and examining the institutions they charter when they choose to do so. States can rely on federal deposit guarantees to protect state citizens' funds and can serve borrowers by chartering new institutions when existing ones fail. States that persist in examining their institutions evidently find that the costs they impose on these banks and thrifts have offsetting advantages, perhaps including state jobs, political contributions, and power.

Changing the Supervision of Holding Companies, Authority to Close Insolvent Institutions, and Mergers of Differently Regulated Institutions

The most important structural problems found from the analysis presented above are: (1) the divided regulation of some holding companies; (2) the fact that the FDIC and FSLIC must get permission from the chartering agencies to close banks or state-chartered S&Ls; and (3) mergers between differently chartered and differently regulated institutions. The first could be solved by having the entire holding company examined by the federal examiner of the lead bank. The second could be dealt with by changing the deposit insurance statutes to give the insurance agency complete authority to close a bank or thrift. The third has been addressed by the Garn-St Germain Act of 1982, at least for failing institutions. The act permits mergers of banks and thrifts in the same states or (if that is not possible) in different states to prevent failures. On the state level, legislators could pass enabling legislation, as has been proposed in Ohio and Maryland, to permit out-of-state banks to purchase failing state-chartered and nonfederally insured savings and loan associations.

To make no other changes in the present system would mean not resolving some inequities. Banks and thrifts would continue to be differently regulated and have different powers, even though they offer essentially the same services to the public. All deposits at giant banks would be *de facto* insured, and there would continue to be uncertainty about deposit accounts that exceeded $100,000 at smaller banks and about the sufficiency of the deposit insurance funds. However, inequities from mispriced deposit insurance would be reduced if it were possible to adjust insurance premiums and equity and subordinated debt capital for risk differences, if all banks were charged for the agencies' cost of monitoring, and if all premiums were charged on all *de facto* insured deposits, including deposits at foreign branches.

Transferring the Insurance Funds to the U.S. Treasury

Making the U.S. Treasury explicitly responsible for deposit insurance payments (though not for administration) has been suggested as a way to eliminate uncertainty about the security of the funds. Although a 1982 Sense-of-Congress resolution stated that Congress would not permit the funds to become bankrupt, the resolution has expired and the mechanism for the funds' replenishment, should their current borrowing authority be insufficient, is not clear. The uncertainty and the possibly costly, though temporary, disruptions could be avoided by transferring the funds to the U.S. Treasury, which would make payments to depositors as requested by the federal deposit insurance agencies. This proposal is not inconsistent with the other suggested structural changes.

A disadvantage of the proposal could be underpriced insurance if the agencies were not concerned about bankruptcy because they assumed that the U.S. government would bail them out. There is reason to believe that this is the case with the FHLBB and S&Ls. However, the Treasury Department and Congress are unlikely to look favorably on this situation; their concern should serve to discipline the agencies.

The Bush Task Group Proposal

The negative effects of duplicative regulation would be reduced primarily by putting the Federal Reserve Board in charge of the supervisory system. State-chartered banks would be examined only by the states if the Fed certified the state as qualified for this purpose. The proposal also would reduce the direct costs of regulation principally by repealing legal requirements for FDIC approval of such things as branching applications, changes in capitalization, and changes in charter.[6]

However, the largest 35 or so holding companies could still be regulated by several agencies: directly by the states, if they chose to impose more restrictive laws and regulations; by the Federal Banking Agency (FBA), if the companies had banks with national charters; and by the Fed. The states apparently still would have the right to examine and regulate state-chartered banks, and to impose fees on these banks, regardless of their certification by the Fed. Certification appears to affect only the Fed's willingness to accept state examinations and supervision.

Inequities stemming from differences between the benefits and costs of deposit insurance would not be affected by the proposals, with the exception of the recommended use of risk-related insurance premiums and the common minimum capital and accounting requirements. However, the allowance for variations in the requirements at the discretion of each agency would seem to reduce the effectiveness of this recommendation.

Considering the "official" status of the Bush Task Group's report, it is desirable to analyze two important proposed structural changes—the roles of the FDIC and the Federal Reserve Board.

The Proposed Role of the FDIC

An important shortcoming of the Bush Task Group's recommendations would be the removal of examination and supervisory responsibility from the agency that had the primary interest in banks' financial soundness—the deposit insurer, the FDIC. This is not to say that the OCC (FBA), the Fed, or the states are unconcerned about bank failures. But they have occasionally conflicting incentives. Furthermore, the recommendation that the FDIC assume responsibility when a bank had been declared (presumably by the FBA, the Fed, or a state) to be troubled would be likely to increase the costs of divided authority. The FDIC would have to obtain and digest very detailed information and insights from the primary supervisor at a time when quick and effective action to prevent a depletion of the insurance funds was required. In practice, it would appear that the primary supervisor would make this determination, and the function of the FDIC would be to wind up a bank that the supervisor decided to close. In this event, it would seem preferable to disolve the FDIC and give its assets to the FBA and the Fed. Then the authority for preventing failures and the cost of failures would be lodged in one office.

The Proposed Role of the Federal Reserve Board

Another important shortcoming of the recommendations would be concentration of authority in the Fed. The Federal Reserve Board now is responsible for the general well-being of the economy, which is the primary determinant of the safety of the banking system. The Fed accomplishes this very important task through its control of bank reserves and the money supply. The failure of individual banks has virtually no effect on this goal; with appropriate last-resort lending and deposit insurance there is no danger that bank failures will result in runs or multiple contractions of the money supply.

Nor is there any need for the Fed to monitor the state of the economy or the condition of individual banks by way of bank examinations. First, as shown in Benston and Marlin (1974), there is no demonstrated relationship between the figure that is unique to bank examinations—the number of substandard loans—and indicators of economic conditions. Second, the Task Group recommended that national banks and some state banks not be examined by the Fed; hence its information would be incomplete.[7] Third, if the Fed wanted specific information, it could obtain it from the examining agencies. Furthermore, in its role as provider of liquidity (lender of last resort), the Fed could lend funds through the FDIC, or directly to banks upon the recommendation and with the guarantee of the FDIC. Even if the Fed lent directly to banks at its own risk, it would have no particular need to know a bank's financial condition until the bank requested funds. At that point, the Fed could ask the bank to give it copies of the examination reports, and could request additional information from the examining agency and the bank in order to evaluate the collateral offered and the bank's solvency. In any event, this is the procedure the Fed would have to follow for banks it did not examine.

In addition, because it would be virtually a monopoly supplier of deposit insurance and principal arbiter of banking regulation, the Fed probably would be overconservative in its administration. Its position as the nation's central bank puts it constantly in the political limelight, particularly when it refuses to take actions that appear to be politically popular. Consequently, the Fed has incentives to over-constrain banks rather than to risk being accused of endangering the financial health of the nation because a bank failed. It has been the Fed's position in the past to resolve goal conflicts in favor of its conception of monetary policy.

Creating a Single Deposit Insurance Agency

This proposal would have the advantage of vesting the respon-sibility for supervision and examination in the agency that has the most interest in preventing insolvencies—the insurance agency. A single insurance agency would facilitate the supervision of holding companies and reduce inequities among institutions stemming from differences in supervision and examination.

An important disadvantage of the proposal would be the cost of combining deposit insurance funds (the FSLIC and NCUIF) that wanted to remain separate. Another important disadvantage would be the loss of diversity of approach from having more than one federal insurance agency. Bankers whose deposits were insured by the FDIC would also object to having "their" insurance funds diluted by the FSLIC's real deficit of unbooked contingent payouts. However, the funds and responsibility for payouts could be moved to the Treasury Department.

Consolidating the Insurance and Regulatory Authorities

Consolidation of all federal regulators into a single agency has been recommended and oppose by several commentators and commissions. A good list of the arguments in favor of consolidation was given by then chairman of the FDIC Frank Wille in 1975 (quoted by Horvitz, 1983, p. 253):

1) Simplification of administration.

2) Elimination of conflicting goals (particularly the Federal Reserve responsibility for both bank supervision and monetary policy).

3) Cost savings from combining the legal, research, data processing and training activities of the separate agencies.

4) Elimination of policy conflicts.

5) Facilitation of the handling of failing banks [footnote reference to the Franklin National failure].

6) Improved regulation of bank holding companies, better coordinating supervision of the holding company and its subsidiary banks.

7) Benefits to bank customers from more uniform rules applying to all institutions.

8) Greater flexibility and ability to adjust to change in the environment.

[Wille listed the following] arguments against consolidation . . .:

1) The present system has worked reasonably well (and the costs of adjusting to a new system would offset many of the benefits).

2) Differences within each agency are as great as interagency differences. Consolidation would not resolve this problem, and perhaps interagency coordination might accomplish much of what consolidation could.

3) Concentration of regulatory power. The present system allows for criticism from within the regulatory structure and not just from the regulated institutions, as in other industries.

4) Benefits of diversity. There may be a greater tendency to experiment and a greater receptivity to change with several agencies than with only one.

Wille concluded that "it would be a grave mistake to consolidate." More recent commentators also opposite consolidation because of the weakness of the FSLIC.

The opposite conclusion has been drawn by other observers. For example, after detailing how conditions have changed since 1975, particularly with respect to thrifts' increased banking and branching powers, the potential for conflict between monetary policy and bank regulatory goals because of the Federal Reserve's dual role, the problems of effecting mergers among differently regulated institutions, and differences in the regulations affecting bank and savings and loan holding companies, Horvitz (1983) concluded that it would be preferable to consolidate the agencies. The consolidation would result in a single federal regulatory agency with responsibility for commercial banks, mutual savings banks, savings and loan associations, and credit unions, including their holding companies. This federal agency would have the power to issue charters, approve mergers, provide deposit insurance, and (presumably) close banks. The states would still be able to charter and supervise depository institutions.

The consolidation proposal would have the advantages of reducing the problems of coordination among agencies to a federal-state concern. Thus, except for the right of states to regulate and supervise holding companies and state-chartered banks, holding companies' supervision would be facilitated, and the responsibility for examining and supervising and (at least for federally chartered banks) closing banks would be vested in the deposit-insurance agency. Consolidation also would offer the advantage of eliminating inequities among depository institutions that offered the same services and products.

A disadvantage of consolidation would be the cost of combining the agencies. The total federal agency costs would likely be somewhat greater because operating economies would probably not be realized, and merger costs might be substantial. Another, perhaps more important, cost would be the loss to the constituents of the existing institutions if uniform regulations were adopted. Many of the laws that impose different regulations on commercial banks, mutual savings banks, savings and loan associations, and credit unions were designed to benefit particular users of their services. For example, the housing industry has objected to consolidation because it fears the loss of subsidies and penalties that direct thrifts' assets toward mortgages. Credit unions are generally small mutual associations with their own constituencies and problems. Commercial bankers have raised objections to combining the much more solvent FDIC fund with the grossly

under-reserved FSLIC fund, unless, perhaps, the Treasury's obligation to pay off insured depositors were formalized.

Introducing Greater Competition Among Deposit Insurers

An opposite recommendation would be to introduce more
competition among federal deposit insurers by splitting the FDIC into
three insurance agencies. One, run by the current FDIC adminstra-
tion, would continue to examine and insure state-chartered nonmember banks. Another would be taken over by the OCC, which
would continue to examine and would now also insure national banks.
The third would insure and examine state-chartered member banks
and be staffed and administered by the current Federal Reserve's bank
supervisors and examiners. The assets of the FDIC would be divided
in proportion to the total domestic deposits of the banks that were
insured by each of the funds. The FHLBB, FSLIC, and NCUIF would
continue as they are now, but banks and thrift institutions would be
free to switch among the five agencies as they might shop among
private insurance companies. However, all depository units in a holding company would be insured by the same agency, which would
supervise all other units of the holding company as required to protect
the insurance fund. Privately provided insurance could supplement or
substitute for federal government insurance, as allowed by the chartering authority.

The deposit insurance agencies would be given the right to
charge variable rate premiums, determine minimum capital, require
the reporting of data, and conduct field examinations. The insurance
agency also could be given the right to close a bank if the agency
determined that the bank's continued operation would result in
payouts from the insurance fund. The chartering authorities, which
would control entry, could prevent the insurance agencies from erect-
ing barriers to entry (which they would be tempted to do, because they
would bear the cost of failures but would not get the benefits from
competition and innovation), and could make sure that depository
institutions had and maintained deposit insurance from a responsible
insurer, public or private. (See Benston, 1983c, for more details).

The proposal would offer several advantages. One would be
that insurance agencies would have incentives to impose on clients
only those regulations and requirements that were cost effective, in
the sense that the marginal costs of restricting and monitoring depos-

itory institutions would tend to be equated with the marginal costs of payouts from insolvencies. If the agency were ineffective in making this tradeoff, it would risk losing at least some banks to other insurers, much as the states lost banks to the OCC when Comptroller Saxon liberalized the regulations governing national banks. As a result, inequitable regulation would likely be reduced, because each regulator-deposit-insurer would have to be concerned about losing its clients, while at the same time it would have to be concerned about institutions that might fail. There is very little evidence that the result would be regulatory laxness. Indeed, because the regulator and the deposit insurer would be the same agency, overregulation would be the greater danger.

The second advantage would be obtained from the reduced necessity for coordinating agencies to monitor a banking organization. The third advantage would be that the same agency that regulated and insured a bank would have the authority and responsibility to close the bank. The agency thus would be in a position to determine the optimal mix of regulation, financial support, cease-and-desist orders, and cessation of operations. Because the same supervisor would be in charge of all aspects, there should be less loss of information than there is today. (This change could be effected independently). A fourth advantage over consolidation would be that the economic, personal, and political costs of combining agencies would not have to be incurred. Indeed, the Federal Reserve's examining staff is already administered and housed separately from the rest of its operations.

Because depositors' funds are protected by deposit insurance, and because the stability of the financial system is assured by deposit insurance and by the deposit insurance agencies' and/or the central bank's provision of liquidity to solvent banks, there is no public interest need for regulations other than those directed towards consumer protection, distributional equity, and limiting concentrations of power. Therefore, it is possible to conclude, there is no reason why the nation's laws on these matters should be administered differently for depository institutions than for other suppliers of financial services or enterprises generally. If this reasoning were accepted, special compliance examinations would not be necessary. Nor would there be a need for regulatory agencies other than the agencies that offered deposit insurance.

A possible disadvantage of the proposal would be the potential capture of the regulator-deposit-insurer by the depository institutions or their constituents. However, this is also a problem (or an advantage, depending on the viewpoint) of the present system. Another disadvantage would be that the separate agencies would probably charge different implicit and explicit prices for what would essentially be the same guarantee. Thus, existing inequities in charging for deposit insurance might not be corrected. However, institutions that believed they were overcharged would have the incentive and ability to transfer to other deposit insurance agencies, subjecting the undercharging agencies to the problems from adverse selection. It should be mentioned, though, that the expected benefits from competition might not be obtained from government-run insurance agencies.

Providing Private (Non-Government) Insurance

Non-government insurance could be provided in several ways. It could be a substitute for or a complement to federal deposit insurance. Private insurance could be offered voluntarily by depository institutions or be mandated in place of some or all federally provided insurance. Private insurance could be sold by insurance companies and/or through cross-guarantees by banks. (See Ely, 1985, for details).

The principal advantage of private deposit insurance would be that the benefits from competition by wealth-maximizing suppliers could be garnered by banks and the ultimate guarantors of the deposit insurance funds, the taxpayers. Compared to having several alternative federal government suppliers, the number of private suppliers would potentially be greater, and the way they would tend to act would be clearer. However, private deposit insurance as a substitute for federal insurance would suffer severely from a lack of credibility. It is possible for private insurers to be unable to meet their promises (as the situation in Ohio and Maryland recently demonstrated), whereas the government's guarantee is absolute—or would be if the Treasury formally assumed responsibility for the insurance. Although an actuarily sound fund (which the one in Ohio was not) would be close to safe, the failure of the Federal Reserve to maintain bank reserves could cause failures of a magnitude beyond the means of a private insurer. Hence, it would be very unlikely that private insurance could be a substitute for federal insurance.

However, private insurance could complement federal government insurance if the government insurance were limited *de facto* as well as *de jure*. One benefit from a complementary insurance system might be useful evidence on the free-market cost of deposit insurance.

Summary and Conclusions

Concerns About the Present System

The present system of regulation, supervision, and examination has been criticized as inadequate, too costly, and inequitable. Analysis and evidence reveals that the principal inadequacies are: (1) difficulties in coordinating supervision when portions of the same banking organization are subject to oversight by different agencies; and (2) the fact that the deposit insurer must obtain agreement by the chartering agency to close an insolvent bank. Laxity in supervision due to competition among agencies is not and probably never has been a serious problem. Indeed, the existence of multiple agencies has resulted in changes that have been advantageous to the public.

The existence of multiple agencies has not resulted in significantly higher costs, with the possible exception of duplicative state and federal supervision and examinations. Multiple-agency regulation, however, does result in different, and hence inequitable, regulation of similar services and products provided by different institutions. But most of these differences have been imposed by laws and reflect political decisions and conflicting social goals. Other inequities are due to mispriced deposit insurance (including capital requirements) and inconsistent deposit-insurance coverage.

Suggested Changes

The following structural changes have been suggested. They are listed in ascending order of the extensiveness of the change required, with a brief assessment of the probable benefits that would be achieved.

1. No change. This would have the advantage of being consistent with previous nonactions. But it would not correct the problems outlined above.

2. Establishing a single supervisor for a given holding company. This change would eliminate the necessity for

interagency cooperation, or at least reduce it to a federal-state problem. Considering the advantages described in Chapter 6 of treating a holding company as an entitity and not attempting to segregate its activities into regulated and nonregulated portions, this change would be beneficial and inexpensive to effect.

3. Giving the deposit insurance agency the right to close an insolvent institution. Considering that the deposit insurer bears the cost of delay, this would appear to be a beneficial change.

4. Charging insured institutions the agencies' costs of monitoring. This change would be a form of risk-related premiums, would correct an inequity, and would be easy to implement. State-chartered institutions still would incur the additional costs of state supervision and examination, but these costs could be eliminated at state option without loss to its citizens.

5. Charging insured institutions risk-related insurance premiums and capital requirements geared to the deposits that actually were insured. This change, even if incompletely implemented, would alleviate the most serious inequities among suppliers of depository services.

6. Transferring the deposit insurance funds to the U.S. Treasury. This proposal would eliminate the uncertainty that depositors might have about the ability of the insurance agencies to meet their promises. Oversight by the Congress over payouts to depositors and the management of deposit insurance would continue, and would be supplemented by the Treasury Department oversight.

7. Consolidating the deposit insurance agencies. The advantage of this proposal would be a reduction in inequities in the supervision and examination of similar suppliers of depository services. However, the costs of combining agencies that wanted to remain separate would probably be significant, and differences in regulations would not necessarily be eliminated. Unless the funds were transferred to the U.S. Treasury, bankers would object to absorbing the FSLIC's considerable deficit.

8. Giving most supervisory authority to the Federal Reserve Board (The Bush Task Group Recommendation). This proposal would remove the agency with the greatest interest in monitoring and dealing with fraud and excessive risk, the FDIC, and give the most power to the agency with no direct interest in bank safety and soundness, the Federal Reserve Board. The Fed could delegate its authorities to state agencies, which also bear little of the cost of bank failures. Although there are useful aspects of the Bush Task Group recommendations (such as putting a single supervisor in charge of a given bank holding company), its proposals would probably result in higher costs and less effective resolution of insolvencies.

9. Consolidating insurance and regulatory authority into a single federal agency. Consolidation would make the equitable application of regulations, supervision, and examinations more likely. It also would facilitate the supervision and merger of institutions that now come under different federal agencies and would reduce problems to those between a federal agency and the states. It is doubtful, however, that consolidation would result in operating cost savings, and the transition would likely be costly. Furthermore, consolidation would mean a surrender or compromise of benefits achieved by some constituents of differently regulated institutions and would necessitate the reconciliation of some divergent goals.

10. Creating additional federal insurance agencies by dividing the FDIC into agencies initially responsible for national banks, Federal Reserve state-chartered member banks, and state-chartered nonmember banks, with banks and thrift institutions free to switch among the insurance agencies. This proposal would increase competition among insurers in the expectation that the result would be more efficient and less unnecessarily burdensome supervision (from the viewpoint of optimally protecting the insurance fund). Although there is little reason to expect supervisory laxness from competition (because it did not occur in the past, and because the insurance agencies would bear the cost of the laxness), it is not possible to predict from economic theory that government agencies necessarily would behave beneficially, as would private companies.

11. Providing private insurance. Because only the U.S. government can guarantee deposits absolutely, and because catastrophic losses such as those experienced in the Great Depression can result from central bank actions, federal government-provided insurance dominates private insurance. It cannot be recommended, therefore, as a substitute for federal insurance. Private insurance, however, can supplement federal government insurance, particularly if government insurance is limited *de facto* as well as *de jure*.

[1]See Golembe and Holland (1983) for a very good and much more complete description of the federal regulatory structure.

[2]See Bush Task Group Report (1984, pp. 32–33) for a concise summary of proposals to reorganize the regulatory structure.

[3]The Bush Task Group Report (1984, pp. 28–32) lists and discusses the following six "existing and potential problems with the current regulatory structure": (1) differential treatment of institutions that provide the same product or service; (2) excessive regulatory controls; (3) overlap and duplication; (4) agency responsiveness; (5) difficulties in the management of shared responsibilities; and (6) overlap and conflict between state and federal requirements.

[4]Bremer (1935) also lists the right to act as insurance agents and as brokers or agents for making or procuring real estate loans for banks in towns with fewer than 5,000 inhabitants, although this power was granted in the National Banking Act of 1864.

[5]Miller (1980b) also attempted to measure the cost of double supervision, but his cost functions were so poorly specified that the results cannot be considered to be meaningful.

[6]The Report recommends other changes that would reduce regulatory costs.

[7]There is no evidence that the Federal Reserve Board has used examination data in any of its decisions on the economy. Indeed, the required data have not even been recorded systematically for many years.

Principal Options and Recommendations for Improving Efficiency and Safety and Soundness of the Banking System

Our review of the problems of ensuring the safety and soundness of the banking system looked at a number of policy options to improve the efficiency, performance, and safety of the system by changing the structure of the deposit insurance system and the bank regulatory and supervisory process. Listed below are the options we considered for achieving these objectives, and our conclusions about their relative desirability.

Three points need particular emphasis. First, the more we examined the issues, the more we became aware of the complex linkages among them. As a result, many of the options cannot stand alone, but must be considered as a package, and we would change our recommendations in some instances if certain parts of the package were not accepted.

Second, a few of the issues and options are covered only briefly in the text of the Report. This is because the initial charge by the American Bankers Association did not include these areas, and it only became clear after the initial phase of the project was completed that some were important.

Finally, we did not address the transitional problems or the political feasibility of adopting the options. These concerns were neither our charge nor our area of particular expertise. For this reason, the recommendations should be viewed in the spirit in which they were prepared—as an aid in identifying the important current policy problems and in focusing the debate on solutions to these problems.

In the following sections, we summarize briefly the policy issues and concerns and indicate specific policy proposals we recommend, reject, or have taken no position on. References to the chapters where the issues are analyzed are also provided.

I. Deposit Insurance and Lender-of-Last-Resort Reform

Our review suggests that reform of deposit insurance and lender-of-last-resort policies are most critical for ensuring the safety and soundness of the U.S. banking system. Several key elements pertain to the structure, quality, and pricing of deposit guarantees and to the functioning of the lender-of-last-resort.

A. Modifications of Deposit Insurance Pricing Structure to Remove Mispricing (Chapter 9)

The mispricing inherent in the present flat-rate insurance premium causes significant distortions and contributes to undue risk-taking by individual depository institutions. We believe the principal solution to these problems is to charge for insurance according to risk by levying risk-related insurance premiums or by using risk-related capital standards. These two alternatives should be viewed as complementary rather than competing options.

1. (Rejected) Use of Restrictions on Activities and Prices as the Means to Limit Risk to Deposit Insurance Agency (Chapter 1)

The present deposit insurance system uses a flat-rate premium structure and employs supervision and examination, together with restrictions on activities and prices, to limit risk-taking. We reject this option as inefficient and detrimental to the efficient operation of banks and other financial institutions.

2. (Recommended) Use of Risk-related Charges for Deposit Insurance Coverage

Risk-adjusted charges for deposit insurance should be adopted to limit the risk exposure of the insurance fund and to limit incentives for undue risk-taking. We have considered the following three options, all of which are preferable to the present system:

a. Use of Risk-Adjusted Deposit Insurance Premiums (Chapter 9)

Risk-adjusted premiums would increase the incentives for bank owners and managers to limit excessive risk-taking by reducing the net returns they could expect from taking on more risky activities.

b. Use of Risk-Adjusted Capital Standards in Conjunction with a Fixed Charge for Insurance (Chapters 9 & 10)

Risk-adjusted capital standards could increase the incentives for owners and managers to avoid excessive risks before imposing losses on the insurance funds. We see risk-adjusted capital standards as desirable, and in some ways preferable, to risk-adjusted insurance premiums, because capital adds a cushion to protect the insurance fund.

c. (Recommended) Use of a Combination of Risk-Adjusted Capital Requirements and Risk-Adjusted Deposit Insurance Premiums (Chapter 9)

Considering the difficulties of developing a fully refined risk-related premium system and the current perceived capital weakness in the industry, a better option may be a combination of risk-related premiums and risk-adjusted capital standards.

3. (Recommended) Base Charges for Deposit Insurance Coverage on Risks Within a Consolidated Bank or, for Banks in a Holding Company System, on the Risks Within the Consolidated Bank Holding Company (Chapters 9 & 7)

Because of the possibilities for risk-shifting within a holding company system and among a bank and its subsidiaries when institutions maximize overall entity profits, we feel it is not possible to isolate affiliates and subsidiaries from risks in the rest of the organization. Therefore, the insurance agency is at risk for all bank holding company activities, and we conclude that charges for deposit insurance should be related to the total risks in the entity. Although our analysis does not deal explicitly with what have become the separable issues of insurance rate and the appropriate base against which that rate should be applied, it is fair to infer that the charge should not be related to total domestic deposits, as is presently the case. Instead the insurance charge should be related to the overall risk of the consolidated institution and levied against all the *de jure* and *de facto* insured liabilities.

4. (Recommended) Calculate Insurance Premiums Considering both On-Balance-Sheet Items and Off-Balance-Sheet Items (Chapter 9)

Risk analysis should be inclusive, considering both on- and off-balance-sheet items. Ignoring off-balance sheet items in assessing risk overlooks major potential liabilities that pose significant risks to the insurance funds. Assessment of the risks in some off-balance-sheet items is extremely difficult. All off-balance-sheet items should be reported. Once items are reported, risk measurement should be attempted.

5. (Recommended) Use of Explicit Charges for Examinations Related to Risk (Chapter 10)

The frequency and extent to which an institution is field-examined should be related to the risk the insurance agency believes an institution imposes on the insurance fund. Consequently, we recommend that all insured institutions pay explicit per diem charges that fully compensate the agency for the costs of examinations and close supervision.

B. Modifications of Insurance Contract

Modifications in the insurance contract are necessary to make market discipline more effective.

1. Insurance Coverage (Chapters 3, 4, & 7)

We could not make a unanimous recommendation from among the options not rejected. However, we feel strongly that all depositors at all banks should be treated the same, and not granted *de facto* differential coverage based on bank size. We also note that, if

100 percent coverage were adopted, a rate ceiling would have to be imposed on the insured deposits to prevent risk-prone (and even dishonest) bankers from taking advantage of the total lack of concern for risk by depositors. On the other hand, if 100 percent insurance were not adopted, at least for transaction accounts, then large banks would have a competitive advantage over smaller banks unless the insurance agency reverses current widespread depositor expectations so that giant banks will not be 100 percent *de facto* insured.

    a. Keep Present Structure (Chapter 7)

There was some support in the group to roll back deposit insurance coverage in the belief that the present *de jure* $100,000 coverage was too great and reduced the potential for market discipline. Others felt that a rollback coverage was impractical and would opt to keep the present maximum limits. No one felt that coverage should be expanded.

    b. Change Coverage (Chapter 7)

        i. Selective Rollback of Coverage

Some of us favored a selective rollback of coverage to an amount significantly less than the present coverage, such as $25,000 or $50,000, in order to increase market discipline.

        ii. (Rejected) Selectively Cover Higher Amounts than Present by Offering 100 Percent Insurance

            a. Transaction Accounts or

            b. Transaction Accounts plus Small Time and Savings Deposits or

            c. Transaction Accounts and all Time and Savings Deposits or

d. All Liabilities

All of these alternatives were rejected because they would reduce market discipline, create incentives to engage in creative redefinitions of uncovered liabilities to qualify for insurance, and raise the need to impose deposit rate ceilings on insured liabilities. Finally, 100 percent insurance of transactions accounts could serve to drive out short-term time deposits.

2. Alternative Sources of Coverage

a. (Recommended) Continue Reliance on Federal Government to Provide Basic or Minimum Deposit Insurance Coverage and Encourage Development of Private Supplemental Insurance (Chapters 3 & 7)

Only the federal government has the resources and credibility to provide perfectly credible guarantees in times of crisis. In this regard, the basic coverage should be high enough to avoid currency runs from the system as a whole (the risk of deposit runs is greatly overstated, as is shown in Chapter 2), yet not so high as to limit market discipline from uninsured depositors. Private supplemental insurance would introduce another source of risk-monitoring and market discipline, and therefore, should be encouraged.

b. (Rejected) Reliance on Private Insurance for Basic Coverage (Chapter 3)

We do not believe that the private sector can provide credible guarantees to prevent destabilizing runs. Moreover, there is a question whether there is sufficient capital in the system to make a system of cross-guarantees among banking organizations work.

C. Changes in Insolvency Resolution Mechanics

We identified serious deficiencies in the present system of resolving failures, which significantly increase the costs of failures to the insurance funds by tending to keep market-value-insolvent institutions open when they should be closed.

1. (Recommended) The Responsible Insurance Agency Should be Given the Authority to Close Economically Insolvent Institutions (Chapter 2, 4, & 10)

Avoiding losses to the insurance funds or the taxpayer requires that institutions legally be declared insolvent promptly when they become economically insolvent. At present, the insurance agency must get the chartering agency to agree to close an insolvent institution. The resulting delays can involve losses that must be borne by the insurance funds or taxpayers. If an institution is closed before economic net worth goes to zero, there will be no losses to uninsured creditors.

A Depository Institution Should be Closed:

a. (Rejected) When the Market Value of Net Worth Goes to Zero

Monitoring costs to catch institutions at the exact instant their net worth goes to zero would be too high to make this a practical alternative.

b. (Rejected) When the Book Value of Net Worth Goes to Zero

This would mean that the market value of assets might already be less than the market value of liabilities, which would result in large insurance losses.

c. (Recommended) When the Market Value of Net Worth Goes Below Some Low, but Positive Percentage, such as 1 or 2 Percent of Assets

This would provide a bigger margin for measurement and reaction error, which would reduce losses and thereby protect the insurance or Treasury General Fund. We also note that increased reliance on uninsured subordinated debt as a source of market discipline provides a buffer that would permit the insurance agency to reduce its monitoring without sacrificing protection of the fund.

2. (Recommended) Use of Trusteeships by the Deposit Insurance Agencies as the Means of Resolving Failures of Banks that May be Too Large to Merge Immediately or To Liquidate Immediately (Chapter 4)

This option provides a mechanism for keeping an institution (which may be too large to sell, recapitalize, or liquidate quickly) operating while it is reorganized. It is critical, however, that costs be imposed upon shareholders and uninsured creditors when estimated net worth goes below zero, and that the new management operates the institution in a safe and sound manner and in the best interests of the trusteeship. Through the trusteeship device, the following proposals would impose some costs on shareholders and uninsured creditors:

a. (Rejected) No Reduction in Claims (Haircut) for Uninsured Creditors (Chapter 7)

This option would provide 100 percent insurance of depositors and creditors, with the result that market discipline would be lost. Furthermore, 100 percent insurance would probably be provided *de facto* for very large banks, which would continue to be favored unfairly over small banks.

b. (Rejected) Impose a Pro Rata Haircut Only for Nondeposit Creditors (Chapter 7)

This option would provide *de facto* 100 percent guarantees of deposits, surrendering market discipline and unfairly continuing to give large banks better guarantees than small banks.

c. (Recommended) Impose a Pro Rata Haircut for both Uninsured Depositors and Nondeposit Creditors (Chapter 7)

This option makes maximum use of the potential for market discipline by uninsured creditors and treats large and small banks equitably. It also eliminates *de facto* 100 percent insurance, increasing the potential for market discipline to work.

3. (Recommended) Impose Management Performance Requirements (Related to the Market Value of the Government Guarantees Provided) to Ensure that Management Acts in the Interests of the Insurance Agency in Regulatory-Assisted Institutions, Including Trustee Relationships (Chapter 4)

Under the present system of mispriced deposit insurance, replacement of management responsible for undue risk-taking will not remove incentives for new management to take similar risks (and thus increase the value of government guarantees). Therefore, specific performance requirements must be imposed on new management to prevent them from following policies similar to those of their predecessors.

D. Need to Eliminate Uncertainties About Quality of Federal Deposit Guarantee (Chapters 3 & 5)

It is important to improve the quality of the federal guarantee of deposits and to put in place a mechanism to deal with market-value insolvencies in the thrift industry. This issue is important, both because the lack of capital in the thrift industry affects banks in the short run, and because problems in the thrift industry and the structure of its deposit insurance system are symptomatic of long-run problems with the structure of deposit insurance for banks.

1. (Recommended) Authorities Should Publicly Announce and Follow Policies to Deal with Failures and Runs. The Specific Insolvency Resolution Procedures and Policies Should be Spelled out to Dispel any Uncertainties about the Availability of Resources to Meet Insurance Commitments in Full. (Chapter 3)

2. Alternative Changes in Insurance Funds to Improve the Quality of the Government Guarantee

Doubts about the sufficiency of resources in the deposit insurance funds create uncertainties about the ability and willingness of the government to live up to its insurance commitments, thereby making destabilizing runs more likely. We did not analyze whether the National Credit Union Share Insurance Fund (NCUSIF) should be treated any differently from the Federal Savings and Loan Insurance Corporation (FSLIC) and Federal Deposit Insurance Corporation (FDIC) funds.

a. Merge the Federal Savings and Loan Insurance Corporation and Federal Deposit Insurance Corporation Funds (Chapter 11)

This responds to the short-run need to inject funds to cover the current thrift problem and reduces the short-run cost to the taxpayer, but does not affect perceptions of government backing of the funds. Again, we did not consider whether the NCUSIF fund should also be included as well.

b. Leave the Two Funds Separate as They Are Presently (Chapter 11)

This option potentially provides the opportunity for competition in pricing and regulation of risk, but does not improve the perception of the government's willingness to stand behind the insurance system.

c. (Recommended) Place the Insurance Funds into the Treasury General Fund but Retain Separate Supervisory, Regulatory, and Premium-Setting Authority (Chapter 11)

This option eliminates uncertainty about the willingness of the government to prevent the collapse of the financial system and backs deposit insurance with the full faith and credit of the U.S. government. However, we also favor giving at least the two insurance agencies authority to supervise, examine, levy insurance premiums on, and regulate depository institutions in order to create some competition in regulation to prevent overly burdensome regulation by a single regulator. It is not necessary to consolidate supervision and examination, administration of insurance pricing, liquidation of insolvent institutions, etc. These issues are considered below.

E. Lender of Last Resort (Chapter 5)

1. (Recommended) The Insurance Agency Should Lend Directly when Necessary to Institutions Experiencing Liquidity Problems. The Funds Could be Borrowed from the Federal Reserve. (Chapter 5)

This option prevents fire-sale losses on liquidations of assets, and, assuming that the appropriate penalty discount rate is employed, prevents insolvent institutions from being subsidized and imposing losses on the insurance funds. In general, credit should not be provided by the deposit insurance agencies to economically insolvent institutions, except in those rare instances where such lending is necessary to forestall a potential financial crisis. The insuring agency and the Federal Reserve should avoid routinely assisting insolvent institutions whose closing has only a remote chance of igniting a national or regional crisis.

2. (Recommended) The Federal Reserve Should Provide Emergency Liquidity, at the Initiative and with the Approval of the Responsible Insurance Agency, to any Depository Institution by Extending Credit on Sound Collateral (Chapter 5)

This option is less attractive than direct lending by the insurance agency because the Federal Reserve would have a residual concern about risk unless there was an explicit guarantee by the insurance agency. With such a guarantee, this option is equivalent to the first. The insurance agency bears the responsibility for certifying the solvency of the institution and for guaranteeing repayment of funds to the Federal Reserve. As noted above, the Federal Reserve should rarely lend to an insolvent institution.

3. (Recommended) Direct Lending in Emergency Liquidity Situations Should be at a Rate that Approximates the Market Rate on Securities with Similar Risk and Duration (Chapter 5)

Credit should not be provided at a subsidized rate, but rather should be related to a market rate.

4. (Rejected) Emergency Lending by the Federal Reserve to Institutions Experiencing Emergency Liquidity or Solvency Problems. (Chapter 5)

This option involves the Federal Reserve in evaluating the solvency of the institution, thus potentially involving it in safety and soundness concerns without bearing the costs of mistakes. The Federal Reserve should be concerned with the overall monetary situation rather than with the solvency of individual banks.

II. Market Discipline (Chapter 7)

A. (Recommended) Increased Reliance on Market Discipline as a Disincentive for Risk-Taking (Chapter 7)

Increased reliance on market discipline, as a supplement to risk-related premiums and/or risk-adjusted capital standards, would reduce incentives for institutions to engage in excessive risk-taking by imposing costs on management (officers and directors), shareholders, and uninsured depositors and creditors. Furthermore, market discipline reduces agency monitoring costs and introduces continual surveillance by the market, which supplements federal examination and supervisory activities.

B. (Recommended) Increased Use of Existing Agency Authority to Remove Officers and Directors of Failing or Problem Institutions (Chapter 10)

Ability to remove management promptly in situations that pose an obvious and continuing threat to the insurance fund curtails incentives for managers to put institutions into unduly risky positions. The agencies should be less hesitant in using their authority under Public Law 95-630, 12 U.S.C. 1818(e).

C. (Recommended) Impose Greater Costs on Stockholders, Uninsured Debtholders, and Depositors When Institutions Fail (Chapter 7)

Market discipline requires that market participants actually believe they are at risk rather than *de facto* insured. This requires the imposition of losses on uninsured creditors, management, and shareholders when institutions fail.

1. (Recommended) Increased Use of Subordinated Debt as a Means to Increase Capital (if it is Determined Additional Capital is Needed) and as a Source of Market Discipline (Chapter 7 & 10)

Much could be gained in the form of increased market discipline, while providing increased protection for the insurance funds, by permitting all institutions to count qualifying subordinated debt towards capital adequacy determinations. Reliance on subordinated debt would be permitted, but not required. The option to use either equity or subordinated debt would alleviate the problems small banks might have in issuing subordinated debt.

a. (Recommended) Only Debt That is Subordinated to Deposits, and is Not Subject to Any Covenants that Would Otherwise Constrain the Insurance Agency's Ability to Resolve Insolvencies Efficiently, Should be Counted Towards Capital Adequacy Requirements (Chapter 7)

Subordinated debt often can contain covenants that restrict the ability of the insurance agency to resolve insolvencies and that effectively converts subordinated debt to nonsubordinated status. Such debt should not be permitted to count toward meeting capital adequacy requirements.

b. (Recommended) The Maturity of Subordinated Debt Should be Required to be Staggered, But in No Case be Less than 30 Days Maturity (Chapter 7)

To maximize the effects of market discipline and force institutions repeatedly to pass the market test, subordinated debt should be required to be of varying maturities. Minimum maturity should be greater than 30 days to prevent debtholders from converting their debt to insured status to avoid the costs of failure.

2. (Recommended) Expand Stockholder Liability in the Event of Failure (Chapter 7)

Institutions should have the option to issue equity with double liability. Such equity would count double toward meeting deposit insurance agency capital adequacy requirements. Expanded stockholder liability would be a way to achieve *de facto* greater capital protection in precisely those instances where such protection is in fact needed. This may be attractive to smaller banks that prefer not to sell subordinated debt. Increased liability could be assured by bonding shareholders.

D. Current-Value Measurement and Public Disclosure (Chapter 8)

Accounts and reports based upon current market value measurement of assets and liabilities would be helpful to the insurance agencies, management, and debtholders. We recognize the practical problems of implementing current-value accounting, but feel that it is a worthwhile goal to pursue.

1. (Recommended) Voluntary Use of Current-Value Measurement for Internal Management Purposes (Chapter 8)

We suggest internal use of current-value estimates for some assets and liabilities as an aid to managers and as a means of obtaining experience that would be useful for implementing a complete current-value accounting system.

2. (Recommended) Use of Current-Value Measurement Should be Required for Insurance Purposes (Chapter 8)

Even with the difficulties, current values of assets and liabilities are required for determining risk-related premiums accurately. Moreover, only if the agencies work with current-value reports can they avoid keeping otherwise insolvent institutions afloat and minimize losses to the insurance fund.

3. (Recommended) Voluntary Current-Value Reporting and Disclosure of Selected Information (Chapter 8)

Public disclosure of key balance sheet items should improve market discipline and act as a constraint on management. We also noted that if short–term subordinated debt were floated, there would be increased incentives to make such disclosures. However, we were unable to agree whether financial institutions should be required to make these data public.

During the transition, reduced premiums and/or capital adequacy requirements might be considered for those institutions reporting on a current-value basis.

4. (Recommended) The Insurance Agencies Should Announce Enforcement Actions when Filed (Chapter 8)

5. (Recommended) Examination Reports and Ratings Must be Given Explicitly to all Directors and Senior Management (Chapter 10)

Not all the agencies disclose bank examination ratings to directors and senior management or give each a copy of the examination report. This reduces the ability of directors to provide discipline on aggressive management, and to limit risk-taking.

III. Examination and Supervisory Reform

Our analysis reveals a number of problems with the current focus and organization of bank regulation, supervision, and examination.

A. Examination Process (Chapter 10)

1. (Recommended) Expand Examination Emphasis to Reveal Fraud (Chapter 10)

Fraud and insider abuses continue to be the most frequent causes and most expensive type of failure to the insurance agencies. Therefore, more emphasis must be given to uncovering these problems.

2. (Recommended) Examinations Should be Directed Toward Verifying Reported Accounting Numbers and Estimates of Current Values of Assets and Liabilities (Chapter 10)

3. (Recommended) Expand Use of Existing Data and Statistical and Computer-Based Methods to Monitor Risks and to Predict and Identify Problems with Possible Increased Frequency of Reporting Significant Information Using Computer Technology (Chapter 10)

Use of these methods and data can enable the supervisory agencies to direct their resources toward potential problems, while reducing examinations of well-run institutions and releasing agency resources for fraud detection.

4. (Recommended) The Agencies Should Charge for Risk Examination of Banks and Savings and Loan Associations and for Bank Holding Company Inspections According to Time Spent (Chapter 10)

As noted previously, this option is another effective way of making an institution's insurance charges sensitive to increased risk.

B. Agency Structure (Chapter 11)

Restructuring the agencies is a separate issue from the structure of the deposit insurance system and the source of its funding.

1. (Rejected) Combine the Federal Agencies into a Single Supervisory and Regulatory Agency (Chapter 11)

This change would have the advantage of unifying regulation and supervision so that institutions offering similar products and services would be subject to similar rules. However, the states would still be free to regulate and supervise state-chartered institutions. The option has the disadvantage of reducing the possibilities for innovation and responsive supervisory change and for competition among the agencies in setting risk-sensitive insurance premiums, examination practices, and supervisory rules.

2. (Recommended) Bank Examination, Supervision, and Regulation Should be Located in Agencies Given Responsibility for Insuring Deposits and for Pricing Deposit Insurance (Chapter 11)

The agencies that directly bear the cost of a failure should be given the authority and responsibility to monitor the condition of the institutions they insure. They should also be given full responsibility for pricing deposit insurance, including direct charges (insurance fees) and indirect charges (including examination fees, capital requirements, etc.).

3. (Recommended) The Federal Reserve Should not be Involved in Bank and Holding Company Examination, Supervision, and Regulation (Chapter 11)

The Federal Reserve is not now responsible for granting bank charters nor for administering a deposit insurance fund. As recommended, its role as lender of last resort should be to lend only with full collateral or through the deposit insurance agencies. Hence, there is no need for the Federal Reserve to be involved in supervision and regulation.

4. (Recommended) Give Federal Supervisory Agencies Insurance Authority (Chapter 11)

Insured depository institutions would have the ability to obtain insurance from at least three agencies (the FDIC, Federal Home Loan Bank Board (FHLBB), and the Office of Comptroller of the Currency (OCC)). This proposal would create more insurance funds to encourage beneficial competition in pricing and regulation of risk. Placing the insurance funds into the Treasury General Fund does not affect this alternative.

5. (Rejected) Bush Task Force Recommendations for Agency Reform (Chapter 11)

In particular, we reject those proposals that would give most of the regulatory and supervisory responsibility to the Federal Reserve. We also reject the proposal that the federal authorities cede their responsibilities to the states, because the states do not provide the funds for deposit insurance. However, the deposit insurance agencies should not have the right to supersede state regulation of banking powers unless it can be shown that these regulations are likely to result in uncompensated losses to an insurance fund.

6. (Recommended) The Insurance Agencies Should be Taken Out of Consumer Protection and Similar Noninsurance-Related Regulation (Chapter 11)

We believe that the agencies with insurance responsibility should not be burdened with and diverted from their responsibility for noninsurance-related regulations.

IV. Other Reform Issues

A. (Rejected) Reimposition of Regulation Q and Similar Deposit Rate Restrictions (Chapter 7)

A large body of research and experience has shown that interest rate ceilings result in inefficiencies without compensating benefits. We do note, however, that some form of rate ceiling, preferably tied to the appropriate Treasury rate, would be necessary if 100 percent deposit insurance were put in place on any type of deposit account.

B. Limitations on Brokered and Insured Deposits

Some limitations on insured deposits will have to be imposed if implicit or explicit risk-sensitive insurance pricing is not introduced. Brokered deposits have been criticized particularly. However, brokerage is but one of several means by which banks can acquire large amounts of funds and trade on mispriced guarantees.

1. (Recommended) The Insurance Agencies Should Monitor Deposit Rates and Fund Flows (Chapter 7)

To provide adequate protection against risky institutions overbidding for deposits when deposit insurance is not properly priced, the insurance agencies should monitor deposit rates and fund flows. Substantially higher-than-market offering rates for insured deposits should serve as a useful early warning device to detect risk-seeking institutions.

2. Limitations on Deposit Insurance Coverage Might Include:

a. Imposing a Lifetime Limit per Depositor on Total Available Insurance

b. Imposing a Maximum Coverage per Depositor at Any One Time Period for Deposits in all Insured Institutions

These limitations would prevent individuals and firms from obtaining government insurance on almost any amount simply by placing deposits in many institutions.

V. Expanded Powers (Chapter 6)

Increased powers do not necessarily lead to increased risk for the institution overall. Furthermore, depository institutions already have the ability to take almost all the risk they want with the existing range of powers. However, with mispriced deposit insurance, the insurance agency has a responsibility to be concerned about the risk potential in new activities for the organization as a whole. We emphasize that such risk is firm-specific. Moreover, whether an activity is financial in nature is not relevant.

A. Criteria For New Activities

1. (Recommended) The Main Criteria for New Activities Should be Related to the Ability of the Responsible Insurance Agency to (Chapter 6)

a. Monitor the Total Risk Implications of the New Activity for the Consolidated Entity

b. Assess the Risk Implications of the New Activity for the Total Risk Exposure of the Entity, and

c. Price the Risk Implications or to Adjust Capital Requirements for the Total Risk of the Firm if the New Activity is Added to the Existing Activities of the Firm

The risks new activities pose for the insurance fund depend upon how much they add to or reduce the total risk exposure of the consolidated entity. These risks depend upon the totality of activities conducted by the firm and do not depend upon whether they are financial or nonfinancial. The risk exposure is dependent, though, on the insurance agency's ability to assess, price, and monitor risk. The intent of this recommendation is to be permissive with respect to new powers for banking organizations. The insurance agency has the responsibility affirmatively to establish procedures to assess, price, and monitor risks. Institutions that want to engage in new activities might pledge government securities or other marketable assets as one means to indemnify the insurance agencies against the risks of new activities.

2. Conflicts of Interest (Chapter 6)

Restrictions on the activities of banks, such as the Glass-Steagall Act's separation of commercial and investment banking and the separation of banking and insurance, are neither necessary nor desirable for reducing conflicts of interest.

In general we believe that conflict-of-interest problems are addressed adequately by other laws and regulations.

3. Concentration of Power (Chapter 6)

Concerns about concentration of power are adequately addressed by existing laws and regulations. The best way to eliminate such concerns is to promote competition aggressively, ease entry and exit restrictions, and enforce existing antitrust statutes.

B. Organizational Structure and the Conduct of New Activities (Chapter 6)

With properly priced insurance, it does not matter whether activities are conducted in separate affiliates or within the insured subsidiary, as long as risk is assessed on a consolidated-entity basis. With the present insurance pricing scheme, placing new activities in separate affiliates cannot reliably protect the insurance agency from risk, because the holding company can shift risk to insured bank subsidiaries.

1. (Rejected) New Activities Should be Limited to Separate Affiliates and Subsidiaries (Chapter 6)

Proposals to limit new activities to separate subsidiaries and affiliates are based on the misconception that it is possible to separate the insured institution from risk-taking in the rest of the organization. At the same time, forbidding banks from conducting activities within their existing organizations can prevent them from achieving desirable economies of scale and offering benefits to their customers.

VI. Additional Concerns

We have identified some additional problems, many of which are not addressed in the Report.

A. International Problems

Important complications are introduced in ensuring the safety and soundness of the financial system when one takes account of international complications. Such complications arise from the operations of not only U.S. institutions abroad but also from those of foreign banking organizations in the United States.

1. Pricing of Deposit Insurance

a. Treatment of Foreign Branches of U.S. Banks

i. (Recommended) Risk Implications of Foreign Activities for the Total Risk Exposure of the Entity Should be Included in the Pricing of Insurance

Foreign activities affect the risk exposure of the insurance fund and therefore should be considered in the pricing of risk. Foreign deposits should, however, be included in the base only to the extent that they are *de facto* insured.

2. U.S. Offices of Foreign Banks

The present policies of *de jure* insuring deposits in the U.S. offices of foreign banks deserves careful reconsideration, especially when the risks to the insurance funds are not solely related to the activities conducted in those offices.

B. Self-Regulation (Chapter 8)

There are several important opportunities to reduce the impact of government regulation by promoting self-regulation by financial institutions. Some suggested opportunities would include:

1. Self-Examination, Audited by the Insurance Agencies

2. Industry Participation as Advisory in Risk-Ratings

3. Identifying Emerging Risks (Such as Daylight Overdrafts and Off-Balance-Sheet Items)

4. Developing Proposals to Assess, Monitor, and Price the Risk Implications of New Activities

5. Developing Methods for Implementing Current-Value Accounting and Disclosure

C. Capital Adequacy

Issues of capital adequacy, especially the relative merits of risk-adjusted capital standards, were not part of the focus of this study but emerged as important complements to risk-related deposit insurance premiums and deposit insurance reform, and are addressed at least partially in the other recommendations.

Aharony, Joseph, and Itzhak Swary. "Contagion Effects of Bank Failures; Evidence from Capital Markets." *Journal of Business* (July 1983): 305–22.

Altman, Edward I. "Predicting Performance in the Savings & Loan Industry." *Journal of Monetary Economics* 3 (October 1977): 433–66.

_____, and Arnold W. Sametz, eds. *Financial Crises: Institutions and Markets in Fragile Environment.* New York: John Wiley and Sons, 1977.

_____. *Corporate Financial Distress: A Complete Guide to Predicting, Avoiding, and Dealing with Bankruptcy.* Wiley: New York, 1983.

Arthur Young & Company. "Assessment of Business Expansion Opportunities for Banking." Prepared for the American Bankers Association, 1983.

Aspinwall, Richard C. "On the 'Specialness' of Banking." *Issues in Bank Regulation* 7, no. 2 (Autumn 1983).

Association of Reserve City Banks. *Risks in the Electronic Payments System: Report of the Risk Task Force.* Washington, D.C., October 1983.

Avery, Robert B., Gerald A. Hanweck, and Myron L. Kwast. "An Analysis of Risk-Related Deposit Insurance for Commercial Banks." Conference on Bank Structure and Competition, Federal Reserve Bank of Chicago, May 1–3, 1985.

Bagehot, Walter. *Lombard Street.* London: Kegan Paul, Trench, Trubner & Co., 1894: 17.

Barth, James R., R. Dan Brumbaugh, Jr., Daniel Sauerhaft, and George H.K. Wang. "Thrift-Institution Failures: Causes and Policy

Issues." Paper presented at the Conference on Bank Structure and Competition, Federal Reserve Bank of Chicago, May 1–3, 1985.

Bartell, Robert H., Jr. "An Analysis of Illinois Savings and Loan Associations Which Failed in the Period 1963–68," in Irwin Friend, ed., *Study of the Savings and Loan Industry*. Prepared for the Federal Home Loan Bank Board, Washington, D.C., vol. 1, 1969: 345–436.

Baumol, William J., John C. Panzer, and Robert D. Willig. *Contestable Markets and the Theory of Industrial Structure*. New York: Harcourt, Brace, Jovanovich, Inc., 1982.

Beighley, F. Prescott. "The Risk Perceptions of Bank Holding Company Debtholders." *Journal of Bank Research* (Summer 1977).

—————, John E. Boyd, and Donald P. Jacobs. "Equities and Investor Risk Perceptions: Some Entailments for Capital Adequacy Regulation." *Journal of Bank Research* (Autumn 1975).

Bennett, Veronica. "Consumer Demand for Product Deregulation." *Economic Review*, Federal Reserve Bank of Atlanta (May 1984): 28–37.

Benston, George J. "Bank Examination." *The Bulletin of the Institute of Finance*, Graduate School of Business Administration, New York University nos. 89–90 (May 1973).

—————, and John Tepper Marlin. "Bank Examiners' Evaluation of Credit: An Analysis of the Usefulness of Substandard Loan Data." *Journal of Money, Credit, and Banking* 6 (February 1974): 23–44.

—————. *Federal Reserve Membership: Consequences, Costs, Benefits and Alternatives*. Trustees of the Banking Research Fund, Association of Reserve City Bankers: Chicago, 1978.

————— "Required Periodic Disclosure Under the Securities Acts and the Proposed Federal Securities Code." *University of Miami Law Review* 33 (September 1979): 1471–84.

—————. "Accounting Numbers and Economic Values." *The Antitrust Bulletin* 27 (Spring 1982): 161–215.

—————. "The Regulation of Financial Services," in *Financial Services: The Changing Institutions and Government Policy*, ed. by George J. Benston. Englewood Cliffs, N.J.: Prentice Hall, Inc., 1983a.

—————. "Federal Regulation of Banking: Analysis and Policy Recommendation." *Journal of Bank Research* 14 (1983b): 216–44.

_____. "Deposit Insurance and Bank Failures." *Economic Review*, Federal Reserve Bank of Atlanta (March 1983c): 4–17.

_____. "Financial Disclosure and Bank Failure." *Economic Review*, Federal Reserve Bank of Atlanta (March 1984).

_____. "Savings and Loan Failures: An Analysis of Proximate Causes." Unpublished manuscript, University of Rochester, 1985.

Black, Fischer, and Myron Scholes. "The Pricing of Options and Corporate Liabilities." *Journal of Political Economy* 81 (May 1973): 257–76.

Board of Governors of the Federal Reserve System. *Annual Report, 1933*. Washington, D.C., 1934: 1–30.

_____. *The Bank Holding Company Movement to 1978: A Compendium*. Study by the staff of the Board of Governors of the Federal Reserve System, 1978.

_____. *Bank Holding Company Acquisition of Thrift Institutions*. Study by the staff of the Board of Governors of the Federal Reserve System, 1981.

Bovenzi, John F., James A. Marino, and Frank E. McFadden. "Commercial Bank Failure Prediction Models." *Economic Review*, Federal Reserve Bank of Atlanta 68 (November 1983): 14–26.

_____ and Lynn Nejezchleb. "Bank Failures: Why Are There So Many?" *Issues in Bank Regulation* 8 (Winter 1985): 54–68.

Boyd, John H., Gerald Fanweck, and Pipat Pithyachartyakul. "Bank Holding Company Diversification." Proceedings of a Conference on Bank Structure and Competition, Federal Reserve Bank of Chicago, 1980.

Bradford, Frederick A. "Discussion." *American Economic Review, Supplement* (March 1932): 239–340.

Bremer, C.D. *American Bank Failures*. New York: Columbia University Press, 1935.

Burke, James. "Bank Holding Company Affiliation and Cost Efficiency," in *The Bank Holding Company Movement to 1978: A Compendium*. Study by the staff of the Board of Governors of the Federal Reserve System, 1978.

Burns, Helen M. *The American Banking Community and New Deal Banking Reforms, 1933–1935.* Westport, Conn.: Greenwood Press, 1974.

Buser, Stephen A., Andrew H. Chen, and Edward J. Kane. "Federal Deposit Insurance, Regulatory Policy, and Optimal Bank Capital." *Journal of Finance* (March 1981).

Bush, George, Chairman. *Blueprint for Reform: The Report of the Vice President's Task Group on Regulation of Financial Services.* Washington, D.C.: U.S. Government Printing Office, 1984.

Cagan, Phillip. *Determinants and Effects of Changes in the Stock of Money, 1875–1960.* New York: National Bureau of Economic Research, Distributed by Columbia University Press, 1965.

Chase, Samuel, and John Prather Brown. "The Role of Bundling in the Provision of Financial Services." Study for the Association of Bank Holding Companies, February 1984.

——————. "The Bank Holding Company as a Device for Sheltering Banks from Risk." Proceedings of a Conference on Bank Structure and Competition, Federal Reserve Bank of Chicago, October 1971.

——————, "The Bank Holding Company—A Superior Device for Expanding Activities?" *Policies for a More Competitive Financial System.* Conferences Series No. 8, Federal Reserve Bank of Boston, 1972.

——————, and Donn L. Waage. "Corporate Separateness As a Tool of Bank Regulation." Prepared for the Economic Advisory Committee of the American Bankers Association, Washington, D.C., 1983.

Cleveland, Harold Van B., and Thomas F. Huetas. *The Bank for All: A History of Citibank 1812–1970.* Cambridge: Harvard University Press, 1985.

Cole, Rebel A. "Risk Implications of the Nonbank Bank." University of North Carolina, School of Business Administration, mimeo, 1985.

Conover, C.T. "Statement of C.T. Conover, Comptroller of the Currency, Before the Committee on Banking, Housing, and Urban Affairs, U.S. Senate, December 10, 1982," in *Hearing Before the Committee on Banking, Housing, and Urban Affairs, United States Senate, 97th Congress, 2nd Session, To Review the Causes, Effects and Implications of the Insolvency and Liquidation of the Penn Square*

Bank of Oklahoma City, December 10, 1982 (Committee Print 97-77, 1983).

_____. *"Testimony" in U.S. Congress, Subcommittee on Financial Institutions Suspension, Regulation and Insurance of the Committee on Banking, Finance and Urban Affairs, Inquiry into Continental Illinois Corp. and Continental Illinois National Bank: Hearings,* Sept. 18 and 19 and Oct. 4, 1984, 91-111, 98th Congress, 2nd Session: pp. 287–88.

Continental Illinois Corporation. *Report of the Special Litigation Committee of the Board of Directors of Continental Corporation.* Chicago: Continental Illinois Corporation, 1984.

Copeland, E. Thomas and J. Fred Weston. *Financial Theory and Corporate Policy.* 2nd ed. Reading, Mass.: Addison-Wesley Publishing Co., 1983.

Corrigan, E. Gerald. "Are Banks Special?" *Annual Report.* Federal Reserve Bank of Minneapolis, 1982.

Crane, Dwight B. "A Study of Interest Rate Spreads in the 1974 CD Market." *Journal of Bank Research* (Autumn 1976).

Curry, Timothy J. "The Performance of Bank Holding Companies." *The Bank Holding Company Movement to 1978: A Compendium.* Study by the staff of the Board of Governors of the Federal Reserve System, 1978.

Cyrnak, Anthony. "Convenience and Needs and Public Benefits in the Bank Holding Company Movement." *The Bank Holding Company Movement to 1978: A Compendium.* Study by the staff of the Board of Governors of the Federal Reserve System, 1978.

Darnell, Jerome. "A Study of the Costs of Complying With Government Regulations." *Issues in Bank Regulation* 5 (Winter 1982): 8–14.

Di Clemente, John J. "What is a Bank?" *Economic Perspectives,* Federal Reserve Bank of Chicago (January/February 1983).

Eiseman, Peter C. "Diversification and the Congeneric Bank Holding Company." *Journal of Bank Research* (Spring 1976).

Eisenbeis, Robert A. "How Bank Holding Companies Should be Regulated." *Economic Review,* Federal Reserve Bank of Atlanta (January 1983a).

_____. "Bank Holding Companies and Public Policy," in *Financial Services: The Changing Institutions and Government Policy*, ed. by George J. Benston. Englewood Cliffs, N.J.: Prentice Hall, Inc., 1983b.

_____. "Inflation and Regulation: Effects on Financial Institutions and Structure," in *Handbook for Banking Strategy*, ed. by Richard C. Aspinwall and Robert A. Eisenbeis. New York: John Wiley and Sons, Inc., 1985.

Ely, Bert. "Private Sector Deposit Guarantees: an Alternative to Federal Deposit Insurance." Unpublished, 1984.

_____. "Yes—Private Sector Depositor Protection is a Viable Alternative to Federal Deposit Insurance!" *Proceedings of a Conference on Bank Structure and Competition*, Federal Reserve Bank of Chicago, May 1985.

Esty, Daniel C., and Richard E. Caves. "Market Structure and Political Influence: New Data on Political Expenditures, Activity and Success." *Economic Inquiry* (January 1983).

Federal Deposit Insurance Corporation. *Annual Report, 1934*. Washington, D.C., 1935.

_____. *Annual Report, 1940*. Washington, D.C., 1941: 61–73.

_____. "Insurance of Bank Obligations Prior to Federal Deposit Insurance," in *Annual Report, 1951*. Washington, D.C., 1952: 59–72.

_____. *Deposit Insurance in a Changing Environment. A Study Submitted to Congress by the Federal Deposit Insurance Corporation*. Washington, D.C., 1983.

_____. *Federal Deposit Insurance Corporation: The First Fifty Years*. Washington, D.C., 1984: 33–53.

Federal Home Loan Bank Board. *Revised Report of the Interoffice Task Force on Market Value Accounting*. Washington, D.C., October 8, 1982 (unpublished).

_____. *Report of the Expanded Task Force on Current Value Accounting*. Washington, D.C., April 12, 1983 (unpublished).

_____. *Agenda for Reform. A Report on Deposit Insurance to the Congress from the Federal Home Loan Bank Board*. Washington, D.C.: U.S. Government Printing Office, 1983.

Federal Reserve System. "Policy Statement Regarding Risks on Large-Dollar Wire Transfer Systems." May 17, 1985.

Fischer, Gerald C. *Bank Holding Companies.* New York: Columbia University Press, 1961.

——————, and Carter H. Golembe. "The Branch Banking Provisions of the McFadden Act as Amended: Their Rationale and Rationality," in *Compendium of Issues Relating to Branching by Financial Institutions.* Subcommittee on Financial Institutions of the Committee on Banking, Housing, and Urban Affairs, United States Senate, 94th Congress, 2nd Session. Washington, D.C.: U.S. Government Printing Office, October 1976.

Flannery, Mark J., and Jack M. Guttentag. "Problem Banks: Examination, Identification, and Supervision," in Leonard Lapidus, ed., *State and Federal Regulation of Commercial Banks.* Washington, D.C.: Federal Deposit Insurance Corporation, vol. 11, 1980: 169–226.

——————. "Deposit Insurance Creates Need for Bank Regulation." *Business Review,* Federal Reserve Bank of Philadelphia (January/February 1982).

——————. "An Economic Evaluation of Bank Securities Activities Before 1933," in *Deregulating Wall Street: Commercial Bank Penetration of the Corporate Securities Market,* ed. by Ingo Walter. New York: John Wiley and Sons, 1985.

Ford, William F. "Banking's New Competition: Myths and Realities." *Economic Review,* Federal Reserve Bank of Atlanta (January 1982): 4–11.

Fraser, Donald R., and J.P. McCormack. "Large Bank Failures and Investors' Risk Perceptions: Evidence from the Debt Market." *Journal of Financial and Quantitative Analysis* (September 1978).

Friedman, Milton, and Anna Jacobson Schwartz. *A Monetary History of the United States, 1867–1960.* Princeton, N.J.: Princeton University Press, 1963.

Galai, Dan, and Ronald W. Masulis. "The Option Pricing Model and the Risk Factor of Stock." *Journal of Financial Economics* (1976): 31–7.

Gendreau, Brian C., and David Burras Humphrey. "Feedback Effects in the Market Regulation of Bank Leverage: A Time-series and Cross-section Analysis." *Review of Economics and Statistics* (1980): 276–80.

General Accounting Office. *Federal Financial Institutions Examination Council Has Made Limited Progress Toward Accomplishing Its Mission.* Report to the Congress of the United States by the Comptroller General. GAO/GGD-84-4: Washington, D.C., February 3, 1984.

Gilbert, Gary G. "Disclosure and Market Discipline: Issues and Evidence." *Economic Review,* Federal Reserve Bank of Altanta (November 1983).

Gibson, William E. "Deposit Insurance in the United States: Evaluation and Reform." *Journal of Financial and Quantitative Analysis* 7 (March 1972): 1575–9.

Glassman, Cynthia, and Robert A. Eisenbeis. "Bank Holding Companies and Concentration of Banking and Financial Resources," in *The Bank Holding Company Movement to 1978: A Compendium.* Study by the staff of the Board of Governors of the Federal Reserve System, 1978.

——————. "The Impact of Banks' Statewide Economic Power on Their Political Power: An Empirical Analysis." *Atlantic Economic Review* (July 1981).

Goldenweiser, E.A. *Bank Suspensions in the United States, 1892–1931.* Material prepared by the Federal Reserve Committee on Branch, Group and Chain Banking, vol. 5, 193X.

Golembe Associates, Inc. "Product Expansion by Bank Holding Companies." The Association of Bank Holding Companies, 1982.

Golembe, Carter H., and David S. Holland. *Federal Regulation of Banking 1983–84.* Golembe Associates, Inc.: Washington, D.C., 1983.

Gorton, Gary. "Bank Suspensions and Convertibility." *Journal of Monetary Economics* (March 1985): 177–94.

Graham, David R., and David B. Humphrey. "Bank Examination Data as Predictors of Bank Net Loan Losses." *Journal of Money, Credit and Banking* (November 1978): 491–504.

Hagerman, Robert L. "A Test of Government Regulation of Accounting Principles." *The Accounting Review* 50 (October 1975): 699–709.

Hamilton, David L. "Bank and Bank Holding Company Involvement with Real Estate Investment Trusts." Board of Governors of the Federal Reserve System, draft, May 19, 1978.

Hammond, Bray. Historical Introduction in Banking Studies. Washington, D.C.: Board of Governors of the Federal Reserve System, 1941: 21.

Hawke, John D., Jr., William J. Sweet, Jr., and Michael B. Mierzewski. "Revised BSC Act Offers Banks New Opportunities." *Legal Times* (December 20, 1982).

Healey, Thomas J., Chairman. *Recommendations for Change in the Federal Deposit Insurance System. The Working Group of the Cabinet Council on Economic Affairs.* Washington, D.C., 1985.

Heggestad, Arnold A. "Riskiness of Investments in Nonbank Activities by Bank Holding Companies." *Journal of Economics and Business* (Spring 1975).

Heinman, John. Testimony before the Committee on Banking, Housing, and Urban Affairs, 172-73, "Tie-ins of the Sale of Insurance by Banks and Bank Holding Companies." *Hearings before the Committee on Banking, Housing, and Urban Affairs, United States Senate*, 96th Congress, 1st Session, June 14, 1979.

Herzig-Marz, Clayim. "Comparing Market and Regulatory Assessments of Bank Conditions." Presented at the 1977 annual meetings of the Southern Finance Association, 1977.

Hill, G.W. "Why 67 Insured Banks Failed: 1960–1974." Washington, D.C.: Federal Deposit Insurance Corporation, 1975.

Horvitz, Paul M. "Stimulating Bank Competition through Regulatory Action." *Journal of Finance* (March 1965): 2–3.

—————. "Reorganization of the Financial Regulatory Agencies." *Journal of Bank Research* 13 (Winter 1983): 245–63.

Humphrey, David B. "Costs and Scale Economies in Bank Intermediation," in *Handbook for Banking Strategy*, ed. by Richard C. Aspinwall and Robert A. Eisenbeis. New York: John Wiley and Sons, Inc., 1985.

Humphrey, Thomas M. "The Classical Concept of Lender of Last Resort." *Essays on Inflation*, Federal Reserve Bank of Baltimore, 4th ed., 1983.

Jacobs, Donald P., H. Prescott Beighley, and John H. Boyd. *Financial Structure of Bank Holding Companies*. Chicago: Association of Reserve City Bankers, 1975.

Jensen, Michael, and William Meckling. "Theory of the Firm: Managerial Behavior, Agency Costs and Ownership Structures," *Journal of Financial Economics* 3 (October 1976): 253–63.

Jesser, Edward A. Jr., and Kenneth H. Fisher. "Guidelines for Bank Holding Company Management." *Bankers Magazine* vol. 152 (Spring 1969).

Johnson, James M., and Paul G. Weber. "The Impact of the Problem Bank Disclosure on Bank Share Prices." *Journal of Bank Research* (Autumn 1977).

Johnson, Rodney D., and David R. Meinster. "Bank Holding Companies Diversification Opportunities in Nonbanking Activities." *Eastern Economic Journal* (October 1974).

Kane, Edward J. "Accelerating Inflation, Technological Innovation, and the Decreasing Effectiveness of Banking Regulation." *Journal of Finance* (May 1981).

_____. "A Six-Point Program for Deposit-Insurance Reform." *Housing Finance Review* 2 (July 1983): 269–78.

_____. "Deregulation and Changes in the Financial Services Industry." *Journal of Finance* 39 (July 1984): 759–72.

_____. *The Gathering Crisis in Deposit Insurance*. Cambridge: MIT Press, 1985.

Karaken, John H., and Neil Wallace. "Deposit Insurance and Bank Regulation: A Partial Equilibrium Exposition." *Journal of Business* (July 1978).

Kaufman, George G. "Measuring and Management Interest Rate Risk: A Primer." *Economic Perspectives*, Federal Reserve Bank of Chicago (January/February 1984): 16–29.

_____. "Bank Failure Fears Are Overdrawn." *Wall Street Journal* (October 12, 1984).

_____. "Implications of Large Bank Problems and Insolvencies for the Banking Industry and Economic Policy." *Issues in Bank Regulation* (Winter 1985): 35–42.

_____. "Implication of Large Bank Problems and Insolvencies for the Banking System and Economic Policy." *Staff Memoranda*, Federal Reserve Bank of Chicago, March 1985.

Kelly, Edward J. III. "Legislative History of the Glass-Steagall Act." *Deregulating Wall Street: Commercial Bank Penetration of the Corporate Securities Market*, ed. by Ingo Walter. New York: John Wiley and Sons, 1985.

Kennedy, Susan E. *The Banking Crisis of 1933*. Lexington, Ky.: University of Kentucky Press, 1973.

Krooss, Herman E. *Documentary History of Banking and Finance in the United States*. New York: McGraw-Hill, 1969.

Lawrence, Robert J. *Operating Policies of Bank Holding Companies, Part I*. Staff Economic Studies 59, Board of Governors of the Federal Reserve System, April 1971.

_____. *Operating Policies of Bank Holding Companies, Part II: Non-Banking Subsidiaries*. Staff Economic Studies 81, Board of Governors of the Federal Reserve System, March 1974.

Maisel, Sherman J., ed. *Risk and Capital Adequacy in Commercial Banks*. Chicago: National Bureau of Economic Research, University of Chicago Press, 1981.

Mayer, Thomas. "A Graduated Deposit Insurance Plan." *Review of Economics and Statistics* 47 (February 1965).

McConnell, C.E., and W.S. Marcias. "Bank Loans to REITs: How Serious the Problem." New York: Keefe, Bruyette, and Woods, Inc., May 2, 1975.

McCulloch, J. Huston. "Interest Rate Risk and Capital Adequacy for Traditional Banks and Financial Intermediaries," in Maisel (1981): 223–48.

_____. "Interest-Risk Sensitive Deposit Insurance Premia: Stable ACH Estimates." *Journal of Banking and Finance* 9 (March 1985): 137–56.

Meinster, David P., and Rodney D. Johnson. "Bank Holding Company Diversification and the Risk of Capital Impairment." *Bell Economic Journal* (Autumn 1979).

Meltzer, Allen H. "Major Issues in the Regulation of Financial Institutions." *Journal of Political Economy, Supplement* (August 1967): 482–501.

Miller, Randall J. "On the Cost of Double Supervision for Insured State Chartered Banks," in Leonard Lapidus, ed., *State and Federal Regulation of Commercial Banks*. Washington, D.C.: Federal Deposit Insurance Corporation, vol. II, 1980a: 375–415.

——————. "Examination Manpower Cost for Independent, Joint, and Divided Examination Programs," in Leonard Lapidus, ed. *State and Federal Regulation of Commercial Banks*. Washington, D.C.: Federal Deposit Insurance Corporation, vol. II, 1980b: 450–70.

——————. "An Analysis of Chartering and Conversions, 1960-1977," in Leonard Lapidus, ed., *State and Federal Regulation of Commercial Banks*. Washington, D.C.: Federal Deposit Insurance Corporation, vol. 11, 1980c: 490–545.

Minsky, Hyman P. *Can "It" Happen Again?* Armonk, N.Y.: M.E. Sharpe, 1982.

Murphy, Neil B. "Disclosure of the Problem Bank Lists: A Test of the Impact." *Journal of Bank Research* (Summer 1979).

Murray, William. "Bank Holding Company Centralization Policies." Prepared for the Association of Bank Holding Companies, Golembe Associates, Inc., February 1978.

Nadler, Marcus, and Jules Bogen. *The Banking Crisis: The End of an Epoch*. New York: Dodd, Mead & Co., 1933: 21–2.

National Credit Union Administration. *Credit Union Share Insurance*. A report to the Congress by the National Credit Union Administration, April 1983.

Natter, Raymon. "Formation and Powers of National Banking Associations—A Legal Primer." Prepared by the American Law Division, Congressional Research Service, Library of Congress, for the Committee on Banking, Finance and Urban Affairs, U.S. House of Representatives, 98th Congress, 1st Session, 1983.

Peach, Nelsen W. *The Security Affiliates of National Banks*. Baltimore: Johns Hopkins University Press (republished by Arno Press, 1975).

Peltzman, Samuel. "Capital Investment in Commercial Banking and Its Relationship to Portfolio Regulation." *Journal of Political Economy* (January/February 1970).

Peterson, Manferd O. "Regulatory Objectives and Conflicts," in *Handbook for Banking Strategy*, ed. by Richard C. Aspinwall and Robert A. Eisenbeis. New York: John Wiley and Sons, Inc., 1985.

Peterson, Richard L., and William L. Scott. "Major Causes of Bank Failures: Determinants and Consequences." *Proceedings of a Conference on Bank Structure and Competition*, Federal Reserve Bank of Chicago, May 1985.

Pettway, Richard H. "The Effects of Large Bank Failures Upon Investors' Risk Cognizance in the Commercial Banking Industry." *Journal of Financial and Quantitative Analysis* (September 1976a).

_____. "Market Tests of Capital Adequacy of Large Commercial Banks." *Journal of Finance* (June 1976b).

_____. "Potential Insolvency, Market Efficiency, and Bank Regulation of Large Commercial Banks." *Journal of Financial and Quantitative Analysis* (March 1980).

_____, and Joseph F. Sinkey, Jr. "Establishing On-Site Bank Examination Priorities: An Early-Warning System Using Accounting and Market Information." 35 *Journal of Finance.* (March 1980).

Phillips, Almarin. "Changing Technology and Future Financial Activity," in *Handbook for Banking Strategy*, ed. by Richard C. Aspinwall and Robert A. Eisenbeis. New York: John Wiley and Sons, Inc., 1985.

Pyle, David H. "Pricing Deposit Insurance: The Effects of Mismeasurement." Unpublished manuscript, Federal Reserve Bank of San Francisco and University of California, Berkeley, October 1983.

Rhoades, Stephen A., and George E. Boczar. "The Performance of Bank Holding Company Affiliated Finance Companies." Staff Economic Studies 90, Board of Governors of the Federal Reserve System, 1977.

_____. "The Effects of Bank Holding Companies on Competition," in *The Bank Holding Company Movement to 1978: A Compendium*. Study by the staff of the Board of Governors of the Federal Reserve System, September 1978.

_____. "The Economic and Socio-Political Issues Raised by Undue Concentration of Resources." *Issues in Bank Regulation* (Spring 1979).

_____, and Roger D. Rutz. "Economic Power and Political Influence: An Empirical Analysis of Bank Regulatory Decisions." *Atlantic Economic Journal* (1984).

Rolnick, Arthur I. and Warren E. Weber. "Free Banking, Wildcat Banking and Shinplasters." *Quarterly Review*, Federal Reserve Bank of Minneapolis (Fall 1982): 10–19.

_____. "The Free Banking Era: New Evidence on Laissez-Faire Banking." *American Economic Review* (December 1983): 1080–91.

_____. "The Causes of Free Bank Failures." *Journal of Monetary Economics* (November 1984): 267–91.

Rose, John T. "The Effect of the Bank Holding Company Movement on Bank Safety and Soundness," in *The Bank Holding Company Movement to 1978: A Compendium*. Study by the staff of the Board of Governors of the Federal Reserve System, September 1978.

_____. "Aggregate Concentration in Banking and Political Leverage: A Note." *Industrial Organization Review* (1978a).

_____. "Bank Holding Companies as Operational Single Entities," in *The Bank Holding Company Movement to 1978: A Compendium*. Study by the staff of the Board of Governors of the Federal Reserve System, September 1978b.

_____, and Samuel H. Talley. "Issues Surrounding Financial Transactions Between A Bank and Affiliate Companies." *Issues in Bank Regulation* 2 (Summer 1978).

Rosenblum, Harvey, and Christine Pavel. "Banking Services in Transition: The Effects of Nonbank Competitors," in *Handbook for Banking Strategy*, ed. by Richard C. Aspinwall and Robert A. Eisenbeis. New York: John Wiley and Sons, Inc., 1985.

Sachs, Jeffrey D. and Steven C. Kyle. "Developing Country Debt and the Market Value of Large Commercial Banks." National Bureau of Economic Research Working Paper No. 1470, Cambridge, Mass., 1985.

Savage, Donald T. "A History of the Bank Holding Company Movement, 1900–1978," in *The Bank Holding Company Movement to 1978: A Compendium.* Study by the staff of the Board of Governors of the Federal Reserve System, September 1978.

_____. "Depository Financial Institutions," in *Handbook of Banking Strategy,* ed. by Richard C. Aspinwall and Robert A. Eisenbeis. New York: John Wiley and Sons, 1985.

Shick, R.A. "Bank Stock Prices as an Early-Warning System for Changes in Condition." St. Bonaventure University and Office of the Comptroller of the Currency, 1978.

Short, Eugenie D., Gerald P. O'Driscoll, Jr., and Frank D. Berger. In "Recent Bank Failures: Determinants and Consequences." *Proceedings of a Conference on Bank Structure and Competition,* Federal Reserve Bank of Chicago, May 1985.

Shull, Bernard. "Federal and State Supervision of Bank Holding Companies," in Leonard Lapidus, ed., *State and Federal Regulation of Commercial Banks.* Washington, D.C.: Federal Deposit Insurance Corporation, vol. II, 1980: 271–375.

_____. "The Separation of Banking and Commerce: Origin, Development, and Implications for Antitrust." *The Antitrust Bulletin* XXVII (Spring 1983): 255–79.

Singer, Mark. "Funny Money." *The New Yorker* April 29, May 22, May 29, and June 6, 1985.

Sinkey, Joseph F., Jr. *Problem and Failed Institutions in the Commercial Banking Industry.* Greenwich, Conn.: JAI Press, 1979.

_____, and Richard H. Pettway. "Establishing On-Site Bank Examination Priorities: An Early-Warning System Using Accounting and Market Information." *Journal of Finance* 35 (March 1980): 137–50.

Smoot, Richard L. "Billion-Dollar Overdraft: A Payments Risk Challenge." *Business Review,* Federal Reserve Bank of Philadelphia, (January/February 1985): 3–13.

Spahr, Walter E. "Bank Failures in the United States." *American Economic Review, Supplement* (March 1932): 208–38.

Spero, Joan Edelman. *The Failure of the Franklin National Bank: Challenge to the International Banking System.* New York: Council on Foreign Relations, Columbia University Press, 1980.

Sprague, O.M.W. *History of Crises Under the National Banking System.* Senate Document, Washington, D.C.: U.S. Government Printing Office, 1910 (reprinted New York: Augustus Kelley, 1968).

Stevens, E.J. "Risks in Large Volume Transfer Systems." *Economic Review,* Federal Reserve Bank of Cleveland (Fall 1984): 2–16.

Stodden, John R. "Survey of the Operating Policies and Performance of Texas Multibank Holding Companies: Preliminary Findings." *Conference on Bank Structure and Competition,* Federal Reserve Bank of Chicago, 1975: 253–59.

Stover, Roger. "The Single Subsidiary One-Bank Holding Company," in *Proceedings of a Conference on Bank Structure and Competition,* Federal Reserve Bank of Chicago, April 27–28, 1978.

_____. "A Reexamination of Bank Holding Company Acquisitions." *Journal of Bank Research* (Summer 1982).

_____, and James M. Miller. "Additional Evidence on the Capital Market Effect of Bank Failures." *Financial Management* (Spring 1983).

Sussan, Sidney Martin. "An Evaluation of the NonBanking Expansion of Bank Holding Companies Under the 1970 Amendments to the Bank Holding Company Act of 1956." Thesis submitted to The Stonier Graduate School of Banking, 1978.

Swary, Itzhak. "Continental Illinois Crisis: An Empirical Analysis of Regulatory Behavior." Working paper, Hebrew University of Jerusalem, January 1985.

Temin, Peter. *Did Monetary Forces Cause the Great Depression?* New York: Norton, 1976.

Thomas, R.G. "Bank Failures—Causes and Remedies." *Journal of Business* (October 1935): 316.

Thornton, Henry. *An Enquiry into the Nature and Effects of the Paper Credit of Great Britain (1802).* New York: Farrar & Rhinehart, 1939: 180.

Timberlake, Richard H. *The Origins of Central Banking in the United States.* Cambridge: Harvard University Press, 1978.

_____. "The Central Bank Role of Clearinghouse Associations." *Journal of Money, Credit and Banking* (February 1984): 1–15.

Tobin, James. *Brookings Papers on Economic Activity,* 1984: 2, 463.

Tussing, Dale. "The Case of Bank Failures." *Journal of Law and Economics* (October 1967): 140–41.

U.S. Congress, House Committee on Banking and Currency, Hearings, *Bank Holding Company Act Amendments,* 91st Congress, 1st Session, 1969a.

_____, House Committee on Banking and Currency, Hearings, *Report to Accompany H.R. 6778,* House Report 91-387, 91st Congress, 1st Session, 1969b.

_____, House Committee on Banking and Currency, Hearings, *Report to Accompany H.R. 6778,* House Report 91-1747, 91st Congress, 2nd Session, 1969c.

_____, Senate Committee on Housing, Banking, and Urban Affairs, Hearings, *One Bank Holding Company Legislation of 1970,* 91st Congress, 2nd Session, 1970.

_____, *Inquiry Into Continental Illinois Corp. and Continental Illinois National Bank: Hearings,* House of Representatives, Subcommittee on Financial Institutions, Supervision, Regulation and Insurance of the Committee on Banking, Finance and Urban Affairs, 98th Congress, 2nd Session, September 18–19 and October 4, 1984.

_____. House Committee on Government Operations, *Federal Supervision and Failure of United American Bank in Knoxville, Tenn.,* and *Affiliated Banks,* Twenty-Third Report, 98th Congress, 1st Session, House Report 98-573, November 18, 1983.

_____. House Committee on Government Operations, *Federal Home Loan Bank Board Supervision and Failure of Empire Savings and Loan Association of Mesquite, Tex.,* Forty-Fourth Report, 98th Congress, 2nd Session, House Report 98-953, August 6, 1984a.

_____. House Committee on Government Operations, *Federal Regulation of Brokered Deposits in Problem Banks and Savings and*

Loan Institutions, Fifty-Second Report, 98th Congress, 2nd Session, House Report 98-1112, September 28, 1984b.

—————. House Committee on Government Operations, *Federal Response to Criminal Misconduct and Insider Abuse in the Nation's Financial Institutions,* Fifty-Seventh Report, 98th Congress, 2nd Session, House Report 98-1137, October 4, 1984c.

Villani, Kevin E. "Electrifying Trends in Housing Finance." *Secondary Mortgage Markets* vol. 1, no. 4 (Winter 1984).

Wall, Larry D., and Robert A. Eisenbeis. "Risk Consideration in Deregulating Bank Activities." Forthcoming in *Economic Review,* Federal Reserve Bank of Atlanta (1984); and "Bank Holding Company Nonbanking Activities and Risk," presented at a Conference on Bank Structure and Competition, Federal Reserve Bank of Chicago, 1984.

Warburton, Clark. *Depression, Inflation, and Monetary Policy: Selected Papers, 1945–1953.* Baltimore: Johns Hopkins University Press, 1963.

Weiss, Steven J. "Bank Holding Companies and Public Policy." *New England Economic Review,* Federal Reserve Bank of Boston (January/February 1969).

Whalen, Gary. "Multibank Holding Company Organizational Structure and Performance." Working Paper 8201, Federal Reserve Bank of Cleveland, March 1982a.

—————. "Operational Policies of Multibank Holding Companies." *Economic Review,* Federal Reserve Bank of Cleveland (Winter 1982b).

White, Eugene N. *The Regulation and Reform of the American Banking System, 1900–1929.* Princeton, N.J.: Princeton University Press, 1983: 74–9.

—————. "A Reinterpretation of the Banking Crisis of 1930." *Journal of Economic History* (March 1984): 119–38.

White, Lawrence H. *Free Banking in Britain: Theory, Experience and Debate, 1800–1845.* Cambridge, U.K.: Cambridge University Press, 1984: 141–48.

—————. *The Regulation and Reform of the American Banking System, 1900–1929.* Princeton, N.J.: Princeton University Press, 1983.

Whitehead, David D. "The Sixth District Survey of Small Business Credit." *Economic Review,* Federal Reserve Bank of Atlanta (April 1982): 42–7.

_____. "Interstate Banking: Taking Inventory." *Economic Review,* Federal Reserve Bank of Atlanta (May 1983).

_____. "Interstate Banking: Probability or Reality?" *Economic Review,* Federal Reserve Bank of Atlanta (March 1985).

Wicker, Elmus. "Interest Rate and Expenditure Effects of the Banking Panic of 1930." *Journal of Economic History* (March 1984): 119–38.

_____. "A Reconsideration of the Causes of the Banking Panic of 1930." *Journal of Economic History* (September 1980): 571–83.

Wu, Hsiu-Kwang. "Bank Examiner Criticisms, Loan Defaults and Bank Loan Quality." *Journal of Finance,* XXIV (September 1969): 667–705.

Young, Ralph. *The Banking Situation in the United States.* New York: National Industrial Conference Board, 1932.

George J. Benston is Professor of Accounting, Economics, and Finance at the Graduate School of Management, University of Rochester, and Honorary Visiting Professor at City University in London, England. He is a C.P.A. He has written more than 70 articles in academic journals and 10 monographs and books in the fields of accounting, economics, and banking and finance. Professor Benston has been a consultant for all of the federal banking regulatory agencies, the World Bank, trade associations, and private banks and corporations, and he has testified before committees of the U.S. House of Representatives and the Senate and of the Canadian Parliament. He holds a B.A. from Queens College, an M.B.A. from New York University, and a Ph.D. from the University of Chicago.

Robert A. Eisenbeis is the Wachovia Professor of Banking in the School of Business Administration at the University of North Carolina at Chapel Hill, and a Consulting Associate with Furash and Company in Washington, D.C. He is the author of more than 40 articles in professional journals, and is coauthor of five books. Much of his academic work has been devoted to policy issues affecting the banking community and financial structure and to internal bank management problems. Professor Eisenbeis was Senior Deputy Associate Director in the Division of Research and Statistics at the Federal Reserve Board in Washington. He has been Assistant Director of Research at the Federal Deposit Insurance Corporation, and Chief of the Financial and Economic Research Section, also at the FDIC. Professor Eisenbeis did his undergraduate work at Brown University. He holds both an M.A. and a Ph.D. from the University of Wisconsin.

P aul M. Horvitz is the Judge James A. Elkins Professor of Banking and Finance at the University of Houston, and a Director both of Ameriway Bank Brookhollow in Houston and of the Federal Home Loan Bank of Dallas. Professor Horvitz writes a monthly editorial column for the *American Banker*. He is the author of two books. His articles have been published in many banking and professional journals. He has served as Senior Economist in the Office of the Comptroller of the Currency, as Director of Research and Deputy to the Chairman at the Federal Deposit Insurance Corporation, and as a Financial Economist with the Federal Reserve Bank of Boston. Professor Horvitz also served as a member of President Reagan's Advisory Task Force on Small Business. He holds a B.A. from the University of Chicago, an M.B.A. from Boston University, and a Ph.D. from the Massachusetts Institute of Technology.

E dward J. Kane occupies the Everett D. Reese Chair of Banking and Monetary Economics at Ohio State University. He is a Research Associate of the National Bureau of Research, and a Trustee and member of the Finance Committee of Teachers Insurance. He has written two books and been published widely in professional journals. Professor Kane has taught at Boston College, Princeton University, and Iowa State University. He has held visiting professorships at Istanbul University and Simon Fraser University. Professor Kane has served as a consultant to the Federal Deposit Insurance Corporation, the Federal Home Loan Bank Board, the American Bankers Association, the Department of Housing and Urban Development, the Federal Reserve System, and the Joint Economic Committee and Office of Technology Assessment of the U.S. Congress. He holds a B.S. from Georgetown University and a Ph.D. from the Massachusetts Institute of Technology.

G eorge G. Kaufman is the John F. Smith Jr. Professor of Finance and Economics in the School of Business Administration at Loyola University of Chicago. He is a trustee of the Teachers Insurance Annuity Association and College Retirement Equity Fund, and is currently on the editorial board of four professional journals. He is the author of numerous books and articles. Professor Kaufman was the Deputy to the Assistant Secretary for Economic Policy of the U.S. Department of the Treasury, and the Senior Economist at the Federal Reserve Bank of Chicago. He has served as a consultant to numerous government agencies and private firms, and was a member of the Federal Savings and Loan Insurance Corporation Task Force on Reappraising Deposit Insurance. He holds a B.A. from Oberlin College, an M.A. from the University of Michigan, and a Ph.D. from the University of Iowa.